Library of
Davidson College

THE POLICY PROCESS IN COMMUNIST STATES

Volume 127, Sage Library of Social Research

RECENT VOLUMES IN
SAGE LIBRARY OF SOCIAL RESEARCH

95 Roberts **Afro-Arab Fraternity**
96 Rutman **Planning Useful Evaluations**
97 Shimanoff **Communication Rules**
98 Laguerre **Voodoo Heritage**
99 Macarov **Work and Welfare**
100 Bolton **The Pregnant Adolescent**
101 Rothman **Using Research in Organizations**
102 Sellin **The Penalty of Death**
103 Studer/Chubin **The Cancer Mission**
104 Beardsley **Redefining Rigor**
105 Small **Was War Necessary?**
106 Sanders **Rape & Woman's Identity**
107 Watkins **The Practice of Urban Economics**
108 Clubb/Flanigan/Zingale **Partisan Realignment**
109 Gittell **Limits to Citizen Participation**
110 Finsterbusch **Understanding Social Impacts**
111 Scanzoni/Szinovacz **Family Decision-Making**
112 Lidz/Walker **Heroin, Deviance and Morality**
113 Shupe/Bromley **The New Vigilantes**
114 Monahan **Predicting Violent Behavior**
115 Britan **Bureaucracy and Innovation**
116 Massarik/Kaback **Genetic Disease Control**
117 Levi **The Coming End of War**
118 Beardsley **Conflicting Ideologies in Political Economy**
119 LaRossa/LaRossa **Transition to Parenthood**
120 Alexandroff **The Logic of Diplomacy**
121 Tittle **Careers and Family**
122 Reardon **Persuasion**
123 Hindelang/Hirschi/Weis **Measuring Delinquency**
124 Skogan/Maxfield **Coping With Crime**
125 Weiner **Cultural Marxism and Political Sociology**
126 McPhail **Electronic Colonialism**
127 Holmes **The Policy Process in Communist States**

THE POLICY PROCESS IN COMMUNIST STATES

Politics and Industrial Administration

LESLIE HOLMES

Foreword by **Roger E. Kanet**

Volume 127
SAGE LIBRARY OF
SOCIAL RESEARCH

SAGE PUBLICATIONS   Beverly Hills   London

For Beenz

Copyright © 1981 by Sage Publications, Inc.

All rights reserved. No part of this book may be reproduced or utilized in any form or by any means, electronic or mechanical, including photocopying, recording, or by any information storage and retrieval system, without permission in writing from the publisher.

For information address:

SAGE Publications, Inc.
275 South Beverly Drive
Beverly Hills, California 90212

SAGE Publications Ltd
28 Banner Street
London EC1Y 8QE, England

Printed in the United States of America

Library of Congress Cataloging in Publication Data

Holmes, Leslie.
   The policy process in Communist states.

   (Sage library of social research; v. 127)
   Bibliography: p.
   Includes index.
   1. Industrial management—Soviet Union. 2. Industrial organization—Soviet Union. 3. Industrial management—Germany (East) 4. Industrial organization—Germany (East) 5. Industrial management—Communist countries. 6. Industrial organization—Communist countries. I. Title. II. Series.
HD70.S63H64   658'.009171'7   81-5610
ISBN 0-8039-1646-9   AACR2
ISBN 0-8039-1647-7 (pbk.)

FIRST PRINTING

CONTENTS

Abbreviations in Chapter Notes		7
Foreword *by Roger E. Kanet*		9
Preface		11
Introduction		15
Chapter 1:	**Structures of Industry**	**35**
	1.1 The Structure of Soviet Industry	36
	1.2 The Structure of East German Industry	45
	1.3 A Brief History of the Development of Soviet Associations	54
	1.4 A Brief History of the Development of East German Associations	58
	1.5 Summary	64
Chapter 2:	**"Demand" Channels**	**81**
	2.1 The Press	83
	2.2 Conferences	85
	2.3 On the Analysis of "Demands"	94
	2.4 Summary	99
Chapter 3:	**The "Demands"**	**105**
	3.1 The Debates	105
	3.2 Claimed Advantages of the Associations	119
	3.3 Calls for Legislation	127
	3.4 Conclusions	129
Chapter 4:	**Party Policy: Macro Policy Statements**	**139**
	4.1 Leadership Views	139
	4.2 References in Official Policy Documents	162
	4.3 Summary	165
Chapter 5:	**Legislation: The Micro Policy Formulation**	**173**
	5.1 The Legislative Process	174
	5.2 The Legislation	183
	5.3 Conclusions	191

Chapter 6:	**Implementation**	**199**
	6.1 Implementation in the USSR	199
	6.2 Implementation in the GDR	208
	6.3 Conclusions	212
Chapter 7:	**Opposition to the Associations**	**219**
	7.1 Opposition to the *Ob"edineniya* in the USSR	219
	7.2 Opposition to the VVBs and Combines in the GDR	236
Chapter 8:	**Conclusions**	**257**
Glossary and List of Abbreviations		287
Bibliography		291
Index		310
About the Author		320

ABBREVIATIONS IN CHAPTER NOTES

The following abbreviations have been used in the chapter notes:

B.Z.	Berliner Zeitung
D.A.	Deutschland Archiv
Die Wirts.	Die Wirtschaft
Ekon. Gaz.	Ekonomicheskaya Gazeta
GBl.	Gesetzblatt der Deutschen Demokratischen Republik
N.D.	Neues Deutschland
P of C	Problems of Communism
Part. Zh.	Partiinaya Zhizn'
Plan. Khoz.	Planovoe Khozyaistvo
S und R	Staat und Recht
SGiP	Sovetskoe Gosudarstvo i Pravo
Sots. Ind.	Sotsialisticheskaya Industriya
Sots. Trud	Sotsialisticheskii Trud
Sov. Kirg.	Sovetskaya Kirgiziya
Vop. Ekon.	Voprosy Ekonomiki
VS	Vertragssystem
Wirts/wiss.	Wirtschaftswissenschaft
WR	Wirtschaftsrecht

FOREWORD

Western analysis of communist society and politics has undergone significant change during the course of the past two decades or so. Most research on the Soviet Union and Eastern Europe published in the 1950s focused on such issues as the struggle for power within the political elite and on the mechanisms of control employed by that elite to maintain its political dominance over a subject population. The totalitarian model, with its emphasis on strict organizational hierarchy and policy-making by command, underlay much of Western scholarly writing. Leslie Holmes's *The Policy Process in Communist States* owes little to that earlier tradition or to its assumptions. Rather it represents the best of more recent research that has emphasized the actual functioning of the political process within communist states.

Industrial organization and management policy is an issue of special importance in communist states, where ultimate control of the economy is in the hands of the political leadership. Both the Soviet Union and the German Democratic Republic introduced major reorganizations of the industrial sector during the 1960s that resulted in the establishment of large industrial complexes called production associations. At one level Mr. Holmes's book is a study of the evolution over a number of years of these associations. The primary purpose of his study, however, is to describe and analyze the policy process by which the production associations were established. In this sense, he has produced a detailed and systematic assessment of the policy-making process in the two communist states that traces the process from its earliest discussion stage to the final enactment of legislation that established a full-scale system of production associations. Included in the discussion is treatment of the "demands" themselves, the interests involved and the political "alliances" established in support of (or opposition to) the new proposals, the channels through which the recommendations were made, the role of the political leadership in the entire process, and, finally, the legislative process itself. Within the limitations of the data available, Mr. Holmes has provided a clear analysis of the factors involved in policy formulation and legislation in an area of major importance for the two communist states. Moreover, he provides the type of comparative microanalytic analysis that should be of interest to all students of comparative politics, not merely to specialists on Soviet or East European politics.

Roger E. Kanet
University of Illinois
at Urbana-Champaign

PREFACE

The present study is basically a comparative analysis of the process whereby an important domestic policy (i.e., as distinct from foreign and/or defense policy) develops and is implemented in a noncrisis situation in two advanced — or, to use Alfred Meyer's term, "mature" — communist states. The latter are defined as highly industrialized, well-established states in which all official policies are allegedly oriented toward the long-term goal of creating a communist society. We examine the way in which the USSR and the GDR (German Democratic Republic) have tackled a similar problem, that of economic administration, in rather similar ways; both states have planned economies, and both have experienced many of the same problems in creating an optimal administrative structure. Moreover, both produced legislation on industrial associations (groupings of enterprises) in the early 1970s, and the study deals largely with the background to and success of this; as a result, the period covered is almost two decades, from the end of the 1950s to the late 1970s. Having considered the kind of organizational problems that have been encountered and the frequently common solutions adopted, explanations are sought for the similarities and differences, and general inferences about the policy process in such states are drawn. It must be emphasized that the study can only serve as a contribution to the gradually increasing body of literature concerned with comparative communist politics, and that in the final analysis many of the conclusions and/or speculations are based on only two case studies or one interstate relationship; only further detailed study of other communist states by scholars knowledgeable about their systems, cultures, and languages can demonstrate the validity of some of the more general hypotheses of the present study. Nevertheless, it is hoped that the overall framework of analysis used — oriented as it is to the particular problems of studying communist states — will serve as a useful contribution to further comparative study of the policy process in what is sometimes called the "second world."

It is always difficult to know when and where to use foreign-language terms in a book aimed both at specialists and at readers with a more general interest in a subject. Certainly, since the organizations with which this study is primarily concerned have different names in the two states, it is necessary to use an English term for those occasions when reference is made to both countries. Nevertheless, there are problems in using English terms. The five most common words used to translate the Russian *ob"edinenie* and the German *Vereinigung* and *Kombinat* — the bodies we are concerned with — are "corporation," "union," "association," "amalgamation," and "combine." The term "corporation" is by now linked in so many people's minds with the Western transnational companies that it would be wrong to use that term in the present context; this point is elaborated in the introduction. Similarly, many automatically think of *trade* unions when they encounter the word "union," so that this rendering must also be rejected. While "association" is an acceptable translation of *Vereinigung,* and "combine" is an obvious and reasonably accurate rendering of *Kombinat,* it is less clear which English word most nearly approximates to the *ob"edinenie*. This is largely because the word does not have a single meaning in Soviet economic vocabulary. It is used to describe groupings of production and other units with very differing levels of integration, which is why one *ob"edinenie* could be described as an amalgamation, while another would more accurately be called an association (i.e., implying a less integrated structure). For these reasons, the German and Russian terms are normally used in this study whenever only one state is being considered. When both states are being discussed — or sometimes merely to avoid excessive repetition of the foreign term — I have used the word most popular among other English-speaking scholars, i.e., "association."

Regarding other terms, it is generally preferable to use the English whenever there is a direct equivalent or a very close approximation to a Russian or German term. Thus the Russian *ministerstvo* becomes "ministry." In some cases, an English term is used for a like-sounding foreign one, even if the concept is slightly different. In such cases, the foreign word is given in parentheses or in a note the first time the English rendering is given (e.g., the "firm" [*firma*]). Elsewhere, the foreign term is included in parentheses even though it bears no resemblance to an English term; this is done where the author knows there may be some disagreement on the most appropriate English-language rendering. Some foreign words are not easily translated into English and/or are commonly used in the English-language literature; in such cases, the foreign term has been used (e.g., *glavk, sovnarkhoz*) with a brief explanation of its meaning and/or a literal translation in the text or notes. Since so much more is known in the English-speaking world about Soviet than about East German economics, this has led to the seemingly incongruous situation whereby the Russian term *glavk* is used, while the East German functional equivalent (*Hauptverwaltung*) is translated.

Where Russian or German terms are used, so is the native plural form. The one exception to this is in the case of sets of initials, when the reader might not otherwise know whether the term was being used in the singular or the plural; thus the plural of VVB becomes VVBs. The Germans and the Russians share a penchant for long titles and for abbreviations of such titles. Therefore, the full title of organizations having particularly long ones is given the first time reference is made to such organizations, after which the Russian or German abbreviation is used (e.g., *Minpribor*). The German umlaut has been replaced by an "e" following the umlauted vowel (e.g., über becomes ueber).

Finally, in order to minimize the confusion that will inevitably arise for many readers not already familiar with Soviet and East German economic vocabulary, a glossary of terms and abbreviations is included at the end of this book.

The study is a substantially revised version of a doctoral thesis submitted to the University of Essex. During the course of my study, I was also fortunate enough to have been awarded scholarships to carry out extended research at universities and research institutes in Leningrad, Moscow, and Berlin. I would like to thank the British Council, the British Social Science Research Council, and the German Academic Exchange Service (DAAD) for their generous funding of these trips. Because of the absence of a cultural agreement — and hence scholarships — between Britain and the GDR during the main period of research (1973-1976), I was unable to study in an East German university. However, through being based in West Berlin I was able to make frequent and regular visits to the State Library in East Berlin, thus having access to documentation not available in the West. This said, there are two main reasons it has not proved possible to provide such detailed answers about some aspects of the East German process as about the Soviet. First, the Soviets publish much more, and give far more detail, about most aspects of their economic system than do the East Germans. Second, we were able to conduct six long (at least half-hour) interviews in the USSR, which provided us with much information that did not appear in available publications. The East German authorities, on the other hand, would not grant us permission to interview economists and the like. The East German data-base is therefore smaller than the Soviet, and our description of what happens there more speculative. This is unfortunate, but at present cannot be remedied; so little is known about the East German political process, however, that it was felt that the (at times relatively detailed) picture drawn here is of some value.

Many people have made comments on various aspects of the research, and for these I am grateful. While it would be impossible to name everyone who has helped me in some way in the academic preparation of this book, I would like to thank in particular my doctoral supervisor, Dr. Mary McAuley, and my examiners, Mr. Peter Frank and Dr. Martin McCauley. I also benefited immensely from discussions with and various other forms of assistance from Dr. Hartmut Zimmermann and Dr. Gero Neugebauer of the GDR section of the Central Institute for Social Science Research in the Free University of Berlin, and my supervisors in the USSR, Professors Leonid Blyakhman and Eduard Dunaev. All errors, omissions, and interpretations are, of course, solely my responsibility.

Help in completing a book is never solely of an academic kind. Three typists, in particular, deserve my gratitude: Jean Stodart, Anne Chapman, and Linda Harty; I shall never know how they coped with my appalling handwriting. Above all, I want to thank my wife, Sue, for her encouragement, tolerance — and never-ending supply of tea; the study would never have been completed without them.

Leslie Holmes
Canterbury, England

INTRODUCTION

The problems of administration are primarily political and not technical ones.

—L. I. Brezhnev
December 1969

The number of books on comparative communism increased markedly in the 1970s, with seminal works being published on topics such as political socialization, political culture, political terror, takeovers, and so on.[1] However, there is still a severe shortage of detailed empirical studies on the policy process in individual communist states, and even fewer comparisons between communist states.[2] This shortage has been commented on recently by A. H. Brown, who writes,

> Our knowledge of the policymaking process within Communist states has advanced very fitfully over the past two decades. There is still no book available that sets out to study Communist states comparatively from a policy process standpoint — very few books, indeed, that are comparative Communist studies at all, in the sense that they apply a common framework of analysis to a variety of Communist states or are unified by a common organising principle.[3]

The present study is offered as a contribution to the overcoming of this deficiency. The basic aims are twofold. The first is to analyze in depth the genesis and development of an important policy in two communist states, in order to demonstrate and explain both the similarities and the differences in their political processes. From this, tentative general conclusions about the policy process in communist states are drawn, which can then be compared with existing, often conflicting views and tested against future analyses of the policy process in other communist states and/or policy areas. The second aim is to highlight particular methodological problems of analyzing the policy process in communist states and to suggest ways in which these difficulties might be handled. The study is therefore both specialized and general in its applications. Let us now consider why the USSR and the GDR were selected as the two states.

The choice of the USSR is relatively simple to explain. First, it is the oldest communist state, and nowadays overtly claims to be nearer to communism than any other state.[4] Thus, in analyzing the Soviet policy process, we will have *some* indications of the possible development patterns of the political process in other communist states. While the similarities between communist states should not be overemphasized — political culture, size, and availability of raw materials being three of the many variables that lead to differences in the politics of different countries — they do, nevertheless, share a fundamentally similar ideology and are organized according to the common principle of democratic centralism. Second, the Soviet Union is a "superpower"; i.e., it plays a leading role in international politics. Not only does this make the USSR of greater interest to people outside the communist world, but it has also often been argued in the past that the Soviet Union has played a major role in the domestic policy process of various East European "satellites." During the 1950s there was certainly some justification for arguing that most of the smaller communist states of Europe, with the notable exception of Yugoslavia, were both politically and economically highly dependent on the USSR. But with the emergence at the end of the 1950s of the Sino-Soviet rift, the situation changed somewhat. Now, countries that had basic disagreements with the USSR could either turn to China for support (e.g., Albania) or use the split to maintain a relatively independent position within the communist world (e.g., Romania) These developments led some writers to talk of the breakup of the Soviet empire.[5] Despite these tendencies of the early and mid-1960s, the Soviet invasion of Czechoslovakia in 1968 and the emergence of what is now popularly known as the "Brezhnev doctrine"[6] demonstrated in a very real way that the new (from October 1964) Soviet leadership was not prepared to allow East European states still relatively loyal to Moscow to wander too far from the general lines for development laid down by the Kremlin. The idea of East European states being satellites of the Soviet Union, even if they had more autonomy than under Stalin, once more gained popularity, while the Chinese intensified their campaign against Soviet "social imperialism."[7]

However, anyone who has made a detailed study of the literature on imperialism will be aware that the concept is highly problematic and used in very different ways. Moreover, there are enormous difficulties — both methodological and in terms of data deficiencies — involved in attempting to "prove" that the economic relationships of imperialism pertain in the communist world. On the other hand, it is possible to examine the policy-making process — as part of the overall policy process — in a so-called satellite to see if it at least appears that the primary factor in this has been Soviet influence. This is not such an ambitious project as trying to study the whole question of imperialism, of course, but it *is* one that can be tested in a real way, and it is not so open to criticisms of subjective definitions of imperialism. Moreover, scholars such as Fejtö did overtly argue in the 1970s that the freedom of maneuver of European communist states in policy-making is limited by their political dependence on the USSR.[8] Thus, in analyzing a significant policy area in the Soviet Union and comparing it with the same policy area in an East European state, such assumptions can be tested against empirical evidence. If Soviet influence did not seem to be the dominant — or even a major — factor in the East European states, we could then attempt to find alternative explanations for particular developments in the history of a policy. But before discussing the choice of policy, the reasons for selecting the GDR as the sample "satellite" or "colony" must be explained; they are basically fourfold.

First, even among writers who were writing in the mid-1960s on the "disintegration" of the Soviet empire, the GDR was seen as "the last bastion of Stalin's empire."[9] It was (and still frequently is) argued that the strategic importance of the GDR both as a "buffer" state and as a possible jumpoff point for any future expansionism on the part of the USSR (e.g., into West Germany and/or France) means that the Soviet leadership has vested interests in keeping East Germany and its leadership well under control.[10] One might add that the Soviets/ Russians traditionally fear the Germans more than any other nation in Europe, which is a linked reason for maximizing control.

Second, the level of trade between the GDR and the USSR is often the highest between any of the East European states and the USSR. Given that the GDR appears to be so dependent on the USSR as the major foreign outlet for its manufactured goods (approximately 40% of East German exports in terms of money value went to the USSR in 1972, and nearly 33% in 1974[11]) and given that the Soviet Union is the GDR's principal supplier of raw materials, it would appear ceteris paribus that the possibilities of policy "leverage" by the USSR on the GDR are greater than in any other East European state.

A third point is that the GDR is the most industrially developed of the communist states, so that it could be argued that the Soviet Union should be learning from and possibly emulating German experience and policies rather than vice versa. Certainly, as has been noted by various Western scholars, the East Germans themselves were arguing in the late 1960s that they had reached a development point at which the GDR could become a development model for other, less advanced communist states; the implication was that the USSR would become correspondingly less influential.[12] Since we are interested in all the possible factors involved in the policy process, including, for example, the influence of interests in a complex society, the GDR's experiences too might thus serve as an indicator of likely future developments in other communist countries.

Fourth, the GDR is a small communist state (with approximately 17 million inhabitants as opposed to over 260 million in the USSR) and as such might have different problems, solutions, and political processes from the vast Soviet quasi-federation. Since other countries, such as Hungary, would have served this purpose equally well, this factor is dependent on the others already cited.

One additional, lesser point is that, in comparison with other communist states, there has been far too little research on the GDR in the English-speaking world.[13]

We now consider how the policy on industrial associations was chosen as the basis for this study. In all the communist states, economic policy is a key — perhaps *the* key — issue; this is certainly true when the economy is doing badly. Given that the official ideologies claim the superiority of the consciously steered economy over the "anarchism" of the capitalist market economy, the credibility of the political system is largely dependent on how well the planned economies fare in comparison with the leading Western states. During the 1950s, all the East European economies enjoyed rapid industrial growth; under such conditions, Ulbricht could make bold claims about the GDR catching up and surpassing the FRG, while Khrushchev made similar claims for the USSR vis-à-vis the USA. Clearly, then, when these growth rates started to fall, it was more than purely economic reasoning that made the political leaderships of Eastern Europe search hard for a solution — the credibility of the communist systems, the very raison d'être of these leaderships, was at stake. The directors of the one-party state can *claim* to be the only ones in the polity to have seen outside Plato's cave, but support for them will wane if they cannot deliver the everyday items the population wants; as Ellman so neatly expressed it, by the 1960s the people of Eastern Europe wanted Marks and Spencer's, not Marx and Engels.[14] Certainly, when the East Germans introduced their New Economic System (NES) in 1963, it was hailed as *the* answer to the major problem that was besetting East Germany at the time — the decleration in growth rates.[15] Similarly, the Soviet Union's Economic Reform of 1965 has probably had more coverage in the Soviet press than any other policy in the last fifteen years, with the possible exception of detente.[16]

In a highly stimulating article, Robert Campbell wrote in 1966, "It is in the deficiencies of this administrative structure that most of the troubles of Soviet-type economies lie,"[17] thus summarizing very neatly the importance of administration and the need to find an optimal structure in a planned economy. The achievement of an optimal administration is, of course, a very political matter. Again, Campbell has put this tersely: "The task of administration is, therefore, the directing of this production establishment *in the service of goals established by the leadership* [emphasis added]."[18] Thus the credibility and legitimacy of any communist leadership is in part dependent on its ability to maximize the efficiency of the machine that implements most of its economic policies, namely the administration.

Hence economic administration is a key policy area in communist states; in the highly industrialized ones, the administration of industry is of particular importance. Within this, there are four major reasons that the development of industrial associations is an especially important and germane policy area for analysis.

First, they are the nearest functional equivalent in the communist world to Western industrial corporations about which we can obtain much information. Interest in the economic and political role of the corporation under capitalism has mushroomed in recent years, but relatively little is known about developments in industrial organizations in states claiming to be socialist.[19] At present, there are no direct equivalents of the multinational or "transnational" in Eastern Europe — or indeed anywhere else in the communist world. There are branches of the Western (and Japanese) corporations in the capitals of most East European states; and there are various communist International Economic Organizations. One or two of these (e.g., Haldex) have been in existence since the late 1950s, but most have been established in the 1970s in the wake of the 1971 CMEA Complex Program, which heralded a new stage of integration in Eastern Europe.[20] They have been described by some as "socialist multinational concerns."[21] But although they do bear some resemblance to Western multinationals, they also differ from the latter in important ways — most notably in that they operate within planned economies and are directly responsible to the state. Moreover, we have at present insufficient information on these bodies to study them from a policy process viewpoint. However, there also exist large organizations (these can be called associations) which link enterprises, lead to specialization and concentration within them, and have the potential for becoming very important politically. There are for comparative purposes two basic types of association in both the USSR and the GDR — as well as in most of the other East European states.[22] On the one hand, there is the production (*proizvodstvennoe*) *ob"edinenie* (USSR)/*Kombinat* (GDR), which is a grouping of (usually) four to ten factories and, perhaps, R and D (research and development) organizations. In the GDR, the factories do not have all the legal and/or economic autonomy that they will previously have had as autonomous enterprises, while in the USSR, the level of autonomy of the component units varies considerably. On the other hand, there is the industrial (*promyshlennoe*) *ob"edinenie* (USSR)/VVB(GDR), which is a higher body, grouping both enterprises and the lower-level associations (i.e., production associations and combines).[23] The units subordinate to an industrial association/VVB normally enjoy a higher level of autonomy than those subordinate to production associations/combines. Finally, whereas the administration of the production *ob"edinenie*/combine is usually situated in one of the production units (such as a factory) of the association, the administration in the higher type of association is generally quite separate from production.

One of the reasons such organizations have the potential for being politically important is that they often constitute monopolistic or oligopolistic organizations for whole subbranches of industry; this concentration could in the long term lead to worker and/or management awareness of bargaining power over government in much the same way as monopolistic or oligopolistic organizations are sometimes argued to exercise power in the West. At present, there is only scant evidence to suggest that these organizations or their work forces ever do pose the same kind of threats as they can in the capitalist world. Nevertheless, their development reveals much that is interesting, particularly to political scientists and economists. In sum, although the *main* focus of this study is not on the economic and social problems of concentration and centralization, many of the problems associated with these processes in any sociopolitical and economic system are touched upon and will be of interest to a wider range of readers than merely specialists in communist affairs.

The second reason relates to the first, in that it concerns the question of power relationships within the economic and political systems. The associations in both countries have developed largely at the expense of both the higher organs (primarily, since 1965, the ministries) and the lower organs (notably the single-factory enterprise) in the industrial hierarchy. They have taken over many rights from these other bodies,[24] a fact that would lead one a priori to expect a certain amount of hostility from people working in the organizations losing powers; this is the main point inherent in the Brezhnev quotation that opens this introduction.[25] Anyone familiar with the veiled allusions in communist leaders' statements will realize that this quotation suggests that the Soviets had been experiencing "political" problems with their own administration. This has indeed been the case, as we shall see; let us now consider why this should be of interest.

With the fading of the Cold War during the late 1950s/early 1960s and the simultaneous upsurge of behavioralist and comparative approaches in political science, Western scholars began seriously to question earlier, generally accepted assumptions about the political systems of the USSR and Eastern Europe. It soon became evident to many that the totalitarian model was less applicable than it might have been at the height of Stalinism. But if this model was wrong, or at least in question, what *did* these political systems look like? How did they function and how similar were they to the Western "liberal-democratic" model, itself rather varied when applied to the individual states of Western Europe, North America, and so on. Several models, ideal types, and approaches were developed, among them Kassof's "administered society" and Meyer's "complex bureaucracy."[26] Many of these writers argue that although the communist states are managed in a different way than the classic totalitarian model would suggest, their political processes are also rather different from those in Western pluralist systems. But one school of thought, subsumed for the sake of simplicity under the heading of the "convergence theorists" went much further and argued that, basically, industrial society has certain laws of its own that are more powerful as homogenizing or unifying agents than the centrifugal forces of differing ideologies. According to this "technological determinism" argument, therefore, the political processes in communist and pluralist states would become increasingly similar.[17] In a strong attack on this school, Brzezinski and Huntington nevertheless conceded that there were certain aspects of the industrial and technological society that cut across ideology to produce very similar processes in allegedly qualitatively different societies. One aspect of this is the role that interests and interest groups can play in the political process.[28] Brzezinski and Huntington did not elaborate on this, but the seed of the idea had been sown.

Thus by the mid- and late 1960s several scholars (mainly North American) had published their ideas on interest groups in communist — and especially the Soviet — systems.[29] Several communist states, including the Soviet Union, officially deny the existence of interest groups altogether in their polities.[30] Yet, just as Bentham and later Bagehot did with respect to British politics, so Western analysts of communist affairs in the 1960s refused to accept constitutional descriptions of the political process as necessarily reflecting the actual nature of politics in the Soviet Union and Eastern Europe. Of course, there was the problem of gathering data for endorsing or refuting the various hypotheses being made. But this difference in studying the impact of interest groups in, say, Britain or the USSR tends to be one of degree rather than quality; politics at the top, where the final decisions are made, remains largely secret in both states. Proof that much could be discovered about groups in Eastern Europe was provided by the publication of various highly detailed studies of them. Many writers maintained that certain groups in such societies were sometimes able to exert influence on the political process, usually by virtue of their functional necessity in a highly industrialized society.[31] While much of this writing seemed persuasive, and was accompanied by considerable data, the "quantitative" presentation sometimes tended to blur the fact that many of these studies were largely only of the social composition and position of various groups, and that evidence of actual involvement in the political process was lacking or scant. Hardt and Frankel, for instance, produced a very useful account of the background (educational, class, and so on) of Soviet managers, referred briefly to their channels of access within the political system without properly examining the importance of this, and yet, based on little more than a priori assumptions, argued that "the core of managerial cadres in industry appears to represent a group with common interests and identification" and that "the managers and economists, as interest groups, may represent forces of institutional change, as contrasted with groups such as the military and the police which stand for the status quo."[32] This they did without examining in detail the role of the two "groups" mentioned as innovators or defenders on a specific policy. For this reason, writers

Introduction

like Griffiths argued for more empirical case studies of the role of groups, whereby the development of a given policy or set of policies — rather than functional groups — would be studied, *after* which one would be in a position to discuss the role in this policy of interest groups.[33] The policy examined here is one that directly affects "the managers" and other functional groups in industry, and which they are therefore more likely to attempt to influence than, for instance, a policy on literary dissidence. As David Lane has succinctly put it, "It is . . . somewhat unreal to describe 'interest groups' without specifying the issues on which the groups may politically intervene."[34] In addition, given the conflicts over rights and authority implied (and therefore recognized) by Brezhnev, the policy looked like one over which we would be as likely to find evidence of political conflict and group involvement as any.

Closely related to this is the fact that the Soviet and East German leaderships have on various occasions in the 1960s and 1970s looked to the associations as the keystone for improving industrial administration and hence economic performance. They constituted the principal innovation of the Soviet Union's 1973 reform of industry — the first major change since 1965 — and their development was looked upon by Leon Smolinskii, for instance, as "potentially the most important of such measures [i.e., industrial reorganization — LTH] in four decades."[35] While past record suggests that much of this "potential" may never be realized,[36] the Soviets themselves certainly had an extensive discussion of the expected advantages of the associations in the period preceding major legislation on them (1973-1974). In the case of the GDR, the former East German leader himself (Ulbricht) claimed that the success of the New Economic System would depend largely on the VVBs, and was enthusiastic about the combines in the late 1960s.

Thus the policy is important and appeared to be as good as any for revealing the minimum tolerated participation levels in the ongoing political process and the relationship between leadership and groups[37] — against which Western descriptions, from totalitarianism through pluralism, could be tested.

The final reason relates to the point made above concerning policy emulation. Interestingly, the development of the two basic kinds of association emerged in reverse order in the two states. In other words, the production associations temporally preceded the industrial *ob"edineniya* in the USSR, whereas the combines were seriously developed in the GDR after the VVBs had already been functioning for some time. Although in the 1960s the East German leadership often appeared to be emulating changes that had been introduced in the USSR (e.g., by reestablishing branch ministries at the end of 1965), they also on occasion introduced significant changes long before rather similar restructurings occurred in the latter state. Even when they do seem to have followed Soviet practice, the emulation has often been only of terminology rather than substance. In the early 1960s, for instance, the East Germans were unquestionably devolving industrial decision-making — even if they did have a central body called the National Economic Council, as the Soviets did—at a time when recentralization measures were being taken in the USSR. Also, the VVBs existed long before the industrial *ob"edineniya* in the USSR and, at least until the end of the 1970s, still appeared to have more extensive authority than their Soviet counterparts. All this runs counter to many of the popular views on the relationship between the Soviet Union and most of the communist states of Eastern Europe already discussed. Yet on the other hand, major pieces of *legislation* on associations in *both* states were ratified within days of each other (in March 1973), which is more than coincidental and the East German leader, E. Honecker, actually stated in May 1973 that

> the Central Committee of the CPSU and the Council of Ministers of the USSR have adopted a decision on measures for further improving the management of industry, careful evaluation of which will be an essential aid to us. It is aimed at a strong increase in the level of concentration of socialist industry, the effective linking of science and production and the extension and development of profit-and-loss accounting. Of particular significance is the high level of agreement between the paths taken in the USSR and the GDR for the improvement of the management of industry. Thus, the Soviet decision is an important confirmation for us, but at the same time a stimulus further to develop our practice too.[38]

In other words, it looked a priori as if suggestions made in the late 1960s by people like Willi Brandt that the GDR was no longer a satellite of the USSR were perhaps premature after all. This particular set of policies might therefore reveal much about both the changing influences in the political process in the GDR and its changing level of political dependency on the USSR. By examining the extent to which statements such as these are mere rhetoric or actually reflect practice, we will be in a better position for explaining the type and scope of political dependency of the smaller state on the larger. We now consider the research approach, some definitions, and the layout.

A variant of the systems approach has been used in this study to analyze the political process and the role of groups, leadership, and the like, within it. Basically, the political process can be seen as a continuum, but in which, for the sake of analysis, we can isolate a four-stage cycle. This runs as follows:

(1) "Demand" Input. As Welsh has pointed out,[39] there are various problems involved in attempting to apply the Eastonian systems approach to communist polities. One of these is that in a polity in which industry is totally or largely state-owned and the industrial managers are almost all members of the communist party (i.e., where there is considerable overlap between the party, the state, and the industrial sector), there are conceptual problems in distinguishing between autonomous demands made on "the state system" or "the party" and what might be interpreted simply as the internal workings of these organizations. However, an acceptably clear distinction can in most cases be made between, on the one hand, industrial managers, local party *apparatchiki* (full-time, professional party functionaries), local state officials, and so on, and, on the other, those directly involved at central levels in making general policy and authoritative statements.[40] It was therefore decided to accept any calls for associations from those not occupying senior positions in the party and/or government apparatuses as subleadership "demands"; for the reasons just elaborated, such "demands" may well emanate from what in liberal democracies might be called "institutionalized" or "insider" groups.[41]

The concept of a "demand" is also difficult to apply to communist polities because of the official attitudes toward interest groups. This problem is, however, more appropriately considered later in the study; for the present, the term "demand" is invariably used in quotation marks when referring to the GDR and the USSR.

(2) Macro Policy Statements. This stage refers to general statements of policy by the political leadership, usually of Politburo rank.

(3) Micro Policy Formulation. By this is meant the elaboration of the details of macro policy statements — the legislation endorsing, amplifying, and explaining the general statements made at party Congresses and so on.

(4) Policy Implementation. Normally, this is the stage at which stages 2 and 3 are put into practice. The success of this can merge with stage 1, and be called a level of "support"; this is, of course, a narrower usage of the term "support" than Easton's.[42] Poor support for the policy can lead to a new round of policy outputs (stages 2 and

3), at the same time that criticisms of the implementation constitute a new round of demands. This ongoing process is rather like what Easton has called the "feedback loop"[43] and will in this study be called simply the "policy process," the "political process," or the "continuum."

Although reference has been made to a continuous four-stage cycle, it is *not* assumed that the history of any policy will necessarily proceed through all four stages. Nor is it assumed that the *numerical* order given above necessarily reflects the *chronological* order of a policy. Leaders may pronounce on a policy *before* there is any overt subleadership demand for change; this would be expected anyway in a communist state, with an allegedly more teleological approach to policy-making than pluralist approaches, which tend to respond to specific demands rather than make decisions linked to some final goal (the "disjointed incrementalist" approach to policy-making, as Braybrooke and Lindblom have called it).[44] Indeed, one reflection of the power of interest groups within a polity would be to examine whether, on any policy where a definite beginning to the continuum can be observed, stage 1 preceded stage 2 or came later. Thus, "demands" in a communist system may be made *after* the political leadership has already called for suggestions for improvement in a given area and/or it has laid down parameters within which the nongovernmental subsystem knows it can and *should* formulate "demands." It might be objected — particularly if the teleological dimension of communist policy-making is considered to be largely theoretical and of little relevance to the everyday realities of running a state and maintaining leaders in power — that stage two may only *appear* to precede stage 1 because stage 4 (implementation) actually merges into stage 1, and that *this* has prompted the leadership to make a pronouncement in the first place. Expressing this by way of example, it could be that poor work attitudes largely resulting from existing policies (and thus representing a low level of support) are perceived as having led to declining growth rates. The leaders respond by saying that a reform of the economic system is needed. They have done this not because of a serious study of the "dialectic" of economic development on the path to communism, but because they know that their own legitimacy is closely related to the performance of the economic system. They are therefore, in one sense, responding to a demand. However, we are concerned in this study with distinguishing overt, articulated demands at stage 1 from responses to falling growth rates and so on. It is for this reason that our conception of "input" is narrower, or at least more deliberately subdivided than in Easton's version. Of course, interests that are in no way aggregated or articulated by a subleadership group can and do influence stage 2. Awareness of hostility or conservatism toward a policy might be assimilated by senior party or governmental bodies (e.g., the Central Committee Secretariat) and be communicated to the leadership, thus being of relevance to the policy-making. But a very clear distinction between the role of interests in this form and interests which are overtly articulated and aggregated by a subleadership interest group should be drawn, since a major component of our argument about the political process in communist states is going to rest on this distinction. It is for this reason that we have not adhered to the more conventional positioning of support with demands (i.e., both at stage 1) but have included support under policy implementation. In the real world, it should be reemphasized, stages 1 and 4 can be adjacent and simultaneous.

In order to qualify as an "interest group," a set of individuals would have to show strong evidence that it was aware of itself as a group with common interests, which it would be prepared to defend or promote in some way; it would, in other words, attempt to influence policy output. Thus, the term "interest group" is used here in the narrow sense of a form of pressure group. This does not mean that we cannot talk of "the managers" as a *group,* but in doing so before the analysis of their political involvement is completed, we are merely referring to a functional and/or social group rather than to an interest group. In searching for interest groups, the sort of evidence looked for has been calls to action in a forum common to the individuals/functional groups (e.g., a journal, a conference) and criticisms or merely recognition of the group by outsiders, especially the political leadership.

Given our premise that the policy process is essentially continuous, the choice of a precise period for analysis was not without difficulties. It was decided to take the legislation on associations passed in the USSR in 1973-1974 and in the GDR in 1973 as the principal fulcrum of the study, from which it would be necessary to work backwards for the inputs and forwards for the implementation. But the question remained, How far back and forward? The main period finally selected was from the late 1950s to 1976, for the following reasons. In the case of the USSR, indigenous economic historians themselves agree that the present generation of *ob"edineniya* dates from 1961, in the sense that that is when the first ones were established. Hence, by analyzing Soviet literature since the late 1950s, we hope to be in a position to explain how and why Soviet associations were created from 1961. The takeoff point for the East German combines is usually given as the late 1960s, so that a priori the mid-1960s represents a logical point at which to start the analysis of their development. The starting point for a consideration of the VVBs is less obvious. It could be argued that the renaming and restructuring of the VVBs undertaken following legislation in February 1958 (see Chapter 1) suggests that the analysis should begin in the mid-1950s. However, it is the intention here to compare like with like to the maximum degree possible, so that the transformation of the VVBs under the New Economic System — in particular, their transfer to profit-and-loss accounting — is taken as the first watershed in their development. This is justified on the grounds that the VVBs were in some important respects closer to the Soviet *glavki* (ministerial subdivisions; see Chapter 1) than to the industrial *ob"edineniya* prior to 1963. Consequently, the period *since* the changes in industrial administration announced in 1958 constitutes the starting point for the main analysis of the GDR.

The choice of a terminal point was not quite so difficult; there are two main reasons that the year 1976 was chosen. First, both the USSR and the GDR held their quinquennial party congresses in that year. Since this seemed a sufficiently long period since the legislation to permit an assessment of implementation, and given that a stock-taking of the situation was undertaken there — by the Soviet leadership at least — these congresses were taken as the principal cutoff points. Second, a major new development in East German policy began to emerge in 1977, and this culminated in new legislation on the combines being passed in November 1979. A thorough analysis of this would have necessitated a further, prolonged study-trip to Berlin — a possibility not open to the author — in addition to which, in terms of the stages of the policy process, the situation at the time of writing was ongoing.[45] Moreover, the recent East German developments have not yet been mirrored in the USSR, so that the adoption of November 1979 as the main cutoff point would have produced a very lopsided "comparative" study. This said, there are important grounds for including in this study references to developments both prior to the late 1950s and since 1976. First, there is, relatively, so little published in English on the associations that reference to the broader history of these bodies is sometimes necessary for an understanding of the context of their development; for instance, without such references most readers would be unable to assess whether a proposal for change was really novel or constituted merely renewed interest in an earlier idea. Second, some readers might be more interested in the associations themselves than the policy process relating to them and will therefore want as much detail on their history as possible. In sum, while the main period for the analysis of the policy process is from the late 1950s to 1976, information on the periods both before and since these dates is included whenever this seems appropriate.

Chapter 1 is predominantly descriptive, outlining the organization of industrial administration in the two states; without this, much of what follows would be difficult to follow for anyone not already having a detailed knowledge of the two systems. The chapter also includes a brief history of the associations. Chapters 2 through 7 reflect the systems approach to the policy process. Chapters 2 and 3 are concerned with the potential channels for "demands," and the calls for the associations (i.e., the "demands" themselves); an analysis of differences of opinion is made, followed by some initial comments on the extent to which interest groups are identifiable. Chapter 4 deals with the leadership views and official policy on the associations (macro policy statements), while Chapter 5 is concerned with various aspects of the legislation on them. In Chapter 6, the implementation of the policy is examined, and it is shown that this stage to some extent temporally preceded the other stages in the USSR. Opposition to the associations and the importance of this to their development forms the basis of Chapter 7. In the concluding chapter, we consider first the impact of factors other than "demands" from below and attitudes on the development of the associations; these include the industrial structure, the foreign trade structure, external influences, political culture, and ideology. We then draw together the various strands of the policy process in the two countries in order to make generalizations about the role of interests and interest groups in communist states, the role of leadership, and so on.

NOTES

1. See I. Volgyes (ed.) *Political Socialization in Eastern Europe* (New York: Praeger, 1975); A. H. Brown and J. Gray (eds.), *Political Culture and Political Change in Communist States* (London: Macmillan, 1977); A. Dallin and G. W. Breslauer, *Political Terror in Communist Systems* (Stanford: Stanford U.P., 1970); T. T. Hammond (ed.), *The Anatomy of Communist Takeovers* (New Haven: Yale U.P., 1975).

2. Even among those books and articles specifically concerned with the policy process in individual states, the emphasis has usually tended to be on policy-making rather than the whole policy process, and has often been of a generalized, inferential rather than a detailed, empirical nature. Although an exhaustive list of studies cannot be included here, interested readers may find the following random selection of use (several other studies are referred to at various points throughout this book):

P. H. Juviler and H. W. Morton (eds.), *Soviet Policy-Making* (London: Pall Mall, 1967); James B. Bruce, *The Politics of Soviet Policy Formation* (Denver: University of Denver Graduate School of International Studies, 1976); S. Ploss, *Conflict and Decision-Making in Soviet Russia* (Princeton: Princeton U.P., 1965); J. M. Starrels and A. M. Mallinckrodt, *Politics in the German Democratic Republic* (New York: Praeger, 1975); O. Ulč, *Politics in Czechoslovakia* (San Francisco: Freeman, 1974), esp. pp. 59-84; P. A. Toma and I. Volgyes, *Politics in Hungary* (San Francisco: Freeman, 1977), esp. pp. 55-73; M. C. Oksenberg, "Policy Making under Mao Tse-tung, 1949-1968," *Comparative Politics*, No. 3, 1971, pp. 323-360. One noteworthy development since the early 1970s has been the appearance of several analyses of the role of particular functional groups in the policy process — partially as a result of criticism that earlier analyses of groups had concentrated too heavily on their social background. In this connection, see T. A. Baylis, *The Technical Intelligentsia and the East German Elite* (Berkeley: University of California Press, 1974); R. B. Remnek (ed.), *Social Scientists and Policy Making in the USSR* (New York: Praeger, 1977); P. H. Solomon, *Soviet Criminologists and Criminal Policy* (New York: Columbia U.P., 1978); R. J. Hill, *Soviet Politics, Political Science and Reform* (Oxford: Martin Robertson, 1980). One of the very rare comparative analyses is G. K. Bertsch's *Power and Policy in Communist Systems* (New York: John Wiley, 1978), esp. pp. 131-145; Bertsch's analysis is considered in our concluding chapter.

3. A. H. Brown, "Policymaking in Communist States," *Studies in Comparative Communism*, No. 4, 1978, p. 424.

4. According to the official Soviet view, the USSR is now at the stage of "developed" or "mature" socialism. For an analysis of this, see A. B. Evans, "Developed Socialism in Soviet Ideology," *Soviet Studies*, No. 3, 1977, pp. 409-428, and the chapter on the USSR by R. J. Hill, T. Dunmore, and K. Dawisha in L. T. Holmes (ed.), *The Withering Away of the State? Party and State under Communism* (London and Beverly Hills: Sage, 1981).

5. For example, G. Ionescu, *The Break-Up of the Soviet Empire in Eastern Europe* (Harmondsworth: Penguin, 1965), passim, esp. p. 41.

6. The basic tenet of the "Brezhnev Doctrine" is limited sovereignty. See *World Communism 1967-1969: Soviet Efforts to Re-establish Control* (Washington, D.C.: U.S. Government Printing Office, 1970), passim, esp. pp. 110-112.

7. J. W. Strong's "The Sino-Soviet Dispute" in A. Bromke and T. Rakowska-Harmstone (eds.), *The Communist States in Dissarray 1965-1971* (Minneapolis: University of Minnesota Press, 1972), esp. pp. 36-37. For the Chinese position both before and since the death of Mao Zedong, see "Diabolical Social-Imperialist Face of the Soviet Revisionist Renegade Clique," *Peking Review*, No. 43, 1968, pp. 8-10; Institute of World Economy of the Chinese Academy of Social Science, "Soviet Social-Imperialism — Most Dangerous Source of World War," *Peking Review*, No. 29, 1977, pp. 4-10, 21. For a Western argument, see A. Avtorkhanov, "The New Phase of Soviet Expansionist Policy," *Bulletin of the Institute for the Study of tussr*, No. 12, 1971, pp. 13-31.

8. F. Fejtö, *A History of the People's Democracies* (Harmondsworth: Penguin, 1974), p. 388.

9. Ionescu, *The Break-Up . . .* , p. 157.

10. Z. K. Brzezinski, *The Soviet Bloc: Unity and Conflict* (Cambridge, MA: Harvard U.P., 1967), pp. 448-449.

11. Trade figures from *Statistisches Jahrbuch der Deutschen Demokratischen Republik – 1974* (Berlin: Staatsverlag der DDR, 1974), pp. 282-283. The mode of presentation of trade figures in the official GDR statistical annuals has now been

Introduction

changed, so that it is no longer possible to use these to distinguish between exports to and imports from the USSR.

12. This idea was inherent in the publication of the book *Politische Oekonomie des Sozialismus and ihre Anwendung in der DDR* in 1969 (Berlin: Dietz Verlag) as recognized in, for example, W. Kalweit and P. Reinhold, "Zum Erscheinen des Buches 'Politische Oekonomie des Sozialismus und ihre Anwendung in der DDR,' " *Wirts/wiss.*, No. 10, 1969, pp. 1442-1457. For a Western view, see Z. Brzezinski, "The Soviet Past and Future," *Encounter*, No. 3, 1970, pp. 13-16.

13. It is significant that in the bibliography to H. G. Skilling's *The Governments of Communist East Europe* (New York: Crowell, 1966) the section on the politics of individual states referred to at least one English-language book on every East European communist country except one — the GDR (pp. 238-239). The situation has marginally improved since then.

14. M. Ellman, *Economic Reform in the Soviet Union* (London: P.E.P., 1969) p. 358. Marks and Spencer's is a British chain of department stores specializing in reasonably priced but high-quality consumer goods.

15. For a useful discussion of the importance attached by the GDR leadership to the NES, see T. A. Baylis, "Economic Reform as Ideology: East Germany's New Economic System," *Comparative Politics*, No. 3, 1971, pp. 211-229. Growth rate figures can be found in the concluding chapter of the present study.

16. On the Soviet reform see Ellman, *Economic Reform . . .* , passim. On reform in Eastern Europe and the USSR, see K. C. Thalheim and H-H. Hoehmann (eds.), *Wirtschaftsreformen in Osteuropa* (Cologne: Verlag Wissenschaft und Politik, 1968); L. A. D. Dellin and H. Gross (eds.), *Reforms in the Soviet and East European Economies* (Lexington, MA: D. C. Heath, 1972); and H-H. Hoehmann, M. Kaser and K. C. Thalheim (eds.), *The New Economic Systems of Eastern Europe*, (London: C. Hurst and Co., 1975).

17. R. Campbell in H. Rosovsky (ed.), *Industrialisation in Two Systems* (New York: John Wiley, 1966).

18. *Ibid.*, p. 187.

19. For an early survey of writing on the Western multinational corporations in politics, see R. L. Heilbroner, "The Multi-National Corporations and the Nation-State," *New York Review of Books*, No. 2, 1971, pp. 20-25. For a more up-to-date bibliography, see the footnotes to T. H. Moran, "Multi-National Corporations and Dependency: A Dialogue for Dependentistas and Non-Dependentistas," *International Organisation*, Winter 1978, pp. 79-100. References to the literature on industrial organization in the socialist states are scattered throughout the present study.

20. On the concept and role of Western "transnationals," see S. P. Huntington, "Transnational Organisations in World Politics," *World Politics*, No. 3, 1973, pp. 333-368. For a lively, up-to-date, but very poorly footnoted analysis of the Western corporations' activities in Eastern Europe, see C. Levinson, *Vodka Cola* (Horsham: C. Levinson, 1980), passim, esp. Ch. 3 and Pt. 5. On the International Economic Organizations, see E. Faude and M. Heinze, "Internationale Oekonomische Organisationen Sozialistischer Laender," *Einheit*, No. 6, 1975, pp. 673-678, and J. W. van Brabant, *Socialist Economic Integration* (Cambridge, England: Cambridge U. P., 1980), esp. pp. 195-216.

21. See J. Bethkenhagen and H. Machowski, *Integration im Rat fuer Gegenseitige Wirtschaftshilfe* (Berlin: Berlin Verlag, 1976), p. 15.

22. For a detailed comparative analysis of the administrative structures in Eastern Europe, see Yu. F. Kormnov and R. N. Yevstigneev (eds.), *Struktura Upravleniya Promyshlennost'yu v Strankakh SEV* (Moscow: Izd. Mysl', 1973).

23. At the time of writing, the VVBs were being phased out, though there still appeared to be some; but see note 45 below.

24. In the GDR this situation was reversed in the early 1970s, although it changed again in the late 1970s; see Ch. 1.

25. This quotation is from L. I. Brezhnev, *Ob Osnovnykh Voprosakh Ekonomicheskoi Politiki KPSS Na Sovremennom Etape: Rechi i Doklady*, Vol. 1 (Moscow: Politizdat, 1975), p. 421.

26. Useful summaries of the various approaches can be found in A. H. Brown, *Soviet Politics and Political Science* (London: Macmillan, 1974), passim; D. Lane, *Politics and Society in the USSR* (London: Martin Robertson, 1978), pp. 178-202; D. Lane, *The Socialist Industrial State* (London: Allen & Unwin, 1976), pp. 19-70.

27. Probably the best account of convergence theories is that by A. G. Meyer in C. Johnson (ed.), *Change in Communist Systems* (Stanford: Stanford U.P., 1970), pp. 313-341.

28. Z. Brzezinski and S. P. Huntington, *Political Power – USA:USSR* (New York: Viking Compass, 1965), passim, esp. pp. 195-196.

29. The standard work on interest groups in the USSR is that of H. G. Skilling and F. Griffiths (eds.), *Interest Groups in Soviet Politics* (Princeton: Princeton U.P., 1971). The seminal article on interest groups in communist states generally is H. G. Skilling's "Interest Groups and Communist Politics," *World Politics*, No. 3, 1966, pp. 435-451. A brief but readily available list of other articles and books concerned with interest groups in communist states is in R. C. Gripp, *The Political System of Communism* (London: Nelson, 1973), pp. 149-150, while Brown, *Soviet Politics* . . . , includes much of the best-known work on the Soviet Union in the footnotes to his Chapter 3 (pp. 120-124).

30. G. Ionescu, *Comparative Communist Politics* (London: Macmillan, 1972), pp. 30-32. Ionescu points out that certain communist states are far more prepared to accept the notion of some form of pluralism than others; pluralism is not per se a bad thing in Yugoslavia, for instance. See the authoritative book by E. Kardelj, *Democracy and Socialism* (London: Summerfield Press, 1978), esp. pp. 115-140.

31. The interested reader will find a useful survey of this "industrialization determinism' argument in Lane, *Politics and Society* . . . , pp. 183-189. An example of the detailed analyses of groups in Eastern Europe was the (unfortunately incomplete) series of volumes published by Macmillan that emerged from a British-based research project coordinated by Prof. G. Ionescu between 1968 and 1971; the series was entitled "Political and Social Processes in Eastern Europe," and included D. Lane and G. Kolankiewicz (eds.) *Social Groups in Polish Society* !London: Macmillan, 1973).

32. J. P. Hardt and T. Frankel, in Skilling and Griffiths, *Interest Groups in Soviet Politics*, p. 173.

33. F. Griffiths, *Ibid.*, pp. 335-377.

34. Lane, *Politics and Society* . . . , p. 234.

35. L. Smolinskii, "Towards a Socialist Corporation: Soviet Industrial Reorganisation of 1973." *Survey*, No. 1, 1974, p. 24.

36. The many drawbacks encountered in the implementation of the 1965 Soviet Economic Reform — perhaps suggestive of what can happen to other attempts at changing the economic structure and mechanism — are described in G. Schroeder's "Soviet Economic Reform at an Impasse," *P of C*, No. 4, 1971, pp. 36-46.

37. The reason we argue that participation will be minimal is precisely because of the importance of the policy to the leadership; this requires explanation. There are

Introduction

various dilemmas facing the leaderships of the maturer communist states, one of which concerns political participation. On the one hand, the leaderships must demonstrate that they are fostering socialist democracy — which implies the extension of political participation — as part of their self-legitimizing exercises. On the other hand, some policies must be kept very much under control to ensure their success, which also relates to regime legitimacy. In the case of the latter sort of policy, often economic, there must be wide participation of specialists (i.e., to maximize the possibilities of achieving an optimal policy), but not of the general public.

38. E. Honecker, *Aus dem Bericht des Politbueros an die 9. Tagung des ZK der SED* (Berlin: Dietz Verlag, 1973), p. 44.

39. W. A. Welsh, "The Usefulness of Social Stratification, Input-Output, and Issue-Processing Models in the Study of Communist Systems in Eastern Europe," (presented at the 66th APSA Conference, Los Angeles, September 1970), esp. p. 10.

40. However, see the comments on Podgorny's contributions at the November 1962 plenum in our conclusions.

41. See, for example, W. P. Grant, "Insider and Outsider Groups" (presented at the ECPR Workshop on Interest Groups, Berlin, March 1977); these "demands" are often called "withinputs."

42. D. Easton, *A Systems Analysis of Political Life* (New York: John Wiley, 1965), passim, esp. pp. 159-161.

43. *Ibid.*, pp. 363-381.

44. D. Braybrooke and C. E. Lindblom, *A Strategy for Decision* (New York: Free Press, 1970), passim, esp. pp. 81-110. For a discussion of the "teleological" approach, see Ionescu, *Comparative Communist Politics*, pp. 48-49; this form of policy-making is essentially the same as what Braybrooke and Lindblom describe as the "synoptic" approach. A fuller discussion of types of policy process is included in the concluding chapter.

45. Since this book went to the publishers, the East Germans have held their Tenth Congress (April 1981). It seems clear from Honecker's speech at this that VVBs have indeed all been disbanded now and replaced by combines. See "Bericht des Zentralkomitees der Sozialistischen Einheitspartei Deutschlands an den X. Parteitag der SED," *N.D.*, 12 April 1981, p. 8.

Chapter 1

STRUCTURES OF INDUSTRY

Before embarking upon a study of the politics of association development, it is essential to have a clear picture of the structure of industry in both the GDR and the USSR, and of the position and functions of the associations within these structures. Most of this chapter is therefore concerned with the arrangement of industrial administration in the two states as envisaged in the legislation of the early/mid-1970s. The approach adopted is to examine the primary production units first, followed by the middle-tier bodies and finally the industrial ministries and other central organs. There are two major reasons that information on the earlier period is also included in this chapter, however. First, some forms of industrial unit have in recent years virtually or totally disappeared; this particularly relates to certain forms of East German enterprise. Therefore, since an appreciation of later chapters depends to some extent on the present one, a description of the role and nature of various types of enterprise as they were until the announcement of a major new nationalization drive in the GDR in June 1972, and of other organs which no longer exist, is included here.[1] Second, an understanding of the changing importance of the associations is necessary for placing subsequent chapters into an overall context; thus a brief historical overview of development is also included. Although the systems approach adopted in this study means that the *detailed* analysis of the development of associations (i.e., implementation) is left to Chapter 6, many of the debates, for instance, make little sense without some appreciation of the major changes in industrial administration over the past twenty years or so. The reader will recall the emphasis in the introduction on the continuous or circular nature of the political process; therefore this division of the history into two parts is not imcompatible with our methodology if it helps to produce a clearer narrative.

A final introductory point is that although the *formal* status of organizations is presented whenever possible, there are some areas in which the status of a given unit is still contentious. In such cases, what appears to be the most commonly accepted definition or conception has been presented.

1.1. THE STRUCTURE OF SOVIET INDUSTRY

Unlike the East German situation, there is no private ownership of industry in the USSR. Thus, in terms of ownership, there is only one type of enterprise, which from most points of view (e.g., planning) is the lowest level of the industrial administrative hierarchy.

THE ENTERPRISE *(PREDPRIYATIE)*

The state enterprise was until the early 1970s considered the basic unit in Soviet industry. Since 1973, however, the production association has also become a "basic (primary) link"; this follows a policy statement to this effect made at the 24th CPSU Congress in 1971.[2] Nevertheless, since the majority of enterprises in Soviet industry are as yet not part of a production association (see below), the enterprise must still be considered as an entity in its own right. The status of the enterprise was laid down in the Statute on the Socialist State Production Enterprise, which was ratified by the Council of Ministers on 4 October 1965, that is, shortly after the announcement of the Economic Reform at the end of September of that year.[3] This document is still in force vis-à-vis those enterprises not forming part of a production association, and "in necessary circumstances" may even be extended to units within the association.[4]

The enterprise is an autonomous legal person in questions of legal transactions, and works on the profit-and-loss accounting (*khozraschet*) principle. Planning works in much the same way as in the GDR, with the enterprise putting forward its own proposals for consideration by higher bodies, which then ratify and/or modify it before returning to the enterprise.[5] The question of pricing in Soviet industry is a large and complex one, and cannot be tackled here; suffice it to say that enterprise autonomy in this field is minimal.[6]

The enterprise is directly subordinate to a ministry; to its subdivision, the *glavk;* to an industrial association; or, sometimes, to a production association.[7] It is headed by a director (or head or manager),[8] who works on the principle of *edinonachalie* or one-person management, a concept existing in the Soviet Union in its present form since 1929;[9] the director is formally obliged to take note of the various "social organizations" within the enterprise, however, when taking important decisions.[10] Below the director are various deputies, who, along with the chief accountant and the head of the department of technical control, are "hired and fired" by representation on the part of the director to his superior organ. In practice, his suggestions are limited by the "nomenclature" system for leading cadres throughout Soviet society. Very briefly, this means that senior posts need party ratification before being filled or vacated.[11]

Brief mention must be made of those enterprises that are subordinate to a production association, by way of comparison; inter alia, this is important for an understanding of the reluctance of some managers to have their enterprise become part of such a body. According to the decree of March 1973, enterprises forming part of a production association are not autonomous legal persons, and do not enjoy the rights granted enterprises under the 1965 statute. Such enterprises are usually called "filials" or "productions" (*proizvodstva*). Hence, if the 1965 Reform had raised expectations of greater autonomy among many enterprise directors and work forces that did not materialize to any great extent, the 1973 changes must have rubbed salt into the wound, in particular for many managers. It should also be noted, however, that there is a clause in the decree allowing certain enterprises to retain their original autonomy.[12] The political significance of all this will emerge more clearly later in the study.

THE PRODUCTION ASSOCIATIONS
(*PROIZVODSTVENNYE OB"EDINENIYA*)

According to the statute on the production associations of 27 March 1974, the production association is "a unified (*edinyi*) production-economic complex, in which are included factories, works, scientific research, design, project-design, technological organizations and other production units."[13] In other words, an *ob"edinenie* is a grouping of production and research units. Until recently, a commonly accepted typology of production associations was in use, and since the press still frequently uses this, an examination of the different types of organization is necessary. It must be borne in mind that the variables employed are those *still* existing in practice, and some forms are not envisaged in the 1973-74 legislation.

The major variables to be considered when attempting to classify a particular production association are

(1) whether enterprises and other organizations are linked "horizontally," "vertically," or both (these terms are explained below);

(2) the degree of autonomy of component units; and

(3) the administrative arrangement.

The majority of early production associations were formed by linking enterprises producing similar goods, that is, according to the horizontal principle.[14] This method has been most popular in the clothing, textile, woolen, footwear, furniture, and glass industries (i.e., in light industry generally). Such a unibranch association is often called a "firm" or *firma*.[15] The level of administrative centralization in a *firma* varies, but the apparatus of the head unit does assume overall leadership of the administrative bodies throughout the *ob"edinenie*.[16] Many firms are large, territorially unified entities, and in such cases are often directly subordinate to a ministry.[17] However, it has sometimes been considered useful to subordinate a firm. along with similar bodies in other parts of the country, to a larger production association, rather than directly to a ministry. For instance, the Tsentrmebel *ob"edinenie* includes firms in Vologodsk, Archangel, Serpukhov, Mytishchin, and the Don area.[18]

But not all unibranch associations are called *firmy*. Another type is the "amalgamated enterprise" (*ob"edinennoe predpriyatie*), in which formerly autonomous enterprises are linked, and all administrative functions are fully centralized. This type of association always has a single account in the state bank, whereas many firms do not. An example of this form of *ob"edinenie* is the Leningrad Optico-Mechanical *Ob"edinenie* (LOMO), where the administrative apparatus was formed on the basis of the apparatuses of all the component units, not merely the most important.[19]

A third type of production association is the "combine" (*kombinat*).[20] Here, production units of different branches are linked because of their common use of raw materials. As in the case of the firm, there is no set pattern in the level of autonomy of the component economic units. This form of association is found mainly in the chemical, metallurgical, food, and wood-processing branches of industry.

Fourth, there is the "trust" (*trest*), which, according to a statute of 1927 still seemingly in effect, is defined as

> a state industrial enterprise, organized on the basis of a special (*osobogo*) charter as an autonomous economic unit with the rights of a legal person and undivided capital assets being under the jurisdiction of one state institution, indicated in the charter, and working on the basis of commercial accounting in accordance with the planned indices confirmed by the institution referred to.[21]

This definition is not very helpful, however, since it makes little distinction between the enterprise and the trust. In practice, a trust links enterprises in one branch or subbranch of industry producing similar goods (i.e., on the horizontal principle). The distinguishing feature of the trust is that the administrative apparatus is quite separate from the production process (i.e., the factories); for this reason, many economists and others within the Soviet Union have criticized them as being superfluous links, particularly as they often constitute an additional tier between other types of association and ministries.[22] In a trust, the component enterprises and so on retain full legal autonomy. Trusts often cover a large territorial area, and are most commonly found in the timber, meat, and milk industries.

Yet another form of the production association is the "science-production association" (NPO),[23] defined in the December 1975 legislation on them as

> a unified science-production and economic complex, in which are included scientific research, design, project-design and technological organizations, works (factories), initiating and modification (*puskonaladochnye*), main assembly and other structural units, depending on the association's tasks.[24]

This type of association, in existence since 1968, includes enterprises, of course, but the central administration is based on an R and D (research and development) institution rather than being in a large production unit or in a separate administrative organ. Since these associations are often intended to supervise and coordinate the scientific research and development of an entire subbranch of industry, it is possible that some of them will be replaced by or in some way transformed into industrial associations (see below), although the reverse process is also feasible.[25]

A distinction is commonly made between three variants of the science-production association, according to the goal. In the first type, the NPO is intended to research, test, and introduce new products; in the second, there is a concentration on developing methods for further automating both the production line and the administrative system; in the third, the primary concern is the design and mastering of new technological processes.[26]

The fact that there is separate legislation on the NPOs from that for other production associations is a good indication of their unique position within the Soviet industrial administrative hierarchy. Moreover, given the intention in this study of comparing like with like to the greatest possible extent, the fact that the East Germans have no direct equivalent of the NPO might suggest that they should not be included here. On the other hand, the science-production associations were often treated in Soviet writing prior to 1973 as a form of production association, a practice to which economists, politicians, and others reverted in the late 1970s. For these reasons, the NPOs are considered in this study, but in much less detail than the main forms of production association.

Sixth, there is the "industrial trade association" (*promyshlenno-torgovoe ob"edinenie*) formed between production units of the consumer goods industry and sales outlets, the administrative arrangement usually being one of minimal centralization. This form of association was particularly encouraged in the late 1970s.

Finally, there is the "agroindustrial association" (*agrarno-promyshlennoe ob"edinenie*). Technically, this is a sort of combine. But many Soviet writers have treated it as a distinct type, and legislation in the late 1970s has endorsed this practice.[27] For this reason, they are treated in this study in essentially the same way as the NPOs are. In the agroindustrial association, farms — both state and collective[28] — link up with factories that process and/or package the farms' produce. One point on which Soviet writers seem to have been in agreement is that if small factories processing and/or packing raw materials are located within collective or state farms, this arrangement does not constitute an agroindustrial association.[29] Rather, the industrial units must be separate from the farm(s).

The head of a production association, according to the statute, is either the general-director or the director, who is to work on the familiar principle of one-person management plus collective deliberation (*kollegial'nost* or "collegiality") on all major questions relating to the running of the association. It is not specified in the statute whether the general-director is head of a body directly under a ministry, and the director of a body under an industrial association, but this does appear to be the case.[30] Each *ob"edinenie* has its own charter, which contains details of its organization and is ratified by its immediately superior organ.[31] The subordination pattern of production associations is treated in the next section. All associations are to be on profit-and-loss accounting.

As stated earlier, the latest statute on the production associations attempts to clarify the position of these bodies, and in particular the position of most enterprises within them. Apart from the aforementioned clause on autonomous enterprises, however, there are other important areas where the statute appears to clarify the ambiguities caused by having so many variations on a theme, only to obfuscate the picture a few lines on; details on this are to be found in Chapter 5. At this point, suffice it to say that the production associations' position is more ambiguous than that of the combine in the GDR.

THE INDUSTRIAL ASSOCIATIONS (*PROMYSHLENNYE OB"EDINENIYA*) AND THE *GLAVKI*

At least since the decrees of 1973-1974, there has been some standardization in Soviet writing of the distinction between the production and the industrial association.[32] The industrial *ob"edinenie* is now the official successor to the ministerial *glavk* (chief administration). Most branches or subbranches of industry are to be headed by an industrial association, which in turn is directly subordinate to a ministry. As is the case with ministries, these associations can be either under all-union or republic control (see next section). Not all branches have industrial associations, however, since it is considered that some are best run on a two-tier (ministry/production association) system.[33]

An industrial association has subordinate to it all the enterprises, R and D institutes, and production associations — other than those that themselves enjoy the rights of an industrial association — of the given branch. Since these organizations were intended to supersede the *glavki*, it is necessary to understand the essential differences between the two.

First, there is the question of financial status. The overwhelming majority of *glavki* were financed from the state budget, whereas the industrial associations are all to be on profit-and-loss accounting.[34]

Second, and following from this, there is supposed to be far greater cooperation between the economic units under the industrial *ob"edinenie* than there was under the *glavk*, and the association is to foster and/or encourage this cooperation.[35]

Third, whereas the *glavk* staff is an integral part of the ministry, the administrative staff of the industrial association is not supposed to be; in fact, it is to be territorially "nearer to production."[36]

The industrial association is responsible for the development of the units below it; encouraging specialization and cooperation; elaborating optimal plans for the branch; publicizing the experience of its enterprises; raising the quality of goods and output; improving administration and seeing that automation is introduced wherever possible; ensuring that the enterprises and so on fulfill their plan targets and their supply tasks; improving the working and participatory conditions of the employees; and developing socialist competition.[37]

In overall charge of such a body is the "head" (*nachal'nik*), again working on the one-person management principle plus collegiality.[38] Below the head are the deputy heads, the leaders of the basic structural subdivisions, the chief accountant, the head of the legal department ("chief legal adviser"), and the leading white-collar workers (*rabotniki*) of enterprises and organizations within the *ob"edinenie*. Again, these personnel are appointed or dismissed by the body above the association on the recommendation of the head of the association. The actual structure of the administration, and the numbers of personnel involved, are laid down by the association's superior body, not the association itself.

Soviet industrial associations are responsible for developing and keeping replenished a "management reserve," and for ensuring that opportunities to improve their qualifications are maximized for the employees.

The industrial *ob"edineniya* also have tasks in the field of cooperation and integration within the CMEA. From the wording of the official statutes on the two types of organizations, however, it would appear that the industrial associations are more subject to supervision in this field than their East German counterparts. For example, suggestions for cooperation with organizations in other CMEA countries require ratification from the ministries in the Soviet case, while the VVBs are themselves fully responsible for such work.[39] Moreover, it should be noted that the rights in this field, and also the limited rights in the field of exports, have been extended only to *all-union* (i.e., national) industrial associations, and not to their republic counterparts.[40]

At the present time, it is not always clear in what ways some types of industrial association — notably the all-union version — differ from some of the less important ministries (i.e., the union-republic ministry of a union republic), and it is hoped that the long-promised new general statute on the latter bodies will clear up this confusion.[41] For the time being, precedent suggests that we treat the various types of ministry as the tier above the associations; but the reader is urged to consult the diagram of the Soviet industrial structure at the end of this chapter for a clearer understanding of a complex picture.

THE MINISTRIES AND OTHER CENTRAL BODIES

Not all ministries are, strictly speaking, "central" bodies. In fact, there are four major types of ministry: the all-union ministry of the USSR, the union-republic ministry of the USSR, the union-republic ministry of a union republic, and the republic ministry. As already stated, a new statute on these bodies has been promised, but for the present the ministries are still working to the law of 2 October 1965 and the general statute of July 1967.[42] According to the more recent of these documents, the distinction between the first three types of ministry named above is as follows:

(1) The all-union ministry of the USSR is formed by the Supreme Soviet of the USSR and is in charge of all the production units in its branch, wherever situated; it deals with them either directly or through organs created by itself.

(2) The union-republic ministry of the USSR leads (*rukovodit*) the branch, as a rule, via ministries of the same name in the republics, and manages those enterprises, organizations, and institutions of all-union importance either directly or through organs created by itself; it is formed by the Supreme Soviet.

(3) The union-republic ministry of a union republic is under dual subordination, both to the ministry of the same name at the all-union level and to the appropriate republic Council of Ministers.

In addition, there are the republic ministries:

(4) The republic ministry is not covered by the two documents referred to above, but is described in the Soviet constitution as a ministry directly subordinate to the Council of Ministers of a union republic; thus it has no direct superior in Moscow, but obviously must conform to general policies on industry emanating from the center. Such ministries sometimes have subordinate to them ministries of autonomous republics.[43]

The functions of the branch ministries — at least of the first three types, and we suspect of the others too — are laid down in detail in the 1967 statute under the general headings of planning; science and technology; capital construction; material-technical supply; finance and credit; cadres, labor, and wages; and economic, scientific-technical, and cultural ties with foreign lands. Generally speaking, their tasks are similar to those of the industrial associations, only on a larger scale (i.e., more coordinatory work) and for longer terms. One important function, though, which is dealt with in the ministerial statute and not in that of the industrial associations, is that of arbitration; the ministries are responsible for resolving problems and disputes that arise within their respective branches of industry. Another important function of the ministry is that of confirming the individual charters of units below the ministerial level, and so having — potentially at least — a very real power to form the branch as it considers appropriate. Third, the fact that ministers sit on the Council of Ministers suggests that they are involved in a much broader range of discussion and decision-making, going beyond the limits of a single industrial branch, than the lower tiers in the industrial hierarchy. In addition to the branch ministries, various nonbranch ministries also play a very important role in the running of industry; one of the most important is the Ministry of Finance.

Apart from the ministries and their subdivisions (the *glavki,* which have already been considered and which have almost been phased out; and the "administrations" [*upravleniya*], which supervise the work of a given branch of industry in a republic when this branch is insufficiently developed to warrant a union-republic ministry of the union republic[44]), there are various other central organs concerned with industry, which are generally subsumed under the title *vedomstva*. The latter term is not readily translated by a single English word, and requires rather a definition. A suitable one is V. S. Pronina's; she describes them as

> the wide circle of central administrative organs, distinguishable by some feature from the ministries, and attached to (*obrazuemykh pri*) the Councils of Ministers of the USSR and the union republics or being organs of the Councils of Ministers (state committees, committees, *glavki*, inspectorates, commissions, councils, and others).[45]

It would be superfluous to list all of these bodies; included here are only those bodies that, for the purposes of this study, appear to have the most important roles in industry. Since several of these bodies are called "state committees," it is useful to attempt to understand the essential difference between these bodies and the ministries; again, Pronina is useful on this point. Having indicated by example the vagueness that exists in Soviet writing on the differences between the two types of institution, Pronina concludes that the ministries are concerned with the actual administration of branches of the economy, whereas the state committees' primary function is the "leadership of economic and sociocultural construction by means of regulating, supervising (*kontrol*) and coordinating the activity of the ministries and *vedomstva*."[46] While this definition does not wholly resolve the problem of distinguishing the two bodies, it does serve as a guideline in an area where it seems to be impossible to obtain an unambiguous differentiation. Let us then list these various organizations:

- The State Planning Committee (*Gosplan*), in overall charge of planning in the economy; it exists at both all-union and republic levels.
- The State Committee for Material-Technical Supplies (*Gossnab*), again existing at both central and republic levels.
- The State Committee for Prices (*Gostsen*).
- The State Committee for Science and Technology.

- The State Committee for Labor and Wages (replaced by the State Committee for Labor and Social Questions in 1976).
- The State Bank of the USSR (*Gosbank*), in which enterprises and the like have their accounts and through which bills are normally paid.
- The All-Union Bank for the Financing of Capital Investments (*Stroibank*), also known as the Construction Bank, which issues investment credit.
- The All-Union Central Council of the Trade Unions, which guides trade union activity in the five-year periods (maximum) between trade union congresses.

At the top of the pyramid, and existing at both all-union and republic levels, are the parliaments (Supreme Soviets) — which often create commissions for the consideration of industrial matters[47] — and the chief executive organs, the Councils of Ministers. All the Supreme Soviets, and the all-union Council of Ministers, have an inner core, the Praesidium. As regards the communist party (CPSU), the Central Committee (all-union) has "departments," some of which are directly concerned with industry. The exact role of these bodies has not received sufficient attention either in Soviet or Western writing, although Avtorkhanov gives those relating to industry two main functions: the registration and allocation of cadres, on the one hand, and the inspection and control of administrative organs, on the other.[48] More recently, Terry Pyper has made a detailed study of these departments, and emerges with similar but expanded findings, listing three primary duties of these bodies: to select and assign personnel throughout the industry concerned; to check and report on the implementation of directives; and to supervise and organize the propaganda function in its particular field of the economy.[49] Since these departments generally cover several branches (e.g., the Department of Heavy Industry), they are less involved in the detailed running of individual branches than the ministries. Above them are the Central Committee Secretariat and the organ generally agreed to be the supreme decision-making body in the Soviet political structure, the Politburo.

1.2. THE STRUCTURE OF EAST GERMAN INDUSTRY

One of the distinctive features of the East German economy when compared with the economies of many other communist states has been the relatively high proportaion of industry not fully nationalized. Thus, at the end of 1972, 78.9 percent of industry was wholly owned by the state, 11.6 percent was partially state-owned, 4.1 percent was cooperatively owned, and the remaining 5.4 percent was in private hands.[50] Even following the nationalization drive of 1972, the percentage of industry privately owned amounted to 3.7 percent at the end of 1973 and 3.6 percent at the end of 1974; the seminationalized enterprises have now virtually all been taken into full state ownership.[51]

The reader is reminded that where bodies still exist, the description of them and their functions is based on the legislation promulgated in 1973. This legislation is *still* valid for the VVBs, but was superseded in November 1979 by the new decree on the enterprises and combines. Most of the points made here, however, still pertain. We again start by examining the lowest tier in the administrative hierarchy, and then move upwards to the central organs. At the lowest level have been four types of enterprise.

(a) THE NATIONALLY OWNED ENTERPRISE (*VOLKSEIGENER BETRIEB* OR VEB)

In the VEB there is no private ownership of the means of production. The activity of the enterprise is governed by the enterprise plan, which is submitted by the enterprise itself to its superior organ for ratification. This organ may be a VVB, a combine, a regional council or "another state organ or organ of economic management."[52] In overall charge of the VEB — though obviously working within parameters laid down by central organs — is the director, who is appointed by the head of the organ immediately above the VEB.[53] The director works according to the principle of *Einzelleitung,* or one-person management, a concept of management essentially the same as that employed in the Soviet Union; as in the USSR, some participation in management is also formally encouraged. Below the director are several "specialist directors."[54] Unlike the overall director, whose function is essentially that of a general coordinator and ultimate decision-maker, these specialist directors are formally and primarily concerned only with one aspect of the enterprise's activities, such as accounts or engineering. They are usually appointed by the VEB director, subject to ratification from the head of the body above the VEB, who also has the right to reserve appointment to himself.

The VEB works according to the principle of profit-and-loss accounting; it plays a minimal role in pricing.[55]

There are certainly many limitations, or at least potential limitations, on the autonomy of the VEB. One example of this has already been mentioned in connection with the appointment of leading cadres. Other important areas include planning and work conditions, in both of which, according to the 1973 decree on the VEB, the enterprise management could find itself having to make allowances for local councils' wishes, perhaps against its will.[56] Nevertheless, it is also quite clear that the VEB is still considered to be an entity in itself, with full legal autonomy. It is not meant to be devoured by higher bodies, even if, in a developing economy, it is considered advisable to link an enterprise with others to form a larger unit; further details can be found in the section on combines and in Chapter 5. This position — whether or not it is largely a formality — contrasts with the position of most Soviet enterprises incorporated into a production *ob"edinenie*.

(b) THE SEMINATIONALIZED ENTERPRISE
(BETRIEB MIT STAATLICHER BETEILIGUNG)

At the sixth plenum of the Central Committee (July 1972), it was announced that socialist production relations had reached a new stage, so that the state bought up the remaining shares in this type of enterprise.[57] Thus, this form of enterprise all but disappeared from East German industry shortly before the 1973 legislation with which we are primarily concerned.

Seminationalized enterprises were administered by the regional economic councils, the appropriate ministry, and sometimes by a VVB. The state provided capital and was entitled to a share of the profits.[58]

(c) PRIVATE ENTERPRISES

Although the state has nationalized wherever it was considered possible and/or advisable, there are still a small number of private enterprises in the GDR. The directors of these units are not appointed by the state, although they are required to operate within certain centrally established parameters. There is a formal subordination to the local economic councils, and sometimes to a VVB. These enterprises are found predominantly in the consumer goods branches of industry; nowadays, however, they are of highly marginal significance to industrial production as a whole.[59]

(d) TRADE PRODUCTION COOPERATIVES
(PRODUKTIONSGENOSSENSCHAFTEN DES HANDELS **OR PGHs)**

Originating in the latter half of the 1950s, these bodies were created by the state in order to encourage craftsmen and artisans to work collectively rather than individually.[60] According to the July 1973 law on local state organs, the PGHs are answerable to the council of the *Kreis* (district) in which they are situated on questions of plan fulfillment and so on.[61] These bodies are, however, of marginal significance to the present study.

Having examined the four types of enterprise that have existed or do exist, we turn to consider the next major tier of industrial administration.

THE COMBINE *(KOMBINAT)* AND FORMS OF INTERENTERPRISE COOPERATION

Unlike Soviet industrial terminology, which has several names to distinguish different types of production association, East German industry now employs only one term, "combine." However, not only do the East Germans have other forms of enterprise linkage (considered below), but there are also several versions of the combine. A minority are granted the rights, responsibilities, and (similar) structure of a VVB, while there are even differences among the more common type, which is subordinate to a VVB or, occasionally, to a regional economic council. One way of subdividing combines is in terms of their management and administrative arrangements. By this criterion, the East Germans themselves have distinguished four basic types. In the first, the combine consists of only one large enterprise, in which is located the central combine management; an example of this type is the Leuna combine "Walter Ulbricht." In the second type, the combine comprises several enterprises, and there is a separate management body (e.g., the "Carl Zeiss" Jena combine); this form of combine is rather similar to the VVB. Third, the combine can consist of several enterprises under a main enterprise (*Stammbetrieb*), the management of which becomes the management for the whole combine (e.g., the Mansfeld combine "Wilhelm Pieck"); according to the 1973 legislation, this is to be the most common form of combine.[62] Finally, there is the combine in which the management is separate and runs component enterprises via the head enterprises (*Leitbetriebe*) of various subordinate product groups (these are defined below); this type of combine is also similar to the VVB. An example of one is the new "Mikroelektronik" combine based in Erfurt.[63]

One way to ascertain whether a combine has the status of a VVB or not is by noting the title of the person in overall charge of it. If that person is simply the "director," then the combine is subordinate to a VVB or a regional council. If the person is referred to as the "general director," the combine is directly subordinate to a ministry. The

Structures of Industry

director (or general director; the two terms will now be used interchangeably unless otherwise stated) works according to the by now familiar principle of one-person management, with collective consideration of basic questions.[64]

Another way the East Germans subdivide combines is in terms of the production process within them. Thus the official *Dictionary of the Socialist Economy* gives the following typology:

(1) A combine for the successive processing stages of raw materials and other materials (e.g., an iron-forging combine, in which the ore is smelted into pig iron, steel is produced, steel is spun and rolled).

(2) A combine in which the individual stages of production have the character of main and subsidiary production (e.g., a combine in which ore is smelted, and building materials are produced from the slag left in the blast furnaces).

(3) A combine for the complex utilization of raw materials (e.g., a mineral oil combine).

(4) A combine of similar production stages and products (e.g., a machine-tool engineering combine).[65]

Like all units in the industrial hierarchy, the combine is subject to parameters laid down by the State Planning Commission, while also working to its own analyses and prognoses. The combine also works on the principle of profit-and-loss accounting, being responsible for its own financing of development and for covering its costs.

Finally, each combine has its own charter, which has to be approved by the head of the body directly above the combine. This charter must, inter alia, delineate clearly the position and tasks of the enterprises within the combine; presumably this helps to alleviate the problems of ambiguity referred to below. As a guideline on this point, the decree on combines states that the functions most suitable for centralization from the individual enterprises to the combine are research and development, investments, material economy, accounts and statistics, sales, raising of professional qualifications, and patent-defending tasks.

Despite the variations in combines, there is *seemingly* less ambiguity in the status of their enterprises than in the comparable Soviet bodies:

> The regulations concerning nationally owned enterprises also apply to enterprises in a combine, insofar as nothing else is laid down in the combine's own regulations (*Bestimmungen*).[66]

Although the second part of this statement confuses the clear picture derived from the first, and despite stipulations that, for instance, the combine director "has the right to issue directives to the directors of the enterprises,"[67] there are certain aspects of the official status of enterprises within a combine that appear to ensure a modicum of autonomy for these units. For instance, there is a stipulation that the former names of enterprises should be retained. Moreover, enterprises in a combine are themselves responsible (*eigenverantwortlich*) for their production process — both the planning and the running of it — even though this is to be within the framework of the development of the combine as a whole.[68] Finally, it is clear that the enterprises in the combines were considered the basic or primary production unit in East German industry in the 1960s and 1970s, which is in marked contrast to the position of most of the component units in a production *ob"edinenie* as envisaged in the 1973 Soviet legislation.[69]

A second method of linking enterprises in the GDR is by the creation of "product groups" (*Erzeugnisgruppen*), which are not unlike the more loosely structured production *ob"edineniya* in the USSR. Originally, a product group was a group of industrial enterprises producing identical or similar products and cooperating with each other under the leadership of the VVB. In fact, the VVB delegated much of its work to a "product-group head enterprise" (*Erzeugnisgruppenleitbetrieb*), which could be a centrally or regionally administered enterprise or combine. An essential difference that used to exist between the product group and the combine was that the former linked enterprises of different forms of ownership, whereas the latter linked only the fully nationalized enterprises. Since about 1972, however, the product group has become simply a formal linking of enterprises — of whatever form of ownership and whether centrally or locally administered — on the basis of a common technology or the production of similar goods. Within itself, it is less integrated than a combine; moreover it can, since 1970, be subordinate to a combine instead of a VVB. Its purpose is to ensure stability, cooperation, specialization, centralization, and concentration.[70]

Yet another form of enterprise linkage has been the creation since 1966 of "cooperation groups" (*Kooperationsverbaende*), which are also known as "cooperation chains" (*Kooperationsketten*). These are loosely organized, vertical groupings of enterprises (possibly of different forms of ownership) cooperating in the production of a complex end-product. There are also "cooperation collectives" (*Kooperationsgemeinschaften*), which, though similar in other ways to the cooperation groups, link enterprises horizontally rather than vertically.[71]

However, none of these forms of cooperation appears to be considered very important in the East German economy in comparison with the combines; for instance, a 1971 standard textbook on the East German economy did not include them in the diagram of the administrative arrangement of the GDR's industry.[72] Moreover, the reader will be aware that this study is primarily concerned with the bodies considered by the Soviets and East Germans themselves as comparable — and the product groups, cooperation groups, and so on have not been compared with the Soviet production associations.[73]

Let us now examine the two bodies that until very recently supervised the majority of combines, and those enterprises not incorporated into a combine, the regional economic councils and the VVBs.

REGIONAL ECONOMIC COUNCILS
(*BEZIRKSWIRTSCHAFTSRAETE* OR BWRs)

The German Democratic Republic is divided into fifteen regions (*Bezirke*), including Berlin. Each of these regions has a council (*Rat*), which in turn has, subordinated to it, an economic council.

In the field of industrial administration, these regional economic councils are responsible for enterprises producing primarily for local requirements, rather than for national or international demand. In practice, this applies primarily to those branches of industry producing nondurable consumer goods. Hence, only a small proportion of industrial production in the GDR is from enterprises directly subordinate to the BWRs. The regional economic councils are subordinate to the regional councils and to the central Ministry for Regionally Administered Industry and the Foodstuffs Industry.[74]

THE ASSOCIATIONS OF NATIONALIZED ENTERPRISES
(*VEREINIGUNGEN VOLKSEIGENER BETRIEBE* OR VVBs)

The associations of nationalized enterprises (hereafter VVBs) are somewhat misleadingly named, since their authority is not limited solely to fully nationalized enterprises and combines. While they do not have the same powers over private enterprises as they do over VEBs — for instance, vis-à-vis cadre appointments — they are, nevertheless, "responsible for the implementation of the state's economic policy in a branch of industry."[75] As such they are to coordinate, to a degree unclear from official documents, the work of *all* units in a given area of the economy.

The tasks of the VVBs can be divided into five broad categories: planning and finance, cadre work, product-group work, CMEA integration, and other.

In the field of planning and finance, the VVBs are responsible for working out both one-year and five-year plans for their branch of industry. The process through which the final plan is reached is a complex one, and it is not necessary to elaborate the details here. Suffice it to say that the VVB has to manage a balancing act between the suggested plans filtering up from the economic units subordinate to it, and the general plan indices which come down to it from the State Planning Commission via the ministries. On the basis of this dual inflow, plus its own prognoses/analyses of demand and so on, the VVB draws up plans that the VVB general director then has to defend before the head of his immediately superior body (i.e., before a minister). Once the plan is accepted or modified by the higher organ, the VVB has to see to its implementation. One important point incorporated in the latest decree is that the VVB may work to indices with built-in "tolerances" (*Toleranzen*), so allowing some flexibility at least in the planning and implementation process.[76] As with all the tiers below it, the VVB works according to the principle of profit-and-loss accounting. It is also responsible for ensuring that the units below it make the required contributions to the state budget.

A second aspect of the VVB's work is cadre work. In line with the general policy of East German industry of rationalizing and avoiding parallelism, the VVB management — and in particular the general-director — is duty-bound to ensure that administrative staffs are continuously "pruned" to the minimum necessary number of personnel. In addition, the general director has to ensure that young persons with suitable qualities, including a good knowledge of Marxism-Leninism, are trained as managers, and that a management reserve is built up and continuously replenished. The general director also appoints the specialist directors of the VVB, by agreement with the head of the superior organ, and these specialist directors "and other leading personnel" of the VVB are responsible for guiding and checking on the corresponding directors in the enterprises and combines under them; the VVB general director himself is appointed by the head of the body above the VVB.[77]

Third, the VVB is responsible for organizing product-group work within the industrial branch. During the 1960s, the involvement of the VVBs in the operation of the private enterprises was predominantly via these product groups.[78]

The fourth major aspect of the VVB's work is "socialist economic integration." According to the VVB decree,

> the VVB bears responsibility for the synchronization (*Uebereinstimmung*) of the development of its branch of industry

with the demands of socialist economic integration with the USSR and the other members of the CMEA.[79]

In practice, this applies particularly to confirming contracts between its own enterprises and similar enterprises in other CMEA countries, mainly on questions of greater specialization and the division of labor. However, the decree does allow for some combines and enterprises to conclude such contracts on their own.

Finally, other tasks of the VVB include the ensuring of a correct pricing system for goods in its branch of industry (though this pricing is not entirely at the VVB's discretion, and requires confirmation from the Office for Prices); the implementation of the state incomes and wages policy in its branch; the provision of adequate opportunities for its employees to improve their qualifications; and the coordination of its work with that of the other VVBs/combines and local state organs. The decree emphasizes, however, that the VVB must use discretion in all its work, recognizing, for instance, that a small enterprise often needs to be dealt with in a manner quite different from a large enterprise.[80]

The VVBs are to be located in various parts of the GDR; this is one of the features that distinguishes them from the next tier in the administrative structure, the ministries.

THE MINISTRIES AND OTHER CENTRAL BODIES

At the central level, East German industry is administered by nine or ten industrial ministries; there is also the Ministry for Regionally Administered Industry and the Foodstuffs Industry.[81] The East German industrial ministerial structure is thus much simpler than the Soviet. Moreover, East German ministries operate according to individual statutes rather than a general guideline.[82] From the writing we have on them, though, their position appears to be similar to that of the Soviet all-union ministries; that is, they act as coordinators and controllers of the various units below them. Two important differences from their Soviet counterparts need to be mentioned, however. The first is that the formal power of the East German ministries has increased in the 1970s. Second, they do not have chief administrations (*glavki*), a factor the significance of which will emerge later in this study.[83]

In addition to the branch ministries there are the various "central state organs." Apart from the aforementioned State Planning Commission and the Office for Prices, the most important for our purposes are

- the State Secretariat for Labor and Wages;

- the Industry and Trade Bank of the GDR, the bank directly dealing with the financial transactions and problems of the enterprises and so on;
- the State Bank of the German Democratic Republic, responsible for the implementation of the party and state financial and credit policies;
- the Executive Committee of the Free German Trade Union Federation (FDGB), responsible for decision-making between trade union congresses; and
- two nonbranch ministries, those for Finance and Foreign Trade.

At the apex of the state structure are the People's Chamber (*Volkskammer*) — which approximates to the Supreme Soviet and similarly has commissions to consider aspects of industry — and the Council of Ministers. Like their Soviet counterparts, both of these elect an inner core, the Presidium.[84] One significant difference between the USSR and the GDR is that the latter state does not have republic equivalents of the parliament and Council of Ministers, due to the absence of a federal structure. There is also an East German body with no direct equivalent in the USSR, the State Council. Since the early 1970s, this has been primarily concerned with issues of diplomacy and foreign affairs, so that it has become of marginal relevance for our purposes. However, it played a major role in economic policy-making during the 1960s, taking many powers in this field from the Council of Ministers[85]; thus it must undoubtedly be included in this overview of the industrial administrative hierarchy.

Mention must also be made of the central party organs. The SED has a Central Committee, which in turn has "departments" (*Abteilungen*), some of which, such as the Department of Raw Materials Industry, are directly concerned with industry. We have little detailed knowledge of the role of these departments, but as in the USSR, they are subordinate to the Central Committee Secretariat. Also as in the Soviet Union, the most important decision-making body in the GDR is the Central Committee's Politburo.[86]

1.3. A BRIEF HISTORY OF THE DEVELOPMENT OF SOVIET ASSOCIATIONS

The concept of amalgamation or association is by no means a new one in Soviet industry. The first Soviet *ob"edineniya* appeared in 1918, and by 1920 there were in the textile industry alone 46 associations, comprising 440 enterprises. Many of these bodies were trusts, but more integrated associations on full profit-and-loss accounting also existed.[87] An exmaple of the later was the L'nopravlenie *ob"edinenie*, organized in July 1921 on the basis of 18 factories and employing more than 20,000 people.[88] However, with the establishment of branch ministries in 1932 (called People's Commissariats until 1946), the concept of the association lost favor, and many were disbanded.[89] By the mid-1950s there were only a few associations left, and these were all either loosely organized trusts or else large unified complexes (combines).[90] In 1957, however, there was a major reform of Soviet industrial administration. The industrial ministries were disbanded and replaced by Councils of National Economy (*Sovnarkhozy*). The basic aim of the reform was to improve administration by moving from a centralized branch principle to a system in which enterprises of most branches would be supervised by local economic councils. It was during this *sovnarkhoz* period that the idea of middle-link administrative organizations gradually assumed greater popularity once again. The first call for a new type of body, the Soviet *firma*, was published in October 1959.[91] Although the term itself was not completely new in Soviet industry, the arrangement advocated was not to be found in the USSR at that time.[92] This new arrangement involved the inclusion not only of production units but also of R and D institutes. The first calls came from officials in Leningrad *sovnarkhoz*, but it was L'vov *sovnarkhoz* (in the Ukraine) that actually established the first *firmy*; these were the shoe firms Progress and Rassvet.[93] Soviet writers therefore refer to the year of the founding of these two *firmy*, 1961, as that in which the present development of Soviet associations began. Within a few months, firms had been established in Leningrad, Moscow, and elsewhere. The growth in their numbers was impressive in the early 1960s, as will be seen in Table 1.[94] Although it is not possible to obtain a definitive set of figures on this growth, it is clear from the table that the proportional increase in numbers from one year to the next in the early 1960s was very large.

In October 1964, however, the Soviet leader Khrushchev was ousted, and the new leadership soon introduced major changes in Khrushchevian policies. Industrial administration was no exception, and in September 1965, as part of the Economic Reform announced at that time, the *sovnarkhozy* were abolished and industrial branch ministries reintroduced. For reasons dealt with later in the study, the numbers of associations declined from then until the early 1970s. Since then their growth has again become positive, particularly accelerating after the 1973 and 1974 legislation on *ob"edineniya*.

Up to this point, no distinction has been made between production and industrial associations. The major reason for this is that until the

TABLE 1 Numbers of Production Associations in Soviet Industry

Year	A	B	C	D	E
1961		2		2	
1962		53		53	
1963	375	351		351	250+
1964	500	486	410	486	<900
1965	600	672			
1966	1200+			500	
1967					
1968					
1969				580	510
1970			608	643	608
1971			879	<900	879
1972				1101	1101
1973				1000+	1425
1974				1541	1715
1975				2300	2314
1976				c.3000	3312
1977				3670	3670
1978					3857
1979				3600	3947

SOURCES/NOTES: See Ch. 1, note 94.

1970s Soviet writers themselves rarely clearly distinguished these two basic types of association. Nevertheless, we can draw a sketch of the development of the *glavk* replacements. Until the ministries returned in 1965, *glavki* did not exist in Soviet industry. However, the *sovnarkhozy* did have subdivisions called "branch administrations," which were functional equivalents of the *glavki*. Senior officials from both L'vov and Leningrad had early argued that the development of production associations/firms would in time render these branch administrations redundant.[95] Yet by 1963, officials from the Leningrad industrial *obkom* (provincial party committee) and Leningrad *sovnarkhoz* had decided that it would be better in some branches to convert these bodies into "production-economic organizations" rather than disband them.[96] They implemented such a change in the ship-building industry, by way of an experiment;[97] this is the earliest example we have discovered of converting the functional equivalents of the *glavki* into organs quite similar to the industrial associations (i.e., making administrative bodies more economically responsible for production in their subordinate units). Over the next three or four years, various bodies called *ob"edineniya* were established that were responsible for whole subbranches of industry and were granted the rights of branch administrations/*glavki*. One such was Melodiya, set up in 1964 to coordinate the work of gramophone/record factories, studios, and record shops.[98] Then, in 1966, the all-union *ob"edineniya* Soyuzmargarinprom and Soyuzparfumerprom were established in the food industry, and became responsible for most of the margarine and perfume factories in the USSR.[99] These bodies differed from the *glavki* primarily in not being located within ministries; apart from this, with the possible exception of the Leningrad ship-building associations, they do not appear to have been on any form of profit-and-loss accounting. For this reason, the real forerunner of the present industrial associations was the Sigma *ob"edinenie,* established in 1965 for the supervision of all enterprises and R and D institutes producing accounting equipment in Lithuania. All the units subordinate to Sigma retained full legal autonomy and considerable economic independence. On 1 July 1966, Sigma was transferred to profit-and-loss accounting and all the other economic methods entailed in the 1965 Economic Reform. It was the first functional equivalent of the *glavk* to be on this economic system. Sigma was subordinate to the Ministry of Instrument-Manufacture, Means of Automation and Administrative Systems (from now on, the Soviet abbreviation for this ministry, *Minpribor* will be used), and in November 1967 a decree was adopted by the All-Union Council of Ministers stating that Minpribor should, by way of an experiment, transfer all of its *glavki* to the new system of planning, economic incentives, and financing.[100] There were further experiments with industrial associations in other branches of industry, especially from 1970 on (see Chapter 6) and in 1973 it was announced that industrial associations were to replace *glavki* in all but exceptional cases. Since that time, the numbers of industrial associations have grown dramatically — from a handful in 1973 to nearly five hundred by June 1977.[101]

In the discussion to this point, the development of associations has been considered largely in terms of growth in the number of units. In order to give some idea of the importance of these bodies in Soviet industry, therefore, it is useful to examine the amount of industrial production for which associations have been responsible. Unfortunately, we have been unable to discover any such figures for the early industrial associations, although it would seem that they had by the late 1970s become responsible for the vast majority of industrial output. What of the production *ob"edineniya?* One problem here is that pre-1973 figures on production emanating from associations relates both to production and industrial *ob"edineniya.* Moreover, there are many difficulties involved in attempting to measure gross output, since economists use different criteria and methods. However, Soviet economists do seem to be in general agreement on this point, and the prime interest here is in discovering whether the *ob"edineniya* have been making a *generally* large or small contribution; if figures only marginally disagree, therefore, this is sufficient for our purposes. The few data available are enough to give us such a general impression. Thus, in 1968 the amount of production sold emanating from the associations accounted for a mere 5.6 percent of the total; by mid-1977 this figure had climbed to 42.6 percent.[102] As at August 1970, associations produced over 8 percent of industrial output; this figure had increased to nearly 12 percent by September 1973, 24 percent by the beginning of 1976, and 45 percent by 1979.[103] Thus, while associations have developed rapidly since 1973, they are still responsible for less than half of Soviet production. Given that they have been in existence since 1961, their growth has not been impressive. Moreover, we shall see in Chapter 6 that qualitative factors have been even more disappointing than these quantitative ones.[104]

1.4. A BRIEF HISTORY OF THE DEVELOPMENT OF EAST GERMAN ASSOCIATIONS

In the GDR, too, the concept and practice of linking enterprises in some way dates back to the earliest days of communist power and even before. Immediately after the collapse of the National Socialist regime in Germany, the eastern part of the country was administered by the Soviet Military Administration for Germany. At the same time (1945), however, there were created for the Soviet zone German Central Administrations, apparently corresponding to the all-German secretariats that had been set up, and fulfilling an essentially coordinatory role — for industry as well as for other sectors of society.[105] In June 1947 a new body, the German Economic Commission, was established for assisting in the administration of industry. Initially, this was merely an advisory body to the Soviet Military Administration — primarily on questions of economic planning. But in February 1948 it was reorganized and granted legislative powers. It had seventeen, later eighteen, "chief administrations" subordinate to it, but these soon lost some of their powers to the new "associations of nationally owned enterprises" or VVBs, established in 1948.[106] These were directly subordinate to the Economic Commission. There were two types of VVB: the VVB(Z) and the VVB(L). The former were responsible for the most important enterprises in a given branch of industry throughout the Soviet zone, while the latter administered the most important enterprises of a given branch in a province (*Land*), excluding those already covered by the VVBs(Z).[107] The remaining nationalized enterprises were under local jurisdiction. These first VVBs were granted full legal autonomy, while the enterprises below them were "extremely limited" in the level of autonomy they enjoyed, in both legal and economic terms. For example, it was the VVBs rather than the enterprises that concluded contracts with other organizations, and enterprise accounts were part of the VVB accounts.[108]

Thus the VVBs preceded the establishment of the GDR itself (7 October 1949). The administrative arrangement described above was relatively short-lived, however. At the end of 1950 — by which time approximately three-quarters of industrial production in the GDR came from the nationalized enterprises — a decree was passed establishing industrial ministries.[109] As a result, the VVBs lost control of all the most important enterprises to the chief administrations of the new ministries, retaining powers only over the smaller units.[110] The VVBs were abolished altogether in their existing form in January 1952, when the nationalized enterprises were transferred to profit-and-loss accounting and granted considerably more autonomy. Between then and 1958 there were bodies in industry called VVBs, but this abbreviation now stood for *Verwaltung* (administration) *Volkseigener Betriebe* rather than *Vereinigung* (union) *Volkseigener Betriebe*, symbolizing their much-reduced role and status. Even in this form, the number of VVBs declined, and were again finally abolished in 1958.[111]

In February 1958, following the October 1957 Central Committee discussion on industrial administration, the ministries and their chief administrations were also abolished.[112] In their stead were created brand new VVBs (with their original title of *Vereinigung* as opposed to *Verwaltung*). There was one for each branch of industry, except for the lignite industry, which had three. The new VVBs differed from their functional predecessors, the chief administrations, in two main ways. First, the new bodies were not parts of a ministry. Second, all of the chief administrations had been situated in Berlin, whereas the new VVBs were spread throughout the GDR, normally being located at the point of greatest concentration of production of a given branch of industry. This was intended to bring the VVBs much nearer to production in both the figurative and the literal sense.[113] We have been able to ascertain the location of many of the VVBs; this partial picture is sufficient to show conclusively that they were indeed spread over the whole of the GDR. Thus, of 41 traced for the year 1958, there were

7 in Leipzig, 6 in both Halle and Karl-Marx-Stadt, 5 in Berlin, 2 in both Erfurt and Meissen, and 1 each in Borna, Chemnitz, Cottbus, Dresden, Eisleben, Ilmenau, Luebeck-Oberfrohna, Magdeburg, Meerane, Plauen, Quedlinburg, Radeburg, and Warnemuende.

Despite these developments in the VVBs, their autonomy was still limited to a considerable degree in practice because of their subordination to the appropriate sections of the State Planning Commission until the middle of 1961, and of the Council of National Economy (established in 1961) from then on. For example, these sections, rather than the VVBs themselves, were responsible for all major planning of a given branch. As before, the VVBs were directly responsible only for the most important enterprises, the enterprises of purely local significance being subordinate to local economic councils.[114]

With the introduction of the New Economic System of Planning and Management (NES) in January 1963, however, many of the powers of central organs were transferred to enterprises and, even more so, to the VVBs. Consequently, the latter bodies' powers were now considerably expanded. In addition, all of the VVBs transferred to profit-and-loss accounting at the beginning of 1964.[115]

Within less than two years, however, important changes were again made in East German industrial administration. Approximately three months after the Soviets replaced the *sovnarkhozy* with industrial ministries, the East Germans similarly abolished their Council of National Economy and reintroduced industrial branch ministries; this was in December 1965. Although it looked as if this would mean the de facto demise of the VVBs, their rights, as well as those of most of the enterprises, actually increased over the rest of the decade, primarily in the fields of foreign trade and pricing.[116] Any threat to the VVBs in the late 1960s was from the combines rather than the ministries.

In the early 1970s, however, the VVBs lost many of their former powers, principally to the ministries and other central agencies. With legislation passed in November 1979, they should disappear altogether in the 1980s, as part of a move toward a predominantly two-tier system in GDR industry (ministry-combine).[117]

The major development of the combines really began *after* the VVBs were well established; if the most significant dates for the VVBs are 1958 (establishment of present generation) and 1963 (major new role for the VVBs as part of the New Economic System), so the takeoff point for the modern combines is 1967; certainly this is how subsequent economic historians have usually portrayed it.[118]

However, this is not to say there were no combines before 1967; indeed, some of the pre-1967 ones were based on similar formations existing even before the GDR had been established, and in the early 1950s many formerly autonomous medium-sized enterprises were administratively amalgamated into large, unified enterprises.[119] This particularly applied in branches where there was complex use of raw materials — most chemical enterprises were called combines, for instance.[120] However, the term "combine" was rarely used at that time in the sense of several production units being linked and retaining a modicum of autonomy. Rather, they were groupings of several factories, of one or more branches or subbranches, all situated in the same location — in this sense multifactory single enterprises.[121] Despite calls from some economists, and the stipulation of an October 1963 decree that a distinction was to be made between the amalgamated enterprise and the combine, no such distinction was generally accepted, with both types of administrative arrangement being seen as variants of the enterprise.[122] Thus, in most East German writing of the period on industrial administration, the combine is rarely treated as sui generis.[123] Moreover, it was often seen as useful at least as much for building (with which we are not concerned here) as for industry. This said, the rather neat distinction in combine history that some communist writers make between the periods before and after Ulbricht's speech at the 2nd plenum of the Central Committee in 1967 is more blurred than they imply. For instance, there were suggestions long before 1967 that combines should in some cases have essentially the same status as the VVBs, in that there were proposals to subordinate combines directly to the Council of National Economy[124]; and at least one combine (Kabelwerk Oberspree) in existence before the second plenum was directly subordinate to a ministry and did enjoy the rights of a VVB from the moment of its establishment on 21 January 1967.[125]

Nevertheless, the idea of creating industrial combines of national significance linking several enterprises was realized — seemingly very rapidly — in the late 1960s. From the beginning of 1969, many new "nationally owned combines" (VEKs) came into being, comprising enterprises that lost most of their former legal autonomy but that retained considerable economic autonomy. Some of these combines were granted the rights of VVBs and in some cases actually replaced disbanded VVBs, while others were subordinate to VVBs or to local state organs.[126] Their development was all part of a structural policy to concentrate efforts on a few branches and products in which the GDR was or could be particularly strong.[127]

However, despite their rapid development in the later Ulbricht years, the combines — like the structural policy — suffered under the present leadership, to the benefit of both the central organs (e.g.,

TABLE 2 Numbers of VVBs in East German Industry

Year	A	Source of Data B	C
1958	86(?)	74	
1959	71		
1960		80	
1961			
1962			
1963	82		
1964	80		
1965			
1966	82		
1967		c.85	85
1968		80+	
1969	71(?)		
1970	71(?)	88	
1971			
1972		52	c.90
1973	71	55	
1974			
1975	55		
1976			
1977			
1978			
1979			

SOURCES/NOTES: See Ch. 1, note 129.

ministries) and the enterprises.[128] Only in the late 1970s has the importance and status of the combines been restored and in some ways even enhanced.

The researcher is faced with rather different problems vis-à-vis the numbers of associations in the GDR from those encountered in analyzing the USSR. In the latter state, the major problem is that until recently different sources have often presented very different figures. In the former, the problem is rather one of obtaining data at all. However, we have been able to construct Tables 2[129] and 3.[130] From these incomplete tables, it is clear that there was a slow decline in the number of VVBs until the mid-1970s, while the number of combines marginally increased; these developments accelerated markedly in the late 1970s. However, until more figures are published, we can only take the word of East German economic historians and politicians that there was a big increase in the number of combines at the end of the 1960s, since we have no earlier figures with which to make comparisons.

Structures of Industry

TABLE 3 Numbers of Combines in East German Industry

Year	Subordinate to Ministries Source A	Source B	Subordinate to VVBs Source C	Total
1966				
1967	<10			
1968				
1969				
1970	37			
1971	37	37		
1972	37		83	120
1973	38	43	86	129 (Max)
1974	40			
1975	43			
1976				
1977				
1978	56		98	154
1979	129			

SOURCES/NOTES: See Ch. 1, note 130.

Once again, numbers of associations do not in themselves reveal very much, and, as in the Soviet case, the most useful indicator of the importance of the associations in the economy is probably the amount of production that emanates from them. In the case of the VVBs, it could be argued that almost *all* industrial production came from enterprises subordinate to VVBs from 1958 till the late 1960s, in the sense that the VVBs were to bear *some* responsibility for all the enterprises in their respective branches, not merely the centrally administered VEBs. It is not clear how much involvement in the affairs of the nonnationalized and locally administered enterprises the VVBs had, however, although the development of product groups (especially in the early 1960s) suggests that in some cases it was probably quite considerable.[131] Even omitting these other enterprises from our calculations for the present, the amount of industrial production manufactured in the centrally administered enterprises amounted to some 70 percent in 1958, and a little more than this by the mid-1960s.[132] Data on the combines are even scarcer than on the VVBs. In July 1970, Walter Halbritter stated that the "overwhelming proportion" of industrial production was already taking place in enterprises that were under centrally administered combines.[133] This might have been an optimistic assessment, however, since the new First Secretary of the SED, Erich Honecker, stated at the party's eighth Congress in 1971 that the combines were now responsible for over one-third of centrally administered industry's output, and almost one-half of all export goods.[134] It was perhaps symptomatic of the leadership's declining interest in the VVBs and combines from then until the later 1970s that no detailed figures on their contribution to the economy were given at the ninth Congress in 1976, even though figures on the contribution by Soviet associations had been given at the CPSU's 25th Congress a few months earlier. However, a 1980 source states that industrial production just from combines directly subordinate to ministries (i.e., omitting combines under VVBs) amounted to 41 percent of the total in 1976, and approximately 88 percent in 1979.[135]

Thus, despite problems of data, it is abundantly clear that the associations of both types have played a far more significant role in the GDR than they have in the USSR.

1.5. SUMMARY

In terms of industrial structure through to the end of the 1970s, there was clearly a remarkable similarity between the GDR and the USSR. However, there were also important differences that should not be overlooked (see Figures 1 and 2). The most important from the point of view of this study are that the position of component units in East German combines was less ambiguous and in some ways more autonomous than in production *ob"edineniya* (they were called enterprises and retained their name, although all lost their status as a legal person); the VVB had more rights than the industrial *ob"edinenie;* the administrative arrangement appeared to be less complex in the GDR than in the USSR (compare the ministerial structures), and has become even simpler since the big nationalization drive of 1972 (and the November 1979 legislation); and the Soviets still had *glavki* through most of the 1970s, while the East Germans did not.

Historically, the two basic types of associations emerge in reverse order in the USSR and the GDR; the associations have accounted for far more production in the GDR than in the USSR, although the industrial associations in the USSR have in the last three or four years become responsible for the major part of Soviet output; and the East German creation of both types of association was much more rapid than the Soviet — especially so in the case of the VVBs and the industrial *ob"edineniya.*

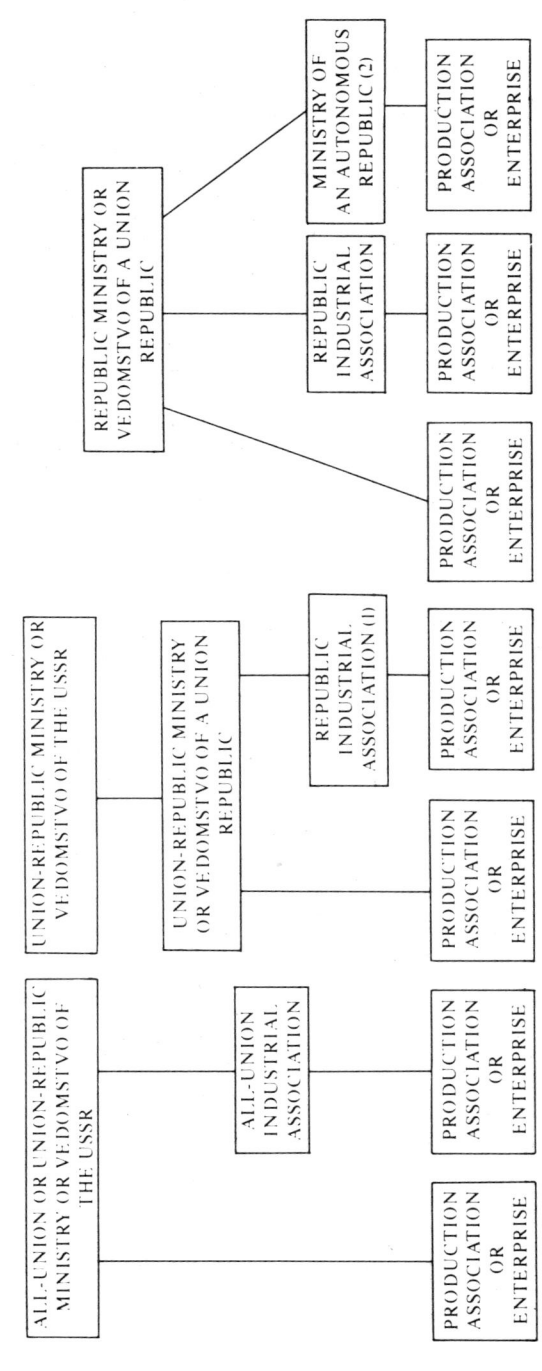

NOTE: *Glavki*, where they still exist, are included within the ministries.

1. Or Ministry of an Autonomous Republic, or Administration of the Executive Committee of a Provincial Soviet.
2. Or Administration of the Executive Committee of a Provincial Soviet.

FIGURE 1
The Administrative Structure of Soviet Industry as Envisaged in the March 1973 Decree

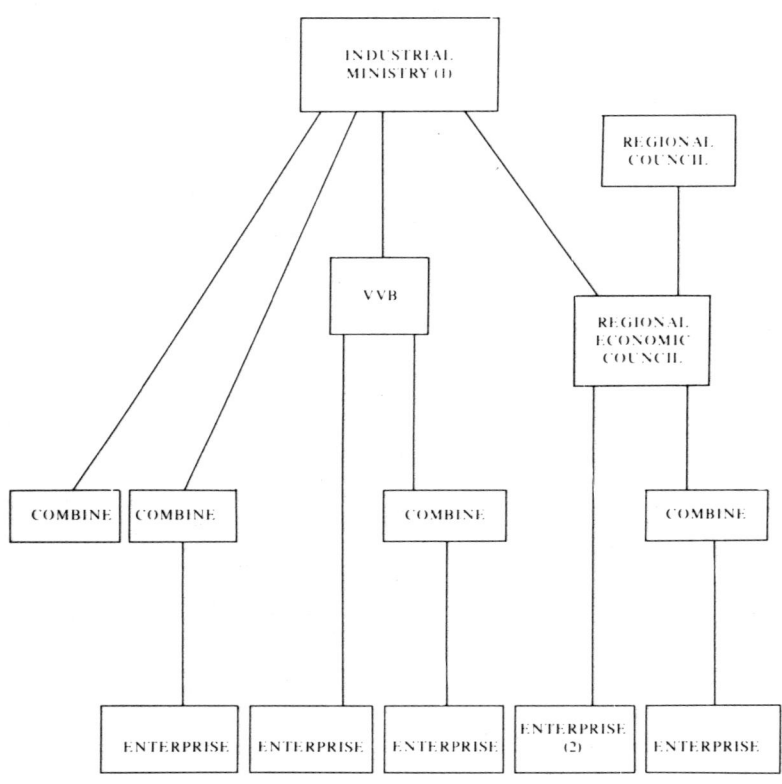

1. Includes the Ministry for Regionally-Administered Industry and the Foodstuffs Industry.
2. Enterprises under a Regional Economic Council can be partially subordinate to a VVB through being in product groups.

FIGURE 2
The Administrative Structure of Nationally Owned Industry in the GDR According to the 1973 Legislation

NOTES

1. See notes 51 and 57 below.
2. See L. I. Brezhnev's statement in *XXIV S'ezd Kommunisticheskoi Partii Sovetskogo Soyuza – Stenograficheskii Otchet*, Vol. 1 (Moscow: Izd. Politicheskoi Literatury, 1971), p. 93.
3. The most important documents regarding the Economic Reform in 1965 were the "Postanovlenie Plenuma TsK KPSS, 29 sentyabrya 1965 g. Ob uluchshenii upravleniya promyshlennost'yu, sovershenstvovanii planirovaniya i usilenii ekonomisheskogo stimulirovaniya promyshlennogo proizvodstva"; "Postanovlenie TsK KPSS i Soveta Ministrov SSSR, 30 sentyabrya 1965 g. Ob uluchshenii upravleniya promyshlennost'yu"; "Zakon ob izmenenii sistemy organov upravleniya promyshlennost'yu i preobrazovanii nekotorykh drugikh organov gosudarstvennogo upravleniya. Prinyat Verkhovnym Sovetom SSSR 2 oktyabrya 1965 g."; "Postanovlenie TsK KPSS i Soveta Ministrov SSSR, 4 oktyabrya 1965 g. O sovershenstvovanii planirovaniya i usilenii ekonomicheskogo stimulirovaniya promyshlennogo proizvodstva." The enterprise statute is, in Russian, "Polozhenie o sotsialisticheskom gosudarstvennom proizvodstvennom predpriyatii." All these documents can be found in *Resheniya Partii i Pravitel'stva po Khozyaistvennym Voprosam*, Vol. 5 (Moscow: Izd. Politicheskoi Literatury, 1968), pp. 640-685 (Economic Reform) and pp. 691-716 (enterprise statute).
4. See the "Polozhenie o proizvodstvennom ob"edinenii (kombinate)," para. 6. This statute can be found in *Resheniya . . .*, Vol. 10 (1976), pp. 138-179.
5. "Polozhenie o sotsialisticheskom gosudarstvennom proizvodstvennom predpriyatii," paras. 43-48. A major new decree on planning and improving the incentive system in Soviet industry was passed in July 1979, but this is not of relevance to the present study; the decree can be found in *Sobranie Postanovlenii Pravitel'stva Soyuza Sovetskikh Sotsialisticheskikh Respublik*, No. 18, 1979, pp. 390-431.
6. For a useful introduction to Soviet pricing, see A. Nove, *The Soviet Economic System* (London: Allen & Unwin, 1977), passim, esp. pp. 172-198.
7. "Postanovlenie TsK KPSS i Soveta Ministrov SSSR, 2 marta 1973 g. 'O nekotorykh meropriyatiyakh po dal'neishemu sovershenstvovaniyu upravleniya promyshlennost'yu," para. 2 (in *Resheniya . . .*, Vol. 9, 1974, pp. 415-426), and "Polozhenie o proizvodstvennom ob"edinenii (kombinate)," para. 6.
8. "Polozhenie o sotsialisticheskom gosudarstvennom proizvodstvennom predpriyatii," para. 89. The Russian terms are *direktor*, *nachal'nik*, and *upravlyayushchii*, respectively.
9. *Ibid.*, para. 4. For a useful history and explanation of the concept, see J. Azrael, *Managerial Power and Soviet Politics* (Cambridge, MA: Harvard U.P., 1966), pp. 42-46.
10. "Polozhenie o sotsialisticheskom gosudarstvennom proizvodstvennom predpriyatii," paras. 4 and 89-104. Also of interest in this connection is the "Polozhenie o postoyanno deistvuyushchem proizvodstvennom soveshchanii" (Statute on the Permanent Production Conference) of June 1973, to be found in *Resheniya . . .*, Vol. 9, pp. 546-551. See esp. para. 7.
11. One of the most enlightening Soviet descriptions of the nomenclature system is that in *Lektsii po Partiinomu Stroitel'stvu – Vypusk 1* (Moscow: Izd. Mysl', 1971), pp. 329-330. Useful Western studies include B. Harasymiw's "Nomenklatura: The Soviet Communist Party's Leadership Recruitment System," *Canadian Journal of*

Political Science, No. 3, 1969, pp. 493-512; J. Hough, *The Soviet Prefects* (Cambridge, MA: Harvard U.P., 1969), pp. 29-30, 114-116, 150-170; and R.W. Theen in G.B. Smith (ed.), *Public Policy and Administration in the Soviet Union* (New York: Praeger, 1980), pp. 38-51.

12. See "Postanovlenie ... O nekotorykh meropriyatiyakh ...," para. 4. Further details on this are to be found in Chapter 5.

The distinction between the "production" and the "filial" is not always clear in Soviet writing. For example, K. I. Taksir (*Upravlenie Promyshlennost'yu SSSR v Sovremennykh Usloviyakh*, Moscow: Izd. Vysshaya Shkola, 1972, pp. 191-192) says that both are part of a production association. The "production" *may* be found some distance from the association headquarters; the filial always is. The production, for Taksir, is based on a former enterprise that has forfeited its legal autonomy by becoming part of an *ob"edinenie;* the same writer implies that, in contrast, the filial is a separate production unit originally set up *after* the association has been established. Another point, made by G. Dzhavadov and E. Dunaev *Proizvodstvennye Ob"edineniya i Khozraschet* (Moscow: Moskovskii Rabochii, 1971, pp. 56-57), is that the filial has a current account, while the production does not. Finally, both the production and the filial are to be distinguished from the "autonomous *tsekh,*" the salient feature of which is that it has a highly specialized production profile, and produces items for use within an *ob"edinenie* or for supply to users having a special cooperation tie with the association (Taksir, p. 191), In sum, the filial appears to have slightly more autonomy (economic at least) than the production, which in turn has more than the autonomous *tsekh*. Legislation has not clarified the situation.

The terms *zavod* (works) and *fabrika* (factory) usually appear in contemporary Soviet writing to refer merely to buildings or small complexes where manufacturing takes place, without implying anything about the legal and/or economic status of the unit.

13. "Polozhenie o proizvodstvennom ob"edinenii (kombinate)," para. 1. As late as the autumn of 1973 (i.e., *after* the legislation on administration and industrial *ob"edineniya*, although before that on production *ob"edineniya*), some felt that there was still no adequate definition of the *ob"edinenie*. See, for example, E. P. Dunaev, *Ob"edineniya Predpriyatii Kak Forma Obobshchestvleniya Proizvodstva* (Moscow: Izd. Moskovskogo Universiteta, 1974), p. 123; Dunaev's own definition is on p. 137. Even following the statute on production associations, many legal specialists felt that the legislation had raised many important problems, including definitional ones, for them to solve; see "Pravovoe polozhenie proizvodstvennogo ob"edineniya (kombinata) i proizvodstvennykh edinits," *SGiP*, No. 9, 1974, pp. 57-67.

14. Taksir, *Upravlenie ...* , p. 122.

15. Some writers have used the term *firma* very broadly; this is especially true of the early 1960s. See, for example, M. I. Radomysel'skii and I. A. Shifrin, *Firmy – Novaya Forma Upravleniya Proizvodstvom* (Moscow: Ekonomizdat, 1963), esp. pp. 57-81.

16. Taksir, *Upravlenie ...* , p. 125.

17. V. D. Shtundyuk, *Khozraschetnye Proizvodstvennye Ob"edineniya* (Moscow: Moskovskii Rabochii, 1973), p. 20.

18. *Ibid.*, p. 20.

19. Taksir, *Upravlenie ...* , pp. 124-125.

20. Some writers have preferred not to classify most combines as *ob"edineniya*. See Dunaev, *Ob"edineniya Predpriyatii ...* , p. 154.

21. Quoted in V. M. Lagutkin (ed.), *Proizvodstvennye Ob"edineniya: Problemy i Perspektivy* (Moscow: Izd. Mysl', 1971), p. 94. We have found nothing to suggest that this is no longer valid.

22. Before 1973, a trust could even be subordinate to a combine. See A. Omarov, "XXIV S'ezd KPSS ob Ekonomicheskoi Politike Partii na Sovremennom Etape," *Plan. Khoz.*, No. 9, 1972, p. 103. It is unclear whether this arrangement still exists, although in theory it should not.

23. NPO is the abbreviation for Nauchno-Proizvodstvennoe Ob"edinenie.

24. "Polozhenie o Nauchno-Proizvodstvennom Ob"edinenii," para. 1. This statute, and the decree on the NPOs ("Postanovlenie Soveta Ministrov SSSR, 30 dekabrya 1975g. Ob utverzhdenii polozheniya o nauchno-proizvodstvennom ob"edinenii") can be found in *Resheniya . . .* , Vol. 11 (1977), pp. 65-113.

25. Authoritative and detailed articles on the NPOs include A. Bachurin, "Nauchno-Proizvodstvennoe Ob"edinenie," *Ekon. Gax.*, No. 9, 1976, p. 21, and V. Pokrovskii, "Rabochaya Baza Nauki," *Sots. Ind.*, 16 April 1976, p. 2.

26. K. I. Taksir, "Nauchno-Proizvodstvennye Ob"edineniya," *Vop. Ekon.*, No. 11, 1972, p. 40. See also S. Tikhomirov "Ot Idei do Voploshcheniya," *Sots. Ind.*, 16 January 1971, p. 2. L. Blyakhman has gone further, subdividing such *ob"edineniya* into seven types (including what he calls science-production complexes). See his article, "Ob"edineniya: Opyt i Perspektivy," *Pravda*, 1 January 1971, p. 3, and also his analysis in A. A. Markin (ed.), *Effektivnost' Khozyaistvennykh Ob"edinenii* (Leningrad: Izd. Leningradskogo Universiteta, 1974), pp. 180-184.

27. For example, M. Baranov, "Problemy Formirovaniya i Razvitiya Agrarno-Promyshlennykh Ob"edinenii," *Vop. Ekon.*, No. 9, 1972, pp. 52-60. Official interest in such bodies became particularly obvious in 1976, when a decree was issued by the Central Committee of the CPSU on cooperation in agriculture ("Postanovlenie TsK KPSS, 28 Maya 1976g. O dal'neishem razvitii spetsializatsii i kontsentratsii sel'-skokhozyaistvennogo proizvodstva na baze mezhkhozyaistvennoi kooperatsii i agropromyshlennoi integratsii," in *Resheniya . . .* , Vol. 11, pp. 316-330). This required the Council of Ministers to adopt decrees delineating the position of, inter alia, the agroindustrial *ob"edineniya* (para. 8). In April 1977, a statute on the joint enterprise and "organization" in agriculture was passed. It is unclear whether this pertains to the agroindustrial *ob"edinenie*, although the opening section defines the joint enterprise (organization) as a "voluntary *ob"edinenie*" of resources of state farms, collective farms, enterprises, and so on. It is possible that this reflects hostility toward the concept of the *ob"edinenie* in the countryside. But this question falls outside the scope of the present study; it is mentioned here for precisely the same reasons as for the science-production *ob"edinenie*. The 1977 legislation ("Postanovlenie Soveta Ministrov SSSR, 14 aprelya 1977g. Ob Utverzhdenii Obshchego polozheniya o mezhkhozyaistvennom predpriyatti [organizatsii] v sel'skom khozyaistve" and "Obshchee polozhenie o mezhkhozyaistvennom predpriyatii [organizatsii] v sel'-skom khozyaistve") is in *Resheniya . . .* , Vol. 11, pp. 653-676.

28. A state farm (*sovkhoz*) is fully state-owned, and its workers are all employees. A collective farm (*kolkhoz*) is a peasant cooperative. For further details, see Nove, *The Soviet Economic System*, passim, esp. pp. 26-30, 120-148.

29. Baranov, "Problemy Formirovaniya . . . ," p. 54. See also E. Pospelova, "Khozraschetnye Ob"edineniya po Proizvodstvu Prodovol'stviya v Strane," *Vop. Ekon.*, No. 9, 1972, p. 129.

30. "Polozhenie o proizvodstvennom ob"edinenii (kombinate)," paras. 16 and 17.

31. *Ibid.*, para. 8.

32. This is not invariably so, however. See Dunaev, *Ob"edineniya Predpriyatii* . . . , pp. 123-138.

33. "Postanovlenie . . . O nekotorykh meropriyatiyakh . . . ," para. 2. See too Figure 1, p. 65.

34. For all the official details on the industrial *ob"edineniya*, see "Postanovlenie Soveta Ministrov SSSR, 2 marta 1973 g. Ob utverzhdenii obschchego polozheniya o vsesoyuznom i respublikanskom promyshlennykh ob"edineniyakh" and "Obschchee polozhenie o vsesoyuznom i respublikanskom promyshlennykh ob"edineniyakh" in *Resheniya* . . . , Vol. 9, pp. 427-459. Here the latter, para. 2. More details on the accounting in these *ob"edineniya* are in paras. 29-36, 97-108, and passim. On the attempt to transfer the *glavki* to profit-and-loss accounting as a failure and/or ill-conceived, see G. Popov and N. Petrov, "Na putyakh k ob"edineniyam," *Pravda*, 12 September 1973, p. 2.

35. See, for example, "Sovershenstvovat' Upravlenie Proizvodstvom," *Pravda*, 4 April 1973, p. 1.

36. "Postanovlenie . . . O nekotorykh meropriyatiyakh . . . ," para. 15, and "V Tsentral'nom Komitete KPSS i Sovete Ministrov SSSR," *Pravda*, 3 April 1973, p. 1. Not only did some writers fail to distinguish between the *glavk* and the industrial *ob"edinenie* before 1973, but at least one failed to distinguish clearly between the latter organization and the ministry. See V. Krylova, *Osobennosti Analiza Khozyaistvennoi Deyatel'nosti Promyshlennykh Ob"edinenii* (Moscow: Ekonomika, 1971), p. 31.

37. "Postanovlenie . . . O nekotorykh meropriyatiyakh . . . ," para. 12, and "Obshchee polozhenie o vsesoyuznom . . . ," para. 4.

38. *Ibid.*, para. 16.

39. Compare *ibid.*, paras. 109-113, with "Verordnung ueber die VEB, Kombinate, VVB," para. 39. The East German decree is to be found in GBl., Pt. 1, No. 15, 1973, pp. 129-141, with slight modifications in GBl., Pt. 1, No. 39, 1973, p. 405.

40. "Obshchee polozhenie o vsesoyuznom . . . ," paras. 109-113.

41. "Postanovlenie . . . O nekotorykh meropriyatiyakh . . . ," para. 18. The decree actually calls for changes to be made in the statute on the ministries (which dates from 1967), in the light of the decree on associations. Such changes would have to be so numerous as to constitute essentially a new document. A new Law on the Council of Ministers was passed on 5 July 1978, but the ministry statute has yet to appear (on the Law on the Council of Ministers, see "Zakon Soyuza Sovetskikh Sotsialisticheskikh Respublik 'O Sovete Ministrov SSSR,' " *Pravda*, 6 July 1978, pp. 1-3).

42. Details of the October law are in note 3 of this chapter. The 1967 statute ("Obshchee polozhenie o ministerstvakh SSSR") is in *Resheniya* . . . , Vol. 6, (1968), pp. 494-507. Additional rights to the Ministers follow the statute; see pp. 507-517.

43. "Obshchee polozhenie o ministerstvakh SSSR," paras. 6 and 7. See also article 142 of the 1977 Constitution.

44. See V. S. Pronina, *Tsentral'nye Organy Upravleniya Narodnym Khozyaistvom* (Moscow: Yuridicheskaya Literatura, 1971), p. 34.

45. *Ibid.*, p. 5.

46. *Ibid.*, p. 33.

47. On the Supreme Soviet commissions, see P. Vanneman, *The Supreme Soviet* (Durham, NC: Duke U.P., 1977) pp. 119-150, and S. Minagawa, "The Functions of the Supreme Soviet Organs, and Problems of their Institutional Development," *Soviet Studies*, No. 1, 1975, esp. 57-70.

48. A. Avtorkhanov, *The Communist Party Apparatus* (Chicago: Henry Regnery Co., 1966), pp. 201-205.

49. T. R. Pyper, "The Central Committee Apparatus of the Soviet Communist Party" (unpublished M. A. dissertation, University of Essex, December 1973), p. 60.

50. *Statistical Pocketbook of the German Democratic Republic – 1972* (Berlin: Staatsverlag der Deutschen Demokratischen Republik, 1972), p. 21.

51. *Statistisches Taschenbuch der Deutschen Demokratischen Republik 1974* (Berlin: Staatsverlag der Deutschen Demokratischen Republik, 1974), p. 25. See too note 57, below.

52. "Verordnung ueber die VEB . . . ," para. 9. For a detailed analysis of the formal position of the VEBs, see K. Glaess, G. Goerner, and H. Tauscher, *Lehr- und Studienmaterial zum Wirtschaftsrecht*, Vol. 6 (Berlin: Staatsverlag der Deutschen Demokratischen Republik, 1974), pp. 15-85.

53. "Verordnung ueber die VEB . . . ," paras. 6 and 22.

54. *Ibid.*, para. 22.

55. On pricing, see M. Melzer in P. C. Ludz (ed.), *DDR Handbuch* (Cologne: Verlag Wissenschaft und Politik, 1979), pp. 850-858.

56. "Verordnung ueber die VEB . . . ," para. 10. The decree does not actually state that this might be against its will; this is simply a possibility. The local councils (*Raete der Volksvertretungen*) are functionally similar to the soviets in the USSR. Their formal position is detailed in the "Gesetz ueber die oertlichen Volksvertretungen und ihre Organe in der Deutschen Demokratischen Republik," in *GBl.*, Pt. 1, No. 32, 1973, pp. 313-335. On the local soviets, see J. Hough and M. Fainsod, *How the Soviet Union Is Governed* (Cambridge, MA: Harvard U.P., 1979), passim, esp. pp. 485-491.

57. At the end of 1971 there were 5658 such units, but within a very short time they were completely eradicated. See W. Jarowinsky, *Aus dem Bericht des Politbueros an die 6. Tagung des ZK der SED* (Berlin: Dietz Verlag, 1972), pp. 5-24, esp. 23-24, and *Statistisches Taschenbuch . . . 1974*, p. 25. Pressure on such enterprises to accept the state as their major shareholder started seriously in 1956, mainly via taxation measures. But, particularly during the latter half of the 1960s, the importance of this type of enterprise (in terms of its proportional contribution to the nation's gross industrial output) increased — a development that some felt jarred with the notion of moving toward communism. See M. Schnitzer, *East and West Germany: A Comparative Economic Analysis* (New York: Praeger, 1972), p. 233, and the appropriate statistical yearbooks for the output figures. Although this kind of enterprise has disappeared from industry proper, there are still a few in, for instance, transport and domestic trade.

58. Schnitzer, *East and West Germany . . .* , p. 233.

59. *Ibid.*, p. 238. See too R. Rytlewski in Ludz, *DDR Handbuch*, pp. 1181-1182.

60. Schnitzer, *East and West Germany . . .* , p. 234. See too *Woerterbuch der Oekonomie Sozialismus* (Berlin: Dietz Verlag, 1973) p. 729.

61. "Gesetz ueber die oertlichen . . . ," para. 39. More details on the PGHs are in P. Mitzscherling et al., *DDR-Wirtschaft – eine Bestandsaufnahme* (Frankfurt am Main: Fischer Taschenbuch Verlag, 1974), pp. 195-198.

62. "Verordnung ueber die VEB . . . ," para. 29.

63. On this see K. Erdmann and M. Melzer, "Die neue Kombinatsverordnung in der DDR [Pt. 2]," *D.A.*, No. 10, 1980, pp. 1048-1051.

64. "Verordnung ueber die VEB . . . ," para. 29. Since the end of 1979, all combines are to be directly subordinate to a ministry, so that they are all to have only

a general director. For the new legislation on the combine and the enterprise, see "Verordnung ueber die volkseigenen Kombinate, Kombinatsbetriebe und Volkseigenen Betriebe vom 8. November 1979," *GBl.*, Pt. 1, No. 38, 1979, pp. 355-366.

65. *Woerterbuch...*, p. 469. These four types are very similar to the typology of Kroemke and Rouscik, except that the fourth one did not appear in the much earlier classification. See C. Kroemke and L. Rouscik, *Konzentration, Spezialisierung, Kooperation und Kombination in der Industrie der DDR* (Berlin: Verlag Die Wirtschaft, 1959), pp. 152-158. A 1971 book goes one further, identifying five types of combines — and arguing that the majority of combines in the GDR do not fully correspond to any of the "ideal types." See D. Graichen and L. Rouscik, *Zur Sozialistischen Wirtschaftsorganisation* (Berlin: Verlag Die Wirtschaft, 1971), pp. 385-395.

66. "Verordnung ueber die VEB...," para. 25.
67. *Ibid.*, para. 29.
68. *Ibid.*, para. 25.
69. See G. Klinger, "Die neue Kombinatsverordnung — ein wichtiges Instrument zur weiteren Vervollkommnung der Leitung und Planung," *S und R*, No. 3, 1980, p. 195. For further details on the combines and their enterprises before 1979, see Glaess et al., *Lehr- und Studienmaterial...*, Vol. 6, pp. 86-130.

70. For an up-to-date introduction to the product groups, see Rytlewski, in Ludz, *DDR Handbuch*, pp. 181-182. For an early Western article on the product groups and their problems, see P. C. Ludz, "Widersprueche im Neuen Oekonomischen System: Organisatorische Probleme der Erzeugnisgruppen," *SBZ-Archiv*, No. 7, 1964, pp. 101-104. In February 1964 there were 620 product groups in East German industry; their numbers increased drastically following a ruling of the Council of National Economy (VWR) in 1962. See *ibid.*, and Dr. W. H., "Erfahrungen aus dem vergangenen Jahr," *Die Wirts*, No. 1, 1964, p. 2. It should be noted that the East Germans sometimes use the term "product group" in the sense of a group of related products (as opposed to enterprises); however, the term is not used in this second sense in the present study.

71. On all these, see Rytlewski, in Ludz, *DDR Handbuch*, pp. 182-183.
72. Graichen and Rouscik, *Zur Sozialistischen Wirtschaftsorganisation*, p. 574.
73. In this connection see U. Kensy, "Wissenschaftliche Arbeitsberatung zu Rechtsfragen der Kombinate bei der Durchfuehrung der Beschluesse des VIII Parteitages der SED," *WR*, No. 6, 1971, p. 361, and Dzhavadov and Dunaev, *Proizvodstvennye Ob"edineniya...*, p. 57.
74. On the BWRs and Regional Councils, see "Gesetz ueber die oertlichen...," passim, and Ludz, *DDR Handbuch*, p. 214.
75. "Verordnung ueber die VEB...," para. 34.
76. *Ibid.*, para. 36.
77. *Ibid.*, para. 46.
78. *Ibid.*, para 40. See too H. B. Zimmermann, "Wandel von Industrieverwaltungen in Sozialistischen Laendern Dargestellt am Beispiel der Vereinigungen Volkseigener Betriebe der DDR" (unpublished thesis for degree of Diplomsoziologe, presented at the Free University of Berlin, February 1970), pp. 103-104.
79. "Verordnung ueber die VEB...," para. 39.
80. *Ibid.*, paras. 34, 43, and 45. For further details on the formal position of the VVBs see K. Hesse, K. Mueller, and H. Richter, *Lehr- und Studienmaterial zum Wirtschaftsrecht*, Vol. 5 (Berlin: Staatsverlag der Deutschen Demokratischen Republik, 1974), pp. 105-128.

81. Nine is in fact the minimum number. The status of some ministries is not clear; alternative classification could give up to eleven industrial ministries. The point about simplicity would still pertain, however.

82. When coordinated legislation on the various tiers in industrial administration was published in 1972-1973, there was a law on the Council of Ministers — which has a general bearing on industrial ministries — but nothing specific on the individual ministries. The best source of information on the latter is M. Benjamin, H. Moebis, and L. Penig, *Funktion, Aufgaben und Arbeitsweise der Ministerien* (Berlin: Staatsverlag der Deutschen Demokratischen Republik, 1973). See too Hesse, Mueller, and Richter, *Lehr- und Studienmaterial . . .*, Vol. 5, pp. 31-36.

83. It should be pointed out that some *nonindustrial* ministries do still have *Hauptverwaltungen* (i.e., chief administrations), so that references to such bodies can still sometimes be found in the East German press.

84. The most detailed analysis of the People's Chamber is P. J. Lapp's *Die Volkskammer der DDR* (Opladen: Westdeutscher Verlag, 1975); this includes a section on the Council of Ministers (pp. 97-108). For formal details on the Council of Ministers, see "Gesetz ueber den Ministerrat der Deutschen Demokratischen Republik," *GBl.*, Pt. 1, No. 16, 1972, p. 253-256, and articles 76-80 of the 1968 Constitution as amended in October 1974.

85. On the role of the State Council in the 1960s see P. J. Lapp, *Der Staatsrat im politischen System der DDR 1960-1971* (Opladen: Westdeutscher Verlag, 1972).

86. As in the USSR, little information on the topmost body is available from official sources. For a formal description of the role of the Politburo in the two systems, see *Ustav Kommunisticheskoi Partii Sovetskogo Soyuza* (Moscow: Izd. Politicheskoi Literatury, 1971), para. 38, and *Statut der Sozialistischen Einheitspartei* (Berlin: Dietz Verlag, 1977), para. 42. These exceedingly brief references are interesting more for revealing the secrecy of the communist parties about their Politburos than for the small amount they tell us about the bodies themselves. For an introductory Western analysis of the role of the Politburo and the Secretariat in the GDR, see W. Voelkel in G. Erbe et al., *Politik, Wirtschaft und Gesellschaft in der DDR* (Opladen: Westdeutscher Verlag, 1980), pp. 105-107. See too G. Neugebauer, *Partei und Staatsapparat in der DDR* (Opladen: Westdeutscher Verlag, 1978), passim.

87. This information is from Dzhavadov and Dunaev, *Proizvodstvennye Ob"edineniya . . .*, p. 9; G. Kh. Popov (ed.), *Sovershenstvovanie Sistemy Vnutrifirmennogo Upravleniya* (Moscow: Izd. Moskovskogo Universiteta, 1972), pp. 13-14. For more details on the *ob"edineniya* during the 1920s, see B. V. Rakitskii, *Formy Khozyaistvennogo Rukovodstva Predpriyatiyami* (Moscow: Izd. Nauka, 1968), pp. 22-36.

88. Popov, *Sovershenstvovanie . . .*, p. 14.

89. Dunaev, *Ob"edineniya Predpriyatii . . .*, pp. 76-102.

90. Popov, *Sovershenstvovanie . . .*, p. 26. It should be pointed out, however, that some new combines were created in the mid-1950s. See, for example, the chapter by L. P. Kalashnikov in A. I. Komlev et al., *Promyshlennye Ob"edineniya i Firmy Odesshchiny* (Odessa: Izd. Mayak, 1973), pp. 65-73.

91. A. Bobrov, "Sovetskaya Firma," *Izvestiya*, 21 October 1959, p. 2. For a reference to this as the first such article, see N. E. Drogichinskii, *Organizatsiya Upravleniya Promyshlennost'yu i Planirovaniya na Sovremennom Etape* (Moscow: Izd. Ekonomika, 1965), p. 47. On the *sovnarkhozy*, see A. Nove, "The Soviet Industrial Reorganization," *PofC*, No. 6, 1957, pp. 19-25, and *Sovnarkhoz i Zhizn'*, (Kharkov: Knizhnoe Izdatel'stvo, 1959).

92. In fact, the term has been traced back at least as far as 1927, when a statute on Soviet *firmy* was issued. This is not to be found in the relevant volume (1) of *Resheniya* . . . , but is referred to in I. Grushetskii, "Sovetskie Firmy — Ikh Nastoyashchee i Budushchee," *Izvestiya,* 18 February 1962, p. 3. For a useful Western analysis of the genesis of the associations and their development through 1973, see A. C. Gorlin, "The Soviet Economic Associations," *Soviet Studies,* No. 1, 1974, pp. 3-27.

93. For details on the early history of these two *ob"edineniya,* see the various contributions in M. T. Meleshkin (ed.), *Pervye Sovetskye Firmy* (L'vov: Knizhkovo-Zhurnal'ne Vidavnitstvo, 1962), pp. 51-84.

94. *Table 1 Notes.* The figures are from different points in the year; a more consistent mode of presentation is not possible with existing data. Most figures explicitly include the science-production associations.

Col. E, 1964: The figure refers to the number of *ob"edineniya* that were to exist by the end of 1964.

See too Chapter 6.

Sources.   Col. A   V. I. Gromov and V. Ya. Kamenetskii, *Proizvodstvennye Ob"edineniya v SSSR* (Moscow: Izd. Ekonomika, 1967), pp. 3-4.

Col. B   Popov, *Sovershenstvovanie* . . . , p. 28.

Col. C   "Upravlenie Proizvodstvom," *Ekon. Gaz.,* No. 37, 1972, p. 1.

Col. D   Various sources:

1961-1964: Official figures of the Central Statistics Office cited in N. D. Baikov et al., *Otraslevye Proizvodstvennye Ob"edineniya v Promyshlennosti* (Moscow: Izd. Ekonomika, 1966), pp. 14-15.

1966, 1969: I. Kuznetsov and A. Tikhomirova, "Voprosy Effektivnosti Organizatsii Upravleniya Otrasl'yu Promyshlennosti," *Vop. Ekon.,* No. 11, 1970, p. 78.

1970: Markin, *Effektivnost'* . . . , p. 38.

1971: N. K. Baibakov, 'Po Voskhodyashchei Linii', *Pravda,* 1 August 1972, p. 2.

1972: Yu. Subotskii, "Ob"edineniya v Sisteme Ekonomiki Razvitogo Sotsializma," *Kommunist,* No. 13, 1973, p. 56.

1973: Popov and Petrov, "Na Putyakh . . . ," p. 2.

1974: E. Kapustin and Yu. Subotskii, "Problemy Razvitiya Ob"edinenii," *Ekon. Gaz.,* No. 17, 1975, p. 7.

1975: A. N. Kosygin in *XXV S'ezd Kommunisticheskoi Partii Sovetskogo Soyuza – Stenograficheskii Otchet,* Vol. 2. (Moscow: Izd. Politicheskoi Literatury, 1976), p. 25.

1976: V. V. Laptev, "Mezhdu Tsekhom i Zavodom," *Sots. Ind.*, 5 January 1977, p. 2.

1977: V. Cherkovets, "Predpriyatie v Sisteme Sotsialisticheskogo Obshchestvennogo Proizvodstva," *Plan. Khoz.*, No. 5, 1979. pp. 88-89.

1979: A. Nagovitsin, "Effektivnost' Vsesoyuznykh Promyshlennykh Ob"edinenii," *Vop. Ekon.*, No. 4, 1980, p. 87.

Col. E Various sources:

1963: Drogichinskii, *Organizatsiya Upravleniya* ..., p. 56.

1964: B. S. Andreev and D. A. Margolis, *Leningradskie Firmy*, (Leningrad: Lenizdat, 1965), p. 118.

1969: Lagutkin, *Proizvodstvennye Ob"edineniya* ..., p. 43.

1970-1979: TsSUSSSR, *Narodnoe Khozyaistvo SSSR v 1979 g.* (Moscow: Statistika, 1980), p. 133.

See too A. V. Bachurin in A. P. Dumachev and A. K. Varsobin (compilers), *Opyt Organizatsii i Raboty Khozraschetnykh Ob"edinenii v Promyshlennosti* (Leningrad: Lenizdat, 1970), p. 72, where there is a reference to the work of 563 *ob"edineniya* in 1969. It is not fully clear whether this figure represents the total number of associations existing at that time; it does constitute a minimum figure, however. Reasons for the discrepancies in these figures are considered in Chapter 6.

95. See Bobrov, "Sovetskaya Firma," p. 2; I. P. Ivonin, "Vygoda Dokazana," *Izvestiya*, 11 May 1962, p. 3. See too A. Alekseenko, T. Patrotskii, and V. Kamenetskii, "Proizvodstvennye kompleksy deistvuyut," *Ekon. Gaz.*, No. 46, 1962, p. 23, for a more detailed investigation of this question by technical specialists (i.e., as distinct from senior officials).

96. Andreev and Margolis, *Leningradskie Firmy*, p. 117.

97. *Ibid.*, p. 117. It is interesting that the shipbuilding industry was one in which experiments were carried out in the GDR too (esp. in 1967), which suggests the importance of this branch of industry to the communist states of Eastern Europe. To the dismay of many Western merchant fleets, the Soviets have in recent years been transporting an ever-increasing proportion of the international cargo.

98. Dunaev, *Ob"edineniya* ..., p. 159.

99. It should also be pointed out that some highly integrated and centralized *production ob"edineniya*, such as the electronics *ob"edinenie* Svetlana (Leningrad), were accorded most of the rights of a *glavk* and were directly subordinate to the ministry. Svetlana was founded in 1962, but we have been unable to discover exactly when it was granted the status of a *glavk;* certainly it enjoyed this by mid-1970 (see G. V. Romanov's paper in Dumachev and Varsobin, *Opyt* ..., p. 27).

100. For details on Sigma, see A. B. Chuplinskas and V. A. Baranauskas, *Tak Rabotaet Ob"edinenie 'Sigma'* (Moscow: Izd. Ekonomika, 1967), passim. See too Taksir, *Upravlenie Promyshlennost'yu* ..., pp. 221-230.

101. Interview data and M. Kashirina, "Srednee Zveno," *Pravda*, 11 June 1977, p. 2; the latter figure refers to all-union and republic industrial *ob"edineniya*.

102. Lagutkin, *Proizvodstvennye Ob"edineniya* . . . , p. 45; A. Tryakin, "Ukreplenie Gosudarstvennoi Planovoi Distsipliny vo vsekh Zvenyakh Khozyaistva," *Plan. Khoz.*, No. 3, 1978, p. 91.

103. P. A. Zdorov, "Proizvodstvennye Ob"edineniya i Effektivnost' Proizvodstva," *Ekon. Gaz.*, No. 33, 1970, p. 3. (This paper can also be found in Dumachev and Varsobin, *Opyt* . . . , pp. 5-14, here p. 8); Popov and Petrov, "Na Putyakh . . . , p. 2; Kosygin in *XXV S'ezd* . . . , Vol. 2, p. 25; A. Nagovitsin, "Effektivnost' Vsesoyuznykh . . . ," p. 87 (this figure *includes* production from NPOs).

104. That some senior officials have considered this growth to be less impressive than it should be can be inferred from the fact that misleading information on the growth of these bodies has been given in the more popular economic periodicals, in the form of official figures; see Ch. 6, note 13. See too the remark about the upward revision of figures on the growth of output in the *ob"edineniya* in P. Hanson, "Economic Development in the Soviet Union in 1972" (unpublished paper presented to the annual conference of the National Association for Soviet and East European Studies, April 1973), p. 24.

105. *Politische Oekonomie* . . . , p. 72.

106. *Ibid.*, p. 74, and N. N. Popov, *Po Puti Sovershenstvovaniya – Primenenie Novoi Sistemy Planirovaniya i Rukovodstva vo Vneshnei Torgovle i v Promyshlennosti GDR* (Moscow: Izd. Mezhdunarodnye Otnosheniya, 1967), pp. 92-93.

107. *Politische Oekonomie* . . . , p. 74. The East German provinces (*Laender*) were abolished in 1952.

108. Popov, *Po Puti* . . . , po. 92-93; K. Pleyer, "Die rechtliche Stellung der VVB im Neuen Oekonomischen System," *D.A.*, No. 2, 1968, p. 113. There appear to have been approximately 75 VVBs at this time; see Bundesministerium fuer gesamtdeutsche Fragen (eds.), *SBZ von A bis Z* (Bonn: Deutscher Bundes-Verlag, 1960), p. 440.

109. Data from *Politische Oekonomie* . . . , p. 135. The decree was dated 22 December 1950, and is referred to in I. P. Il'inskii et al., *GDR – Osnovy Gosudarstvennogo Stroya* (Moscow: Yuridicheskaya Literatura, 1971), p. 171.

110. For a writer arguing that such centralization was necessary (because of sabotage and wrong attitudes at many lower levels), see G. Friedrich, *Aufgaben und Arbeitsweise der VVB* (Berlin: Verlag Die Wirtschaft, 1959), p. 5.

111. *Ibid.*, pp. 5-18 and *SBZ* . . . (1960), p. 440.

112. For a fuller discussion of this period, see Baylis, *The Technical Intelligentsia* . . . , pp. 219-232, and Ch. 4 of the present study.

113. Friedrich, *Aufgaben* . . . , p. 21.

114. Popov, *Po Puti* . . . , p. 94.

115. *Ibid.*, p. 96.

116. For a useful survey of pricing reforms in the late 1960s, see M. Keren, "The New Economic System in the GDR: An Obituary," *Soviet Studies*, No. 4, 1973, pp. 554-587, esp. 565-568 and 572. Regarding foreign trade, a "guideline" published in June 1966 called for more autonomy of VVBs and large enterprises in the field of foreign trade. This idea was endorsed at the 14th plenum of the Central Committee in December 1966, and more formal legislation to this effect was issued on 13 February 1967. For details of experimentation, see S. Domdey and S. Hohl, "Ein Experiment im Dienste hoeherer Effektivitaet," *Die Wirts.*, No. 4, 1967, pp. 4-5; H. Soelle, "Neue Schritte auf dem Wege zu wachsender aussenwirtschaftlicher Effektivitaet,"

Die Wirts., No. 8, 1967, pp. 4-5; S. Domdey and D. Albrecht, "Mit dem neuen Instrumentarium lassen sich wichtige aussenwirtschaftliche Probleme loesen," *Die Wirts.*, No. 15, 1967, pp. 3-4. However, see too Ch. 6 of the present study.

117. In fact, this concept of a two-tier system is not entirely clear, since the enterprise will continue to exist, and *formally* retains much autonomy. For an awareness of the apparent contradiction here, see Klinger, "Die neue Kombinatsverordnung . . . ," p. 196. See too Note 45 to Introduction.

118. See, for instance, K. Heuer, "Die planmaessige Weiterentwicklung der Rechtsstellung der volkseigenen Kombinate," *WR*, No. 4, 1970, p. 207; *Statistisches Jahrbuch der Deutschen Demokratischen Republik – 1970* (Berlin: Staatsverlag der Deutschen Demokratischen Republik, 1970), p. 96. A Soviet article has distinguished between the combines that existed before the late 1960s and the "new" sort that developed in the late 1960s. See P. Velichko and F. Shevyakov, "Razvitie Proizvodstvennykh Ob"edinenii v Promyshlennosti GDR," *Vop. Ekon.*, No. 7, 1972, p. 110. However, see too Ch. 4, where there is a discussion of a reference made in an authoritative source to 1966 as the "takeoff" year.

119. Graichen und Rouscik, *Zur Sozialistischen Wirtschaftsorganisation*, p. 385.

120. Kroemke and Rouscik, *Konzentration . . .* , pp. 76-77 and 118.

121. See *ibid.*, pp. 136-179 on combines; here esp. pp. 136-140.

122. L. Penig, "Rechtsbeziehungen der Planung und Leitung volkseigener Industriekombinate," *VS*, No. 11, 1967, p. 661.

123. See, for example, H. Such, *VVB und Wissenschaftlich-Technischer Fortschritt* (Berlin: Staatsverlag der Deutschen Demokratischen Republik, 1964). On p. 42 Such discusses various forms of cooperation between enterprises without mentioning the combines.

124. See F. Bandel in *Das Neue Oekonomische System der Planung und Leitung der Volkswirtschaft in der Praxis* (Berlin: Dietz Verlag, 1963), p. 181.

125. "Kombinat der Kabelwerke," *Die Wirts.*, No. 5, 1967, p. 6.

126. *Statistisches Jahrbuch . . .* , 1970, p. 96. For an example of a VVB (the VVB Luft- und Kaeltetechnik) being transformed into a combine, see the announcement to this effect in *effekt*, No. 6, 1970, p. 56.

127. This policy of prioritization led to the emergence of the concept of "structure-determining tasks" — i.e., tasks within industry that were considered to be of key importance to the restructuring of the mix of industrial product output.

128. For a detailed analysis, see E. Lieser-Triebnigg, "Ein neues Organisationsrecht fuer die Wirtschaft in der DDR," *D.A.*, No. 8, 1973, pp. 825-835.

129. *Table 2 Notes.* We are not alone in experiencing difficulties in obtaining data; see D. Granick, *Enterprise Guidance in Eastern Europe* (Princeton, NJ: Princeton U.P., 1975), p. 139. Figures are from different points in the year.

Col. A It is unclear whether the 1958 figure includes the construction industry or not, though we believe it does.

1969, 1970: Based on the fact that there were 71 branches of industry. However, some VVBs were already being replaced by combines, so that the figures are questionable.

Sources.   Col. A   1958: *Die Wirts.*, No. 34, 1958, p. 2

                         1959: Friedrich, *Aufgaben . . .* , p. 23.

                         1963: *ND*, 16 July 1963, Sonderbeilage, p. 12.

1964. *Das funktionelle Wirken der Bestandteile des neuen oekonomischen Systems der Planung und Leitung der Volkswirtschaft* (Berlin: Dietz Verlag, 1964), pp. 14, 22, 23.

1966: D. M. Gvishiani et al. (eds.), *Upravlenie Sotsialisticheskimi Promyshlennymi Ob"edineniyami i Predpriyatiyami,* Vol. 1 (Moscow: Progress, 1974), p. 238.

1969, 1970: See notes above.

1973: "Intensivierung der Sozialistischen Reproduktion — Teil 2 — Diskussion," *Sitzungsberichte der Akademie der Wissenschaften der DDR,* No. 12/2, 1973, (Berlin: Akademie-Verlag, 1974), p. 40.

1975: *Vsesoyuznaya Nauchnaya Konferentsiya 'Problemy Razvitiya Ob"edinenii v Sisteme Otraslevogo Upravleniya' – Tezisy Dokladov,* Vol. 1 (Moscow: Institut Ekonomiki AN SSSR, 1975), p. 182.

Col. B 1958: G. Rossmann et al., *Geschichte der SED – Abriss* (Berlin: Dietz Verlag, 1978), p. 375.

1960: *SBZ* . . . , p. 440.

1967, 1972: Mitzscherling, *DDR-Wirtschaft,* p. 75.

1968, 1973: A. Nagovitsin, "Promyshlennye Ob"edineniya v GDR," *Plan. Khoz.,* No. 2, 1974, p. 89.

1970: East German source cited in Granick, *Enterprise Guidance* . . . , p. 139.

Col. C 1967: Bundesministerium fuer gesamtdeutsche Fragen (eds.), *A bis Z – Ein Taschen- und Nachschlagebuch ueber den anderen Teil Deutschlands* (Bonn: Deutscher Bundes-Verlag, 1969), p. 693.

1972: Granick, *Enterprise Guidance* . . . , p. 139 (Granick has reservations about the figure).

130. *Table 3 Notes.* The figures are from different points in the year. A more consistent mode of presentation is not possible with existing data. The 1967 figure in Col. B is inferred from the reference in the source to "90 VVBs and directly subordinated combines and enterprises." Locally administered combines are not included; they appear to have been of marginal significance anyway. 1978 and 1979 figures explicitly include construction combines as well as industrial combines.

Sources.

Ministerial Subordination, Col. A:

1967 *Die Wirts.,* No. 34, 1967, p. 4.

1970 Rossmann, *Geschichte* . . . , p. 500.

1971 Granick, *Enterprise Guidance* . . . , p. 143.

1972 *Studieneinfuehrung fuer die Seminare zum Studium der politischen Oekonomie des Sozialismus und der*

Wirtschaftspolitik der SED −2. Studienjahr (Berlin: Dietz Verlag, 1972), p. 110.

1973 As for Table 2, Col. A, 1973.

1974 "25 Jahre DDR — ein Vierteljahrhundert Kampf fuer Frieden, Demokratie und Sozialismus," *Die Wirts.*, No. 15, 1974, p. 12.

1975 As for Table 2, Col. A, 1975.

1978 M. Melzer and A. Scherzinger, "Wirtschaftssystem der DDR im Umbau?," *Vierteljahrsheft zur Wirtschaftsforschung*, No. 4, 1978, p. 381.

1979 M. Duesterwald, "Genauere Leistungsrechnung der Kombinate," *Die Wirts.*, No. 1, 1980, p. 16.

Ministerial Subordination, Col. B:

1971, 1973 Nagovitsin, "Promyshlennye . . .', p. 89.

VVB Subordination, Col. C:

1972: *Studieneinfuehrung* . . . , p. 110.

1973: "Intensivierung der . . . ," p. 40.

1978: Melzer and Scherzinger, "Wirtschaftssystem der DDR . . . ," p. 381.

131. Friedrich (*Aufgaben und* . . . , p. 19) states that the VVBs bore full responsibility for the enterprises formally subordinate to them and also exercised some functions over *all* the enterprises in the respective branch, including the locally managed enterprises.

132. Zimmermann, "Wandel von Industrieverwaltungen . . . ," p. 42; Popov, *Po Puti* . . . , p. 95.

133. Referred to in O. Schoth, "Kombinate — Zentren der Leistungskraft unserer Gesellschaft," *ND*, 19 July 1970, p. 5.

134. E. Honecker in *Protokoll der Verhandlungen des VIII. Parteitages der Sozialistischen Einheitspartei Deutschlands*, Vol. 1 (Berlin: Dietz Verlag, 1971), p. 86. It is possible that Honecker was referring only to production from combines directly under ministries, and Halbritter to combines under ministries and VVBs.

135. M. Duesterwald, "Genauere Leistungsrechnung . . . ," p. 16. See too "Erfahrungen aus Kombinate," *Die. Wirts.*, No. 12, 1979, p. 5. However, it should be made clear that this is probably partially explained by the fact that many VVBs have been disbanded recently, so that their combines would then be subordinate directly to ministries — although many brand new combines have undoubtedly been established since January 1979.

Chapter 2

"DEMAND" CHANNELS

In discussing interest groups and demands within a political system, the point is not always sufficiently emphasized that the mere existence of what would appear to an outside observer to be the common interest of a group (because its members fulfill similar functions, have similar backgrounds, and so on) does not in itself signify that there will be awareness of that interest by members of the group or pressure to promote or defend that interest. For such pressure to exist, the group must first become aware of its common interest (through comparing opinions on a given topic), then make its views known — either to the general public and/or to the senior political decision makers — and finally attempt more directly to influence decisions to ensure that these are maximally favorable toward the group interest. Thus for analytical purposes we can subdivide the "demand" channels into those through which views are expressed predominantly amongst peers (i.e., at which perception of a common group opinion and possibly interest could emerge) and perhaps generally publicized, and those through which such views directly reach the senior decision makers. Three points must be strongly emphasized here. First, information on both the type and amount of access to the senior political actors in both the USSR and the GDR is extremely limited. This problem is not limited to the communist states, of course; although considerably more information on such access can be obtained about countries such as Britain or the USA, there are still areas of political communication even in these states about which the political scientist must often make intelligent inferences. Second, as was pointed out in the introduction, it is more appropriate to define "demands" at the end of this study than here; for the present, "calls," "views," and "opinions" will be used as well as "demands." Third, these channels are not as distinct in the real world as in the analyst's study. In the GDR, particularly in the 1960s, the fora at which opinions might be aggregated were often attended by the most senior decision makers (i.e., members of the Politburo) so that the division outlined above is difficult to sustain. Indeed, important conferences in the GDR other than party gatherings have very often been organized by the Central Committee of the SED itself, which further blurs the line between the different types of channel. This problem pertains far less to the USSR, where conferences of specialists have rarely been attended by members of the Politburo or organized by central party bodies; it also pertains much less to the GDR in the early 1970s. Consequently, we have decided to concentrate in the next two chapters on subleadership calls for associations in all fora *other* than central party gatherings (which are considered in Chapter 4), fully aware that this distinction cannot always be so clearly made. The justifications for this are that any comparative study must have a common framework for analyzing the individual states and that the study would look very imbalanced if all "demand" channels were considered in one place, with the statements made only by senior leadership being analyzed somewhere else. Since leadership views are very important, such an imbalance could excessively distort the reader's perception of the significance of the different stages of the political process. The content of these subleadership "demands" is examined in Chapter 3; for now, we are concerned with the ways such "demands" are initially articulated and possibly aggregated.

The three main channels for publicizing views are the press, conferences, and radio/television. Although we have little information on the third of these, there are strong grounds for arguing that this particular channel of communication is of little relevance. Thus we have seen a VVB director on East German television discussing the work of his organization, proclaiming its good work, and hence in one sense promoting the VVB concept.[1] However, whereas debates in the press frequently refer to points made at conferences and vice versa, we have found no significant references to arguments made on television or radio, suggesting that these are not important channels. In the USSR, too, there have been broadcasts specifically concerned with the *ob"edineniya*;[2] but the remarks on the GDR pertain here too, in addition to which all our interviewees said that these channels were of no real importance as debating fora. Hence, only the press and conferences are considered here. The term "press" is used broadly to include all published material — newspapers, journals, and books — and for this reason even our distinction between "the press" and "conferences" must often be hazy. This is because conference papers often appear in newspapers, journals, and books either before or after the conference has taken place. Not all conference papers are publicly available, however, and we would argue that in any case it is valid to distinguish between isolated articles and books, on the one hand,

and papers that are aggregated and that might directly interact at some specific meeting, on the other. Unfortunately, we were not able to attend conferences in either the USSR or the GDR, so that the scale and nature of *oral* debates at such meetings cannot satisfactorily be assessed; we do have some information on this, however, which is presented in the sections on conferences.

2.1. THE PRESS

The position of the press in both the GDR and the USSR has to be understood in a rather different way from that of the press in most Western states. First, there are no legal private presses in the states we are looking at — certainly not for discussing economic policy.[3] In this sense, there is a state monopoly. Second, and as a corollary of the first point, the press works within narrower parameters than the press in, for example. Britain. Whereas in the latter state one is at liberty to subscribe to newspapers and books offering totally different philosophies, the press in East Germany and the Soviet Union is essentially committed to a Marxist-Leninist approach to all the basic questions in society, and no fundamentally different *Weltanschauungen* are popularly available.[4] This said, it should be borne in mind that the "Marxist-Leninist" conception of the world is not a static or noncontentious one; as the debates between the Chinese and the Russians over the past two decades have clearly shown, two states, both claiming to be adherents to the same ideology, can have significant differences. Therefore the overall commitment to something rather vague called communism does not preclude major disagreements within these societies over concrete policy proposals.

Of course, censorship operates in the East European press, as it does to *some* extent (particularly on matters of state security) in the press everywhere.[5] But the fact that censorship exists does not in itself tell us how strict this is, how frequently and under what circumstances it is applied, and so forth. Thus, in assessing the usefulness of the press as a "demand" channel and a medium for articulating different opinions, we must examine the practice rather than the principle. In doing so, we find that there is plenty of "hack" writing that merely eulogizes the existing leadership and its policies (i.e., serving an ideological, supportive role).[6] But it is also true, as we shall see in the next chapter, that very different viewpoints on various issues are published in both the Soviet and the East German press. There do appear to be constraints on these views, however. For instance, neither in the Soviet nor in the East German debates on associations have we found any arguments that clearly transcend the broad parameters of Marxism-Leninism. Moreover, we have found no book or article in which the author openly condemns the concept of the association, although the press does occasionally refer to people opposed to it.[7] While these latter references are rare, *veiled* criticisms of the concept are not, and there are frequently criticisms of specific types of association. This lack of *open* rejection does suggest some form of censorship. But this raises the question of whether such censorship is direct or indirect. By the latter we mean that writers may themselves be aware of the limits of discussion — that they have *internalized* certain norms — and that this could explain the phenomenon as well as the direct intervention of the censor; their understanding of limits would be based on their knowledge of laws, of what senior political actors have said, and so on. For example, at the 1968 Soviet conference, one speaker (A. M. Aleksandrov) proposed that *ob"edineniya* should have rights of direct access to foreign markets, and had his suggestion firmly rejected by the Chairman of Gosplan, Baibakov. We have been unable to find any further suggestions that the associations should have direct access to external markets following this incident.[8] Such internalized censorship clearly acts as a constraint on the openness of debate. But if it constitutes the (a) major form of censorship, this gives us a different perspective on the scope and nature of control of the press in the USSR and the GDR. Moreover, it is not clear that censorship, direct or indirect, accounts for *all* cases of allusive writing. Sometimes a writer might be circumspect in his or her criticisms or suggestions that people or organizations be replaced, because he/she works for or with them. In 1972, for instance, the man in charge of the most progressive Soviet ministry in terms of experimentation with the industrial associations (K. Rudnev of Minpribor) argued that the powers of a minister are in no way diminished if *ob"edineniya* replace *glavki* — in a way that appeared as if he were trying to allay the fears of fellow ministers.[9] In sum, although there clearly are restraints on writers, it should not be assumed that this necessarily indicates frequent and/or strict direct censorship.

It might be objected that this potential for *relatively* open debate is, after all, only in line with the official description of the political process in communist states, namely, democratic centralism. According to this concept, there is "open" debate on any given topic before a decision on it is taken, after which everyone has to accept the leadership's ruling.[10] It is therefore an interesting aspect of the debates studied here that disputes have occasionally continued *after* official policy announcements and legislation. For instance, in 1974 A. Markin argued very much in favor of a more territorially oriented approach to industrial administration (à la *sovnarkhozy*) at a time when the Soviet leadership was still, apparently, firmly committed to the essentially branch principle of administration (ministries).[11] This is examined in more detail later in the study, but for now this fact endorses the general point that censorship is not always strictly applied.

The publications in which views on the associations are expressed can be divided into two types. On the one hand there are the more specialized publications aimed at relatively select readerships; most of the journals and books would come under this heading. On the other, there are the "popular," mass publications, mainly daily newspapers.[12] The debates have been conducted in both types (although it is noticeable that there have been far fewer articles in the East German mass press than in the Soviet). Moreover, there is no evidence to suggest that a particular journal or the like will publish only one viewpoint on any of the many issues concerning the associations. Finally, the fact that very differing views have appeared in the East German press would suggest that the relatively small number of articles in that press in comparison with the Soviet Union is less a reflection of the existence of censorship than other factors (less contentious issues because of clearer and earlier legislation; the simple fact that there are likely to be so many more people wanting to express their views in a country the size of the Soviet Union; and so forth).

In conclusion, the press in the two countries does serve a positive role as a reflector of differing views, and it is far from certain that the limitations on the divergences of opinions expressed are always the result of an interfering censor.[13] It should be reiterated, however, that the Soviet press is generally more critical and open than the East German.

2.2 CONFERENCES

When we talk of conferences in the two states, this again is understood fairly broadly to include any discussion forum (other than central state and party fora), including "seminars" and "round table discussions."

Nowadays, in both states, the number of conferences concerned with technical and scientific matters (this includes economics) is vast. The number of all-union scientific and scientific-technical conferences, sessions, symposia, seminars, and so on in the USSR in 1975 was to have reached almost 1400, for instance.[14] While we have not found a similar breakdown for the GDR, the reporting of economic conferences and the like in the economic journals there gives the impression that such fora are equally important in that system, and some have suggested, in fact, that there are too many.[15] It would thus be impossible — indeed, superfluous — to note every conference at which we know *some* mention of associations was made. It was therefore decided to analyze only those conferences and similar gatherings that we know were either totally or partially concerned specifically with problems of administration and associations; by "partially," we mean that at least one workshop or session was primarily concerned with this subject.

The method used for discovering conferences was as follows. In the USSR an annual of economic affairs (*Ekonomicheskii Ezhegodnik*) was published for the years 1965, 1967, and 1968. This had a section on the "most important" conferences and gatherings for the respective years. For other years, the main initial sources of information were the reports of conferences in the economic and legal specialist journals (*Planovoe Khozyaistvo, Voprosy Ekonomiki, Sovetskoe Gosudarstvo i Pravo,* and *Ekonomicheskaya Gazeta*), which were scanned methodically. Beyond this, discovery was ultimately random — from references in footnotes of books, speeches, and the like. The same methods were used for the GDR (with no annual reference book); the journals scanned there were *Wirtschaftswissenschaft, Vertragssystem, Wirtschaftsrecht, Die Wirtschaft, effekt,* and *Staat und Recht.*

Moreover, the conferences have to appear to have been of national significance; there have been many gatherings at which associations have been discussed, but included here are neither very small sessions of specialists meeting to discuss primarily marginal aspects of the association, nor regional- or town-level gatherings of essentially only local participants. One reason for this omission is that the interest in this study focuses on meetings that appear potentially "influential"; these will therefore be attended by representatives of the central agencies most directly involved in the general policy of creating associations and/or will be reported in detail in the national press. Another is that detailed information on such local meetings is not usually available.

Unfortunately, the amount of information we have been able to obtain on different conferences varies considerably. In the case of one or two Soviet conferences, we have had access in the USSR to the complete collection of papers delivered. In contrast, our information on some conferences, especially East German, has been collected from reports in just a few pages of a journal. Despite this problem, sufficient information is available in the economic and legal journals and some books to be able to list and, to a varying extent, analyze the most important conferences. The type of information of particular interest is the following:

(1) Who convened the conference? We have examined the extent to which the same agency (-ies) are involved all the time, whether these are always central bodies, and whether some organizations that might be expected to be involved are conspicuous by their absence.
(2) How are conferences organized? This relates to the way conferences are publicized as well as to the methods by which papers and participants are chosen.
(3) Who participates? Here we consider both who attends the conference and who actually presents papers. We also consider whether members of the Politburo, ministers, and Central Committee secretaries are present and deliver papers, since this constitutes concrete evidence of leadership interest/concern on the topic and will be useful for the consideration later in the study of the direct channels of access to leaders.
(4) What is the format of conferences? The main interest here is in how much discussion there is and how conference recommendations are agreed upon.

SOVIET CONFERENCES

Much of this section is based on the interviews the author carried out in the Soviet Union in the autumn of 1975; where possible, this material is endorsed with evidence from printed sources.[16]

Since the early 1960s, the following meetings appear to have been the most important regarding the *ob"edineniya:*[17]

- the 47th Sitting of the "Business Club" (*Delovoi Klub*), early 1963
- the L'vov Conference, early 1963
- the Conference on Administration, June 1965
- the All-Union Conference, June 1966
- the L'vov Conference, September 1967
- the All-Union Conference, May 1968
- the Leningrad Seminar, August 1970
- the All-Union Conference, July 1972
- the All-Union Conference, March 1975[18]

We consider first the question of who convenes the conference. From Table 4[19] it is clear that the most frequent organizer of conferences has been the state planning agency, *Gosplan*. Another signific-

TABLE 4   The Conveners of Soviet Conferences

Convener	1963(1)	1963(2)	1965	1966	1967	1968	1970	1972	1975
Central Committee of the CPSU						•			
Gosplan		•		•		•		•	•
Journals	•				•				•
Academy of Sciences, USSR				•				•	•
Academic Bodies (Universities etc)		•	•					•	
Local Party and State Bodies		•			•	•			
All-Union Council of Scientific-Technical Societies				•			•		
Ministries								•	
State Committee for Science and Technology				•				•	•
Others	•				•				

SOURCES/NOTES: See Ch. 2, note 19.

ant feature is that local bodies were often involved in the organizing of a conference of nationwide importance — at least until the 1970s. Whether this has pertained since the issuance of a major decree on conferences in May 1969 is not answerable on the small amount of data we have.[20] According to this document, *all* all-union scientific and technical meetings, conferences, congresses, symposia, and seminars can only be called by ministries, other central bodies (*vedomstva*), and the USSR Academy of Sciences. This is done on the basis of annual plans, which have to be ratified by the State Committee for Science and Technology by the first of October in the year preceding that in which the conference is to be held. This initially appears to be a form of strict, central control of all important fora, although two major reasons given for introducing this decree put it in another perspective. These were that it was hoped unnecessary duplication of conferences would be avoided, and that anyone with an interest in a particular area would be able to discover in advance from one central body all the conferences and like gatherings during the following year that would be of relevance to him or her. This does not alter the fact, however, that central bodies — and in particular one state committee — have a right of veto on conferences or sections of conferences they do not consider to be fit for discussion. The decree also means that if a particular problem arises over a very short period of time, any formal discussion of this at the all-union level has to be delayed — unless in practice this regulation is sometimes overruled.[21] A final point emerging from the table is that, since there have been major disputes on the question of financing in *ob"edineniya*, it seems surprising that the Ministry of Finance has not initiated a conference on this problem.[22]

The detailed organizing of conferences is carried out by an "organizing committee" (hereafter, *orgkomitet*) composed of people appointed by, and frequently from, the various bodies convening the meeting. It is this *orgkomitet* that actually decides which papers are to be presented, edits them, and circulates them to the conference participants. Perhaps the most interesting question to be answered here is how participants and papers are chosen. Details of this vary from conference to conference, but the general picture is as follows. The *orgkomitet* will invite certain specialists or prominent functionaries personally to give plenary speeches on themes related to the particular conference, and/or to head workshops. It will then circulate information to organizations it considers will be interested in the topic (and occasionally advertise in the press). These organizations publicize the forthcoming conference among their members, and request volunteers to deliver papers. Some people will offer papers for the workshops; others will ask simply if they may attend. Our interviewees were agreed that specific titles for papers are *not* issued by the *orgkomitet*, which only gives broad outlines of the areas it wants the conference to concentrate on. However, they also agreed that papers are sometimes considerably edited — or, more accurately, that authors are requested to make alterations themselves in line with suggestions from the *orgkomitet*. In some cases papers are outrightly rejected; apparently, this happens only rarely.

Clearly, then, the *orgkomitet* is a powerful body for determining what is and what is not debated in the Soviet Union.[23] However, as with the press, *potential* veto rights do not necessarily mean that they are frequently used. The only way we can attempt to judge the extent to which conferences are "controlled" by the *orgkomitet* is to study the conferences themselves, which we have done. We would argue that there is sufficient evidence to suggest that conferences are not usually rigidly steered, since very differing opinions are expressed at them, albeit often in somewhat Aesopian language.

The next question to be considered is that of participation at the conferences. Unfortunately, the reports on conferences tend to use different categories for classifying the people attending, so that any attempt to put this into tabular form would have to include so many notes explaining different classifications and so on that it would be of little value.[24] However, the following is clear. First, the number of people attending is usually high. The May 1968 conference was attended by more than 5000 participants, whilst 1000 is by no means unusual. Second, at only one of the nine conferences examined (the May 1968 conference) were members of the Politburo present, whereas ministers and Central Committee secretaries often attend. Third, the vast majority of papers are given by officials from the central ministries and *vedomstva*, academics, senior staff from the *ob"edineniya*, and staff from scientific research institutes. Papers from workers or even middle-management are rare, while even Politburo members do not appear to have spoken; the "technical specialists" dominate.

The Soviets were quite informative on the actual format of a conference; the following picture emerges from the interview data. The papers are always circulated in advance. At the conference, plenary speeches are given at the beginning, and these last perhaps 50-60 minutes each, rarely longer. After these, the participants break up into work groups. At this stage, the picture varies from conference to conference. Often, delegates who have written papers will present a résumé of their argument, and this might last up to 30 minutes. There will then be a discussion, at which anyone can speak, lasting perhaps 10-15 minutes. In other words, discussion time in such a situation seems somewhat restricted. At other conferences, this recapitulation of papers does not take place, a discussion starting immediately through some delegates asking the paper's author specific questions on what he or she has written. This discussion stage is never published, although odd details from it might appear in reports in specialist journals.[25] Finally, the conference reunites for the final speech(es) and perhaps to adopt recommendations. These recommendations are usually drawn up and circulated *before* the conference by the *orgkomitet*, and will be discussed at workshop stage. Our interviewees assured us that changes in these recommendations *are* made in the light of discussion. The decision to adopt the final recommendation is taken through a vote. Allegedly, these votes are not invariably unanimous. It also seems probable that even where they are, this is sometimes achieved by omitting any reference to contentious issues.[26] Let us now consider the East German conferences.

TABLE 5   The Conveners of East German Conferences

Convener	1961	1962	1963	1967(1)	1967(2)	1970	1971	1975
Central Committee Bodies	•	•	•	•			•	•
Council of Ministers	•	•	•	•		•		
Academy of Sciences								•
Others					•			

SOURCES/NOTES: See Ch. 2, note 27.

THE EAST GERMAN CONFERENCES

Since we were not permitted to interview in the GDR, this section is less detailed and authoritative than the Soviet. Our other introductory caveat is to remind the reader that some conferences are included here which would fit almost as well into Chapter 4; inclusion here is justified primarily in that they are different types of meetings, notably from Central Committee plena — more specialized, having more participants, and not requiring all or almost exclusively Central Committee members to be present — and in that this makes comparisons and contrasts with the Soviet picture easier. This said, speeches by Politburo members are considered in Chapter 4. Bearing these reservations in mind, it appears that the most important conferences have been the following:

- the Economic Conference, October 1961
- the Economists' Conference, December 1962
- the Economic Conference, June 1963
- the Economic Seminar, September 1967
- the Legal Conference, October 1967
- the Meeting on Combines, July 1970
- the Scientific Work Consultation, September 1971
- the 14th Session of the Scientific Council for Economic Research, June 1975

Once again, the question of who convenes is presented in tabular form. From Table 5[27] it is clear that the Central Committee itself (or its various committees and attached institutes) and the Council of Ministers have been the main organizers of important conferences on the associations. It is also noticeable what a small role both the local organs and the State Planning Commission have played. Neither the Ministry of Finance nor the Ministry of Foreign Trade appears to have convened conferences, even though the questions of financial and foreign-trade rights of the association have been important issues in the GDR. Thus, although conferences on similar topics in both the USSR and the GDR are largely organized by central organs, it is not the case that functionally equivalent bodies in both states perform the same role vis-à-vis such meetings.

Legislation on the organization of conferences appeared at the beginning of the last decade, a decree on the implementation of conferences being issued in November 1970. An authoritative book was also published in 1973, which gives us a detailed picture of how such meetings are to be organized.[28]

As in the USSR, an organizing committee (in this case, *Organisationsbuero*) is created, the maximum number of members of which is supposed to be four.[29] If this is the maximum number in practice, German conferences are organized by a smaller number of people than their Soviet counterparts.[30] The committee is, once again, created by the overall convener of the conference. It is this convener (it is unclear whether this is a single individual or an organization) who decides the aim of the conference, the size and complexion of the list of participants, the length of duration of the meeting, and, in fact, all basic organizational issues. The committee is thus constrained within fairly specific parameters when working on the details of the conference. The organizational committee normally works in the same location as the conference convener, and is formally subject to the convener's control.[31] It is this committee, as in the USSR, that decides which papers are to be presented, circulates them in advance, and so on.

The method of choosing participants for East German conferences looks virtually identical to the Soviet. Thus, prominent personalities receive personal invitations to conferences. As for other people, the convener sends out posters and reply cards to individuals and/or organizations, and individuals are requested to fill in one of these cards and return it if they wish to attend. All this should happen some six months before the conference is due to take place. Sometimes, the conference is also advertised in the press, and posters can be put up announcing it.[32] One point made in the book on conferences is that everyone who has expressed interest in attending the conference is to receive a formal invitation.[33] This apparent lack of differentiation, however, must be seen in the context of there being a recommended maximum number of participants for many conferences, and of there not being completely open access to the initial reply cards; the possibility of a contradiction between these two principles is, unfortunately, not explained in the literature.

As regards registering East German conferences, the situation appears to be less complicated than in the Soviet Union. Thus, the conferences we are interested in normally have to be registered with the Ministry of the Interior through the local police at least ten days before they are to take place.[34]

As for participation in the GDR, numbers again tend to be large, and the same categories of people as in the USSR present the papers — with one significant difference. Far more senior people were likely to have attended conferences and presented papers in the smaller state until the 1970s. Not only members of the Politburo, but the head of the party and state himself often participated in the East German conferences during the 1960s; the situation in the early and mid-1970s much more closely resembled the Soviet picture. All this means that we can say with certainty that the East German senior leadership was aware of what was being said at conferences on the associations, whereas we have almost exclusively circumstantial evidence of this for the Soviet Union. In fact, Ulbricht often referred to the views of others expressed at the conferences; and, when he and/or another member of the Politburo gave the concluding remarks at such a gathering, they would often praise or criticize individual speakers.[35] No cases of this occurring in the USSR have been found.

The format of conferences is also similar to the Soviet. Thus there will be a welcoming introductory paper, followed by general papers covering the main areas to be discussed. These will be followed by discussions of the papers, usually in work groups, after which concluding remarks are made to the whole gathering.[36] One can infer that these concluding remarks are not necessarily drawn up in advance, or at least that they can be modified as a result of the conference discussions, since materials evaluating the meeting are supplied up to three months *after* it has taken place.[37]

In principle, there is less centralized control of conferences in the GDR than in the USSR; unfortunately, we do not know whether the practice is very different. But of course it is often higher-ranking bodies that convene the important conferences anyway. It is also interesting to note that the main book on the organization of conferences in the GDR does state that the function of such gatherings is primarily educative, to impart information; hence there is no formal acceptance that the conference is a "demand" channel or even a forum for resolving conflicting opinions *within* parameters laid down by the senior leadership.[38] Although we shall see in the next chapter that differing views *are* expressed at East German conferences, these are usually couched in even more veiled terms than at Soviet gatherings. Also, the division of labor between papers at most East German conferences has been far more noticeable than at the Soviet meetings, so that often there is only one paper concerned with one aspect of associations. In such a situation, it is not possible for "group" awareness on a given question to be detected just from the conference papers — unless, of course, there are references in papers or elsewhere to groups, which is not the case.

2.3. ON THE ANALYSIS OF "DEMANDS"

Having examined the channels for articulating views, we come to the question of how articles and the like were chosen for analysis, and what method was used for this analysis.

SELECTION METHODS

In looking for "group" views, one method is to examine a large number of written units (a unit being any single piece of writing on associations, whether book, article, or conference paper). Given the abundance of such units since the beginning of the 1960s, it would not be feasible for one person — especially attempting to categorize views in two states — to cover everything written. The approach adopted by some content analysts of choosing a proportion of the total, analyzing these and then drawing inferences about the total population, is not without problems. This method can be useful if one is *only* looking for opinion groupings, although we show in the next section why this could not be done satisfactorily in our case.[39] However, we were also looking for possible group influence on the senior political leadership, and would argue that policy makers who themselves have to select articles they wish to read about industrial administration do not approach their reading in a random way, but more probably based on which writers they know personally, whom they are advised to read, and so on. A senior member of *Gosplan* is surely more likely to have his or her views read by leaders than is a young economist from Vladivostok, for example; but how can allowance be made for this in sampling? The notion of weighting units according to potential influence is so questionable and problematic that it would not be acceptable. Thus, after long consideration, our first chosen method of selecting units was based on what can be called "involved-person perception." By this is meant that we selected articles and other writings by people whom we knew to have been involved in the policy process (notably those members of the commission who drew up the legislation on associations, and ministers whose ministries have been affected and/or who have been required to ratify the legislation) and then examined their references to other units. In practice, there proved to be a relatively high level of mutual reference, that is, a comparatively limited number of people in relation to the total number who have written on the associations have most frequently referred to the opinions of other people within the micro policy-making group. It is noticeable in Soviet writing, for example, how many criticisms of the ideas of the two legal specialists, A. G. Pevzner and V. V. Laptev, there have been.[40]

While this first method would give an indication of the views of many of those whom we knew to have been most influential in the micro policy (legislation) stage, it would not necessarily tell us either whether these people themselves had been influenced by others or that they were the most important influences on senior leaders. As we have indicated, the question of direct access to leaders is treated later in the study; but at this stage, we were interested in other possible ways the leaderships could be influenced, notably through views expressed in the press or at conferences. Therefore, our second method for selecting units was to analyze all units concerned with associations, both in the press and at conferences, for one year before and six months after any major policy statement or legislation. The aim was to see if opinion groups were discernible and, if so, whether they at least *appeared* to be attempting to pressure (influence) policy makers. If these views came *before* the policy statements/legislation, we would be justified in arguing that they may well have influenced the policy makers in some way. If they came *after* such events, it would imply that opinion groups were merely endorsing leadership views.

Finally, we scanned all the main journals and newspapers used over the whole period, selecting for analysis all articles appearing to deal with the most contentious issues emerging from the first and second methods. Given the particular importance of conferences for the analysis of group views, all the papers not covered by the first and second methods were also analyzed. Particularly in the case of the GDR, this meant that we had by this stage covered most of the articles, books, and conference papers to which we have access, so that the selection was de facto fairly comprehensive.

METHOD OF ANALYSIS

Within a few months of starting the research, a general picture of the major areas of debate had already been formed; since debates revealed preferences for different kinds of associations — as well as misgivings about these bodies — they constituted a major part of the search for differing views and possibly demands. Moreover, if preferences could be classified, we could then attempt to correlate these with data available on the people showing these preferences; for example, we could see whether or not a person's functional role was a good predictor of his or her views.

Having isolated what appeared to be the eight most contentious aspects of the associations, an attempt was made to classify units according to these eight variables. For reasons that shall now be explained, this attempt at methodical content analysis ultimately proved to be unworkable. Nevertheless, some aspects of the exercise did produce insights into opinion groupings (see Chapter 3). The exercise is discussed partially because of this, and partially to highlight some of the problems that can be encountered in trying to apply content analysis to communist writing. We start by presenting two of the Soviet variables, since the subsequent discussion will be clearer if the reader can refer to these:

Variable 2: Preferred method of forming the administration in a production association.

(1) Use the best administrators from all component enterprises.
(2) Convert the administration of the head enterprise only into the administration of the association.
(3) Unclear.
(9) No reference.

Variable 6: On the role of the *glavk*.

(1) Eradicate the *glavk* and, whenever possible, do *not* replace it with an industrial *ob"edinenie*.
(2) Transform it into an industrial *ob"edinenie*.
(3) Restructure (mainly through transfer to profit-and-loss accounting), without replacing it with an industrial *ob"edinenie*.
(4) Retain *glavk*, with very little change (mainly, do *not* transfer to profit-and-loss accounting).
(5) Unclear.
(9) No reference.[41]

One of the most serious problems was the question of how to interpret "nonreference." In other words, was it permissible to infer from a writer's lack of reference to industrial *ob"edineniya* or *glavki* in a unit allegedly concerned with the whole administrative structure of industry that he or she did not favor these bodies? There is no foolproof method for assessing the relevance of this sort of omission, and the researcher ultimately has to use intuition. As justification for this and by way of concrete example, mention can be made of one Leningrad economist whom we interviewed, who did not refer to branch ministries in his writings on administration, preferring to concentrate on the alleged advantageousness of a *Gosplan* with increased powers plus a network of industrial associations. When questioned on this, the economist admitted that "in his personal opinion" (this was constantly repeated) there were far too many ministries, and they could usefully be substantially reduced in number; in the long term, many could be abolished altogether, and their functions divided between the industrial *ob"edineniya* and *Gosplan*. In other words, our inference had been correct that the writer was deliberately not referring to ministries because he was (covertly) opposed to them. Perhaps the best example, however, was the attitude found toward the replacement of *glavki* with industrial *ob"edineniya*. We were informed that the reason so little had been published on the new bodies was that there had been too little experience with them for much to have been written. One Moscow economist even suggested that we omit these bodies altogether in our research and concentrate on the production associations; the same man favored a two-tier system in industrial administration "whenever possible" in his writings. The implication is clear. He and other economists were not interested in industrial *ob"edineniya* because they felt that these "new" bodies would simply extend the status quo and thus undermine a major aspect of the association reform.[42] On the other hand, we were also informed that many ministerial officials favored a three- or more-tier arrangement, doubtless in many cases being aware that they could thus essentially retain the existing structure. In view of the fact that the 24th Party Congress had referred to the possibilities of a three-tier arrangement in some branches, and that Brezhnev's own references there to the *ob"edineniya* manifested a vagueness about them (that is, it is not clear that he was aware at that time of the distinction that has subsequently emerged between the two basic types of association), one must assume that some writers, well versed in the ways of suggesting change within accepted parameters (i.e., official party policy), make subtle criticism or show disguised preferences through this nonreference technique.[43] There remains, however, the problem of classifying such nonreferences, and trying to distinguish between "significant" and "nonsignificant" nonreference. This last point is part of a more general problem, to which we now turn.

Particularly at conferences, it is abundantly clear that some speakers present general papers — concerned with industrial administration as a whole and the role of different types of association within this — while others simply describe the detailed work of the association they happen to work in, without concerning themselves in any meaningful sense with general problems of the association policy.[44] However, given certain accepted norms in Soviet writing, the latter type of speaker frequently ends the paper with a general call for his/her type of association. There is thus a serious methodological problem of how to distinguish real preferences — someone who is arguing in favor of the *firma* against the *kombinat*, shall we say — from the argument of someone who is only really saying that the *ob"edinenie* he now works in functions better than the individual enterprises constituting it did before amalgamation, without considering the question of whether the new association would have been more effective still had it been formed in a different way. In practice, one can often intuitively distinguish the two types of paper, although there are certainly some problematic units. Even dismissing the question of the latter sort, however, we still require some acceptable "objective" standard for categorizing units. Many units contain phrases such as "better than . . ." or "preferable to . . ."; many more do not, however, thus creating difficulties for a coder.

Finally, there was the question of whether it was justified to distinguish between "no reference" and "preference unclear" on any given variable. We felt that it would be of interest to distinguish these two, largely in view of the "significant nonreference" point made above. In other words, we would ideally have distinguished between the writer who made no reference — e.g., to industrial associations — and the writer who did mention them in a context revealing either no opinion on them or an unclear opinion. In the final analysis, however, it proved impossible to divide the "no reference" category into "significant," "nonsignificant," and "unclear," owing to the doubts already expressed about how this could be done at all satisfactorily. Rather, it has proved more useful merely to refer to certain writers who did not mention, for instance, industrial associations when they might have been expected to.

Because of all thes problems, it was felt that any attempt at excessive "quantification" could not be justified. In the case of the GDR, the even more Aesopian language in which debates are couched, the relatively small number of accessible units concerning associations, and the existence of difficulties similar to those in Soviet writing (e.g., nonreference) meant that an attempt at rigorous content analysis was not possible either. Thus, the method of analysis adopted was to use a mixture of partial content analysis (we started with our original analytical framework of eight variables) and more traditional, subjective methods of interpretation[45] (when coding problems and the like precluded the more formal content analysis).

2.4. SUMMARY

We have seen in this chapter that despite a state monopoly on communications, the press and conferences are potentially useful media for articulating differing views and making "demands" within certain parameters — although East German conferences have often in theory and practice been the least useful forum for this. It has also been argued that several methodological difficulties ultimately prevented us from analyzing the press and conferences in as quantitative a way as had originally been intended, but that this very attempt revealed much about the ways in which views are articulated in communist states. Let us now consider the views themselves.

NOTES

1. Gerhard Hauschild, general director of the VVB Energy Supply, on the 1st Program (GDR Television), 12 September 1974.
2. See V. Kovalenko, "Shagi Ob″edineniya," *Sots. Ind.*, 14 May 1972, p. 2.
3. On the press in the GDR, see J. Sandford, *The Mass Media of the German-Speaking Countries* (London: Oswald Wolff, 1976), pp. 184-209. For the Soviet position see M. W. Hopkins, *Mass Media in the Soviet Union* (New York: Pegasus, 1970). Of course, there are illegal press channels (e.g., the *samizdat* publications in the USSR), but these are not concerned with detailed discussions of economic policy of the sort being examined here. Even if they were, it is hardly conceivable that any "demands" made there would be considered by the senior decision makers.
4. Sandford, *The Mass Media . . .*, esp. pp. 185-186 and 192-202; Hopkins, *Mass Media . . .*, passim, esp. pp. 19-52, 109-149.
5. In Britain, for example, there are the D-notices.
6. Such articles will usually also give details of a particular association — without in any real sense contributing to the debate — and/or will merely publicize current official policy. For examples, see V. Manaev, "Ob″edinenie i Otrasl," *Pravda*, 17 November 1973, and H., "Echte Partner der zentralen Planung und Fuehrung," *N.D.*, 25 January 1969, p. 3.
7. See note 1 to Ch. 7.
8. For details of this dispute, see A. V. Bachurin et al. (eds.), *Sovershenstvovanie Planirovaniya i Uluchshenie Ekonomicheskoi Raboty v Narodnom Khozyaistve* (Moscow: Izd. Ekonomika, 1969), pp. 88-89, and N. K. Baibakov, "Zadachi Sovershenstvovaniya Planirovaniya i Uluchsheniya Ekonomicheskoi Raboty v Narodnom Khozyaistve," *Ekon. Gaz.*, No. 21, 1968, p. 10.
9. See D. M. Gvishiani and S. E. Kamenitser (eds.), *Problemy Nauchnoi Organizatsii Upravleniya Sotsialisticheskoi Promyshlennost'yu* (Moscow: Izd. Ekonomika, 1974), p. 171.

10. On democratic centralism, see K. von Beyme, "A Comparative View of Democratic Centralism," *Government and Opposition*, No. 3, 1975, pp. 259-277; L. T. Holmes, "Democratic Centralism in the GDR" (ECPR Conference Paper, April 1975); K. Hanf in L. H. Legters (ed.), *The German Democratic Republic – A Developed Socialist Society* (Boulder, CO: Westview Press, 1978), pp. 17-59.

11. See Markin, *Effektivnost'* . . . , pp. 38-42. For an East German view at odds with existing legislation and policy, see note 64 to Ch. 3.

12. Included here under "specialized" publications are not only the (usually) monthly journals, such as *Planovoe Khozyaistvo* or *Wirtschaftswissenschaft*, but also the weeklies, *Ekonomicheskaya Gazeta* and *Die Wirtschaft* (which recently became a monthly). Some of the "dailies" in fact appear four or five times per week (e.g., *Sotsialisticheskaya Industriya*).

13. One possible exception to this should be noted, however. In 1968 the journal *effekt* began to be published in the GDR; it was aimed primarily at higher management. The journal suddenly ceased appearing in 1970, with no warning and no explanation. If it was closed because of a feeling in the higher party ranks that the managers were becoming too self-aware as a group with independent interests, then censorship can be seen to have been taken to its extreme (i.e., closure of a particular communication medium). There was little serious debate in *effekt* concerning associations, however, so that this case is not of major relevance for the present study.

14. "Effektivnost' Nauchnykh Soveshchanii," *Pravda*, 15 May 1975, p. 1.

15. See K. H. Burghardt, C. Pobuda, and K. Weber, *Organisation von Konferenzen und Beratungen* (Berlin: Verlag Die Wirtschaft, 1973), p. 58. For a similar Soviet criticism, see *Resheniya* . . . , Vol. 7, p. 546.

16. In order not to compromise these interviewees, they are not named.

17. It may seem incongruous that in the case of both the USSR and the GDR, a conference has been included which took place *after* the legislation with which we are primarily concerned; there are three main reasons for this. First, we wanted to ascertain whether the opinions of specialists on certain issues were publicly expressed for the first time only after official policy statements and legislation; i.e., were these opinions mere endorsement of leadership views or did they predate leadership statements? Second, we wanted to know whether there is ever specialist criticism of legislation and/or leadership views shortly after these have become known publicly? Finally, the conference papers often contain the most detailed analyses of implementation that are available to Western researchers.

18. Details of these meetings are from (early 1963) "Sovetskie Firmy," *Ekon. Gaz.*, No. 6, 1963, pp. 9-18; (L'vov 1963) "Ekonomicheskii Eksperiment Podtverzhdaet: Firmy — Eto Khorosho," *Ekon. Gaz.*, No. 27, 1963, pp. 35-36; (June 1965) *Ekonomicheskii Ezhegodnik – 1966* (Moscow: 1966), pp. 198-200; (June 1966) D. M. Gvishiani and S. E. Kamenitser (eds.), *Problemy Nauchnoi Organizatsii Upravleniya Sotsialisticheskoi Promyshlennost'yu* (Moscow: Izd. Ekonomika, 1968), and D. M. Gvishiani et al. (eds.), *Materialy K Vsesoyuznoi Nauchno-Tekhnicheskoi Konferentsii "Problemy Nauchnoi Organizatsii Upravleniya Sotsialisticheskoi Promyshlennost'yu,"* 7 vols., (Moscow: 1966); (L'vov 1967) *Ekonomicheskii Ezhegodnik – 1967* (Moscow: 1968), p. 133; (May 1968) Bachurin, *Sovershenstvovanie* . . . , passim, and Baibakov, "Zadachy Sovershenstvovaniya . . . ," pp. 3-10; (August 1970) D. A., "Proizvodstvennye Ob"edineniya: Opyt i Perspektivy," *Vop. Ekon.*, No. 11, 1970, pp. 152-154, V. Vorotnikov, (Report), *Plan. Khoz.*, No. 9, 1970, pp. 94-96, and Dumachev and Varsobin, *Opyt Organizatsii* . . . ; (July 1972) "Ob"edineniya; Ikh Raznovidnosti, Obshchee i Spetsificheskoe v Ikh Deyatel'nosti," *Sots. Trud*, No. 10, 1972, pp. 18, 52-70, Gvishiani and Kamenitser, *Problemy Nauchnoi Or-*

ganizatsii . . . (1974), and *Vtoraya Vsesoyuznaya Nauchno-Tekhnicheskaya Konferentsiya "Problemy Nauchnoi Organizatsii Upravleniya Sotsialisticheskoi Promyshlennost'yu,"* 11 vols. (Moscow, 1972); (March 1975) Kapustin and Subotskii, "Problemy Razvitiya Ob"edinenii," p. 7, and the articles under this heading by A. V. Bachurin, *Ekon. Gaz.,* No. 20, 1975, p. 9, B. F. Bratchenko, No. 22, 1975, p. 4, V. V. Dementsev, No. 25, 1975, p. 8 (the full collection of papers is in *Vsesoyuznaya Nauchnaya Konferentsiya 'Problemy Razvitiya Ob"edinenii'* . . . , 5 vols.

19. *Table 4 Notes.* The 1970 Seminar was organized by the Council of Economic-Social Development of the Leningrad *obkom,* on the basis of a decision of the Central Committee of the CPSU. The "others" category includes the All-Union *Sovnarkoz* (1963) and an institute of the Ukrainian Academy of Sciences (1967). *Sources.* See note 18.

20. For this decree, see *Resheniya* . . . , Vol. 7, pp. 426-427. See too "Effektivnost' Nauchnykh . . . ," p. 1.

21. We were informed that it was theoretically possible for someone other than a member of the organizations that convene conferences to suggest a meeting, but that this rarely, if ever, happens.

22. See, for example, the papers in *Vtoraya Vsesoyuznaya* . . . , Sbornik 3 (in fact, this is the fifth of the eleven volumes), the shortened version of this in Gvishiani and Kamenitser, *Problemy Nauchnoi* . . . (1974), pp. 262-331, and "Ekonomicheskii Eksperiment . . . ," p. 36.

23. It is of interest and relevance that one of the major organizers of conferences has been D. M. Gvishiani, who, inter alia, is the son-in-law of A. N. Kosygin. The significance of this is discussed in the concluding chapter.

24. Compare the highly detailed breakdowns of the 1966 and 1972 conferences in Gvishiani and Kamenitser, *Problemy* . . . (1968 and 1974), pp. 614-615 and 706-707, respectively, with the breakdown of the 1970 seminar in Dumachev and Varsobin, *Opyt Organizatsii* . . . , pp. 3-5.

25. For example, "Ob"edineniya; Ikh Raznovidnosti . . . ," pp. 57-61.

26. This may well have been the case at the L'vov 1963 conference (see "Ekonomicheskii Eksperiment . . . ," p. 36).

27. *Table 5:* Details of these meetings are from (October 1961) W. Ulbricht, *Probleme der Sozialistischen Leitungstaetigkeit* (Berlin: Dietz Verlag, 1968), pp. 104-116, and various contributions in *Die Wirts.,* Nos. 42-43, 1961, pp. 1-24, and No. 44, 1961, pp. 3-6 and 10; (December 1962) Various contributions under "Wirtschaftskonferenz," *N.D.,* 7-8 December 1962, pp. 1-6 and 3-8, respectively; (June 1963) *Das Neue Oekonomische System* . . . , and in *Die Wirts.,* No. 26, 1963, pp. 1-48; (September 1967) *Der Weg zur Durchfuehrung der Beschluesse des VII. Parteitages der SED auf dem Gebiet der Wirtschaft, Wissenschaft und Technik* (Berlin: Dietz Verlag, 1967), and W. Ulbricht, " Der Weg zur Durchfuehrung der Beschluesse des VII. Parteitages der SED auf dem Gebiet der Wirtschaft, Wissenschaft und Technik — Schlusswort," *Die Wirts.,* No. 41, 1967, pp. 3-9; (October 1967) R. Streich, "Sozialistische Wirtschaftsfuehrung und Recht," *Wirts/wiss.,* No. 1, 1968, pp. 146-151; (July 1970) "Oekonomisches System in den Kombinaten," *N.D.,* 18 July 1970, p. 2, Schothe, "Kombinate — Zentren . . . ," p. 5, E. Ladwig and D. Kiermeyer, " Das Niveau der Leitung und Wirtschaftsfuehrung bestimmt massgeblich den Konzentrationseffekt," W. Halbritter, "Leistungsstarke Kombinate — bedeutsamer Faktor bei der Erhoehung der Effektivitaet unserer Volkswirtschaft," and the lead article in *Die Wirts.,* No. 31, 1970, pp. 1 and 4-6; (September 1971) U. Kensy "Wissenschaftliche Arbeitsberatung zu Rechtsfragen der Kombinate bei der Durchfuehrung der Beschluesse des VIII Parteitages der SED," *WR,* No. 6, 1971,

pp. 361-363; (June 1975) K-H. Graupner and W. Krzyzanowski, "14. Tagung des Wissenschaftlichen Rates fuer die wirtschaftswissenschaftliche Forschung," *Wirts/wiss.*, No. 9, 1975, pp. 1386-1403.

Notes. Included under "Central Committee Bodies" are the Central Committee Secretariat and the Central Institute of Socialist Economic Management, which is attached to the Central Committee. Included under "Council of Ministers" is the Work Group on the Formation of the Economic System of Socialism. Under "others" are included various research and higher educational institutes.

28. Burghardt et al., *Organisation* . . . , and *GBl.*, Pt. 2, No. 10, 1971, pp. 69-71.
29. Burghardt et al., *Organisation* . . . , p. 16.
30. For numbers of Soviet conveners, see the details on conference organization in the reports of conferences detailed in note 18 above. The 1972 conference, for example, was organized by a committee consisting of 44 people, although there was a subgroup of 6 within this.
31. Burghardt et al., *Organisation* . . . , p. 17.
32. *Ibid.*, pp. 24-26.
33. *Ibid.*, p. 36.
34. *Ibid.*, pp. 19-20.
35. Ulbricht, "Der Weg . . . ," pp. 4, 8, and 9. See too Apel's remarks at the 1963 conference, esp. pp. 277-278, 284.
36. Burghardt et al., *Organisation* . . . , p. 21.
37. One example of spontaneity during concluding remarks is the interruption of Apel's speech by Ulbricht at the 1967 seminar; see *Der Weg* . . . , p. 270. See too Burghardt et al., *Organisation* . . . , p. 24.
38. *Ibid.*, p. 37. It should be noted, however, that the authors do say that there is an exchange of both information and "thoughts" at conferences, which could be interpreted as mild recognition of possibly conflicting views.
39. The best-known study applying such techniques to Soviet politics is M. C. Lodge, *Soviet Elite Attitudes Since Stalin* (Columbus, OH: Merrill, 1969). Lodge's book has been the subject of considerable criticism; see, for example, Ionescu, *Comparative Communist Politics*, pp. 19-24. Lodge is not alone in drawing conclusions from very questionable content analysis. R. Judy, in a study of "the economists" in the USSR, conceded that "many authors did not fit easily into the category where they were finally placed; alternative interpretations of their contributions to the debate might place them differently." Yet Judy still felt justified in tabulating views and basing his argument on such tabulation. The quotation is from Skilling and Griffiths, *Interest Groups* . . . , p. 237.
40. See note 6 to Ch. 3. For a writer disagreeing with Laptev, see A. Seleznev, "Khozyaistvennyi Raschet i Deyatel'nost' Organov Upravleniya Promyshlennykh Ob"edinenii," *Ekonomicheskie Nauki*, No. 10, 1974, p. 53.
41. For reference purposes, the other six variables were
(1) views on level of centralization of enterprise rights within a production *ob"edinenie*
(3) preferred location for administration
(4) preferred form of production *ob"edinenie*
(5) preferred principle in creation of production *ob"edinenie*
(7) preferred number of industrial tiers
(8) reference to foreign experience

We did not perform this exercise at all rigorously vis-à-vis the GDR, since it had by that stage become clear that this method was too problematic.

42. As shall be shown in Ch. 6, this fear has since 1973 proved to be well founded. It is interesting to note that some writers have explicitly stated that the industrial associations are to be short-term bodies only; see, for example, G. Kh. Popov in *Vsesoyuznaya Nauchnaya Konferentsiya "Problemy Razvitiya . . . ,"* Vol. 1, p. 30. Moreover, the little writing there has been on the industrial *ob"edineniya* has often been concerned with production associations that expanded and were subordinated directly to the ministry (e.g., Sigma, Melodiya), rather than with bodies that replaced *glavki*. It is primarily since the mid-1970s that the industrial *ob"edineniya* have been considered in detail, and then more by legal specialists than by economists; but for early examples see V. Laptev, "Pravovoe polozhenie ob"edinenii v promyshlennosti," *SGiP*, No. 8, 1973, pp. 9-18; V. A. Rakhmilovich, "Khozraschet v promyshlennykh ob"edineniyakh," *SGiP*, No. 8, 1973, pp. 19-25; I. K. Il'in, "Promyshlennye ob"edineniya i sovershenstvovanie upravleniya proizvodstvom *SGiP*, No. 11, 1973, pp. 3-11.

43. The first observer to have noted this nonreference technique appears to have been Victor Zorza in 1957. See the reference to this in Ploss, *Conflict and Decision-Making . . .* , p. 17.

44. An example of the Soviet general paper is N. M. Oznobin's in Gvishiani and Kamenitser, *Problemy Nauchnoi Organizatsii . . .* (1974), pp. 197-204, while that by L. V. Puzynya in Dumachev and Varsobin, *Opyt Organizatsii . . .* , p. 145-152, exemplifies the specific paper. For East German examples, compare Halbritter, "Leistungsstarke . . . ," passim, and the paper by H. Fritzsche in *Das Neue Oekonomische System . . .* , pp. 129-136.

45. Of course, most content analysis is also to some extent subjective.

Chapter 3

THE "DEMANDS"

In this chapter, the calls *for* the associations from the subleadership levels are considered. In the first section we examine the debates on these bodies. On the one hand, this shows the extent of disagreement and that the "demands" have not all been for the same types of association. On the other, an appreciation of the variety of opinions is necessary for the subsequent discussion of ambiguous legislation and the ways in which differences can be exploited by those hostile to the associations. In the second part, the claims made about the associations by their advocates are elaborated. Such claims are often accompanied by overt calls for these organizations; but many are not, and have therefore to be treated as "implied demands." The brief third section deals with calls for legislation, and is followed by the conclusions to the chapter.

3.1. THE DEBATES

We consider here the major areas of debate that have emerged from our analysis of the press and conferences. Some questions have been collapsed into one (i.e., the number of debates has been reduced in comparison with the original attempt at content analysis) for the sake of a clearer and more concise presentation. One factor to be borne in mind is that many of the polemics in both states have been concerned with marginal details rather than fundamental issues that affect the development of the associations. Time and space — and not a little concern to avoid often highly technical and sometimes trivial issues — have restricted the investigation here to the basic issues rather than every dimension of the debates. Moreover, we have tended to cite representatives of the more extreme views on any given issue. This has been done to make the disagreements as clear as possible — often they appear in very subtle wording. But this should *not* give the impression that all writers/speakers fall neatly into one or another "camp"; just as in the West, many people follow a middle-of-the-road, compromising line.

THE SOVIET DEBATES

The seminal article for the debate on the *ob"edineniya* is that written by A. Bobrov (Deputy Chairman of Leningrad *sovnarkhoz*), which appeared in *Izvestiya* in October 1959. In it are contained many of the points that have subsequently proved to be so disputed, and in this very first article Bobrov admitted that "In the very idea of the production *ob"edineniya* there is much that is contentious."[1] Indeed, for a long time — certainly until the 1973-1974 legislation on production and industrial *ob"edineniya* — the most fundamental and controversial debate on these bodies was undoubtedly that on their exact nature.

The Concept of the *Ob"edinenie*

In some cases, apparently different answers to the question, "What is an *ob"edinenie*?" merely reflect imprecision, a lack of conceptual clarity among writers. In other cases, however, differing views reflect very different ideas on the ways to improve Soviet industrial administration.

Bobrov, in the article just cited, referred at one point to an *ob"edinenie* of works and factories (*zavody* and *fabriki*), at another to an *ob"edinenie* of enterprises (*predpriyatii*), and at a third to the merging of three enterprises into one, thus implying that the *ob"edinenie* is an enterprise.[2] He seems to have been unaware of the illogicality of this, since he did not discuss why he had adopted different (and conflicting) definitions. Other writers also appear to have missed the point that there are *two basic* conceptions of the association.[3] The one is of a largely administrative organ above the enterprise, similar to but not necessarily having exactly the same rights as the *glavk*. The other is of a much more integrated grouping of former enterprises, which essentially constitutes a new, larger enterprise.

While some have been vague, others have either clearly understood the two basic conceptions and urged the adoption of one of these (occasionally both), or else have not openly admitted the existence of two meanings but have consistently interpreted the term *ob"edinenie* in only one way. The question of which conception to adopt was no mere semantic nicety, for, as Radomysel'skii and Shifrin pointed out in 1963, the legal position and status of both the *ob"edinenie* itself and its component units were very different in the two conceptions. They argued that if the *ob"edinenie* was understood as an association of enterprises, then the status quo would not be greatly affected; the enterprises would retain their autonomy, and the *ob"edinenie* would be a middle-tier, largely administrative organ. If, on the other hand, the *ob"edinenie* itself was an enterprise, then its component units could not *also* be enterprises. It was further argued that the latter conception represented a radical departure from the status quo, and required major new legislation.[4] Not everyone agreed with this, however, some arguing that the concept of the enterprise was dynamic, and that the *ob"edinenie* could be seen as merely a more up-to-date enterprise than the former predominantly one-factory arrangement, not a qualitatively new body.[5] Such an argument was clearly at odds with that of someone like the legal specialist A. G. Pevzner, whose conception of the *ob"edinenie* has most frequently been singled out for attack by those — mainly economists — who have advocated the highly integrated association. In 1968 Pevzner saw the development of *ob"edineniya* as

> the formation of huge production complexes, of economic systems, by means of the organizational and economic uniting of enterprises, *with the retention of their economic and legal autonomy,* but with the centralization of several functions fulfilled by each enterprise autonomously before the *ob"edinenie* is formed [emphasis added].[6]

This question of the status of component units was one of the main areas of disagreement vis-à-vis the concept of the *ob"edinenie*, so that it needs to be considered in some detail. The three main questions here concern the legal, economic, and titular rights of component units.

There has been a fundamental disagreement, primarily between legal specialists on the one hand and economists on the other, over the legal position of units incorporated into an association; economists have generally been far less concerned that these units retain the rights of a legal person. The actual meaning of "legal person" is not unambiguous, but at the most general level it means that the unit can draw up contracts with other units (rather than via the *ob"edinenie* administration) and can independently make claims on other parties for losses caused by these parties.[7]

The major point of debate over economic autonomy concerns the type of accounts the component units in an *ob"edinenie* should have. Most economists have favored giving these units only a current account (*tekushchii schet*), leaving the right to have a capital account (*rasschetnyi schet*) only to the association.[8] In other words, the former enterprises would have an account for covering day-to-day expenses (e.g., the wages bill), but would centralize some of their former funds to the association for items such as capital investment.

This capital account would be subdivided into various association funds — for capital investment, better housing for the workers in the association, creches, and so on.[9] But there has been considerable disagreement as to how much should be centralized and what funds were to be formed. At the 1963 conference in L'vov, for instance, an official from the State Bank (*Gosbank*) argued against excessive centralization of finance in an *ob"edinenie*. He argued that each case must be taken on its merits, and then emphasized that the management board of the all-union *Gosbank* had issued instructions to local branches of banks that they could open capital accounts for filials of an association by agreement with the head of the appropriate *firma* and of the *sovnarkhoz*; this could be applied, for instance, to filials that were a long way from the head unit.[10] Not all would agree that this was necessary or advisable, however, and it can be argued that *Gosbank* is seen here to have vested interests in *not* supporting extreme centralization in the *ob"edineniya*, since this could mean that many small branches would have drastically reduced workloads, which in turn would lead to closures or at least redundancies in some branches.

The third question concerns whether or not the name of a former enterprise is retained. This question has not concerned Soviet writers to the same extent that it has their East German colleagues, but it has been raised. At the 1975 Moscow conference, for instance, Ye. I. Kapustin and Yu. V. Subotskii (both of the Institute of Economics) made the point that even such a "seemingly unimportant" aspect of *ob"edinenie* formation as the question of the retention of former names of component units is important, not only from the point of view of the people working in the factory, but also from that of the consumer. A factory can build up a reputation for producing high-quality goods, and this reputation should not get lost in administrative rearrangements.[11]

So far, we have concentrated on the association which primarily affects and can even replace the enterprise. But many of the Soviet debates on the *glavki* also represent calls for the other basic conception of the *ob"edinenie*. These arguments can be reduced to two basic questions. First, can the *glavki* be transferred to profit-and-loss accounting, Second, if the answer to this is in the negative, should *glavki* be replaced with bodies that do operate on the profit-and-loss principle, and what should these be called? It is at this juncture that what is now known as the industrial association emerges.

A minority of writers have argued that there is no point in even attempting to introduce profit-and-loss accounting into the work of either the ministries or the *glavki*, and have been content to retain existing arrangements.[12] Others have argued that the *glavki* can and should be transferred to profit-and-loss accounting, although they have disagreed on the best way to do this. Pevzner, for instance, argued that there are two basic types of *glavk*; he maintained that while the ideal would be to transfer all *glavki* to profit-and-loss accounting, this was only practicable for one of the types.[13] The views of Laptev and Kamenitser also fit into this opinion grouping, although their views are not identical to Pevzner's.[14]

Although such people have called for change in the *glavki*, these calls are not usually for their replacement with industrial associations. But another group of writers has argued that profit-and-loss accounting in a *glavk* can at best be partial, or even that it is conceptually unsound, and has therefore called for the replacement of the *glavki* with industrial associations.[15] While some have felt that the latter would be to a large extent merely profit-and-loss versions of the former, others have appreciated that there is more change involved than merely one of name.[16]

Most of the arguments so far cited have been relatively moderate, calling either for a change in the working style of the *glavki* or for their replacement with bodies that are not necessarily very different from the *glavki*. Much more radical proposals have been mooted, however — sometimes overtly, sometimes covertly. The basic point of such proposals is that there should be no replacement of the *glavk* at all. Some writers will propose industrial associations (i.e., which others could take to mean some form of modernized *glavk*) when they really want powerful production asssociations (i.e., based on the enterprise). We know from interviews that although such writers have interchanged the terms "industrial *ob"edinenie*" and "production *ob"edinenie*" seemingly in ignorance in their writings, they are fully aware of the distinction and are merely making radical proposals covertly.[17] Others have overtly called for a reduction in the number of administrative tiers; the detailed proposals, if implemented, would mean that not only the *glavki* but also their functional replacements would disappear. N. Drogichinskii, for example, has increasingly openly proposed a basically two-tier administrative structure (simplified ministry, large production association) whenever possible in the branches of Soviet industry.[18] A. A. Markin has made similar suggestions, except that his scheme appears to involve abolition of the ministries and their replacement with some form of territorial administration of powerful production associations.[19]

Consideration of the fate of the *glavki* and the number of tiers in industry has brought us back to the question of confusion and preferences. We have seen that some writers who appear to be vague — using the terms industrial *ob"edinenie* and production *ob"edinenie* interchangeably — were in fact aware of the difference but were loath openly to call for the abolition of a tier in industrial administration. Their calls for associations, though outwardly similar to the calls from a "moderate" such as Pevzner, were, in fact, for much more radical change.

In sum, the different conceptions of the association have been far more than academic pedantry. On the other hand, the use of the same noun, *ob"edinenie*, for two very different concepts, has meant that many did not realize that apparently identical calls could, in fact, contradict each other. Although some, such as the Moscow economist G. A. Dzhavadov, have criticized the East Germans for using only one term for several different arrangements (i.e., the *Kombinat*), at least the East German use of two completely different nouns for fundamentally different types of association (*Kombinat* and *Vereinigung*) has meant that everyone has a clearer appreciation that there are qualitatively different organizational forms.[20]

While this has been the most significant Soviet debate, there have been others of major relevance to the development of the associations.

When Should an *Ob"edinenie* Be Formed?

In a book written by economists from Leningrad University on the production associations, A. A. Markin argued against the views of G. Popov and others from Moscow University concerning the appropriate stage of economic development at which *ob"edineniya* should be formed. The Moscow economists had argued in 1972 that there should be a process of concentration and specialization between enterprises (either producers of the same products or those commonly involved in a complex end-product) *before* an *ob"edinenie* is formed.[21] In other words, they were calling for an essentially organic, staged development, with the *ob"edinenie* appearing as a logical next step in an ongoing process. But Markin — who showed considerable concern at the slow development of the *ob"edineniya* since the mid-1960s — argued that there needed only to be the *potential* for concentration and specialization.[22] In this, he was in agreement with G. Sazontov, who maintained that there was a time lag between the act of creating an *ob"edinenie* and the achievement of technological unity.[23] Clearly, the creation of *ob"edineniya* would be an easier and faster process were Markin and Sazontov's views adopted rather than those of Popov et al.

Another aspect of this debate is whether the *ob"edinenie* should be formed of small and medium-sized enterprises or of large enterprises. While most writers have favored the former idea, A. Aleksandrov has argued that associations should only be created out of units which are themselves already large; this prerequisite would certainly delay the development of a large network of associations.[24]

How Should the *Ob"edinenie* Administration Be Formed?

As emerged in the debate on the concept of the *ob"edinenie*, some people have wanted the administration of an association to be separate, while others have preferred it to be in the head unit of the association. Since the problem is so closely linked with the basically different conceptions of *ob"edinenie*, there is no need to elaborate on it here.

Another question, however, is that of the *composition* of the apparatus in those *ob"edineniya* where the administration is to be located in the head enterprise; thus we are looking here only at production associations. The basic question is whether the administration of the newly formed *ob"edinenie* should be identical with that of the head enterprise as it was before the association was formed, or whether it should be based on the best people from all the component units. The majority of writers appear to have accepted unquestioningly that the apparatus of what has become the head enterprise should assume leadership of the whole association,[25] while some, such as M. Panfilov, have argued that it is better both in terms of efficiency (best person for the job) and morale ("fair play") to create a new apparatus from among the best of all the former administrative staff.[26] But how should the head enterprise itself be chosen?

Choice of the Head Enterprise of an Association

Two Ukrainian party officials (V. Slyusarenko and B. Krupenchik) realized very early in the 1960s that the selection of the head unit for an association or *firma* is not always as obvious as might, a priori, be expected. Although many writers seem to have accepted that the head unit should be the largest enterprise, Slyusarenko and Krupenchik argued that it is sometimes better to choose a unit with the most experience (of what is not clear). They argued that this is often better than choosing according to a third criterion — that is, choosing the unit that appears to have the best development perspectives.[27] Other suggested criteria include the level of technical sophistication (i.e., the technically most advanced factory should head the *ob"edinenie*);[28] the amount of modern equipment (one assumes that this is often the same thing);[29] and the proximity of the different units to a capital or a provincial center.[30] Regarding the last point, Markin, for one, has criticized the practice of choosing as head unit the one nearest to a capital — which some have seen as the most important criterion — arguing that it is not sensible if that unit is not the biggest and/or the best-equipped; he cited Ukrlakokraska as an example of the inappropriateness of this criterion.[31]

While most writers have accepted that a production enterprise would head a production association, others have called for science-production associations, which would be headed by research institutes rather than production enterprises.[32]

THE EAST GERMAN DEBATES

The tracing of East German debates proved to be more difficult than was the case with Soviet debates. Access to most specialist conference reports was not possible, despite persistent attempts in East Berlin, and debates in the press have been less widespread and less overt than in the Soviet Union. Moreover, as was stated in the introduction, we are *primarily* concerned with the buildup to the 1973 legislation in both the USSR and the GDR. Although mention is made of debates on the VVBs around 1958 and, to a greater extent, 1963, these watersheds are of less relevance to this study than the more modern period. Thus, it is important to note that in the only full-length Western study of the VVBs (that of H. B. Zimmermann), the author refers to the marked decline of interest in the VVBs manifested in the East German press since 1967.[33] This is in line with our own findings, and means that there is much more in this section on the combines than on the VVBs.

All this said, there have been real disagreements on some issues. These are outlined below.

The Concept of the Association

It has been shown that there has been considerable disagreement in the USSR on what is meant by the term *ob"edinenie*. In the GDR, the fact that two completely different terms, VVB and *Kombinat*, are used for the two most basic conceptions of association (one of legally autonomous enterprises, one in which enterprises have some restrictions on their legal autonomy) has meant that this particular debate did not occur. This does not mean that the conception of the VVB or the combine has gone unchanged or unchallenged over the years, however.

The "Demands" 113

Debates on the definition of the VVB are difficult to find, and we have found nothing to suggest that the change in the conception in 1963 or 1973 (see Chapters 4 and 5) was in response to "demands" or even suggestions from the subleadership level. However, we can say the following. When the VVBs were reintroduced in 1958, the new situation was moving, if only marginally, in the direction of the kinds of changes that had been advocated by two of the most outspoken subleadership critics of the existing industrial administrative arrangement in the 1950s, Prof. Dr. Fritz Behrens (head of the Central Office for Statistics from 1955) and his colleague from the Institute of Economic Sciences in the German Academy of Sciences, Dr. Arne Benary. Although the two wanted a major decentralization of industrial decision-making (primarily to the enterprise level), which did not emerge, the new conception of the VVB in 1958 did, at least, testify to a marginal decentralization of decision-making.[34] More rights and the new status of the VVBs in 1963 were preceded by debates. However, although many views on ways to improve the economy were published in the months preceding the announcement of the New Economic System, the concept of the VVB was not seriously questioned, and the new definition in 1963 appears to have been used first by Ulbricht. This is not to say that there were no suggestions for increasing the rights of the VVB prior to 1963. There were.[35] But this is not the same as calling for a changed conception, and in any case the suggestions were rare. Similarly, the changed definition of 1973 was seen first in the legislation, not debates; indeed, there was very little discussion of the VVBs either in the press or at conferences in the early 1970s.

In contrast, disagreements on the concept of the combine *are* perceivable in the East German press and at conferences. During the 1960s, and contrary to official legislation, writers seem to have considered both the type of association in which several similar enterprises are linked (i.e., horizontally) and that in which enterprises are linked because of their various contributions to a complex end-product (i.e., vertically) as combines. The former type had officially been designated as "amalgamated enterprises" in 1963, but the term was never popular amongst East German economists, legal specialists, and so on.[36] Moreover, during the mid-1960s there was general agreement that the combine was a unified enterprise (VEB) because of its status as a legal person; if there was any distinction to be drawn, it was between the combine and the VVB rather than the combine and the enterprise.[37] Thus, although there was some disagreement on whether or not nonnationalized enterprises could be included in a combine,[38] the concept of the combine itself was not questioned.

But the picture had changed by the end of the 1960s. By that time, there was a growing awareness of a possible illogicality in the popular conception of the combine. There was concern — primarily among legal specialists — over the status of former enterprises becoming parts of combines. Now, the bland assertion that the combine was merely a new type of enterprise was put in doubt, and the East Germans recognized that if the combine itself was an enterprise, it could not be made up of various units also having the status of enterprise. By 1970-1971, East German legal specialists were arguing that the concept of the combine was unclear, and called for a clarification of their legal position. This cannot be understood without referring to the level of autonomy of component units within an association; hence it is to this question we now turn.

The question did not pertain to VVBs, since no one suggested that enterprises would lose autonomy under them. There were complaints of excessive interference by the VVBs in the work of the enterprises, but this is not the same as a theoretical debate about the legal and economic status of the enterprises — merely criticism of the VVBs abusing their rights. Such debate as there was concerned the question of whether the rights of the enterprise vis-à-vis the VVB should be *increased* or remain essentially the same — but not reduced.[39] As for the combines, some argued that component units should enjoy varying degrees of autonomy, depending on such factors as the distance from the head unit, the amount of participation in the most important scientific-technical work, and so on.[40] But this idea of differing degrees of autonomy was considered too vague by many, who argued that it would be useful to start overcoming the confusion by distinguishing clearly between legal and economic autonomy.[41] This division in the debate persisted from the late 1960s, with the arguments about the economic position of component units being considerably less in significance and number than those on the legal situation.

The legal debate hinged largely on the question of whether the component parts of a combine were enterprises or not and, if not, what their exact legal status was. K. Mueller and H. Such published an article in 1970 that illustrated nicely the dilemma in which many legal specialists found themselves. They argued in the early part of the article that the combine is a form of enterprise. Later on, they cite those aspects of a combine that distinguish it from the enterprise.[42] The obvious contradiction here was soon spotted by H. D. Ebbecke and J. Niebelschuetz, who argued that to overcome Mueller and Such's dilemma it would be more useful to distinguish between the combine and the enterprise which does not have any combine characteristics. Ebbecke and Niebelschuetz concluded by insisting that component units should be known as "combine enterprises," which should retain considerable legal autonomy but would be distinguishable in law from "enterprises."[43] Others, such as L. Penig, had argued that the component units should be called "works" (*Werke*, as opposed to enterprises), and that these should enjoy a relatively high level of economic but no legal autonomy.[44]

For Penig and many others in the late 1960s, the question was a simple one of a unit either being or not being a legal person. For him, if the combine is a legal person the component units cannot also be legal persons; thus, they cannot have legal autonomy.[45] But this was *too* clear-cut for many legal specialists who were concerned about the loss of status of units going into a combine, and a solution to the dilemma soon began to emerge. The basis of this solution was to question the very notion of a "legal person" (*juristische Person*), which was one of the major stumbling blocks to the differentiation between the combine, a component unit of a combine, and an enterprise. Already in 1969, G. Klinger and W. Panzer had argued that the concept of the legal competence (*Rechtsfaehigkeit*) of an economic unit is not the same as the concept of the legal person, the former being a *variable* concept. This meant that the combine and its parts could have differing or graduated legal status, whereas the concept of the legal person was rigid.[46] Although there was still disagreement as to how far attempts to classify different units into one or another of several different classes of legal status should be taken,[47] the broader problem now seemed to have been overcome. Indeed, at the 1971 meeting on combines most of the East German participants, as well as the Soviet legal specialist V. V. Laptev, agreed that the concept of a "legal person" was a category of bourgeois law and represented in essence a capitalist method for limiting the liability of companies to the minimum. Under socialism, it was argued, organized collectives of workers are not seeking to limit their liability but rather to demonstrate their social responsibility.[48] Not everyone accepted this line of argument, however, some participants suggesting that a new conception of the legal person could be developed. In support of this argument, the point was made that some conception of the legal person was required if trade were to continue with capitalist countries (because firms in the capitalist world still operated according to the notion of the legal person, and there would have to be some common norm for working together). The outcome of this conference debate was that a proposal to grant full autonomous liability to the combine enterprises was accepted, while it was further agreed to treat the question of the liability of the combine itself as a subsidiary matter.[49]

We have been unable to find detailed discussion of funds and accounts — generally, the question of the economic autonomy of component units — in the GDR such as there was in the Soviet Union. In line with the concern to avoid excessive centralization in combines, however, there were calls to ensure some self-financing of units.[50]

The question of the retention of enterprise names for component units of a combine, on the other hand, has been one of the most openly and fiercely debated in the GDR. As in the USSR, those favoring retention have referred to the economic benefits that accrue from keeping brand names (i.e., names derived from the enterprise name), which the national and international markets know and respect, and have also mentioned the negative effect on work attitudes caused by the imposition of a new, impersonal name on a component unit.[51]

On the question of whether the concept of the association could be confused with that of the ministerial chief administration, it will be recalled that these were abolished in 1958, since when no one appears to have suggested their return. Indeed, since the Soviet writer V. V. Laptev explicitly stated in the journal *Wirtschaftsrecht* and elsewhere that the major reason the East Germans had been so much more successful in their association development than the Soviets was precisely because they did not have the functional equivalents of the *glavki* to deal with, it seems improbable that there would be any call for such bodies.[52] However, this is not to say that their successors, the VVBs, have not been put in question. For instance, the combine director H. Wedler argued at the 1967 seminar that there was a lot to be gained from subordinating combines directly to ministries. This suggestion implied a two-tier system where possible; hence the abolition of some VVBs.[53] Such views are rare, however, and it is easier to find support for three or even more tiers of industrial administration, implying retention of the VVB; as in the USSR, it would appear that economists tend to favor fewer tiers than the legal specialists, although the very limited number of articles dealing with this question means that we cannot be certain of this.

In conclusion, although the confusion, real or apparent, over terms that characterized the Soviet debates has not been a feature of the East German, this is not to say that there has been no ambiguity in what people have called for. In many cases it is not possible to ascertain whether a call for more combines is radical (i.e., that this type of association should replace the VVB) or more moderate (i.e., that the combine would be subordinate to the VVBs). Certainly, if many of the calls for more rights to combines — especially in the fields of pricing and foreign trade — were to be implemented, there would be little justification for the continued existence of the VVBs.[54] But the very necessity of drawing such inferences gives some indication of just how veiled many calls for major change are.

When Should an Association Be Formed?

The question of the right time and circumstances for creating a VVB has not been debated in the GDR as a general point in the period under consideration.[55] Since 1958, the general rule of one VVB per subbranch was not contested until the late 1960s, when combines could be granted the status of a VVB. In the latter situation, however, it appears to have been the case that a VVB was to be created if a new branch was formed, unless it could be demonstrated — or at least convincingly argued — that a combine would be more appropriate. It is therefore to these latter bodies, once again, that we must turn for the debates.

As a general rule, combines were advocated wherever it looked as if the advantages of specialization, concentration, centralization, and cooperation would be enjoyed more fully by the creation of one, in particular in the structure-determining branches of industry. In Wedler's important speech at the 1967 seminar it was further argued that it is a good idea for a combine to develop out of a product group (i.e., develop organically), where the component units have already enjoyed several years' common experience.[56] While disagreement over these principles has not been overtly articulated, it is clear that some writers or speakers have favored a much more cautious approach to the formation of combines than others. In some cases, indeed, the warnings about having the "right" conditions appear, in typical Aesopian manner, to represent some opposition to the very concept of the combine. A good example of this is the article by "F. K." that appeared in *Neues Deutschland* in January 1968. Having praised the advantages of the combine, F. K. finished by arguing that

> the combine remains, however, an exception for the organization of the unified production process, applicable only in those cases where concrete economic and technical conditions exist.[57]

Such caution reflects at the very least a much more conservative approach than that of someone like Wedler.[58]

Formation of the Association Administration

In the case of the VVBs, there do not appear to have been any disagreements between East German writers on how the VVB administration is to be formed; it will be situated near to the main center of production of a given subbranch, and will comprise many of the personnel that formerly worked in ministerial chief administrations.[59]

In the case of the combines, there has been some disagreement among the few writers that dealt with this topic. Thus L. Penig, writing in late 1967, argued that the type of administrative arrangement existing in the recently formed Kabelwerk Oberspree (KWO) could be recommended for general application. In KWO, the administration of the head enterprise became the administration of the combine as a whole. Although Penig acknowledged that this could lead to problems — in that the management (e.g., the various specialist directors) would have more work to do — he did not consider this to be an insurmountable problem, arguing that it could be overcome by improving the information services within the combine and by making the work of the staff organs more efficient and qualified.[60] W. Mothes, however, disagreed with this, arguing that there were many cases in which a combine could and should have a separate management body; this is particularly so, according to Mothes, when a combine comprises several vertically cooperating tiers and manufactures a wide variety of products.[61] Although Mothes is not explicit on this, it seems probable that his suggestion would involve the formation of a brand new administration, not necessarily comprising the same individuals as managed the largest or most modern enterprise.[62]

This debate virtually ceased following a decision of the Council of Ministers in May 1969, according to which the management of a combine was to be simultaneously the management of the head enterprise.[63] However, some writers did still occasionally point out that there could be real drawbacks in identifying the management of the head enterprise with that of the combine generally, on the grounds that the combine management can become too involved with day-to-day details, to the detriment of more long-term functions.[64]

Choice of Head Enterprise of a Combine

Once again, the evidence we have suggests that the East Germans have been even less concerned than the Soviets with the choice of the head enterprise of a combine. At the 1967 seminar, H. Wedler did sketch the outline of the good head enterprise: It would have lots of experience in R and D, and a good supply of cadres already well qualified or else currently undergoing training in management and the like. But this description hardly constitutes a major interest in the topic.[65] Similarly, the important April 1968 article by members of the Central Institute for Socialist Economic Management devoted very little of its sixteen newspaper pages to the question, the following being all that was mentioned on the subject:

> in this [forming combines] an important precondition is that there be available as the core (*Kern*) an enterprise which is economically stable and which has the material-technical and staff (personnel) facilities for decisively promoting the creation of the combine. Such a suitable head enterprise must acquire for itself the necessary authority, through efficient management in product-group work or in a cooperation group.[66]

Later on in the article there is a reference to the tasks to be taken over by the combine director, with no attempt to explain how he or she is to be chosen.[67] This highlights nicely one of the reasons the East German debate is not a mirror image of the Soviet one; since the combines were normally to develop from already-existing forms of cooperation between individual enterprises, the choice of head enterprise had usually either de jure or de facto been made.[68]

3.2. CLAIMED ADVANTAGES OF THE ASSOCIATIONS

This section is concerned with the various benefits that advocates of the associations claim for them. It must be emphasized that we are interested in these claims primarily because they represent overt or implied calls for the associations, and an examination of their validity belongs to a later part of the study (see Chapters 6 and 7).

SOVIET CLAIMS

In this section, the advantages claimed primarily for the production associations are considered first (moving from advantages that are common to virtually all types of production association to those more specifically related to a particular form), followed by the far fewer ones claimed for the industrial *ob"edineniya*. For the sake of clarity, the benefits of the production *ob"edineniya* are further subdivided into "economic" and "social," although in practice and theory the dividing line is frequently hazy.

The four main economic advantages claimed for the *ob"edinenie* over a system of isolated, individual enterprises are specialization, concentration, centralization, and cooperation. Let us consider each of these.

A major, frequent criticism of Soviet industry from Soviet writers themselves is the existence of "parallelism" or "duplication."[69] Two or more enterprises unnecessarily produce identical goods and both/all these factories often make a wide range of items, all or most of which are manufactured in an essentially small-scale fashion. In other words, the manufacture of each of these products in the individual enterprises is highly labor-intensive and basically inefficient.[70] In an *ob"edinenie* there can be a conscious division of labor, especially if the component units lose most of their autonomy. In ending a situation in which several small enterprises all attempt to produce a wide variety of goods, at least three major benefits are held to accrue. The first is that there is a higher level of concentration, to be discussed below. Second, there is greater harmonization between supply and demand; the switch, under the 1965 Economic Reform, to sales instead of gross output as an indicator of performance helped to alleviate the problem of unwanted production, but it is argued that the *ob"edinenie* can also make a useful contribution in this field. The point is best understood by taking a concrete example. Before the Frunze Dairy combine was set up in January 1968, many of the smaller enterprises in the Chui Valley were concentrating on producing butter (which is a profitable commodity), even though this was not necessarily in line with demand. Once the *ob"edinenie* was established, this situation was rectified.[71] As Popov wrote, "In production *ob"edineniya*, the unity of production and the market is better provided for."[72] The third benefit claimed is that as a result of specialization there are much-improved opportunities for introducing more automated production than when individual units are producing a wide range of goods (because there is larger-scale production of a reduced number of articles). This in turn increases labor productivity, a point frequently and strongly stressed in Soviet journals.[73] And, it is argued, as complexity in production grows, so the advantages and the need for specialization will increase.[74]

The dividing line between "specialization" and "concentration" is sometimes a thin one in Soviet administrative theory. In an *ob"edinenie*, component units can be expanded or closed down in the process of both specialization and concentration, for instance. Equipment can be moved around and concentrated in different units in the specialization process.[75]

One area in which there is no such ambiguity is that of funds. It is argued that by concentrating funds from small enterprises into a larger unit, the overall benefit to each unit (averaged out) is greater than it would have been had the unit utilized only its own funds (e.g., for minor capital investment).[76]

Concentration and centralization also sometimes appear to be synonymous when used by Soviet advocates of the *ob"edineniya*. Some will talk of concentrating administration, while others will talk of its centralization. For clarity's sake, it is assumed here that concentration refers to equipment, centralization to services and personnel. Thus, concentration is said to permit a greater and better use of the "automated systems for the administration of production" (ASUP), an important aspect of which is the use of computers.[77] Not only does the concentration of funds permit the purchase of such equipment for general use, but it is likely to be more fully utilized since it is serving several production units. Smaller units (the majority of Soviet enterprises as of 1973 still employed less than 200 people) simply could not afford such equipment or make full use of it.[78]

By centralizing administrative personnel, it is argued, the problem of parallelism can be overcome. Rather than having a full administration in each of many small production units, most functions can be carried out by the streamlined and more automated *ob"edinenie* administration. Superfluous personnel can be "released" for other work, thus reducing administrative costs while increasing efficiency; the space formerly occupied by their offices can be turned into a manufacturing area.[79] The same argument about personnel is put forward in connection with services such as repairs and transportation.[80]

Turning now to the question of cooperation, anyone having even a slight knowledge of Soviet industry will be aware of the perennial problem for enterprise managers of securing supplies, and of the effect this worry has when the time comes for compiling suggested plans for future output. The situation has improved somewhat since 1965 (as profit-and-loss accounting has spread), though the problem still exists. Advocates of the associations argue that the supplies position can be greatly improved with the establishment of *ob"edineniya*.[81] Cooperation in an *ob"edinenie* is not limited to supplies, however, according to its supporters. Labor and material resources can more quickly and easily be moved around; R and D organizations can be more informed about each other's work, and thus avoid duplication while also being better able to assist each other; by pooling financial resources, the stronger units can assist the weaker to develop (here, cooperation overlaps with concentration). Finally, communications between units can be vastly improved.[82]

If these four basic advantages of the *ob"edineniya* are accepted, then the relatively very low cost, in most cases, of forming one is also frequently cited as a major attraction.[83] In general, the point is made that resources are more rationally utilized, and productivity — always of major importance to Soviet economists and politicians — rises in the *ob"edinenie*.

Referring briefly to some of the benefits attributed to particular types of *ob"edineniya*, Soviet writers have argued that the agroindustrial association can overcome seasonalness and increase agricultural yields;[84] that the science-production association can considerably reduce the time lag between new techniques being developed and actually introduced into production, while also orienting research work more toward the concrete problems of production;[85] that the industrial trade *ob"edinenie* can relate production to consumer demand much more accurately;[86] and that the combines are particularly advantageous for reducing wastage, by using scraps that would otherwise be disposed of.[87]

There are many social advantages claimed for the *ob"edinenie* by Soviet writers. Just as *ob"edineniya* are usually most able to introduce expensive, sophisticated techniques in both administration and production, so it is argued that often only an *ob"edinenie* has the necessary resources for vast social undertakings such as the building of houses of culture, sports complexes, holiday hostels, and so on. Not only does the *ob"edinenie* have the material funds, but the building of such projects can be justified on the grounds that the much greater number of workers would suggest that these facilities will be fully and rationally used.[88]

A second point put forward by some Soviet writers is that work attitudes improve in the *ob"edinenie*.[89] There are greater possibilities for competitions, the necessary funds to make work places more pleasant and hygienic, and sufficiently large labor forces to justify the provision of more and better night classes, thus enabling workers to improve their educational qualifications.[90] The argument is also put forward that creativity among workers increases, since suggestions tend to be implemented or at least discussed more in the *ob"edinenie* than in the individual enterprise.[91] Finally, it is maintained that good ideas can spread to a greater number of work units more quickly and efficiently when these units are in an *ob"edinenie*.[92] All these factors, which can be subsumed under the heading "improvements in working conditions" and imply greater job satisfaction, are said to have the concrete result of helping to ease the perennial problem of high labor turnover.[93]

Third, there is the important point that an *ob"edinenie*, once it has been organized on the basis of already-existing enterprises and institutes, can create completely new factories, R and D institutes, and the like. As a writer in the newspaper *Pravda Vostoka* pointed out with reference to Uzbekistan, these new units can be established in small towns where there is a good labor supply. This eases the load on industry in large towns suffering from labor shortages, while also creating jobs.[94]

Turning to advantages peculiar to specific types of *ob"edinenie*, one form that allegedly brings important social benefits is the agroindustrial *ob"edinenie*. The chairman of a collective farm in L'vov province pointed to the fact that there should be a unified system of wages and bonuses in an *ob"edinenie*,

> independent of where they (employees) labor — in the factory, on the farm (*ferma*), in the field, or on the construction site. In this way the socialist principle of "for equal labor, equal pay" will be realized.[95]

This in itself should help to reduce labor flow from the fields. But as the farm chairman further argued, collective farm workers in an *ob"edinenie* will also have better opportunities for raising their qualifications (e.g., by becoming qualified mechanics for agricultural machinery) because of the improved extracurricular activities, more night classes, and so on.[96] This, too, helps to raise income and so retard the migration from agriculture. In sum, it is argued that the standard of living in the countryside can be brought up to that of the townfolk more quickly and surely through the *ob"edinenie*.[97]

The science-production association is held to be particularly beneficial from the point of view of the job satisfaction mentioned above. Scientific research workers allegedly perform better on account of the "sociopsychological benefit" of witnessing their ideas being planned, tested, and brought into use in a considerably shorter period than before, since the transition time from plan to reality can be drastically reduced.[98]

A very important aspect of social advantages, we would maintain, is the degree of worker participation in the decision-making process. It is therefore interesting to note that some advocates of associations argue that workers' interests are much better represented in these bodies than in small enterprises, through both party and trade union organizations.[99]

So far, we have considered primarily the benefits claimed for the production associations. We turn now to an examination of the alleged advantages of the industrial *ob"edinenie*. It should be reiterated at this point, however, that Soviet writers were frequently vague on the distinctions between the industrial and production associations prior to the 1973 legislation. For this reason, it has had to be assumed that when someone writes of the advantages of an *ob"edinenie* in which the units all retain their economic and legal autonomy (where production units, for instance, are still classified as enterprises) and/or talks of the type of *ob"edinenie* that replaces a *glavk* and has an administration separate from all the production or R and D organizations, then it is the industrial *ob"edinenie* to which reference is being made.

One of the most frequently cited advantages of the industrial *ob"edinenie* over the *glavk* was that it could go onto full profit-and-loss accounting, which the latter body cannot.[100] However, we have already seen that this point was very controversial.

A second point is that whereas the *glavk* really only represents the branch principle of administrative organization, the industrial association can successfully blend both the branch and the territorial principles. The *glavki* have been situated within the ministries (so that all the all-union ministerial *glavki* have been in Moscow), whereas the industrial associations are supposed to be "nearer to production." Thus, if a particular branch or subbranch is situated primarily in one region of the country, then the industrial association can also be located there.[101]

Third, it has been argued that the branch structure is constantly changing, and that the *glavki* can be a hindrance to the optimal administrative structure at any given point in time. Thus, some enterprises should, because of developments, changing specializations, and so on, be under one *glavk* rather than another. But officials in the *glavki* have often been loath to transfer enterprises. The abolition of the *glavki* and their replacement by industrial associations, it has been argued, could lead to a rationalization of this.[102]

EAST GERMAN CLAIMS

In order to avoid unnecessary repetition, only brief reference is made here to East German claims that are identical to Soviet ones; this is followed by an examination of different points. As with the Soviet section, the combines are considered here first.

The advantages of specialization, concentration, centralization, and cooperation in industry were certainly recognized in the GDR by the 1950s, although it was argued in the major 1950s East German work on this subject that the first study of the advantageousness of such processes in postwar communist industry was that by the Soviet economist, L. J. Berri.[103] At that time (the late 1950s), however, the combine was seen as advantageous primarily in the complex use of raw materials (that is, in the same context as the Soviet combine, as distinct from the production association generally).[104] There were other forms of cooperation that were also seen as advantageous at that time, and this was to some extent a function of the incomplete nationalization of East German industry. In other words, the combine was a way of linking only nationalized enterprises (VEBs), so that organizations that linked enterprises of various forms of ownership — notably the product groups — for a long time seemed more appropriate. This general picture of the type of situation in which a combine was considered most valuable was valid until the latter half of the 1960s, except that by the early 1960s it was also occasionally argued to be a useful form specifically for local nationalized industry and the construction sector.[105] Since the late 1960s, however, the advantages claimed for the combine have been similar to those claimed for the Soviet production association, with a few differences of emphasis and a narrower range of viewpoints published.[106]

By the late 1960s, then, the sort of argument that had pertained earlier (i.e., that combines were only relevant for fully nationalized enterprises) was being modified. Gerstner argued in 1968, for example, that many semistate and private enterprises could in fact be linked to the combines (and thereby enjoy the advantages of the process of concentration, specialization, and so forth) by concluding long-term contracts to supply the combines.[107]

Another difference of emphasis has been that the East Germans have considered the social advantages of the combines rather less than their Soviet colleagues. Certainly social questions have been considered (for instance, in the plans for creating combines), but economic advantageousness has been emphasized even more than in the USSR.[108] Moreover, some of the social advantages claimed by the Soviet advocates of the production associations do not appear to have been considered by the East Germans. One example of this is the point made by some Soviet writers that the production association can create new filials in towns where there is an abundance of labor, and thus ease the strain on component units in towns where labor shortages are acute. This concept of "job creation" was, in fact, tacitly criticized by the Deputy Chairman of the State Planning Commission for Territorial Planning and Construction in 1969, when he wrote that he did *not* consider it advantageous for combines (or, indeed, VVBs) to create production units away from the main concentration of production units in a given town or district.[109]

The East Germans have also more strongly linked the advantageousness of the combine over a large number of individual enterprises to the international division of labor. Ever since the early 1960s, the East Germans have been among the most enthusiastic advocates of a clear-cut division of labor within CMEA — much to Romania's disapproval — and many writers have argued that international production cooperation and avoidance of duplication is easier to secure between a few large units than between lots of small enterprises.[110] Moreover, the combines have often been seen as having a very useful role to play in improving the administration of foreign trade, a point not usually mentioned by Soviet writers.[111]

Until recently, the East Germans have not shown any interest in the concept of the science-production association (NPO), unlike the Russians. This does not mean that they have not been interested in linking science and production more closely, however; in fact, the opposite is true, and already at various meetings of SED central bodies in the 1950s there were strong calls for a closer linking of science and production, with various measures being taken to ensure this.[112] It has often been argued by East Germans that the combines are a prerequisite for even closer ties between scientific research and production.[113] Unlike the Soviets, however, the East Germans did not envisage this through the creation of NPOs. Rather, they have seen it through the creation of R and D bodies inside but not heading the combines, or else in combines commissioning R and D work on a contractual basis; the latter method was considerably increased at the beginning of 1969.[114]

Our final point is that the arguments surrounding the creation of many new combines at the end of the 1960s focus largely on the advantageousness of the combines to the new structural policy of that period. Indeed, many East German writers actually cite this as the primary reason for the emphasis on establishing new combines at that time. Combines were argued to offer major benefits in terms of efficiency and for making products on which the GDR was to concentrate to render it more competitive in the international market.[115] Since the Soviets did not have an overt skewing policy of this sort in the period being examined in this study, it is clear why such an advantage was not mentioned by Soviet advocates.

When the VVBs returned in 1958, many of the advantages claimed for them over the chief administrations appear to be very similar to the points made by Soviet advocates of the industrial associations in the 1960s and 1970s. Thus, the fact that they were nearer to production than the ministerial subdivisions made them potentially more efficient in running the enterprises below them.[116] This point was further endorsed by the fact that individual VVBs had on average fewer enterprises to supervise than the chief administrations had had — which also meant that they could employ fewer staff than their predecessors.[117] Finally, the greater geographical proximity also had the advantage, it was claimed, that workers could participate more in the running of their own branch than had been the case under the ministerial arrangement.[118]

The main advantages claimed for the changed status of the VVBs in the early to mid-1960s hinged on their transfer to profit-and-loss accounting. This, it was argued, raised their responsibility for the work of the units below them.[119] In particular, their new status was said to have greatly increased their responsibility for linking science and production. One writer even argued that although the VVB itself is not a producing unit, its management of R and D under the New Economic System meant that it was very directly involved in production.[120]

As with the combines, one area in which a major advantage claimed for the VVB is in marked contrast to the position in the USSR is that of foreign trade. Whereas A. M. Aleksandrov's idea for improving the administration of foreign trade in the USSR was soon rejected,[121] the VVB was seen by the mid-1960s as having a potentially important role to play in foreign trade. The fact that it was on profit-and-loss accounting and had very close linkups directly with the producing units (that is, it was much nearer than any centralized Ministry of Foreign Trade or the like) was said to be a major advantage if foreign trade were to increase.[122]

Of course, many VVBs were replaced by combines in the late 1960s and the early 1970s. This does not mean that they were seen as essentially superfluous bodies, however. Rather, some now considered the VVBs to be particularly appropriate in certain circumstances, the combines more suitable in others.[123]

3.3. CALLS FOR LEGISLATION

SOVIET CALLS FOR LEGISLATION

Calls for legislation on the *ob"edineniya* have come from a multitude of sources. In the *sovnarkhoz* period (i.e., until 1965) each *ob"edinenie* worked according to its own individual charter, which was confirmed by the *sovnarkhoz*. This situation was soon criticized. Writing in 1962, for instance, A. Savitskaya called for an all-union law on the *firmy*/production associations to clarify all sorts of legal questions that had not been answered in the individual *ob"edinenie* charters (e.g., the property position of the association).[124]

Following the 1965 statute on the enterprises, it was generally accepted that there now was some (if not totally satisfactory) legislation to cover those *ob"edineniya* in which there was a very high degree of centralization — where, in short, the association became a new, larger enterprise. However, there was still no general legislation on those associations in which the enterprises retained much of their former autonomy, or for those *ob"edineniya* in which there was a mixture of relatively autonomous enterprises and units with very few rights.[125] Despite persistent calls both from individuals and in the form of resolutions from economic conferences at which the associations were discussed, the legislation did not appear until 1973-1974 for the production and industrial associations, and the end of 1975 for the science-production associations.[126]

It is useful to note two facts about these requests. First, the overwhelming majority of "demands" were vague in terms of setting a deadline to be aimed for in the issuance of such legislation. In fact, at only one of the many conferences studied (the May 1968 one) was a definite date proposed (the end of 1968).[127] Second, there has been disagreement as to whose responsibility such legislation should be. The most commonly named body for this has been *Gosplan*, from whom a general statute was frequently demanded.[128] Other bodies proposed include the State Committee for Labor and Wages, the State Committee for Light Industry, and "ministries and *vedomstva*."[129] At the important July 1972 conference on administration, *Gosplan* was called upon to organize the drawing up of general schemes of administration of the national economy and its branches along two- and three-tier lines, while the Ministry of Justice — "enlisting the cooperation" of the State Arbitration Board, the State Committee for Material-Technical Supplies, "MF" (presumably the Ministry of Finance) of the USSR, and the Institute of State and Law of the USSR Academy of Sciences — was to accelerate the work on the systematization and improving of economic legislation.[130] In the end, the legislation was drawn up by a commission under the aegis of *Gosplan* (see Chapter 5). However, for some time *Gosplan* did not appear to accept that the model statute should be its responsibility. At the 1968 conference, for instance, the Chairman of *Gosplan* (N. Baibakov) talked of the need for statutes (i.e., in the plural). He argued that one should be drawn up for the *ob"edineniya* and *glavki* in each branch of industry — immediately after having said that the individual ministries must work out well-planned programs for the transfer of *glavki* to profit-and-loss accounting and the establishment of a general network of associations.[131] The implication was that Baibakov considered the charters or statutes to be the responsibility of the ministries, not *Gosplan*. If this was the case, he was being either optimistic, ingenuous, or irresponsible to believe that the ministries would voluntarily produce charters that would to some extent threaten their own position. In all events, such disagreements are not conducive to the emergence of legislation.

EAST GERMAN CALLS FOR LEGISLATION

Subleadership calls for legislation on the VVBs can be found throughout the period from the late 1950s; such "demands," and suggestions on what such legislation should include, were particularly numerous around the time a draft decree on the VVBs was published (1967).[132] Ulbricht criticized the draft, however, after which there was a marked decline in both general calls and detailed proposals.[133]

The relatively small number of calls for combine legislation emanated primarily from legal specialists. There were calls both before and after the October 1968 legislation.[134] Even following the December 1969 legislation (which eliminated many of the ambiguities of the earlier law), there were charges that the existing legislation was too vague; one speaker at the 1970 meeting, for instance, said that the failure to delineate rights clearly within their organizations was not so much the fault of the combine directors as of the legislators, since the latter should have produced a general directive to guide directors.[135] Following the emergence of the new leadership in the GDR in 1971, calls for combine legislation appear to have declined, although there were still a few.[136]

In comparing these requests with the Soviet ones, the following points are significant. First, the East German calls have not been any more specific than the Soviet ones in terms of deadlines and so on. Second, the evidence suggests that there has not been the debate in the GDR that there was in the Soviet Union over whose responsibility legislation should be; but a full discussion of this cannot be undertaken until we have considered leadership statements and the legislative process in the two states.

3.4. CONCLUSIONS

We have seen that debates on the associations have been similar in both states, although the East German ones have been rather more legalistic and less concerned with the formation stage of combines/production associations. The advantages claimed by proponents of the associations have also been largely the same; however, unlike the

East Germans, the Soviets have not generally accepted that the production associations are useful for improving the foreign-trade organization, nor was the development of these bodies linked to a structural policy. In both states, calls for legislation on the associations can be found, and most of these have been vague; the Soviet debate on the responsibility for legislation does not seem to have been repeated in the GDR.

General pleas for the development of associations have come from a wide variety of sources in both the USSR and the GDR. Such calls do not obviously correlate with any particular functional grouping. For instance, conference resolutions sometimes include such calls — and conferences include representatives from many functional groups. Since the resolutions are usually adopted unanimously, discrete interest groups cannot be identified by this method.

Nevertheless, some pattern in the groupings of advocates of *particular* types of association is discernible. In the Soviet Union, the most obvious cleavage is between economic and legal specialists.[137] The former have tended to favor the more integrated conception of an *ob"edinenie* and a more streamlined industrial administration, whereas the latter have often been concerned with retaining as much autonomy for component units as possible. This cleavage has been noticed by Soviet writers themselves, so that we can safely assume that "the economists" and "the legal specialists" have constituted relatively distinct opinion groups.[138] This said, we have also seen that there have been differences among "the economists" on issues such as the timing of the establishment of an association.[139] As for groupings of managers, ministers, and other people working in industry (whose interests would be directly affected by the development of associations), we have too little evidence to argue that they constituted interest groups making "demands" at this input stage, or even that they represented opinion groups. For instance, we have found no references to such functional groupings as opinion groups by third parties at this stage of the political process. In the GDR, the debates have been dominated by legal specialists, or at least people concerned with legal aspects of the associations. Economists have been less involved, while significant contributions from ministerial officials, managers, and the like are too few to suggest groupings. Thus, there is a little evidence of conflicting opinion groups related to function in the USSR, but not in the GDR. The question of interest groups and "demands," however, is still not answerable, since we have not considered enough of the political process to draw conclusions.

NOTES

1. Bobrov, "Sovetskaya Firma," p. 2. Although the article was written by Bobrov, it was essentially a report of a discussion held between several officials of Leningrad *sovnarkhoz* in the late 1950s.
2. *Ibid.*, p. 2. Types one and three certainly, and two possibly, are not necessarily mutually exclusive.
3. For example, N. F. Podymalov in Markin, *Effektivnost'* . . . , pp. 145-155. Dunaev (*Ob"edineniya Predpriyatii* . . . , pp. 179-181) has argued that disagreement in Soviet writing on profit-and-loss accounting in *ob"edineniya* is often the result of writers insufficiently distinguishing between the two most basic types of association. By 1966, many *Gosplan* officials were aware of *fundamental* differences between different types of *ob"edinenie*, and by 1971 at least one *Gosplan* department had officially recognized the difference between an *ob"edinenie* of the primary link and one of the middle link (see Baikov, *Otraslevye* . . . , pp. 44-49, and Dzhavadov and Dunaev, *Proizvodstvennye Ob"edineniya* . . . , p. 46). Nevertheless, the authors of a 1972 book criticized the fact that "the overwhelming majority" of Soviet writers still understood the *ob"edinenie* in only one sense — as a body similar to the *glavk*, rather than the enterprise (see Popov, *Sovershenstvovanie* . . . , p. 35).
4. Radomysel'skii and Shifrin, *Firmy* . . . , pp. 13-17. These authors favored the conception of the *firma* as a new sort of enterprise, and included the combine in their definition of the *firma* (p. 23).
5. For example, N. Drogichinskii, "Nazrevshie Voprosy Sovershenstvovaniya Upravleniya Promyshlennost'yu," *Plan. Khoz.*, No. 5, 1962, p. 17.
6. A. G. Pevzner, *Khozraschet v Proizvodstvennykh Ob"edineniyakh* (Moscow: Izd. Ekonomika, 1968), p. 4. For examples of the rejection of Pevzner's conception, see Popov, *Sovershenstvovanie* . . . , pp. 35-36; Markin, *Effektivnost'* . . . , pp. 29-30; and Rakitskii, *Formy* . . . , p. 36. Although Pevzner's 1968 conception is the one usually criticized, he had in fact already made his position clear in an earlier book he had written with Yu. V. Subotskii; see their *Pravovye Osnovy Upravleniya Promyshlennost'yu* (Moscow: Izd. Ekonomika, 1966), pp. 34-35. Pevzner and Subotskii have not been alone in their conception. For instance, the First Deputy Minister of Light Industry of the USSR (V. I. Solov'ev) adopted a similar position at the 1970 seminar; see Dumachev and Varsobin, *Opyt* . . . , p. 259.
7. For example, compare the views of Chuplinskas and Baranauskas (*Tak Rabotaet* . . . , passim, esp. p. 17) with those of Radomysel'skii and Shifrin (*Firmy* . . . , passim, esp. pp. 20, and 104-105) or Taksir (*Upravlenie* . . . , p. 130). Some Soviet writers have argued that the concept of autonomy must always be relative anyway; see G. Ya. Kiperman, *Tsentralizm i Samostoyatel'nost' Predpriyatii* (Moscow: Izd. Politicheskoi Literatury), passim, esp. pp. 33-35.
8. For evidence of early disagreements on this, see "Ekonomicheskii Eksperiment . . . ," p. 36. See too I. Ivonin in Meleshkin, *Pervye* . . . , pp. 22-24.
9. For a writer arguing in favor of the formation and centralization of such funds, see A. A. Vilkov in Lagutkin, *Proizvodstvennye Ob"edineniya* . . . , pp. 216-251, esp. pp. 226-234. See too O. Lenev and T. Apse, "Ob"edinenie v Puti," *Pravda*, 24 January 1972, p. 2.
10. For the views of this official (Broide), see "Ekonomicheskii Eksperiment . . . ," p. 36.

11. Kapustin and Subotskii, "Problemy . . . ," p. 7. In the early 1960s, some Soviet writers were opposed to the name *firma*, on the grounds that such a foreign term was inappropriate for Soviet industry. See Grushetskii, "Sovetskie Firmy . . . ," p. 3.

12. See S. N. Bratus', "Reforma i Pravo," *Ekon. Gaz.*, No. 4, 1967, pp. 15-16.

13. Pevzner, *Khozraschet v* . . . , pp. 52-54.

14. See the views of S. E. Kamenitser and V. V. Laptev at the 1966 conference (Gvishiani and Kamenitser, *Problemy Nauchnoi* . . . , 1968, pp. 46-53, 162-173). Rakitskii (*Formy* . . . , pp. 137-145) argued that ministries and *glavki* could be on some form of profit-and-loss accounting, but that they would have to be transferred immediately if such accounting at enterprise level were to be properly implemented; his views were therefore different from those of the "gradualist" Kamenitser. At the 1968 conference, the chairman of *Gosplan* announced that his organization was working on a plan to put the *glavki* onto profit-and-loss accounting; see Baibakov, "Zadachi Sovershenstvovaniya . . . ," p. 7.

15. See V. Nevelyuk, "Firmy: Ekonomika, Organizatsiya," *Pravda*, 19 May 1970, p. 2; Dzhavadov and Dunaev, *Proizvodstvennye Ob"edineniya* . . . , p. 19; A. P. Dumachev, *Khozraschetnye Ob"edineniya v Promyshlennosti* (Leningrad: Lenizdat, 1972), p. 82.

16. Compare the views of Baibakov ("Zadachi Sovershenstvovaniya . . . ," esp. pp. 5, 7) with those of Bachurin (Dumachev and Varsobin, *Opyt Organizatsii* . . . , pp. 70-87, esp. p. 81).

17. See too the views of A. A. Pushkin in Gvishiani and Kamenitser, *Problemy Nauchnoi* . . . , 1968, pp. 180-182, and G. Dzhavadov in *Vsesoyuznaya Nauchnaya* . . . , Vol. 1, pp. 94-102, esp. 99-100.

18. Compare the following pieces by Drogichinskii: "Nazrevshie Voprosy . . . ," pp. 16-23; *Organizatsiya Upravleniya* . . . , passim, esp. p. 123; and his paper at the 1972 conference (*Vtoraya Vsesoyuznaya* . . . , Vol. 1, pp. 114-139).

19. Markin, *Effektivnost'* . . . , pp. 32, 38-42, 73-75.

20. G. A. Dzhavadov, in Dzhavadov and Dunaev, *Proizvodstvennye Ob"edineniya* . . . , p. 57.

21. Popov, *Sovershenstvovanie* . . . , pp. 36-37.

22. Markin, *Effektivnost'* . . . , pp. 13-14.

23. G. Sazontov, *Sotsial'no-ekonomicheskie Problemy Kontsentratsii i Razmeshcheniya Promyshlennogo Proizvodstva* (Moscow: Izd. Ekonomika, 1971) p. 219.

24. A. M. Aleksandrov in *Vsesoyuznaya Nauchnaya Konferentsiya "Problemy Razvitiya* . . . ," Vol. 1, pp. 56-62, esp. 56.

25. For example, Radomysel'skii and Shifrin, *Firmy* . . . , pp. 18, 30.

26. M. Panfilov, *Sovetskaya Firma Deistvuet* (Leningrad: Lenizdat, 1964), pp. 75-76 and Taksir, *Upravlenie* . . . , p. 125.

27. V. Slyusarenko and B. Krupenchik in Meleshkin, *Pervye* . . . , pp. 8-9, 11-12.

28. Drogichinskii, *Organizatsiya* . . . , p. 52.

29. B. Z. Mil'ner in *Vsesoyuznaya Nauchnaya* . . . , Vol. 4, p. 49.

30. M. M. Blufshtein in *ibid.*, p. 56.

31. Markin, *Effektivnost'* . . . , p. 36.

32. See, for example, the papers by G. V. Romanov and A. I. Golenishchev in Dumachev and Varsobin, *Opyt* . . . , esp. pp. 25-26, 217-218.

33. Zimmerman, "Wandel von . . . ," p. 137.

34. See M. Jaenicke, *Der Dritte Weg* (Cologne: Neuer Deutscher Verlag, 1964), pp. 104-106.

35. See the contribution by T. Halbauer at the 9th plenum of the Central Committee in July 1960 in 9. *Tagung des Zentralkomitees der Sozialistischen Einheitspartei Deutschlands* (Berlin: Dietz Verlag, 1961), p. 156. For the 1962 debates, see esp. the series of articles relating to the December conference, which commenced in *Die Wirts.*, No. 22, 1962.

36. L. Penig, "Rechtsbeziehungen . . . ," p. 661.

37. See L. Schramm, "Rechtsfragen der Leitung," *VS*, No. 3, 1965, p. 125.

38. It was in this context that L. Penig proposed "economic groups" (*Wirtschaftsverbaende*), i.e., combines plus nonnationalized enterprises; see "Entwicklungstendenzen in der Wirtschaftsfuehrung," *VS*, No. 1, 1969, p. 16.

39. See, for example, H. Langer, G. Pflicke and R. Streich, "Theoretische Aspekte der gesetzlichen Regelung der Rechtsstellung der volkseigenen Betriebe," and R. Streich, "Zur Rechtsstellung der VVB in der zweiten Etappe des neuen oekonomischen Systems," in *S und R*, No. 2, 1967, pp. 177-196 and 196-210, respectively.

40. Gerisch, "Organisatorische Probleme . . . ," pp. 7, 9.

41. See, for example, E. Baltrusch, "Dispute in Rahnsdorf," *effekt*, No. 2, 1968, pp. 50-51.

42. K. Mueller and H. Such, "Zur Rechtsstellung des Kombinats und der Kombinatsbetriebe," *WR*, No. 6, 1970, pp. 338, 340.

43. H-D. Ebbecke and J. Niebelschuetz, "Nochmals zur Rechtsstellung der Kombinate und der Kombinatsbetriebe," *WR*, No. 11, 1970, pp. 666-667.

44. L. Penig, "Rechtsbeziehungen . . . ," pp. 662-663.

45. *Ibid.*, pp. 662-663.

46. G. Klinger and W. Panzer, "Sozialistisches Wirtschaftsrecht und Organisationsstruktur der Volkswirtschaft," *VS*, No. 2, 1969, p. 102. See too Heuer, "Die planmaessige Weiterentwicklung . . . ," pp. 208-209.

47. Compare G. Pohlan and Dr. Schmiechen, "Zur Rechtsstellung der Teilsysteme eines sozialistischen Industriekombinates und zur kombinatsinternen Kooperation," *WR*, No. 7, 1970, pp. 420-423, and Ladwig and Kiermeyer, "Das Niveau . . . ," p. 6.

48. Kensy, "Wissenschaftliche Arbeitsberatung . . . ," pp. 361-362.

49. *Ibid.*, p. 362. This reflected a desire to ensure the parts of a combine considerable autonomy, although, of course, it was a negative right (liability) that was being urged.

50. For example, H. Wolf, "Die Rolle der Eigenverantwortung im Oekonomischen System," *effekt*, No. 2, 1969, p. 5.

51. Compare the views of K. Hilbert (editor of *Die Wirtschaft*) in his articles "Kombinatsbildung und Effektivitaet," *Die Wirts.*, No. 24, 1969, p. 11, and "Firmennamen und Warenzeichen — Symbole fuer Wertarbeit und Weltmarktfaehigkeit der Erzeugnisse," *Die Wirts.*, No. 36, 1969, p. 2, with those of G. Pohlan, "Warenzeichen und firmenrechtliche Probleme bei der Kombinatsbildung beachten," *Die Wirts.*, No. 22, 1969, p. 9. See too S. Schroeter, "Kombinate, Warenzeichen und Namen," *effekt*, No. 3, 1970, pp. 26-27.

52. V. V. Laptev, cited in "Wissenschaftliche Arbeitsberatung . . . ," p. 361.

53. H. Wedler in *Der Weg zur Durchfuehrung . . .* , pp. 43-44.

54. See, for example, E. Faude, "Zur Rolle der Kombinate in der Aussenwirtschaft," *Sozialistische Aussenwirtschaft*, No. 6, 1968, pp. 12-19, esp. p. 15.

51. It is true that, since the VVBs established in 1958 did not correspond exactly to the ministerial chief administrations they replaced, there must have been some

debate on the division of the economy. But such a debate lies beyond the scope of this study. For our purposes, it was a case of one VVB per subbranch of the economy (with the exception of the lignite industry), so that the question was not of whether a VVB should be set up or not, but rather that of how the economy should be subdivided.

56. H. Wedler in *Der Weg zur Durchfuehrung* . . . , pp. 42, 45.

57. F. K., " Das Kombinat," *N.D.*, 10 January 1968, p. 2.

58. The term "conservative" is used here merely in the sense of status-quo-oriented; no value judgment about such a position is implied. In the concluding chapter it will be shown why the use of the term "conservative" in the context of the policy being analyzed could be misleading.

59. See, for example, Dr. H., "Vor Gruendung der VVB Baumwolle," *Die Wirts.*, No. 13, 1958, p. 3.

60. Penig, "Rechtsbeziehungen . . . ," pp. 662-663. A similar view was held by Gerisch et al. in "Organisatorische Probleme der Kombinatsbildung," *Die Wirts.*, No. 15 (Beilage), 1968, p. 12.

61. W. Mothes (under "Leserwort"), *VS*, No. 3, 1968, pp. 147-148.

62. In one sense, Mothes and Penig are talking about different things, and Mothes is really calling for an extra administrative tier in some circumstances. From this point of view his argument could have been included in the earlier debate on the meaning of a combine. However, he himself contrasts his views with those of Penig, which are clearly concerned with the way in which the administration is formed. It is for this reason that the disagreement is included here.

63. See Ch. 5 and Die Redaktion, "Kombinatsleitung kein Dachorgan," *VS*, No. 8, 1969, p. 447.

64. Ebbecke and Niebelschuetz, "Nochmals zur Rechtsstellung . . . ," p. 668.

65. H. Wedler in *Der Weg zur Durchfuehrung* . . . , p. 42.

66. Gerisch et al., "Organisatorische Probleme . . . ," p. 6.

67. *Ibid.*, p. 6 and passim.

68. The reader is reminded that neither the Soviets nor East Germans consider product groups and so on to be comparable to the production *ob"edineniya*. Therefore the question of the choice of head enterprise in such an arrangement lies beyond the parameters of the present study.

69. For example, Taksir, "Nauchno-Proizvodstvennye Ob"edineniya . . . ," p. 50.

70. See A. Malevanyi, "Effekt Obshchikh Usilii," *Sov. Kirg.*, 15 December 1970, p. 3.

71. *Ibid.*, p. 3. It is not explained in this article why butter would be profitable if there were no demand for it. The most likely explanation is that the ministry to which these enterprises were subordinate was rewarding them on the basis of output rather than sales. This might be because the enterprises were not yet on the system envisaged in the Economic Reform of 1965. Even if they were, however, a frequent criticism of the Reform by Soviet writers has been that "sales" as an indicator of enterprise performance is not always effective while ministries continue to be judged on the gross output of their branch.

72. Popov, *Sovershenstvovanie* . . . , p. 38.

73. V. Shtundyuk, "Vygody Ochevidny," *Sots. Ind.*, 10 March 1971, p. 2.

74. Yu. Subotskii, "Ot Otraslevoi Tsentralizatsii i Spetsializatsii v Promyshlennosti," *Vop. Ekon.*, No. 7, 1972, p. 24.

75. Pospelova, "Khozraschetnye Ob"edineniya . . . ," p. 133.

76. A sophisticated approach to this question is N. Kozlov's "Fond Razvitiya," *Sots. Ind.*, 28 April 1972, p. 2.

77. E. Slastenko and M. Guseva, "Magistral'nyi Put'," *Sots. Ind.*, 19 February 1971, p. 2. See also Lenev and Apse, "Ob"edinenie v Puti," p. 2.
78. Yu. Subotskii, "Ob"edineniya v Sisteme . . . ," p. 53.
79. See, for example, A. Tikhomirov and V. Novikov, "Effektivnost' Upravleniya Cherez Proizvodstvennoe Ob"edinenie," *Plan. Khoz.*, No. 8, 1972, pp. 117-121. This article is based largely on mathematical arguments, and I am indebted to Alistair McAuley, Department of Economics, University of Essex, for invaluable help in discovering that the mathematical "proofs" are largely convincing.
80. For example, Baikov, *Otraslevye* . . . , p. 53.
81. P. Borodin, "Gigant i Ego Sputniki," *Sots. Ind.*, 24 February 1971, p. 2.
82. These points are from P. Suprun and V. Bobrov, "Shakhterskaya Nov'," *Sots. Ind.*, 25 February 1971, p. 2; A. Kosar', "Ot Zamysla do Vnedreniya," *Sots. Ind.*, 29 January 1971, p. 2; Malevanyi, "Effekt Obshchikh Usilii," p. 3; and A. Kashmanov, "Kontsentratsiya Podskazyvaet," *Sots. Ind.*, 9 April 1972, p. 2.
83. Slastenko and Guseva, "Magistral'ny Put'," p. 2.
84. M. Baranov, "Problemy Formirovaniya . . . ," p. 54. The reason given is that agricultural workers can work in factories during the winter. Perhaps the industrial workers can also help with the harvesting.
85. S. Tikhomirov, "Ot Idei . . . ," p. 2.
86. D. Polyakov, "Ne Tol'ko Posrednik," *Sots. Ind.*, 7 January 1971, p. 2.
87. Taksir, *Upravlenie* . . . , pp. 129-130.
88. (Various contributors), "Kompleksno, s Perspektivoi," *Part. Zh.*, No. 10, 1972, p. 18.
89. For example, M. Vasin and Yu. Zakharov, "Kto Upravlyaet Firmoi?," *Pravda*, 13 June 1972, p. 3.
90. R. Shakhbazyan, "Ot Prostogo k Slozhnomu," *Sots. Ind.*, 16 September 1972, p. 2. See too G. Romanov, "Novye Usloviya — Novye Trebovaniya k Kadram," *Kommunist*, No. 5, 1972, pp. 53-54.
91. Vasin and Zakharov, "Kto Upravlyaet Firmoi?," p. 3.
92. In many cases this is linked to the fact that R and D work is centralized in the *ob"edinenie*. See Gromov and Kamenetskii, *Proizvodstvennye Ob"edineniya* . . . , pp. 92-96.
93. Shakhbazyan, "Ot Prostogo . . . ," p. 2.
94. Sh. Tuldashev, "Firmy: Vygody i Perspektivy," *Pravda Vostoka*, 18 February 1971, p. 2. See too G. Engibaryan, "Luchi "Armelektrosveta," *Sots. Ind.*, 11 March 1971, p. 2.
95. Baranov, "Problemy Formirovaniya . . . ," p. 59.
96. *Ibid.*, p. 54.
97. V. Boldin, "Vazhnoe Zveno," *Pravda*, 15 March 1972, p. 2.
98. Taksir, "Nauchno-Proizvodstvennye Ob"edineniya," p. 47.
99. Zdorov, "Proizvodstvennye Ob"edineniya . . . ," p. 3; A. Smirnov, "Slovo — za Ministerstvami," *Ekon. Gaz.*, No. 37, 1970, p. 7; Vasin and Zakharov, "Kto Upravlyaet Firmoi?," p. 3; A. Lazutkin, "Rukovoditeli Vystupaet Pered Rabochimi," *Part. Zh.*, No. 11, 1972, pp. 51-53; Taksir, *Upravlenie* . . . , pp. 132-134.
100. See note 15 above and V. Nikishova, "Ob"edinenie — Osnovnoe Zveno Otrasli," *Vop. Ekon.*, No. 12, 1972, p. 145.
101. Bachurin in Dumachev and Varsobin, *Opyt* . . . , esp. pp. 79-84.
102. See, for example, Subotskii, "Ob Otraslevoi . . . ," pp. 15-26, esp. pp. 23-26.
103. Kroemke and Rouscik, *Konzentration* . . . , p. 5. L. Ya. Berri's work *Spetsializatsiya i Kooperirovanie v Promyshlennosti SSSR* (Moscow: Gosudarstvennoe Izd. Politicheskoi Literatury, 1954) appeared in the GDR in 1955 as *Spezialisierung*

und Kooperation in der Industrie der UdSSR (Berlin: Verlag Die Wirtschaft, 1955). Berri's conception of combination and amalgamation, however, was very much along the lines of the combine, and he definitely understood this as being one enterprise, rather than an association of enterprises (as did Lenin many years earlier). See p. 188 (Russian edition) and p. 162 (German edition).

104. Kroemke and Rouscik, *Konzentration* . . . , passim, esp. p. 24.

105. A. Haupt, "Probleme der oertlich geleiteten Industrie Leipzigs," *Die Wirts.*, No. 43, 1962, p. 9.

106. Perhaps the best terse delineation of the advantages of combines is that given in the authoritative article by Gerisch et al., "Organisatorische Probleme . . . ," pp. 5-6.

107. K-H. Gerstner, "Kombinat fuer Oberkleidung wird gebildet," *B.Z.*, 17 July 1968, p. 3.

108. However, see W. Biermann, "Ein Kombinat ist mehr als die Summe seiner Betriebe," *N.D.*, 24 July 1972, p. 2, for an example of an article that refers to social (e.g., more holiday places for the workers) as well as economic benefits.

109. R. Mueller, "Betriebe, Kombinate und Bezirke," *effekt*, No. 4, 1969, p. 26.

110. See Ionescu, *The Break-Up* . . . , pp. 125-128, and K. Heuer and G. Klinger, "Einige Fragen der Verordnung ueber die Aufgaben, Rechte und Pflichten der volkseigenen Betriebe, Kombinate und VVB," *S und R*, No. 7, 1973, pp. 1076-1077.

111. *Politische Oekonomie* . . . , p. 446 and Biermann, "Ein Kombinat . . . ," p. 2.

112. For example, legislation on linking science and production in 1955; the introduction of the Plan for New Technology, and its role as the base point for planning, in 1961; and the fact that the state decided to participate in some enterprises (i.e., the semistate) was allegedly to speed up ties between R and D and production in such enterprises. On all this see Such, *VVB und* . . . , pp. 16-17, and *Politische Oekonomie* . . . , pp. 169-170.

113. Graichen and Rouscik, *Zur Sozialistischen* . . . , p. 79.

114. See H. Seickert, "Die Wissenschaft als Faktor oekonomischen Wachstums," *Wirts/wiss.*, No. 3, 1969, p. 3.

115. See Ebbecke and Niebelschuetz, "Nochmals zur . . . ," p. 666, and H. Koziolek, "Oekonomisches System und sozialistische Wirtschaftsfuehrung," *effekt*, No. 3, 1968, p. 5.

116. Friedrich, *Aufgaben* . . . , p. 21.

117. *Ibid.*, p. 24.

118. *Ibid.*, p. 24.

119. Such, *VVB und* . . . , passim, esp. pp. 38-72.

120. *Ibid.*, p. 52. Under the New Economic System, for the first time, the VVBs were made responsible for basic R and D work. In order to ensure their success in this, Scientific-Technical Centers (WTZs) were established in VVBs at the beginning of 1964 for the coordination and management of all R and D work in the branch.

121. See Ch. 2, note 8 and accompanying text.

122. See, for example, G. Grote, "Zur Verwirklichung der Mitverantwortung von VVB und VEB fuer den Export," *Die Wirts.*, No. 1, 1964, p. 12, and R. Grossmann, "Unser Experiment orientiert Aussenhandelsunternehmen und VVB auf ein gemeinsames Ziel," *Die Wirts.*, No. 8, 1967, p. 6.

123. For example, Graichen and Rouscik, *Zur sozialistischen* . . . , pp. 78-80; their reasoning follows very closely that of *Politische Oekonomie* . . . , pp. 694-709, esp. p. 703.

124. A. Savitskaya in Meleshkin, *Pervye Sovetskie Firmy*, p. 105. See too F. F. Kovalenko at the early 1963 meeting ("Sovetskie Firmy," pp. 11-12), where he

says that the forthcoming legislation on the enterprise that was announced at the November 1962 plenum should include regulations on the production of *ob"edineniya*.

125. For examples of Soviet criticisms of the pre-1973/1974 legislation, see Laptev in Gvishiani and Kamenitser, *Problemy Nauchnoi* . . . , 1968, p. 173; Popov *Sovershenstvovanie* . . . , pp. 30-31; and Bachurin in Dumachev and Varsobin, *Opyt* . . . , p. 79. At least one commentator has argued that the position of *ob"edineniya* in which there are both relatively autonomous and highly integrated units is *still* unclear (despite the detailed 1973-1974 legislation); see V. V. Laptev, "Khozyaistvovanie i Khozyaistvennoe Pravo," *Kommunist*, No. 1, 1975, p. 48.

126. See Ch. 5 for details of the legislation. Calls for legislation include A. A. Smirnov, "Slovo . . . ," p. 7; Gvishiani and Kamenitser, *Problemy Nauchnoi* . . . , 1968, p. 608; Bachurin, *Sovershenstvovanie Planirovaniya* . . . , p. 381.

127. Bachurin, *Sovershenstvovanie Planirovaniya* . . . , p. 381. The conference also called for a statute on the *glavki* on profit-and-loss accounting. (p. 381). It is worth remembering that this was the only conference at which members of the Politburo were present.

128. See, for example, D.A., "Proizvodstvennye Ob"edineniya . . . ," p. 154. Sometimes the calls are for a statute, sometimes for guidelines on typical arrangements for different types of *ob"edineniya*. See too R. Bakalo, "Nerealizovannye Vygody," *Sots. Ind.*, 11 July 1972, p. 2.

129. Under "ministries" is often included a reference specifically to the Ministry of Finance. See for this point Bachurin, *Sovershenstvovanie Planirovaniya* . . . , p. 381; V. Nikishova, "Ob"edinenie . . . ," p. 146; Smirnov, "Slovo . . . ," p. 7.

130. Gvishiani and Kamenitser, *Problemy* . . . , 1974, p. 697.

131. Baibakov, "Zadachi Sovershenstvovaniya . . . ," p. 7.

132. W. Klampfl and H. Lehmann, "Rationalisierung der Leitungsprozesse verlangt wissenschaftlich begruendete Organisationsarbeit," *Die Wirts.*, No. 46, 1962, p. 9; U-J. Heuer, "Rechtsfragen der Leitung," *Wirts/wiss.*, No. 6, 1966, p. 933; R. E. Loos, "Die VVB muss fuer die weitgehende Uebereinstimmung zwischen Zweig, Betrieb und Volkswirtschaft sorgen," *Die Wirts.*, No. 14, 1967, pp. 4-5; H. Marr, "Detailfragen eigenverantwortlich loesen," *ibid.*, pp. 4-5. See too references in note 24 to Ch. 5.

133. See Ch. 4, note 75.

134. U-J. Heuer, "Zur weiteren Entwicklung der Wirtschaftsrecht in der DDR," *N.D.*, 9 February 1968; Penig, "Rechtsbeziehungen . . . ," pp. 662-663; Heuer "Die Planmaessige . . . ," p. 210.

135. The speaker was Dr. Scholl, and he was indirectly answering criticisms of the combine directors that had been made by Walter Halbritter. See Ladwig and Kiermeyer, "Das Niveau . . . ," pp. 4, 6.

136. For example, Kensy, "Wissenschaftliche Arbeitsberatung . . . ," passim.

137. Our classification of writers as economists/economic specialists or legal specialists is based on three criteria. The first, dominant one is the nature of a person's academic qualifications; the second is current post; and the third is reference to the person's function by someone else.

138. Dzhavadov and Dunaev, *Proizvodstvennye Ob"edineniya* . . . , p. 36.

139. It should also be noted that *some* economists have favored less integrated *ob"edineniya* (a point acknowledged by Dzhavadov and Dunaev in *ibid.*, pp. 37-38), while a very few legal specialists (notably A. A. Pushkin) have preferred the highly integrated association.

Chapter 4

PARTY POLICY: MACRO POLICY STATEMENTS

The present chapter divides into three sections. First, we consider leadership views on associations. This is followed by a description of official party policy on these bodies, after which the findings of the chapter are summarized.

4.1. LEADERSHIP VIEWS

Western commentators are generally agreed that, de facto, the most important policy-making body in both the USSR and the GDR is the Politburo; the few individuals who constitute this body can be seen as the *senior* leadership. However, there are several reasons we cannot treat decisions taken at Politburo meetings as authoritative policy. The first is a legalistic one: In both states, the party Congress is the highest party organ, to which the Central Committee and its Politburo are formally subordinate.[1] Another, more important reason is that Soviet and East German writers cite a variety of sources when they wish to refer to "official" policy, but almost never Politburo decisions. Finally, we have depressingly little information on Politburo meetings; indeed, this factor helps to explain the previous point. Consequently, the main sources of information on both senior leadership views and party policy in both states are reports from party Congresses and Central Committee plena.

Although indigenous writers often refer both to the views of (most frequently) the General Secretary of the CPSU/SED or the Chairman of the Council of Ministers, on the one hand, and party directives of one sort or another, on the other, as if they were interchangeable and both official policy, it is useful for our purposes to separate these here. Although the two are often virtually indistinguishable, there have been instances when senior leaders do not agree among themselves. For instance, the First Secretary of the SED and the Chairman of the East German Council of Ministers had differing views on the combines in the late 1960s, so that it could be misleading to refer to the general policy adopted by the Congresses as the policy of "the senior leaders." However, it is not only senior leaders who speak at the fora at which such differences are made known. A wide range of party members speak at party Congresses, for instance, from regional party bosses to representatives of factory workshop committees. Some of these contributions appear to be as important as some of those of Politburo members (other than the General Secretary or Prime Minister), so that a division between senior leaders and the rest seems questionable. This said, it also seems odd to include our workshop representatives in a discussion of leadership views. The solution to this dilemma reveals itself during an analysis of speeches at such meetings. There is in most cases a perceptible division between those speakers who are making general points for consideration by Congress — or, by inference, the Politburo — and those who merely praise the party and deliver a very narrow, factual report on the rise of labor productivity in their workshops. In practice, those who give the former are never lower-ranking party members but high-ranking political actors — such as republic or regional party secretaries and senior ministers — who can therefore be included under "leadership." Hence the term "leadership" in this study includes but is broader than the membership of the Politburo.[2] In our section on leadership views, therefore, we concentrate on the views of heads of party and state, and anyone else at official party fora who has shown strong views on the associations. We also consider statements by members of the *senior* leadership at gatherings other than official party ones. The section on official party policy, on the other hand, is concerned with Congress resolutions and directives, plenum directives, and party programs.

Although the 1973-1974 legislation has been adopted as the main fulcrum of this study, it was also emphasized that the political process is continuous, and that it was intended to study the implementation of policy as well as the input stage. Mainly for this reason (but also because of the shortage of secondary material on association policy) we have taken the last Congresses of the CPSU and the SED (both 1976) as the main terminal points in this chapter, rather than the party gatherings prior to the 1973-1974 legislation. For reasons already outlined, however, a brief description of developments in the GDR to November 1979 is included.

Before we begin the analysis of plena and so on, a few words on the comparability of data from the two states are required. In the case of Congresses, we do have all speeches given for both countries. The situation regarding Central Committee plena is less clear-cut. Basically, the East Germans have usually published — and still publish — the main speech and *some* of the other speeches at all plena. The Soviets, on the other hand, published all speeches during the later Khrushchev years, and into 1965. Thereafter, for the period considered here, only one, partial report was published, that of the July 1968 plenum.[3] Until recently, this meant that there was very little information on the plena, other than when they were held, the identity of some of the speakers, and a general idea of what was discussed (industrial policy, agriculture, foreign policy, and so on). Since the mid-1970s, however, several collections of speeches by senior party and state functionaries have appeared in both the USSR and the GDR, some of which include speeches made at plena. Thus, we at least know now some of the contents of Brezhnev's speech at the crucial December 1969 plenum, for instance.[4]

SOVIET LEADERSHIP VIEWS

The first specific leadership references to *firmy* and the like were made at the only party gathering during the Khrushchev era at which the associations were discussed in some detail, the November 1962 Central Committee plenum. The plenum is best known as the one in which plans were announced to bifurcate the party and reduce the number of *sovnarkhozy*. But at this session, Khrushchev also spoke of the need for greater specialization and concentration in industry. Whereas he had been referring at recent conferences primarily to territorial units in this context (and of course still was to some extent), he now also spoke of these processes at the enterprise level. He asked rhetorically what the future of the small and medium-sized enterprise was to be, and said that in this connection he had read many suggestions about the creation of various forms of production *ob"edinenie*, namely, the *firmy* and *kombinaty*. While the leader saw the development of such bodies as a correct long-term aim, he also warned of the danger of forming them without sufficient preparation; if the job were not done properly, the associations could bring more harm than good. Khrushchev's speech at the plenum revealed that he was fully aware of the kinds of legal problems that could arise in this process, and he agreed that the status of enterprises in the new arrangements needed formal legal elaboration. He did not give any deadlines for this new law, however, nor did he name any bodies that would be responsible for its drafting.[5]

Few speakers at this session made any meaningful references to the *ob"edineniya*. Of those that did, the strongest advocates without any doubt were Podgorny of the Ukraine and Tolstikov of Leningrad.

Thus, the First Secretary of the Ukrainian CP (and later President of the USSR) stated that his party supported the initiative of the L'vov *sovnarkhoz* in its development of the *ob"edineniya*; it is clear from his speech that it was the single-branch association with a head enterprise to which reference was being made.[6] Podgorny argued that since the concentration of various functions meant that the directors of the new type of enterprise (the *firma*) would have more responsibility for a wider range of tasks, he endorsed what he called Khrushchev's suggestion (although in fact the party leader had not made this point at the plenum) to broaden the rights of the heads of the enterprises.[7] The recently appointed First Secretary of the Leningrad provincial party committee, V. S. Tolstikov, was enthusiastic about the enlarging of the economic regions announced at the plenum, mainly because he felt that the development of the *ob"edineniya (firmy)* would be more effective in the larger territorial units. Tolstikov cited advantages such as the greater possibilities for concentrating technical personnel and reducing parallelism in their work in his argument strongly favoring the associations.[8]

Although Khrushchev did not make many public statements of note on the associations over the next two years, it appears that he remained somewhat wary of them, and also that he preferred the single-branch, horizontally integrated *firma* to the multibranch, vertically integrated *kombinat*. He was, like Ulbricht in the early 1960s, strongly in favor of the combine for the construction industry, however.[9]

Within only a few months of the Brezhnev-Kosygin leadership coming to power, the chairman of the Council of Ministers (Kosygin) stated at a *Gosplan* meeting on the new five-year plan that the need for greater specialization in industry required constant refining of the branch system and the creation of specialized *firmy* and other types of *ob"edineniya*. We know that K. Rudnev (who later headed the first ministry to experiment with industrial associations) was present at this *Gosplan* meeting, and we would expect that he, and possibly the Chairman of the Ukrainian Council of Ministers, Tikhomirov, spoke in favor of the *ob"edineniya*. Alas, though, we have no record of this.[10]

In his speech announcing the Economic Reform (September 1965), Kosygin argued that the *sovnarkhoz* arrangement had led to serious drawbacks for the national economy.[11] While not rejecting all the claimed advantages of the territorial principle, he maintained that the economy fared better under a predominantly branch-oriented arrangement. Therefore the *sovnarkhozy* were abolished, and branch ministries restored. However, another of Kosygin's criticisms was that the departure from the branch principle had resulted in an overcomplex structure in which enterprises had too many administrative tiers above them. Since the associations often represented an intermediate tier between enterprises and *glavki*, one could be forgiven for expecting them now to be rendered superfluous. But this was not the case. Kosygin argued that the associations were related to the development of Soviet industry, and that the advantages — especially those of increasing specialization, cooperation, and concentration of production — were as relevant to the new organizational arrangement as to the old.[12] It should be noted, however, that while Kosygin went into considerable detail about the role of ministries and enterprises, the *ob"edineniya* received scant attention. Nothing was said about their various forms and which the leadership preferred (unlike Khrushchev), nor were any specific development plans for the future given.

In his speech at the same September 1965 plenum, the party First Secretary (Brezhnev) criticized parallelism in industry. But Brezhnev saw the solution to this problem in the restructuring of industry along branch lines, rather than in the removal of "superfluous" tiers such as the associations. He saw production associations, in fact, in the same light as union-republic ministries: useful for combining the principles of centralization and local initiative.[13]

It is clear then that both the head of state and the head of the party had positive but weak views on the *ob"edineniya* at the September plenum, and this stance continued over the next four years. One small piece of evidence endorsing our own research on this point is that in a 1969 article on associations, the author had to go back to March 1965 (i.e., to Kosygin's speech at the *Gosplan* meeting) for a strong, authoritative statement on the Soviet associations;[14] it is normal practice in both the USSR and the GDR to cite as recent a policy statement as possible to support an argument. Thus, at the 23rd Congress in March and April 1966, Prime Minister Kosygin made few references specifically to the associations, though in his detailed discussion of different branches of industry, he praised the achievements of the combines (especially in the chemical and engineering branches), noting their advantageousness in helping to expand and improve production. Nor did Brezhnev have much to say about the *ob"edineniya*, although in not criticizing them and including them in his generalized view of the Soviet administrative structure, it may be inferred that they were still in favor and considered an integral part of industry.[15] It is interesting to note that none of the individuals or their functional replacements who had argued strongly for the associations at the November 1962 plenum made any reference to these bodies at the 23rd Congress. Tolstikov, still First Party Secretary to the Leningrad provincial party committee, said nothing at all about them, his main new interest being the need for social as well as economic plans for enterprises and other collectives.[16] The new Chairman of the Praesidium of the Supreme Soviet, Podgorny, similarly made no reference, nor did his replacement in the Ukraine, Shelest. In fact, nobody at the Congress made a strong case either in favor of or against the *ob"edineniya*.[17]

The whole question of these bodies appears to have faded into the background as far as senior state and party officials are concerned — though not, as we saw in the last chapter, among economic and legal specialists — while the Economic Reform was being implemented after the September 1965 plenum. Interest focussed more on the new ministries, and especially on the enterprise and its new economic methods. By late 1968, however, it was becoming clear that the Economic Reform was not being implemented as well as or quite in the way that the leaders had hoped. A decree was passed calling for closer links between science and production, and advocating as one aspect of this the creation of a new type of *ob"edinenie*, the science-production association.[18] We have not been able to find any reference at plena to this kind of association in the late 1960s, so that we cannot say who advocated them at this time. However, the fact that Leningrad developed them first suggests that Tolstikov was probably one of their leading advocates.

In December 1969, a plenum of the Central Committee was held to discuss plans for the development of the economy in 1970. Although we have only (lengthy) extracts from one of the speeches at this gathering, Brezhnev's, we do know from Soviet sources that this plenum constituted a milestone in the history of policy on the associations. Brezhnev himself, for instance, said at the 24th Congress in 1971 that the question of the administration of industry and the role the associations were to play in this was discussed primarily at this plenum.[19] Yet, while Brezhnev spoke at length on the need to improve the administration of industry, there is *no* reference to the *ob"edineniya* as such in the extracts of his speech published in 1975.[20] While it is possible that the General Secretary made references in an unpublished part of the speech — and perhaps, because the association policy has not been implemented as well as the leadership would like, did not want this section published — it is far more likely that here, as well as elsewhere since October 1964, Brezhnev was not too involved in details of industry, preferring to leave this to the Chairman of the Council of Ministers and other state officials while he concentrated on questions of agriculture and, even more so, foreign policy. From what we have been told by a senior official of *Gosplan*, the strongest and most influential advocate of the associations at the December plenum was the man who had called for their development more than seven years before, V. S. Tolstikov. Although we have no details on his speech, it can safely be assumed that the chief of the Leningrad party machine cited the many achievements of his city's industry that had accrued as a result of the policy there of developing the associations. According to Meissner, the plenum was held in a tense atmosphere, as party and state officials were disagreed on how the relatively low level of success of the 1965 Reform could be improved. He maintains that Brezhnev (who had already upset some state officials by discussing industry at all) was in favor of at least as much centralization of economic decision-making as existed at that time, while others (all unnamed!) felt that the way forward was to give the enterprises more autonomy than they had been granted under the so-called Reform.[21] If Meissner is correct about this division, Tolstikov's renewed emphasis on the *ob"edineniya* could be seen as a happy compromise between the two factions.

By the time of the 24th CPSU Congress (March-April 1971), it was clear that the *ob"edineniya* were intended to replace the enterprise as the basic economic link of future Soviet industry. As Brezhnev stated,

> Accumulated experience shows that only large associations are up to the task of concentrating a sufficient number of qualified specialists, providing rapid technical progress, and making better and fuller use of all resources. The policy of creating associations and combines must be carried out more decisively — in the long term, they must become the basic profit-and-loss links of social production.[22]

Kosygin, too, went into considerable detail at the Congress on the advantages of the associations over the individual enterprise. He argued that it was difficult for the individual enterprise to gauge demand, organize supplies and sales, improve specialization and cooperation, centralize auxiliary services, and so forth, on its own; these functions could be far better fulfilled by the production association.[23]

From the wording of their statements, both Brezhnev and Kosygin appeared to be primarily concerned with the production as opposed to the industrial association at the 24th Congress. However,

Brezhnev did refer to the pressing need to continue the process of putting enterprises, farms, and "the higher economic links" onto profit-and-loss accounting.[24] Since there was a well-publicized debate in the press on the difficulties of transferring the *glavki* onto this system, it is possible that the General Secretary was thus obliquely referring to the necessity of replacing the *glavki* with industrial associations.

But what of other papers at the Congress? In direct contrast to the 23rd Congress, several speakers referred to the *ob"edineniya* in more or less positive terms. The man who spoke most strongly in favor of the associations was Tolstikov's successor, G. V. Romanov, whose ideas on industrial administration were fully in line with the arguments his predecessor had been putting forward for almost a decade. Whereas most of the speakers who mentioned associations at all merely said that they agreed with the party line on these bodies, and perhaps gave a few statistics on the development of them in their own particular republics, Romanov devoted no less than eleven paragraphs to this topic.[25] He clearly favored the science-production associations as an important development in the struggle to link science and production more closely, and saw all types of *ob"edineniya* as more favorable for the introduction of ASUP (automated administrative systems) than small units. He went into more detail than anyone else at the Congress on the advantages of the associations, one of the most important of which was that it was easier for central organs to manage a few, large production units than several thousand small enterprises. With a network of associations, he argued, the central organs would be able to concentrate more than they did at present on long-term, general questions.[26]

Since the main promotional bases for the association at the November 1962 plenum had been Leningrad and the Ukraine, it is instructive to note what the First Secretary of the Ukrainian Communist Party, P. E. Shelest, had to say now on the *ob"edineniya*. In comparison both with Romanov at this Congress, and Podgorny in the early 1960s, Shelest's advocacy of the *ob"edineniya* was low-key. He certainly referred to them and the way they had helped to raise labor productivity and production; in general, they were justifying themselves. But he devoted only one paragraph to them, and did not go into any detail — of their advantages, their problems, or why they should replace the enterprise (in its old meaning) — in the way the Leningrad representative did.[27] Similarly, the First Secretary of Moscow *gorkom*, V. V. Grishin, spent less than a paragraph on the new organizations, and, while arguing that their creation was "of great significance," did not discuss their advantages in any detail; he concluded by saying that the possibilities they offered were not always used. He did not explain what he meant by this, however, nor did he suggest ways of improving the situation.[28] If the head of Moscow *gorkom* was thus reserved in his praise of the *ob"edineniya*, the First Secretary of Moscow *obkom*, V. I. Konotop, did not even mention them, although he devoted part of his speech to the problems of making better use of existing equipment without large capital inflows, raising productivity, and so on.[29] Indeed, the only other person to make significant references to the production association was the First Secretary of the Belorussian Communist Party, P. M. Masherov, whose main point was that his republic wanted to develop the new bodies but was being hindered by the lack of support of several (named) ministries.[30] However, several speakers called either directly or indirectly for science-production *ob"edineniya*. Apart from Brezhnev, Kosygin, Masherov, and Romanov, the following also called for better links between science and production via the science-production associations: M. V. Keldysh (President of the USSR Academy of Sciences), A. Yu. Snechkus (First Secretary of the Central Committee of the Communist Party of Lithuania), and V. V. Shcherbitskii (Candidate Member of the Politburo and Chairman of the Council of Ministers of the Ukraine).[31] Of the three, Shcherbitskii is the most interesting in that once again the Ukraine emerged as a major advocate of associations (of one kind or another). It should also be mentioned that apart from the above references to the associations by party generalists and the head of the Academy of Sciences, the Minister of *Minpribor* (K. Rudnev) also spoke on the experiments in his ministry, and warned against overestimating the ability of computers to improve the economy.[32] This, in conjunction with some of the less positive — indeed openly critical — papers on the lack of success of the 1965 Economic Reform helped to set the scenario for the most important legislation on the associations, the March 1973 decree.[33]

But there is one other party gathering of relevance to us before the issuance of this legislation, and that is the Central Committee plenum of December 1972; once again, only limited concrete information is available on this. In his speech, Brezhnev considered the difficulties that had so far been encountered in implementing the ninth five-year plan, and said that there would have to be correctives. He went on to make a highly critical attack on the lack of success of what he called "the implementation of measures which have received the title of economic reform." What was needed now, according to the General

Secretary, was a real *system* of the whole economy. One very important aspect of this was the systematization of industrial administration, so that at long last leaders at each level of the hierarchy would know exactly their own rights and responsibilities, and their position relative to other parts of the system. On one level, this involved strengthening the role of the central organs, which, according to some observers, Brezhnev had wanted ever since 1965.[34] At another, there could be a simplification, and the party leader called for a more rapid transfer to "huge *ob"edineniya* and combines" as the basic production units in the Soviet economy.[35] What Brezhnev had in mind when he called for an acceleration of the transfer is not clear from the available extracts of his speech, since no figures and no dates are given. In fact, there are grounds for believing he did not prescribe any targets, in that he rarely has in those speeches of which the full text is available.

In the cases of both the December 1969 and this December 1972 plena, we know who gave papers, but not the content of these papers. A straight comparison of the eight speakers at both (excluding the General Secretary and the readers of the official reports on the plan for the following year) is revealing, however, in view of what we know both from Congresses and from the November 1962 plenum. Thus, the following spoke at the 1969 plenum:

(1) V. V. Shcherbitskii (Chairman of the Ukrainian Council of Ministers)

(2) V. F. Promyslov (Chairman of the Executive Committee of Moscow Soviet)

(3) D. A. Kunaev (First Secretary of the Central Committee of the Communist Party of Kazakhstan)

(4) I. P. Kazanets (Minister of Ferrous Metallurgy for the USSR)

(5) V. S. Tolstikov (First Secretary of the Leningrad provincial party committee)

(6) G. A. Aliev (First Secretary of the Central Committee of the Communist Party of Azerbaidzhan)

(7) I. I. Kiselev (Director of Gor'kii Automobile Factory)

(8) V. D. Shashin (Minister of the Oil-Producing Industry for the USSR)[36]

At the December 1972 plenum, the following participated in the discussions:

(1) N. D. Khudaiberdyev (Chairman of the Uzbek Council of Ministers)

(2) B. Ashimov (Chairman of the Kazakh Council of Ministers)

(3) G. V. Romanov (First Secretary of the Leningrad provincial party committee)

(4) G. S. Zolotukhin (First Secretary of the Krasnodar provincial party committee)

(5) V. V. Shcherbitskii (First Secretary of the Central Committee of the Communist Party of the Ukraine)

(6) I. P. Kazanets (Minister of Ferrous Metallurgy for the USSR)

(7) D. Rasylov (First Secretary of the Central Committee of the Communist Party of Tadzhikistan)

(8) E. E. Alekseevskii (Minister of Melioration and Water for the USSR).[37]

We know already that these gatherings were important in the development of the policy of the associations, but also that this question was not the only one discussed at the plena. From what we know of their arguments elsewhere, as well as from what the author has been told by interviewees in the Soviet Union, there is thus very strong evidence that the most influential people advocating the *ob"edineniya* at Central Committee plena have been

(1) the First Secretary of the Leningrad *obkom* (Tolstikov, then Romanov), and

(2) the Chairman of the Council of Ministers and/or the First Secretary of the Central Committee in the Ukraine (Podgorny, Shcherbitskii).

In view of their lack of interest in the associations at other meetings analyzed, it is improbable that either Kunaev or Ashimov from Kazakhstan, or Kazanets, or indeed any of the other speakers with the probable exception of Kiselev and Shashin (whose own ministry simplified to the three-tier system, with the associations in the middle, in 1970) made any particularly important comments on the associations. In other words, the policy appears to have been pushed at the top of the party by a very small number of individuals.

In the period since the appearance of the 1973-1974 legislation on associations, the only detailed and significant evidence we have of leadership views is from the 25th Congress, held in February-March 1976.[38] For the first time, the General Secretary stated explicitly that he would not deal in detail with economic questions, and would concern himself only with essential matters. He complained that the restructuring of the administrative mechanism and the policy of intensification of production had been implemented more slowly than had been intended, without at this point specifically referring to the *ob"edineniya*. Later he stated that there needed to be an acceleration of this restructuring, and specifically referred to the need to create even more production and industrial *ob"edineniya*. In this connection, the central organs were to speed up their work on proposals for such change. Elsewhere, he made the familiar call for better links between science and production, briefly mentioning the science-production associations. Apart from these references, though, the General Secretary made no significant statements on the associations.[39] Nor did any of the other speakers at the Congress, with the notable exceptions of Romanov and Kosygin. The Leningrad secretary — by this time a full member of the Politburo — produced a familiar argument in favor of the *ob"edineniya* (especially of the science-production variety), although it was less detailed than that at the 24th Congress.[40] The Prime Minister agreed with Brezhnev that much work remained to be done in improving Soviet industrial administration. He was very positive about production *ob"edineniya*, especially the ways they linked science and production, and called for more *ob"edineniya* (and enterprises) to open their own shops in order to link production more closely with demand. But even Kosygin's treatment of the *ob"edineniya* was noticeably less detailed, enthusiastic, and optimistic than it had been at the 24th Congress.[41]

EAST GERMAN LEADERSHIP VIEWS

As explained in the introduction, the main concern in this study vis-à-vis the VVBs is with their development as "economic organs" since 1963. The starting point for this is taken as the late 1950s, in the aftermath of their reintroduction as Unions of Nationally Owned Enterprises in February 1958. A *detailed* analysis of the economic debates amongst the leadership before the 1958 decision therefore lies beyond the scope of this book. Nevertheless, a summary of them is necessary both for understanding subsequent developments and for appreciating the degree to which ideas and policies that emerged in the 1960s were new at senior levels, In other words, since leadership interest in the associations has a longer history in the GDR than in the USSR, the present section covers a longer period than its Soviet counterpart.

Following the June 1953 uprising, the East German leadership had to consider ways of improving many aspects of life in the GDR. This included industrial organization. As part of its search, the leadership established various commissions both to consider different views on improvement and to participate in the actual management of the economy. Perhaps the most important for our purposes were the three commissions established under the auspices of the Council of Ministers in November 1955 for the coordination of economic management, and two organizations set up in the wake of serious economic problems in 1956: the Economic Council of the Council of Ministers (established in April 1957 on the basis of a Central Committee resolution of the previous February), and the commission convened in the autumn of 1957, on the basis of a resolution of the 32nd plenum of the Central Committee (July 1957), to make suggestions for improving the state apparatus.[42] It appears that the most important voices on these commissions were those of Oelssner, Leuschner, and Selbmann. Oelssner had been a full member of the Politburo since 1950, Leuschner was head of the State Planning Commission and had been a candidate member of the Politburo since 1953, and Selbmann was a member of the Central Committee and deputy premier. According to Richert, Oelssner and Selbmann had fundamental disagreements with Ulbricht on the management of the economy. Basically, the latter believed that the party could to a large extent direct the economy, while the former argued that there were certain economic laws with which not even a communist party could successfully tamper.[43] During 1957, the views of Oelssner, Selbmann, and the like-minded Central Committee secretary for the economy, G. Ziller, seemed to be gaining ascendancy over Ulbricht's. At the 33rd plenum in October, for example, Ulbricht had to concede that the existing targets in the five-year plan were unrealistic, as a result of which they were lowered. It was in the same year, 1957, that Selbmann, as a member of the commission established by the 32nd plenum, advocated the creation of VVBs that would perform more of a management rather than merely an administrative role.[44]

But the apparent victory of Oelssner, Selbmann, and Ziller proved to be short-lived. Following the start of a purge of the SED's higher ranks in October 1957, Ziller seems to have foreseen his own imminent fall, and committed suicide in December. At the 35th plenum (February 1958), Oelssner was expelled from the Politburo. This was primarily because of his differences with Ulbricht over economic policy. In addition to the disagreements referred to above, both Oelssner and Selbmann had criticized the suggestion that the GDR should emulate the USSR's policy of creating *sovnarkhozy*. Selbmann was strongly criticized, both at the plenum and in the press, for "managerialism," and lost his seat on the Central Committee. The charges of technocratic and managerial leanings made against Selbmann imply that, had his views been implemented, the VVBs would have been granted considerably more autonomy in 1958 than was actually the case.

In contrast to Oelssner and Selbmann, Leuschner had restrained his criticism of Ulbricht's approach to economic management, and was rewarded with full membership of the Politburo in 1958. However, it seems that his views on economic management were in similar vein, if less extreme, to Selbmann's.[45] Thus, he was in all probability a, perhaps the, major advocate of the kind of moderate change in the VVBs that occurred in 1958.

This said, Ulbricht appears to have decided that he would need to keep the GDR's leading economic advisers more fully under his control in future. Not only did he downgrade and thereby dispose of his most outspoken critics, but he also implemented various organizational changes in line with this policy of closer supervision. The Economic Council of the Council of Ministers was dissolved, and its powers given to the enhanced State Planning Commission under Leuschner. An economic commission that had hitherto been subordinate to the Central Committee was now replaced by one directly responsible to the Politburo. The head of this was Erich Apel, the secretary Guenter Mittag; both these men were elected candidate members of the Central Committee by the 5th Congress (July 1958). Mittag launched a critical attack on the managerial ideas of Selbmann in the party journal *Einheit* in August 1958.[46] For the present, the leadership had clearly rejected ideas that could lead to greater managerial autonomy, including the suggestion that the VVBs would become real economic organs.

But it was not very long after the reintroduction of VVBs as "unions" rather than "administrations" that senior leaders started to think of ways to improve them. By the early 1960s, Ulbricht was already making concrete proposals on this that were later incorporated into the 1963 reform of these bodies. Two of the most important methods were the transfer to profit-and-loss accounting (which he mentioned at the October 1961 conference) and the granting of far more direct responsibility for ensuring the optimal linking of scientific research and production in their respective branches. He dealt with the latter question in some depth both at the 17th plenum in October 1962 and at a speech to the Research Council in November 1962.[47] It was also at the latter meeting that he first mentioned that the VVB could play the role of the "management of a large concern (*Konzern*)."[48]

The new conception of the VVB announced at the 6th Congress in January 1963 did not, therefore, represent some totally unexpected development in the senior leadership's thinking — and indeed, as hinted at by Richert, actually incorporated some of the ideas of Selbmann and others who had been demoted in 1958.[49] Nevertheless, the New Economic System that was announced did involve considerable, real change, and the party leader argued at length that a qualitatively new stage of economic development had been reached, necessitating a decentralization of much industrial decision-making. This, he stated, would involve the devolution of many of the powers of central organs to enterprises and, even more so, to the VVBs. One of the major tasks of these bodies now was to ensure maximum rationalization along the lines of concentration, specialization, cooperation, and combination. The VVBs were to be transferred to profit-and-loss accounting at the beginning of 1964, and, generally, manage via economic rather than their former predominantly administrative methods. Their enterprises, however, were to retain full legal autonomy.[50]

This major upgrading of the VVBs was not as acceptable to some members of the Politburo as to others, and the differences emerged rather more clearly at the June 1963 conference on the New Economic System.[51] Four members of the Politburo spoke at this: Ulbricht, Neumann, Apel, and Mittag (the latter two had recently been promoted to candidate membership). The meeting had been called to discuss a forthcoming official directive on the New Economic System (the "guideline"; see next section), and considerable attention was paid to the new role of the VVBs. Ulbricht, Apel, and Mittag were all enthusiastic about this new role and were highly critical of the attitudes toward it that were to be found among many of the functionaries working in the central state organs.[52] Neumann, on the other hand — who was Chairman of the central body in overall charge of running industry, the National Economic Council — paid lip service to the general line of increasing the rights and responsibilities of the VVBs, yet covertly disagreed with Ulbricht on the way this was to affect the central state bodies. Ulbricht had said that some of the subdivisions of the National Economic Council (the so-called general departments) could be disbanded as the VVBs took over more responsibilities, whereas Neumann argued that the activity of these bodies would have to harmonize better with the production principle.[53] In other words, Ulbricht wanted to abolish these departments,

Neumann wanted to improve them. Moreover, Neumann accused certain (unnamed) VVB-directors of having a very limited knowledge of modern methods of economic accounting, thus probably implying that it was too soon to transfer these bodies to profit-and-loss accounting.[54]

Although Ulbricht and others went into more detail on the role of the VVBs over the following couple of years, the next meeting of major importance to the development of policy on the VVBs was the 11th plenum (December 1965). The general theme of this gathering was the long-term plan to 1970, and much of the main speech — by Ulbricht — was devoted to a stock-taking of what had been achieved already under the New Economic System and what future developments were to be. It has been argued by some[55] that the 11th plenum constituted the beginning of the end of NES and of the new role for the VVBs that had been elaborated in 1963. Much of this argument is based on the fact that it was at this gathering that the National Economic Council was abolished and replaced by eight industrial ministries plus a ministry of material-technical supplies. There are strong objections to the thesis, however. First, just as Kosygin had done with regard to the new Soviet ministries introduced just three months earlier, so Ulbricht stressed that the new ministries were not the same as those that had existed prior to 1958.[56] Second, Ulbricht also announced that the first stage of the reform was now almost over, and that 1966 marked the beginning of a new stage. But far from this meaning a recentralization, the rights and duties of both the VVBs and the enterprises were to increase. Thus, the First Secretary argued that VVBs and enterprises were still not acting sufficiently responsibly regarding investments, frequently attempting to obtain more — Ulbricht called it "using tricks" — for financing projects than the budget could afford. In order to overcome this, he announced that both the VVBs and the nationalized enterprises would in future bear more responsibility than hitherto for financing projects; such finance was to come both from profits and from repayable credits. The central state budget would provide funds only for very large-scale projects and for structure-altering investment. In addition, the VVBs (as well as enterprises and research institutes) were to work out the details of individual R and D projects themselves; until now, this had been done by central planning and other central bodies, who would now issue the VVBs only with general parameters within which to plan and finance research and the like. In general, then, the ministries and other central organs were to fulfill primarily coordinatory and supervisory functions, not to limit any of the relatively new autonomy of the VVBs and lower bodies.⁵⁷ The final objection is that since the National Economic Council had had functional departments corresponding closely to the new ministries, there is no inherent reason for the new bodies to have had any more (or, for that matter, fewer) powers over subordinate units than their predecessors.

In fact, the call for even more autonomy for the lower organs in the economy continued for some time. At the 14th plenum (December 1966), for instance, Ulbricht again called for greater responsibility for the middle and lower tiers of the industrial hierarchy.⁵⁸ The main reason for this was a concern to raise initiative in expanding foreign trade.

But by the time of the 7th Congress (April 1967), it was clear that the First Secretary was not entirely satisfied with the development of the VVBs or the New Economic System, although his views on the ways to improve the situation were still only forming. One symbol of a desire for change was the essentially cosmetic one of renaming the New Economic System the Economic System of Socialism.⁵⁹ Ulbricht had four main ideas at the Congress for further improving the economy: to increase and improve exports, to upgrade economic law, to increase nationalization, and to improve long-term planning. The first point was to affect the VVBs: They were to have more direct foreign links in the future.⁶⁰ The second point also directly related to the VVBs, as well as to other tiers in the industrial administrative hierarchy. Ulbricht clearly felt that one of the reasons there was still excessive interference by higher organs in lower — including by VVBs in the work of enterprises — was that there was no clear legislation on how each tier related to the next. Points three and four, it was argued, would also affect the VVBs, though it was not elaborated how.

But the idea that was potentially to have a far greater impact on the VVBs, the development of a network of combines, does not appear to have emerged until the 2nd plenum in July 1967.

Ulbricht had shown interest in combines at the beginning of the 1960s. In April 1961, for instance, he had argued that the creation of combines or head enterprises in the regions (*Bezirke*) could help to involve local enterprises more in scientific-technical development.⁶¹ He made a similar point in November 1962, when he argued that one of the ways science and production could be better linked was to locate R and D laboratories in large enterprises *and* in the combines which were to be built.⁶² However, his interest in them was not sufficient to go into any detail, and can be seen to have declined still further after the introduction of the New Economic System. Although he seemed to favor combines at the 6th Congress, his enthusiasm was clearly restrained in comparison with his interest in the VVB.[63] Moreover, despite the fact that he criticized the National Economic Council at the June 1963 conference for approaching the creation of combines with insufficient courage, and despite praising Leipzig region for creating combines that were very useful for locally run industry, the First Secretary went on to state,

> We recommend the Regional Economic Councils to study their [Leipzig Council's] experiences, and only to create a combine where all the prerequisites are met.[64]

In other words, he was by no means strongly advocating the creation of the combines, and indeed for the next four years or so appeared to be more interested in cooperation through product groups or contracts between enterprises.[65] None of the other leaders, either, appear to have been strongly in favor of the combines at this stage.[66]

However, as Ulbricht became increasingly concerned about rationalization, foreign trade, and long-term planning, so the idea of greater concentration, and hence the combine, became important. But exactly when the First Secretary became really enthusiastic about these bodies is open to some debate. The official *History of the SED* published in 1978 states that the Politburo adopted a decision to create combines in the autumn of 1966;[67] but there is no reference to any source, and the evidence available suggests that the statement is at best misleading. For instance, at the December 1966 plenum, Ulbricht argued that the scientific-technical revolution had led to the possibility and necessity of a new stage of cooperation between enterprises, but in this context he emphasized the value of loose cooperation chains.[68] Similarly, it would be wrong to suggest that the party leader showed very great interest in the combines qua combines at the 7th Congress. Certainly, two combine directors (Wedler and Gallerach) did report to the Congress on the work of their organizations, and this could have been at Ulbricht's instigation. But the focus of their speeches was on experiments being conducted in their organizations rather than the advantageousness of the organizational form itself.[69] And it was not only Ulbricht whose interest in these bodies was marginal; other leaders, too, still seemed more sympathetic toward other forms of cooperation. Stoph, for example, strongly advocated the looser product groups.[70] The evidence would therefore suggest that in the period between the Congress (April 1967) and the 2nd plenum (July 1967), Ulbricht decided that the progressiveness of the two combines was not merely a function of

Party Policy

their dynamic directors, but also of their organizational structures. Since (as shall be demonstrated below) some other leaders remained relatively unenthusiastic about the combines, it seems unlikely that the Politburo adopted a *general policy* of creating combines in 1966. It is far more likely that a decision to establish two *particular* industrial combines (KWO and the Ruhla timepiece combine) was taken; such a decision did not obviously represent any major new development, given the evidence already cited (Chapter 1) on other combines in the 1950s and early- to mid-1960s.

Ulbricht himself delivered the main speech at the July plenum, and in it dealt with the organization of the state organs and their workstyle.[71] The party chief called for the development of a *model* of the management of socialist society as a whole, as well as for a reduction in expenditure on state administration and a simplification of the state management system. He dealt in some detail with the role of various parts of the industrial administrative system (the Council of Ministers, the State Planning Commission, and so on) before coming to his main point. This was that at present subgroupings within the economy were primarily of a horizontal nature, whereas vertical linkage should take an ever more prominent role in the future. Ulbricht went on to say that the vertically organized combine, in which supply enterprises and end-producers are organically linked, was a major new development within the economy, and that other types of combine should also spread (namely, combines of enterprises producing similar goods under the leadership of one strong enterprise). All this restructuring would require changes in the management system, including the transfer of some (supply) enterprises to other VVBs so that they would be subordinate to the same body as the end-product enterprise. Ulbricht stated that this process would inevitably render some VVBs superfluous.[72] Having made these points, the First Secretary focused his attention on the VVBs and their relationship with the combines. He complained that implementation of the New Economic System had been only partial in many VVBs. While there had been agreement at the 7th Congress that the VVBs as a whole had basically proved themselves, there was still too much use of administrative, bureaucratic methods and too little use of the preferred economic methods in the running of several branches of industry. One aspect of this, for example, was that many VVBs used their scientific-technical centers for administrative purposes. This had to be overcome, and Ulbricht suggested that the VVBs' R and D capacities should be transferred to appropriate large enterprises whenever possible.[73]

For these reasons — administrative style and a move to vertical linkups — Ulbricht said that the role of the VVBs needed to be defined more precisely. He went on to make a statement that can be seen as a watershed in the relative demise of the VVBs and the intensive development of combines from the beginning of 1968:

> Thus it is a matter of creating all the preconditions for making the VVBs effective as the economic organs of management (*oekonomische Fuehrungsorgane*) of their branches. Where the objective prerequisites for this do not exist, we will develop combines or other organs for economic management.[74]

This statement, taken in conjunction with what else Ulbricht said at the plenum, constituted an overt threat to the VVBs to modernize their style in line with party policy or be replaced. The First Secretary continued by saying that the most important factor in management was to render the actual producing units, the enterprises, maximally effective. In the light of all this, Ulbricht stated that a draft decree on VVBs, which had been issued at the beginning of March, needed to be revised.[75]

At the September 1967 seminar (see Chapter 2), there were papers by three members of the Politburo (Honecker, Stoph, and Ulbricht). From these, it is clear that there was not complete agreement on the future development of East German industrial administration. Honecker's speech was nonspecific, representing primarily a call to implement properly the Economic System of Socialism.[76] Stoph, on the other hand, did talk in some detail on the various administrative and producing tiers within industry. The interesting point is that he spoke very little about either the VVBs (other than to criticise "ten or twelve" for operating unprofitably) or the combines, devoting far more attention to the role of ministries (which was to increase), the State Planning Commission, and the enterprises. When he did talk about the combines, his support for them was reserved; as at the 7th Congress, he was far more interested in the looser forms of enterprise cooperation, such as the product groups and cooperation groups.[77] Ulbricht, in contrast, was clearly very much in favor of the combine. He criticized the low levels of cooperation in East German industry, praised the papers by the combine directors Gallerach and Wedler, and argued that a really important advantage of the combines was their potential contribution to the development of cooperation and to structure-determining tasks. Elsewhere in his speech, the First Secretary revealed that he was very concerned that the economic plan for

1967 would be underfulfilled in the latter crucial area.[78] Because of his enthusiasm for the combines, Ulbricht disagreed with Stoph that technical prerequisites were necessary before cooperation measures could proceed, arguing that the real barrier was not these technical aspects but people's attitudes. He thus lacked the cautiousness Stoph had shown. In fact, where Stoph called merely for more of the loose forms of cooperation between enterprises, Ulbricht argued that existing product groups should be more complexly integrated (suggesting they become more like combines), and in this connection singled out for praise the work of the Suhl region.[79]

Ulbricht was more circumspect about the VVBs at the September 1967 seminar than he had been at the 2nd plenum in July. Whereas at the earlier gathering the leader had said that the overall number of VVBs might well decline as the combines developed, he now argued that the size of staff in VVBs would be reduced, without mentioning the actual abolition of VVBs.[80] He did, however, also mention that the development of the combines would affect the ministries (without specifying how)[81] — which seemed to be a very different viewpoint from Stoph's. The latter, it will be remembered, had called for raising the role of ministries.

The main speech at the next plenum (November 1967) was delivered by Mittag. He continued to emphasize the advantages of combines, saying that they had proved themselves and that they were to be given more autonomy at the expense of the VVBs. However, although he maintained that the combines were not to affect their autonomy more than was necessary, it is clear from his speech that Mittag expected the combines to affect *enterprises* as well as the VVBs. It was therefore probably in order to placate potential opposition to the combines from enterprise management that Mittag expressed his approval of the combine directorate recently formed in KWO; this body included the directors of all the component enterprises. Mittag also emphasized that the enterprise, as well as the combine, was in future to play a greater role in foreign trade. Like Ulbricht, Mittag argued that the best way to form combines was on the basis of already-existing product groups. Finally, what by now seemed obvious was officially revealed — that the Politburo and the Central Committee Secretariat had agreed as a general principle that combines should be developed as part of the program to increase concentration and cooperation in East German industry.[82]

The events in Czechoslovakia in 1968, however, led to more blurring of the official line on the level of autonomy to be granted to various sections of the industrial hierarchy. At the October 1968 plenum, for example, there was strong criticism of what had been happening in Czechoslovak industry (or at least of what some Czechoslovak economists had been calling for, as the East Germans interpreted this), and much stronger attacks on self-administration by enterprises than there had been for some time.[83] It would be wrong, however, to take the East German criticisms at this time at face value, without taking into consideration what was actually happening in the GDR (which is examined elsewhere) and what the theoretical line on the autonomy of different levels was a few months after the main furor of the August 1968 events had receded somewhat. Thus, the 10th plenum, held in April 1969, is more instructive regarding party policy than the slightly hysterical tone of the 8th plenum; it also reveals that some speakers were by now more openly critical of the combines than they had been earlier. The main report was delivered by Honecker, who had not often spoken on industry up to this point. Honecker did make favorable comments on the combines, but warned that only those functions really belonging together (largely research and automation plans) should be taken over by a unified management. He praised certain centrally administered combines; but he also had a far more positive evaluation of the VVBs than Ulbricht had had, and repeatedly emphasized that the autonomy of the enterprises should not be affected more than was necessary.[84] The general impression is of a preference for the situation of the mid-1960s, before the development of the combines on any meaningful scale. This emerged both in his praise of the way six (named) VVBs had improved their work in comparison with 1968, and in the way in which he criticized the work of the engineer-buros of some VVBs — yet called for this to be improved by the VVB general directors: When Ulbricht had criticized the VVBs for their poor record on R and D at the 2nd plenum, the First Secretary had called for a transfer of such work to the combines, and, in fact, had virtually ceased to mention his erstwhile favorites, the VVB general directors, in the previous two to three years. Finally, Honecker repeatedly criticized the poor work of some combines, most notably in the chemical industry.[85] If this interpretation seems fanciful, a report that appeared in *Die Wirtschaft* soon after the 10th plenum endorses the impression. This report referred to the "critical words" at the April plenum directed against the combines. While the author of the article goes on to explain that these criticisms should not be construed as directed against the combine as a general principle — saying that what was being criticized was the creation of combines without sufficient preparation, and the practice in some combines of stifling enterprise autonomy — the very fact that a member of the editorial board of the leading economic journal in the GDR felt it necessary to "correct" a false impression means that many economic functionaries *did* interpret some of the remarks at the plenum as an attack on the very concept of the combine.[86]

At the next plenum of relevance, the 13th in 1970, the main speaker (Mittag) stated that the combines had basically proved themselves. But this is almost all he said on the new bodies, which undoubtedly must be seen as very low-key support in comparison with the enthusiasm of both Ulbricht and Mittag himself in 1967 and 1968.[87]

By the time of the 8th Congress in June 1971, Ulbricht's leadership of the party was over.[88] The new First Secretary was Erich Honecker, who has been far less concerned with industrial questions — at least until the late 1970s — than his predecessor. Although Honecker made a few remarks about the general desirability of combines, these were of little significance, and he made no statements about the VVBs.[89] However, just as Kosygin had done less than three months before at the CPSU's 24th Congress, so now the East German premier, Willi Stoph, announced that the administration of industry was to be simplified, with either a two-tier (ministry-combine) or three-tier (ministry-VVB-combine) structure.[90] This was, we would argue, merely symbolic of the new leadership's greater display of loyalty to the USSR, since the omission of the enterprise as a tier does not correspond to subsequent policy and practice. Moreover, although Stoph reported that "mighty economic units" (i.e., combines) were being established — which had led to the disbandment of some VVBs — he did not go into detail on the advantages of the combine.[91] In fact, interest in both the VVBs and the combines was very low at the 8th Congress, and even Mittag seemed much more interested in the product groups.[92] In other words, the lack of interest in the combines was *not* matched by a renewed emphasis on the VVBs. Rather, the interest focused mainly on the ministries and the enterprises, at the expense of the middle tier; NES/ESS was quietly being buried.

From 1971 to late 1977, leadership interest in associations appears to have been low. Honecker did refer to the necessity for and possibility of further developing the combines at the 9th plenum (May 1973).[93] However, he did so in the same speech in which he referred to the new Soviet legislation on associations, and this can be seen as official endorsement of Soviet policy as much as genuine enthusiasm for the combines. To our knowledge, moreover, no other speeches at the 9th plenum were concerned with the development of the combines.[94]

This lack of interest in either the VVBs or the combines was still manifest at the 9th Congress in May 1976, at which very few meaningful references to these bodies were made. Honecker did say that the combines — and their enterprises — had proved themselves since the 8th Congress in 1971, and that the existing combines were to be strengthened. However, he gave no detail on what he meant by "strengthening," nor did he say that any new combines were to be formed. He said even less about the VVBs.[95] The Chairman of the Council of Ministers, Horst Sindermann, had nothing significant to say about the combines or the VVBs — nor did anybody else.[96] East German leadership interest in both the VVBs and the combines was never lower in the period since the late 1950s than it was between 1971 and 1977.

In October 1976, following indications that there would be increasing economic problems in the late 1970s, major changes were made within the East German leadership. For our purposes, the most significant were that Willi Stoph reassumed the post he had held until October 1973 (Prime Minister), while Guenter Mittag again became the Central Committee secretary for economic affairs. The latter change suggested that Honecker and his team might be looking more sympathetically at the formerly discredited New Economic System, and Western observers were quick to realize this.[97] By 1977, it was obvious that the Politburo was indeed prepared to reassess its views on *some* aspects of the New Economic System; the most important of these was a reevaluation of the usefulness of the combines. At the 7th plenum (November 1977), for instance, Kurt Hager announced that the Central Committee Secretariat, in line with recent guidelines from the Politburo, had decided to create various combines in the automobile and electronics branches of industry.[98] Honecker has also shown enthusiasm for the combines recently, most notably at the 8th plenum in 1978, as has Mittag.[99] It was in line with such renewed interest that the new legislation on the combines was published in November 1979.

4.2. REFERENCES IN OFFICIAL POLICY DOCUMENTS

We have seen that either the leaders in both states have disagreed about associations, or else sub-Politburo level leaders were much more enthusiastic about these bodies than the senior leaders. We now consider how this was reflected in official directives.

USSR

Although the CPSU Party Program and the directives of the 22nd Congress (both 1961) are sometimes cited as authoritative statements in favor of the *ob"edineniya*,[100] in fact very little reference to these bodies was made in either. Certainly the idea that there was a need for a higher level of specialization and cooperation was mooted both at the Congress and in the program, and there were calls for a reduction in the management apparatus plus a raising of enterprise initiative.[101] But the nearest we come to a call for the associations was a brief reference in the program to the need for an "appropriate combination of related enterprises" as one of the long-term objectives of the party.[102]

Similarly, despite Tolstikov's and Podgorny's strong advocacy of the *ob"edineniya* at the November 1962 plenum, the plenum recommendations made no reference to the associations.[103]

The associations were not directly referred to in the directive from the September 1965 plenum, but on the following day (30 September) a joint resolution was passed by the CPSU Central Committee and the Council of Ministers that *did* see the *ob"edineniya* as integral parts of Soviet industrial administration.[104] There were no specific references to the associations in the directives from the 23rd Congress (1966), although, in endorsing the September 1965 plenum, the directives implicitly accepted them as part of the Soviet industrial administrative structure.[105] The Congress was generally far more concerned with the enterprise than with any other administrative tier, although there were certainly repeated references to the need for more specialization and cooperation, and for intensive as opposed to extensive development. The associations fitted in with the spirit of such development, but were not singled out.[106] The report of the December 1969 plenum only referred to the one-year plan, so that we do not know the directives on the association from this crucial meeting.[107] But the resolution of the 24th Congress on the Central Committee's report did explicitly refer to the associations, although it mentioned only the production *ob"edineniya*, science-production *ob"edineniya*, and combines, not the industrial associations.[108] However, the Congress directives on the 1971-1975 plan, as well as referring to "huge *ob"edineniya* and combines," also juxtaposed the *glavki* and the *ob"edineniya* of industrial ministries, thus revealing either that there was official recognition of the two basic types of *ob"edinenie* or that even at the top levels of the party there was confusion about the different types of *ob"edinenie*.[109]

The only significant policy statements since then (as opposed to detailed legislation) to which we have access were those made at the 25th Congress. The format changed at this Congress, so that Brezhnev's speech was now taken to be the official party policy; this speech has already been considered. The Congress directives on the five-year plan to 1980 are not unambiguous. On the one hand, they called for the completion of the policy of reducing the numbers of tiers in industrial administration and creating *ob"edineniya*.[110] On the other, they stated that the structure and functions of the apparatuses of ministries and interbranch functional organs needed to be improved. While this should probably be taken to mean "streamlined," the term "improvement" (*sovershenstvovanie*) is open to interpretation (i.e., ministers would not necessarily feel compelled to reduce their staffs on the basis of this directive).[111] Moreover, there were no calls for science-production associations in a section dealing with the linkups between science and production.[112] Finally, the directives clearly stated that the role of branch ministries and *vedomstva* in foreign trade was to increase.[113] All in all, the support for *ob"edineniya* looked lower-key than it had been in 1971.

GDR

It was at the SED's 6th Congress (January 1963) that, for the first time, the new, greatly enhanced role of the VVBs was publicly made official policy. According to the resolution of the Congress, the VVBs were to be transformed from administrative into economic organs.[114] However, Ulbricht himself later said that the detailed directives on this were those approved by the June 1963 conference,[115] which appeared as the "guideline," and it is to these that we soon turn. Before doing so, however, it should be noted that the Party Program adopted by the 6th Congress contained no significant references to the VVBs, and said of the combines only that they were a useful long-term development for locally administered industry.[116]

The "guideline" for the New Economic System appeared in July 1963, technically as a resolution of the Praesidium of the Council of Ministers.[117] It can be seen both as a general directive and, in its length and detail, a form of legislation. Because of this ambivalence, we refer here to the *general* points made in the document, considering the details in the next chapter. The "guideline" endorsed Ulbricht's statement at the 6th Congress that VVBs should become economic organs of management for the industrial branches. It also stated that experiments that had been carried out in four VVBs indicated, inter alia, that all VVBs could and should be transferred to profit-and-loss accounting from the beginning of 1964.[118] No other general statements were made, probably for the simple reason that there was already a VVB for each branch, so that a call for more was unlikely and unnecessary. On the combines, the "guideline" called for the elaboration of initial proposals for the staged creation of these bodies in regionally administered industry, and an extension of the system of head enterprises for coordinating enterprises of different forms of ownership.[119] This was all very much in line with Ulbricht's views at the 6th Congress and the June conference. However, the "guideline" also stated that combines or "amalgamated industrial undertakings" could be built within the framework of a VVB.[120] We have been unable to trace the genesis of this vague directive.

The 7th Congress (1967) did not produce any significant directives on the associations, the resolution stating only that the VVBs had proved themselves.[121] By the time of the 8th Congress (1971), references to the VVBs had all but disappeared. The only directive on combines was that concentration in industry should continue and existing combines should be strengthened.[122] Thus, there were no calls for *more* combines; indeed the section in the directives concerned with economic administration concentrated on the ministries and, to a lesser extent, the enterprises. The directives of the 9th Congress (1976) stated that the administrative structure in industry was to be simplified and expenditure on it reduced — without making significant reference to the associations; rather, the call was for more product groups, implying a move away from the combines.[123] Finally, the new Party Program adopted by the 9th Congress contained nothing significant on either the combines or the VVBs.[124]

It is clear that in the GDR, as in the USSR, official policy documents tend to be very much in line with the statements of the First/General Party Secretary, and that they are often of a generalized nature.

4.3. SUMMARY

The interest of the First/General Secretary of the CPSU in the associations has varied over time, but it has never been *very* strong. Khrushchev was reservedly in favor of them, particularly single-branch *firmy*. Brezhnev appears to have had little interest during the mid-1960s, although he certainly does not seem to have opposed them. As problems arose with the 1965 Economic Reform, however, he was prepared to listen to leading party and state functionaries — especially those from Leningrad and the Ukraine — who were eager to point out the advantages of the *ob"edineniya*. These people had been silent on the associations at the 23rd Congress, however, when the senior leadership clearly had alternative ideas for improving the economy and was not seeking advice. The Chairman of the Council of Ministers since 1964, Kosygin,[125] has been much more enthusiastic about the associations than the head of the party, although his support, too, was low-key in the mid- to late 1960s; it is strange that Kosygin does not appear to have spoken at the crucial December 1969 plenum. In comparison with the 24th Congress, all of the leaders seemed to have become less optimistic about the associations by the time of the 25th.

We have been unable to find such overt cases of disagreement on the associations among Soviet leaders as among their German colleagues, although it is useful to remember Zorza's argument that silence from a Soviet leader can signify disagreement with the views of his colleagues.[126] Silence is not always explained by this factor; probably some leaders have simply not been interested in industrial administration. But Zorza's hypothesis does at least compel us to allow for greater differences of opinion among Soviet leaders than we have evidence of.

The East German picture is very different. There, the party leader himself was enthusiastic about an enhanced role for the VVBs in the early 1960s — having essentially rejected proposals along similar lines made in 1957-1958 — while the Chairman of the National Economic Council (Neumann) did not share this enthusiasm. As the VVBs proved to be less successful than he had hoped, Ulbricht began to look to the combines. In doing so, he more or less overtly (it varied over time) threatened the VVBs that they would be either transformed into or replaced by the combines if they did not improve. Toward the end of the Ulbricht era, other senior leaders started to reveal fairly open disagreement with the leader's views. Honecker preferred the VVB to the combine, while the Chairman of the Council of Ministers (Stoph) preferred the product groups to the combines. Following Ulbricht's ouster, interest in *both* types of association declined to the benefit of the ministries and individual enterprises. However, loyalty to the Soviet Union meant that the East German leadership praised its own system of industrial administration — including the role of the VVBs and combines in this — when Soviet leaders showed rather more serious interest in the associations in the early 1970s. Since the late 1970s, the East German leadership has again become enthusiastic about combines, but appears to have rejected the VVBs altogether.

In both states, party directives on the associations have often been very general, although this pertains rather more to the USSR than to the GDR. Soviet directives have also been open to varying interpretations more frequently than German ones. In both states, there has usually been a high correlation between statements by the party leader and official policy directives. In the USSR, however, the General Secretary has in recent years stated explicitly that authoritative pronouncements on economic matters are primarily the responsibility of the Chairman of the Council of Ministers rather than himself. Although Honecker does not appear to have made a similar statement, East German practice since 1971 has generally accorded with this division of labor.

NOTES

1. *Ustav* . . . , p. 29. However, the Soviet Central Committee and the Politburo are to direct the party on behalf of the Congress between congressional sessions. See *ibid.*, pp. 31-33. The same applies to the GDR; see *Statut* . . . , pp. 16-19.

2. There is sometimes a problem in deciding whether a speaker is making an authoritative policy statement or is articulating demands and/or citing the advice of specialists; this point is more appropriately considered in our concluding chapter.

3. Extracts from Brezhnev's speeches in particular are now often published at the time of plena, but this does not pertain to the main period considered in this study. However, the speeches on the economy delivered to the Supreme Soviet in December each year (which are published) are probably similar to those presented to the Central Committee a few days earlier. But as yet, we still do not know many details of other speeches (i.e., possibly discussions) as we do for the Khrushchev period (though see following text). Cessation of publication is in one sense less "democratic," because there is more secrecy; but it could also suggest more open debates, precisely because of such secrecy.

4. Brezhnev, *Ob Osnovnykh* . . . , Vol. 1, pp. 414-429.

5. N. S. Khrushchev, in *Plenum Tsentral'nogo Komiteta Kommunisticheskoi Partii Sovetskogo Soyuza 19-23 Noyabrya 1962 g. - Stenograficheskii Otchet* (Moscow: Gosudarstvennoe Izd. Politicheskoi Literatury, 1963), pp. 5-99, esp. p. 45.

6. *Ibid.*, p. 121.

7. *Ibid.*, p. 122. Khrushchev might have made the point at some other gathering, of course.

8. *Ibid.*, p. 145.

9. *Ibid.*, pp. 40, 44, and the reference in E. Utkin, "K Voprosu o Firmakh," *Vop. Ekon.*, No. 10, 1963, p. 34. For Ulbricht, see *Das Neue Oekonomische System* . . . , pp. 47-50.

10. A. N. Kosygin, "Povyshenie Nauchnoi Obosnovannosti Planov — Vazhneishaya Zadacha Planovikh Organov," *Ekon. Gaz.*, No. 16, 1965, p. 4.

11. A. N. Kosygin, "Ob Uluchshenii Upravleniya Promyshlennost'yu, Sovershenstvovanii Planirovaniya i Usilenii Ekonomicheskogo Stimulirovaniya Promyshlennogo Proizvodstva," *Pravda*, 28 September 1965, pp. 2-3.

12. *Ibid.*, p. 3.
13. L. I. Brezhnev, "Rech' Pervogo Sekretarya TsK KPSS Tovarishcha L. I. Brezhneva," *Ekon. Gaz.*, No. 40, 1965, p. 3.
14. See N. M. Konin, "Sovershenstvovanie Pravogo Regulirovaniya Organizatsii i Deyatel'nosti Khozyaistvennykh Ob"edinenii," *SGiP*, No. 2, 1969, p. 113.
15. *XXIII S'ezd Kommunisticheskoi Partii Sovetskogo Soyuza – Stenograficheskii Otchet*, Vol. 1 (Moscow: Politizdat, 1966), pp. 51-63, esp. pp. 55, 59; also *ibid.*, Vol. 2, pp. 4-68.
16. *Ibid.*, Vol. 1, pp. 140-148.
17. *Ibid.*, pp. 130-140, 233-247, and passim.
18. The decree ("On Measures for Raising the Efficiency of the Work of Scientific Organizations and Speeding Up the Use in the National Economy of the Achievements of Science and Technology") may be found in *Resheniya . . .*, Vol. 7, pp. 111-136; see esp. para. 18.
19. L. I. Brezhnev in *XXIV S'ezd . . .*, Vol. 1, p. 90. See too Kuznetsov and Tikhomirova, "Voprosy . . . ," p. 75.
20. Brezhnev, *Ob Osnovnykh . . .*, Vol. 1, pp. 414-429.
21. B. Meissner, "Die Sowjetunion auf dem Wege zum XXIV. Parteitag (1)," *Osteuropa*, No. 6, 1971, pp. 378-380. See too G. Hodnett, "Succession Contingencies in the Soviet Union," *P of C*, No. 2, 1975, p. 8.
22. Brezhnev, *XXIV S'ezd . . .*, Vol. 1, p. 93.
23. *Ibid.*, Vol. 2, pp. 50-52.
24. *Ibid.*, Vol. 1, p. 94.
25. Romanov, in *XXIV S'ezd . . .*, Vol. 1, pp. 166-167.
26. *Ibid.*, p. 167.
27. Shelest, *ibid.*, pp. 149-156, esp. p. 150.
28. Grishin, *ibid.*, pp. 141-148, esp. p. 145.
29. Konotop, *ibid.*, pp. 435-441, esp. pp. 437-438. This surely constitutes a classic example of what in Ch. 2 was called "significant nonreference."
30. Masherov, *ibid.*, pp. 175-183, esp. p. 180. Apart from these speakers, Shakhirov and Bodyul also spoke a little on associations (the latter on agroindustrial ones), but their references were of marginal relevance.
31. See *ibid.*, pp. 272, 338, and Vol. 2, p. 72.
32. Rudnev, *ibid.*, Vol. 2, p. 203.
33. For a more detailed analysis of the economic discussion at the Congress, see P. Knirsch, "Stand und Entwicklungstendenzen der Sowjetwirtschaft," *Osteuropa*, Nos. 8-9, 1971, pp. 628-650.
34. B. Meissner, "Die Sowjetunion . . . ," p. 379.
35. Brezhnev, *Ob Osnovnykh . . .*, Vol. 2, esp. pp. 252-254.
36. "Informatsionnoe Soobshchenie," *Pravda*, 16 December 1969, p. 1.
37. "Informatsionnoe Soobshchenie," *Pravda*, 19 December 1972, p. 1.
38. The December 1973 plenum was probably also of some relevance, but again, with the exception of Brezhnev's, we know nothing of the content of the speeches at this gathering. Therefore, since it also took place after the 1973 legislation calling for a restructuring of industry, we have not included it in the main body of the text (i.e., there seems even less justificaiton for speculating on the position of leaders than at the earlier plena, since the main output with which we are concerned had already been issued). The list of speakers at the plenum can be found in "Informatsionnoe Soobshchenie," *Pravda*, 11 December 1973, p. 1, and 12 December 1973, p. 1. Extracts from Brezhnev's speech are in his *Ob Osnovnykh . . .*, Vol. 2, pp. 341-361. It appears from this that the General Secretary said very little about the *ob"edineniya*

Party Policy

other than that the change envisaged in the legislation must not be a mere formality (see *ibid.*, pp. 354-356).

39. Brezhnev in *XXV S'ezd* . . . , Vol. 1, pp. 26-115.
40. Romanov, *ibid.*, p. 147.
41. Kosygin, *ibid.*, Vol. 2, pp. 23-6.
42. On all this see E. Richert, *Macht ohne Mandat* (Cologne and Opladen: Westdeutscher Verlag, 1963), pp. 130-131; S. Doernberg, *Kurze Geschichte der DDR* (Berlin: Dietz Verlag, 1965), pp. 328-329; M. McCauley, *Marxism-Leninism in the German Democratic Republic* (London: Macmillan, 1979), pp. 94-95, 102-107.
43. Richert, *Macht ohne Mandat*, esp. pp. 130-133.
44. Baylis, *The Technical Intelligentsia* . . . , p. 199.
45. *Ibid.*, esp. pp. 193-194.
46. *Ibid.*, p. 203.
47. Ulbricht, *Probleme* . . . , pp. 115, 151-155; Ulbricht, *Zum Neuen Oekonomischen System der Planung und Leitung* (Berlin: Dietz Verlag, 1967) pp. 36-37.
48. Ulbricht, *Probleme* . . . , p. 152.
49. E. Richert, *Die DDR-Elite oder Unsere Partner von Morgen?* (Reinbek bei Hamburg: Rowohlt, 1968), p. 23.
50. *Protokoll der Verhandlungen des VI. Parteitages der Sozialistischen Einheitspartei Deutschlands*, Vol. 1, (Berlin: Dietz Verlag, 1963) pp. 28-250, esp. 98-113.
51. Details from *Das Neue Oekonomische System* . . . , passim.
52. *Ibid.*, pp. 5-127 (Ulbricht); 261-291 (Apel); 160-170 (Mittag).
53. Compare Ulbricht, *ibid.*, p. 85 with Neumann, *ibid.*, pp. 174-181, esp. p. 176.
54. *Ibid.*, p. 180. The disagreement never reached crisis proportions, however, and Neumann has been a full member of the Politburo continuously since 1958.
55. See, for example, A. M. Hanhardt Jr., *The German Democratic Republic* (Baltimore: Johns Hopkins Press, 1968) pp. 96-97. Not all agreed with this interpretation, however; see D. Miller and H. G. Trend, "Economic Reforms in East Germany," *P of C*, No. 2, 1966, pp. 29-36, esp. p. 36.
56. Ulbricht, *Zum Neuen* . . . , p. 705.
57. *Ibid.*, pp. 663-751, esp. pp. 682-690, 704-711. Ulbricht also called for more involvement of the VVBs in foreign trade (p. 715).
58. Ulbricht, *Probleme* . . . , pp. 473-496, esp. p. 478.
59. *Protokoll der Verhandlungen des VII. Parteitages der Sozialistischen Einheitspartei Deutschlands*, Vol. 1 (Berlin: Dietz Verlag, 1967), pp. 25-287, esp. p. 99.
60. *Ibid.*, pp. 133-164, 206-215.
61. Ulbricht, *Probleme* . . . , pp. 95-96.
62. *Ibid.*, p. 154. For an article in which it is argued that the formation of combines as a new form of management was suggested at the 17th plenum (October 1962), see H. Zschunke, "Erste Erfahrungen in Leipzig mit der zweigmaessigen Leitung der oertlichen Industrie," *Die Wirts.*, No. 48, 1962, p. 5. Although we have been unable to find such a reference, this is not crucially important, since we have discovered much earlier references (see note 61 above).
63. *Protokoll der Verhandlungen des VI. Parteitages* . . . , Vol. 1, p. 114.
64. Ulbricht in *Das Neue Oekonomische System* . . . , p. 101; see too p. 98, *ibid.*
65. See, for example, Ulbricht, *Probleme* . . . , pp. 428, 452-453.
66. Based on an analysis of speeches by Politburo members at party Congresses, Central Committee plena, and the economic conferences referred to in Ch. 2.
67. Rossmann, *Geschichte der SED*, p. 499.

68. Ulbricht, *Probleme* . . . , pp. 483-485.
69. *Protokoll der Verhandlungen des VII. Parteitages* . . . , Vol. 1, pp. 352-355, 391-395.
70. *Ibid.*, pp. 457-459; see too text accompanying note 82 below.
71. Ulbricht's speech is to be found in *Probleme* . . . , pp. 580-636.
72. *Ibid.*, pp. 619-622.
73. *Ibid.*, p. 622.
74. *Ibid.*, p. 622.
75. *Ibid.*, p. 622.
76. Honecker in *Der Weg zur Durchfuehrung* . . . , pp. 11-13.
77. Stoph in *ibid.*, pp. 15-23.
78. Ulbricht, "Der Weg zur Durchfuehrung . . . ," pp. 4, 5, 8. His complaints about low levels of cooperation were not based on general impressions, but on a report on this which had been compiled by the Statistical Office.
79. *Ibid.*, pp. 8-9
80. *Ibid.*, p. 8.
81. *Ibid.*, p. 8. Ulbricht merely stated that ministerial management structures would have to be simplified.
82. G. Mittag, "Aus dem Bericht des Politbueros an die 3. Tagung des ZK der SED," *N.D.*, 24 November 1967, pp. 2-8.
83. The 9th plenum was held from 22 to 25 October 1968; speeches from it appeared in *N.D.* from 25 to 30 October. It is our view that the attacks on self-administration made at the plenum were largely criticisms of Czechoslovakia and any East Germans sympathetic to the pre-August 1968 developments in that state. But some would argue that the Czechoslovak events merely confirmed a declining faith in the New Economic System among East German leaders, and that the type of statements made at the October plenum would have been made anyway. See. K. Erdmann, "Das Ende des Neuen Oekonomischen Systems," *D.A.*, No. 9, 1968, pp. 998-1001.
84. E. Honecker, "Aus dem Bericht des Politbueros an die 10. Tagung des ZK der SED," *N.D.*, 29 April 1969, pp. 3-8, here esp. 3-5.
85. *Ibid.*, p. 4.
86. U. L. (Ursula Leupold?), "Volkseigene Kombinate," *Die Wirts.*, No. 22, 1969, p. 11.
87. G. Mittag, "Die Durchfuehrung des Volkswirtschaftsplanes im Jahre 1970," *N.D.*, 11 June 1970, pp. 3-6, esp. pp. 4-5, and 12 June 1970, pp. 3-4. However, it is implied that Mittag was very much in favor of the combines at the 13th plenum in Schoth, "Kombinate . . . ," p. 5; although the quotation given by Schoth is accurate, Mittag did not seem to be advocating new combines, and was critical of several aspects of existing ones. Moreover, he frequently referred to enterprises and combines interchangeably in his speech, implying that he was not particularly concerned with emphasizing the latter as sui generis.
88. Ulbricht "resigned" at the 16th plenum in May 1971. For an analysis of his fall, see P. C. Ludz, "Continuity and Change since Ulbricht," *P of C,* No. 2, 1972, pp. 56-58, and P. C. Ludz and M. Croan, "Meinungen zum Fuehrungswechsel in der SED," *D.A.*, No. 6, 1971, pp. 572-578.
89. Honecker in *Protokoll der Verhandlungen des VIII Parteitages* . . . , Vol. 1, pp. 34-121.
90. Stoph, *ibid.*, Vol. 2, p. 32.
91. *Ibid.*, p. 33.

92. G. Mittag, *ibid.*, Vol. 2, p. 148.
93. E. Honecker, *Aus dem Bericht . . . an die 9. Tagung . . .* , pp. 44-45. Honecker also said that the VVBs performed a useful function — but this hardly constitutes a significant reference.
94. See *Aus den Diskussionsreden auf der 9. Tagung des ZK der SED* (Berlin: Dietz Verlag, 1973). There were references by other speakers to the combines — indeed, W. Frohn devoted his entire speech to a report on the petrochemical combine at Schwedt, of which he was the director — but nothing resembling strong views either in favor of or against them. Frohn's speech is on pp. 41-44.
95. *Protokoll der Verhandlungen des IX. Parteitages der SED,* Vol. 1 (Berlin: Dietz Verlag, 1976), pp. 31-151, esp. pp. 101, 106.
96. Sindermann, *ibid.*, Vol. 2, pp. 41-42. Stoph did not refer to the economy at all — merely giving the opening, welcoming speech at the congress — while Mittag did not even give a speech.
97. H-D. Schulz, "Fortsetzung des NOeSPL in Sicht?," *D.A.,* No. 2, 1978, pp. 117-121, esp. 120-121.
98. For Hager's speech, see "Dokumentation — Das 7. Plenum des ZK der SED (24. und 25. November 1977), 'Aus dem Bericht des Politbueros,' " *D.A.,* No. 1, 1978, pp. 82-108, esp. 90.
99. E. Honecker, "Aus dem Bericht des Politbueros an die 8. Tagung des ZK der SED," *N.D.*, 25 May 1978, p. 4. It does seem that Honecker still wants enterprises to retain considerable autonomy, however, which is probably in contrast to some of the other leaders such as Mittag; this would help to explain the ambiguities of the November 1979 legislation noted in Ch. 1. For Mittag's views, see, for example, G. Mittag, "Zielstrebige Verwirklichung der Hauptaufgabe," *Einheit*, No. 10, 1978, p. 1010, and "Vorzuege des Sozialismus fuer hoehere Effektivitaet nutzen," *N.D.,* 26/27 August 1978, p. 3. Honecker's views on enterprise autonomy are also clearly out of line with those of some East German specialists who have wanted a reduction in enterprise autonomy; see, for example, R. Gerisch and W. Hofmann, "Aufgaben und Probleme der Entwicklung in den Kombinaten zur Erhoehung der volkswirtschaftlichen Effektivitaet," *Wirts/wiss,* No. 2, 1979, esp. pp. 143-144, 147-148.
100. See, for example, I. Ivonin in Meleshkin, *Pervye Sovetskie Firmy,* p. 19.
101. *Programme of the Communist Party of the Soviet Union* (Moscow: Foreign Languages Publishing House, 1961), pp. 69, 79, and *XXII S'ezd Kommunisticheskoi Partii Sovetskogo Soyuza – Stenograficheskii Otchet,* Vol. 3 (Moscow: Gosudarstvennoe Izd. Politicheskoi Literatury, 1962), pp. 205-227, esp. p. 218.
102. *Programme . . .* , p. 69.
103. *Plenum . . . 19-23 Noyabrya 1962 g.*, pp. 446-458.
104. "Postanovlenie TsK . . . Ob Uluchshenii . . . ," para. 1.
105. *XXIII S'ezd . . .* , Vol. 2, pp. 321-382.
106. *Ibid.*, esp. pp. 329-332.
107. For details on the report, see note 36 above.
108. *XXIV S'ezd . . .* , Vol. 2, esp. pp. 231-232.
109. *Ibid.*, pp. 306-310.
110. *XXV S'ezd . . .* , Vol. 2, pp. 240-241.
111. *Ibid.*, p. 241.
112. *Ibid.*, pp. 237-238, 281-283.
113. *Ibid.*, p. 305.
114. *Protokoll der Verhandlungen des VI. Parteitages . . .* , Vol. 4, pp. 440-441.
115. Ulbricht, *Zum Neuen . . .* , p. 379.

116. *Programm der Sozialistischen Einheitspartei Deutschlands* (Berlin: Dietz Verlag, 1963), esp. p. 81.
117. "Richtlinie fuer das neue oekonomische System der Planung und Leitung der Volkswirtschaft," *N.D.* (Sonderbeilage), 16 July 1963, p. 2.
118. *Ibid.*, pp. 5, 33.
119. *Ibid.*, p. 12.
120. *Ibid.*, p. 29.
121. *Protokoll der Verhandlungen des VII. Parteitages* . . . , Vol. 4, p. 52.
122. *Protokoll der Verhandlungen des VIII. Parteitages* . . . , Vol. 2, p. 376.
123. *Protokoll der Verhandlungen des IX. Parteitages* . . . , Vol. 2, p. 454. There was also a call to strengthen central state planning and raise the responsibility of VVBs, combines, and enterprises (p. 447), but this was very general, and cannot, in the absence of any detail, be taken as a meaningful policy statement.
124. *Ibid.*, Vol. 2, pp. 209-266, esp. pp. 231-233, where references would have been most expected.
125. Kosygin resigned this post on October 22, 1980, and was replaced by N. A. Tikhonov. Kosygin has subsequently died.
126. See Ch. 2, note 43.

Chapter 5

LEGISLATION: THE MICRO POLICY FORMULATION

We have already seen who was arguing for what among leaders, economists, legal specialists, and the like at party gatherings, conferences, and in the press. The next stage is to consider the process by which all these ideas are adopted or rejected, and concretized into actual laws or decrees. The first section of this chapter deals with the legislative process itself, the second with the resulting legislation, and the third summarizes and draws conclusions from the preceding analysis.

In considering the buildup to the 1973-1974 legislation, the following legislation is examined in this chapter:

Soviet Legislation (General)
- The statute on enterprises, October 1965
- The decree on the administration of industry, March 1973
- The statute on industrial *ob"edineniya*, March 1973
- The statute on production *ob"edineniya*, March 1974[1]

Soviet Legislation (Specific, i.e., referring to particular branches of industry, and constituting a lead-in to the general legislation)
- The statute on the *glavki* of *Minpribor*, November 1967
- The decree on *Minpribor*, March 1970
- The decrees on the chemical, oil, and coal industries, May 1970[2]

East German Legislation (General)
- The guideline on the New Economic System, July 1963
- The guideline on the creation of combines and amalgamated enterprises, October 1963
- The decree on nationalized enterprises, February 1967
- The draft decree on VVBs, March 1967
- The decrees on combines, October 1968
- The resolution on combines, May 1969

- The resolution on combines, December 1969
- The decree on nationally owned enterprises, combines, and VVBs, March 1973[3]

East German Legislation (Specific)

- The resolution on experimentation in four VVBs, January 1963[4]

It is clear from the above that there has been considerably more general legislation in the GDR than in the USSR.

5.1. THE LEGISLATIVE PROCESS

Detailed information on the legislative process of most political systems is difficult to obtain; this is particularly true of communist states. Nevertheless, some picture can be formed. We present here the information about both states that has been gathered from published sources (which appear in the notes to this chapter) and about the USSR from the interviews we were granted there (which are not covered in the notes). Our interview data relate almost exclusively to the most important legislation on the associations — that of 1973 and 1974 — so that the rest of the information is based primarily on printed sources. The main focus of this stage of the research was on the identity of those who initiate legislation, those who actually draw it up, how much consultation there is, whether there are differences of opinion, how important such differences are, and how they are resolved; not all of these questions can be equally satisfactorily answered.

THE SOVIET PROCESS

The December 1967 statute and the March 1970 decree that put *Minpribor* onto a system very similar to that announced for all branch ministries in 1973 were based on suggestions from *Gosplan* and *Minpribor* itself. A *Gosplan* official told us that this was for two reasons. First, the Minister of *Minpribor*, K. Rudnev, had a reputation as a very progressive minister who was anxious to experiment. Second, watches and other timepieces are a good export product, and are particularly useful for earning Western currency. These two organizations required the agreement of several other bodies, however, before the 1970 experiment described in the decree could be embarked upon. These were (1) the State Committee for Science and Technology, (2) the State Committee for Labor and Wages, (3) the Ministry of Finance, (4) the State Committee for Prices, and (5) the All-Union Central Committee of Trade Unions.[5]

Although various detailed aspects of the new work of *Minpribor* had to be agreed upon with other bodies (such as the State Committee for Material-Technical Supplies, the Construction Bank, and so on), it seems to have been these five bodies that actually sanctioned the overall experiment. Much of the detail of the experiment was elaborated by an interdepartmental commission within *Gosplan* and *Minpribor*. The following bodies were responsible for presenting the first results of the experiment to the All-Union Council of Ministers in the latter half of 1970: (1) *Minpribor* itself, (2) *Gosplan*, (3) the Ministry of Finance, and (4) the State Committee for Labor and Wages.[6] In addition, a *Gosplan* interdepartmental commission and *Minpribor* were responsible for working out and ratifying the instructions for transferring the ministry to the new arrangement, and were to do this within three months.[7]

According to the May 1970 decree on the chemical industry, many of the same bodies were responsible for drawing up the draft general charter on the state industrial association. Thus, the organizations to be involved in this drafting were (1) *Gosplan*, (2) the Committee of People's Control, (3) the All-Union Central Committee of Trade Unions, (4) the State Committee for Labor and Wages, (5) the Ministry of Finance, (6) the Central Statistical Office, (7) the Legal Commission attached to the Council of Ministers, and (8) the Academy of Sciences.[8] This draft was to be prepared within three months, and the compilers were to discuss proposals with ministries and *vedomstva* that would be affected; the legislation was to be coordinated with that on ministries and enterprises.[9] Unfortunately, we do not know whether this draft ever materialized; all that can be said is that work both on it and on modifications to the enterprise statute (to clarify the position of the production *ob"edineniya*) was in progress by August 1970.[10] However, if it *was* produced, it must have been rejected, since shortly after the 24th Congress (in 1971) the Chairman of *Gosplan* issued an order formally establishing a commission to draw up the long-awaited decrees.[11] *Gosplan* appointed N. Drogichinskii to head the commission, and it was primarily he who chose its members. However, in deciding who should sit on the commission, Drogichinskii had to adhere to a general principle of a division of labor. It was explained to us that this meant "something like" ten academic economists, ten academic legal specialists, a few *ob"edinenie* directors, and so on, but it proved impossible to obtain more detail than this. Eventually, approximately 50 (maximum) people sat on this body. The commission met every 1-3 months, discussing various aspects of the decree on industrial administration and the statutes on the industrial and production associations. Not all the meetings were held in Moscow; some took place in Leningrad, for instance. A member of this commission told the author that there were some "real" discussions (i.e., disagreements) on certain parts of the legislation, such as the legal and economic status of enterprises situated some distance away from the head enterprise of a production association. That such disagreement existed is also strongly suggested if we examine the known views of those members of the commission who have been identified. They amount to something over one-half of the total, and are classified according to their institution or simply as academic if they are from an institution of higher education:

SOVIET LEGISLATIVE COMMISSION BY INSTITUTION/FUNCTIONAL BASE
(Number Identified — 26)

Gosplan	Drogichinskii, N. E. (Chairman)
	Oznobin, N. M.
	Pevzner, A. G.
	Rakitskii, B. V.
	Tatevosyan, M. G.
State Committees	Lagutkin, V. M. (Material-Technical Supplies)
	Subotskii, Yu. V. (Material-Technical Supplies)
Central Committee (i.e., Secretariat)	Zdorov, P. A.
Academy of Sciences	Laptev, V. V.
Industry	Budinskii, A. A.
	Chuplinskas, A. B.
	Panfilov, M. P.
Academia	Deineko, O. A.
	Dunaev, E. P.
	Dzhavadov, G. A.
	Gromov, V. I.
	Kamenitser, S. E.
	Kozlova, O. V.
	Kruk, D. M.
	Lisitsyn, V. N.
	Oligin-Nesterov, V. I.
	Omarov, A. M. (Higher Party School)
	Petrov, A. S.
	Popov, G. Kh.
	Shubnikov, A. K.
	Slezinger, G. E.

Because of the same difficulties encountered in the attempt to classify views at conferences, it was not possible to categorize members of the commission in a systematic way. Nevertheless, we know, for instance, that A. G. Pevzner and M. Panfilov were both members and that their views on enterprise autonomy in *ob"edineniya* were very different.[12] While the most radical advocate of *ob"edinenie* autonomy in the field of foreign trade, A. M. Aleksandrov, was *not* on the commission, he was consulted by it. We were unable to discover who else was consulted at this decree-drafting stage.

Another point emerging from this list is that the participants were all "specialists," i.e., there were no party or trade union generalists. Obviously, it could be that such people were among those members of the commission who have not been identified. But two interviewees, on different occasions, told us that the commission was composed entirely of people who had written "learned" books or papers concerned with associations and/or who were directly involved with problems of the *ob"edineniya* because of the function they fulfilled. One economist emphasized that there were no party functionaries from local organs; this applied even to A. Dumachev (a Leningrad party secretary), despite the fact that he is by any standards a specialist on the *ob"edineniya*.[13] Moreover, the ministries were hardly involved at this stage of the discussion other than, perhaps, in a consultative capacity.

The commission produced draft legislation, which was then sent to selected enterprises and *ob"edineniya* for discussion. Regretfully, we were unable to obtain any information on this, merely a comment from one economist that this stage was *not* important in the legislative process. Once back from the enterprises, the drafts were sent to four senior bodies for ratification. These were (1) the State Committee for Prices, (2) the State Committee for Labor and Wages, (3) *Gosplan*, and (4) the Ministry of Finance. Without endorsement from all four of these organizations, the legislation could not have materialized. Having said this, we were informed by our *Gosplan* interviewee (who was himself a member of the commission) that three individuals from these organizations had pushed hard for the *ob"edinenie* legislation, had been in favor of the associations, and had in fact been more influential than anyone else in getting the decree and statutes published in their final form. These three were (1) V. K. Sitnin (Chairman of the State Committee for Prices), (2) A. V. Bachurin (Deputy Head of *Gosplan*), and (3) B. M. Sukharevskii (Deputy Chairman of the State Committee for Labor and Wages). This was partially endorsed by another interviewee, who said that the four bodies referred to above were the ones which really had most influence in the decision on what was and what was not to be included in the legislation, and that the delay in the ratification of the statute on production *ob"edineniya* — it appeared just over a year after the decree on administration and the statute on industrial associations — was primarily due to criticisms of the draft from the Ministry of Finance.[14] Only after several compromises had been reached with this ministry did the statute appear. In other words, the interviewee was saying that only one of the four bodies was taking what might be called a cautious or even obstructive approach to the association legislation, and thus implied that the other three were at least neutrally and, more probably, positively disposed toward the issuance of the statutes.

It should be pointed out that, notwithstanding the fact that two different sources agreed on which bodies were most influential and had the final say, the 1973 decree on administration called on a large group of bodies jointly to prepare within six months a draft statute on the production association. The organizations entrusted with this task were (1) the Ministry of Justice, (2) *Gosplan*, (3) the State Committee for Labor and Wages, (4) the State Committee for Science and Technology, (5) the State Committee for Material-Technical Supplies, (6) the Ministry of Finance, (7) the Academy of Sciences, (8) the State Bank, (9) the Central Statistical Office, and (10) the All-Union Central Council of Trade Unions.[15] Presumably, it was hoped that in broadening the range of bodies responsible for a draft there was a greater chance of producing a generally acceptable one and overcoming the resistance that had already been encountered.[16] Moreover, responsibility for a draft does not necessarily mean that a new commission had to be set up, nor that the bodies that were to ratify the draft were different from before. There is thus no inherent contradiction between the information obtained from published sources and that gleaned from interviews.

Returning to exclusively interview data, we learned that once the four bodies had agreed to the decree and statutes, the Council of Ministers' endorsement was forthcoming with no further discussion. The Supreme Soviet appears to have played no significant role at any stage of the decree, a finding that accords with Vanneman's research on this body.[17]

THE EAST GERMAN PROCESS

Although this section is incomplete and often tentative, it was considered useful to present the information available in the hope that it will form a basis for further research if access to East German sources improves.

Before the 1963 guideline was adopted, it was discussed at length at the June conference referred to earlier. However, the conference was only one small part of the process by which the guideline was produced and accepted as binding. Between late 1962 and April 1963 a vast number of working parties was established — some directly by the Politburo itself — to consider and make recommendations on specific aspects of the New Economic System. Of these, it would appear that two of the most important, from the point of view of industrial administration, were the one established in December 1962 under Willi Stoph and that set up in March 1963 under Walter Halbritter. Stoph was at that time First Deputy Chairman of the Council of Ministers and a member of the Politburo; the rest of the group was also composed of members of the Politburo and the Council of Ministers. Halbritter's thirteen-member group, too, consisted of leading state and party functionaries. Halbritter himself was Deputy Minister of Finance and was shortly to become a Deputy Chairman of the State Planning Commission. Among the other members were the two men seen by many as having been Ulbricht's leading advisers on the New Economic System: Erich Apel (a candidate member of the Politburo, Chairman of the State Planning Commission, and a Deputy Chairman of the Council of Ministers) and Guenter Mittag (also a candidate member of the Politburo, and Central Committee Secretary for Economic Affairs). Two other members have also subsequently become leading figures in the administration of the GDR's economy: Gerhard Schuerer (at that time First Deputy Chairman of the State Planning Commission) and Siegfried Boehm (Director of the Central Committee's Department of Planning and Finance). Although there is evidence that subordinate groups did include and/or consult lower-ranking party and state functionaries (including VVB general directors), it seems that these two groups were the most influential in the formulation of the final guideline.[18] But there is one other group that must be singled out for mention, namely, the central working party established by the Council of Ministers in January 1963 and attached to the National Economic Council. The group's brief was to coordinate both the experiments that were to be conducted in four VVBs (see Chapter 6) and the legal regulations pertaining to this experimentation. It was headed by the two First Deputy Chairmen of the National Economic Council, E. Markowitsch and H. Wittik.[19]

Early in June 1963, the proposals of the various working parties were discussed by representatives of the Central Committee and the Council of Ministers. The recommendations were then discussed by the Politburo (between June 11 and 18) before being presented to the economic conference. On the day following the end of the conference (June 26) the Politburo again met, and took a final decision on the guideline. It was then ratified by the Praesidium of the Council of Ministers (July 11) and the State Council (July 15).[20]

Information on the legislative process surrounding the rest of the legislation considered here is much sparser. When the draft decree on the VVBs appeared in *Die Wirtschaft* in 1967, it was preceded by a little information on its genesis. Thus, a working party of the Central Committee and the Council of Ministers had produced it.[21] It is likely that this working party either included some members of two groups about which we have limited information and/or consulted them. The first was the Legal Commission of the Research Council, established in 1963. One of the tasks of this commission was to research problems of the state's management of scientific-technical progress, which included consideration of the role of the VVBs in this.[22] The other was the permanent working party attached to the Praesidium of the Council of Ministers, which was established in November 1963 and headed by Walter Halbritter. This group's brief was to monitor and make recommendations on all aspects of the New Economic System.[23] The Chairman of the Council of Ministers (Stoph), who was directly responsible for issuing the draft decree, listed the people from whom he wanted comments on the document. These were (1) the general directors of the VVBs, (2) the ministers and heads of other central state organs, (3) the chairmen of Regional Councils and the chairmen of the Regional Economic Councils, and (4) the directors of the nationalized large enterprises. Stoph requested these people to convey their opinions on the draft to the head of the Council of Ministers' Office by the end of March — i.e., less than a month from the date the draft was allegedly issued, and only *one day* after it appeared in *Die Wirtschaft*.[24] It is clear from the above that only relatively senior members of the industrial administration hierarchy were expected to make comments. There was no call for comments from academic economists or legal specialists, although this could well be because the working party itself was composed of the leading experts in this field from academia. It would also seem that since the deadline was so close, there would have been very little time for those people specified above to digest the document *and*, having done this, arrange consultative meetings with trade union officials, party workers, or even enterprise directors. While it is true that views intended for consideration by the legislators were still appearing in the press as late as May, it is far from clear that the legislative group would take note of them, since a Council of Ministers working party was already revising the draft by the time these suggestions were published.[25]

Although we know no more about the compilation of this draft, some of the above information is of relevance to later legislation in that it suggests that a suspicion we already had — that the legislation on industrial administration in the late 1960s and early 1970s was drafted by a working party about which we do have some information — could well be correct. At the 3rd plenum in late 1967, Guenter Mittag announced that a working party (permanent) had been set up to deal with problems of the elaboration and implementation of the Economic System of Socialism.[26] This group, once again under the leadership of Walter Halbritter, seems to have been largely concerned with the combines, as seen both in its involvement in the convening of the July 1970 meeting on these bodies and in the publication of a set of instructions and recommendations for the implementation of the Economic System of Socialism in the combines during 1969 and 1970; this appeared in *Die Wirtschaft* at the end of 1969.[27] Inasmuch as the introduction to these recommendations stated that one of the reasons for their publication was to encourage ideas for further work on the regulations on combines, it can be seen as a form of draft charter on these bodies; This emerges even more clearly from the editorial comment on the document.[28] At the time the recommendations were published, they had already been discussed by (1) experts (*Praktiker*) working in the combines, (2) representatives of the industrial ministries and other central state organs, and (3) the working party itself.[29] Comments were invited, and again the deadline for the submission of these was only about a month away. This time, however, there was no listing of the type of people who should be making comments. All suggestions were to be sent to the secretary of the group, Dr. Scholl; since the editorial board stated that this should all help in the drafting of a decree on the combines and their enterprises, it is reasonable to infer that this working party was closely involved in any combine legislation being formulated at that time. The only caveat to this inference is that the group was disbanded at some unknown point in the early 1970s, so that it is unclear how influential it was in the compilation of the 1973 decree.

But there was another group at this time that clearly also had an important role in the discussing and drafting of legislation on the combines and possibly the VVBs; this was the Working Party on Constitutional and Economic Law. The first reference we have found to this group dates from late 1967, and it was probably formed very near the time that Halbritter's new group came into existence.[30] It appears that the body was disbanded in the middle of 1972, which would probably be late enough for it to have had some involvement in the series of decrees on the different tiers of the industrial administrative hierarchy that appeared between October 1972 and July 1973.[31]

We have been unable to discover the total number of members of this group, but of the eighteen identified, all were specialists — more in law than in economics — from institutions of higher education and the Ministry of Justice. They were responsible for a series of authoritative interpretations/explanations of new legislation on industrial administration after decrees and the like had been announced, primarily in the journal *Wirtschaftsrecht* but also in more "popular" publications such as *Die Wirtschaft*.[32]

WORKING PARTY ON CONSTITUTIONAL AND ECONOMIC LAW
(Number Identified - 18)

Head:	Spitzner, O. (until 1969)
	Supranowitz, S. (from 1969)[33]
Members:	Badestein, H.
	Bergmann, S.
	Boettcher, H.
	Grass, K.
	Heuer, K.
	Hoffman, B.
	Knupfer, W.
	Kreutzer, C.J.
	Lassak, S.
	Panzer, A.
	Ramminger, B.
	Richter, A.
	Sauer, M.
	Schramm. L.
	Wedler, M.
	Willma, B.

Judging by their publications and the fact that authoritative interpretations of legislation have appeared from their members, it is highly probable that three further bodies played important roles in the legislative process. These were:

(1) The GDR Council of Research into Economic Law. At the 7th Congress (1967), there had been calls for a consistent body of socialist economic law. In line with this, the Politburo decided in October 1968 to create this council; the decision was followed by a Council of Ministers' resolution to this effect at the end of April 1969. The founding meeting of the council took place in Berlin in June 1969; it was initially headed by the State Secretary for Constitutional and Economic Law, O. Spitzner. The council's brief was

specifically to advise on the formation and practical implementation of a consistent body of socialist economic laws by 1975.[34]
(2) The legal department of the Office (*Buero*) of the Council of Ministers, headed by Prof. Dr. Gunther Klinger.
(3) The Economic Law Group at the Central Institute for Socialist Economic Management, attached to the Central Committee of the SED and headed by Prof. Dr. Uwe-Jens Heuer.[35]

Unfortunately, we have no further details on the latter two bodies. Indeed, the only other information we have on the legislative process leading up to the 1973 decree is that some time early in that year the Council of Ministers discussed a draft of it, following numerous deliberations on the document in enterprises and institutes.[36]

5.2. THE LEGISLATION

No attempt is made here to précis the considerable body of legislation listed at the beginning of this chapter, one reason being that many of the details were included in Chapter 1. Instead, the intention is to concentrate on those parts of the legislation that give formal, if not always clear, answers to the contentious aspects of associations discussed earlier in the study. These answers are presented in the same order as the issues in Chapter 3. However, descriptions of the legislation are often much briefer than descriptions of the areas of disagreement. For this reason — i.e., to avoid absurdly short sections — we have collapsed the legislation into only two subdivisions. This said, the fact that the East Germans have produced so much more legislation means that the section on the GDR is longer and more complex than that on the USSR.

SOVIET LEGISLATION

The Concept of the *Ob"edinenie*

The 1965 legislation stipulated that the enterprise was the basic link in the national economy. But was the *ob"edinenie* also seen as an enterprise, as some specialists had argued it should be? The only reference to *ob"edineniya* (of various sorts) was the following:

> The combine, trust, firm, or other economic organization in which are included production units which are not autonomous enterprises operates in accordance with the present statute as a production enterprise.

The combine, trust, firm, or other economic organization to which are subordinate autonomous enterprises operates in relation to these enterprises as an organ of economic administration.[37]

Thus, the legislation did not settle the contentious issues. The *ob"edinenie* could be an enterprise or it could be a body above autonomous enterprises. Since there was no legislation on the "organs of economic administration" (the *glavki* have always worked according to individual charters drawn up by their own ministry), there was still no general guideline for the running of such bodies.

This latter deficiency was rectified by the 1973 decree — which at long last made an official distinction between the "production" and "industrial" *ob"edineniya* — and the statute on industrial associations. Although the organ above enterprises and production *ob"edineniya* now had its legal position set out in detail, the position of the production association was still ambiguous. In the 1973 decree, the production *ob"edinenie* was not called an enterprise. But it was described as the basic (primary) link in production, and was to have the rights described in the 1965 enterprise statute, plus additional unspecified ones, until its own statute materialized.[38] It was normally to consist of factories and works (as opposed to enterprises), but could, if part of a two-tier arrangement, include autonomous enterprises also enjoying the rights of the 1965 statute.[39] This confused situation was exacerbated when the 1974 statute appeared. Whereas before only production *ob"edineniya* in a two-tier scheme could include autonomous enterprises, there was now no stipulation of the conditions under which autonomous enterprises could be part of such an association.[40] This said, the very promulgation of the 1974 statute, and the continued validity of the 1965 statute, meant that there was now, at least formally, a clear distinction between the enterprise and the production *ob"edinenie*.

Let us now consider in more detail the position of component units in a production association. The 1973-1974 legislation does recognize the illogicality of calling such units enterprises unless they actually enjoy enterprise status. Nevertheless, their legal position is still not wholly clear; indeed, one Soviet commentator has stated enigmatically that the component units are "semilegal" persons under the 1974 legislation.[41] Certainly they cannot conclude contracts independently, one point which was made more explictly in the 1974 statute than in the 1973 decree.[42]

The 1974 statute rendered the economic position of component units even less clear than the 1973 decree had done. In the earlier document, every production unit could have its own balance, and any unit located away from the main body of the association was to have a current account.[43] According to the statute, on the other hand, *any* production unit (not merely those some distance from the head unit) could have a current account, subject to the agreement of the *ob"edinenie* general director and the local branch of the state bank. In addition, the distant unit could now have an account for financing capital investment, a point not mentioned in the 1973 decree.[44] However, it is clear from the 1974 statute that only the *ob"edinenie* itself (and possibly autonomous enterprises) could have a capital (*rasschetnyi*) account.[45]

Regarding the names of production units, the 1974 statute stipulated that units were to have their own title (*naimenovanie*), although there was to be a reference in this to the name of the *ob"edinenie* (in contrast to the East German picture).[46]

According to the 1973 decree, *glavki* were usually to be replaced by either industrial or production associations, but could be retained in certain, unspecified cases. The legislation was reasonably specific that industrial associations should be located nearer to the main centers of production, and that where *glavki* were retained they were to be on profit-and-loss accounting.[47]

The legislation has not given a clear ruling on the number of tiers there should be in industrial administration. The 1973 decree stated that most of industry should be on either a two- or a three-tier system, and that there was to be an eradication of superfluous tiers. However, provision was also made for a four-tier arrangement in "exceptional" (unspecified) cases.[48] It should also be pointed out that since the 1974 statute allowed for the inclusion of autonomous enterprises in production *ob"edineniya* on a three- or more-tier arrangement, the legislation can hardly be seen to have given clear indications of a preference for as streamlined an administrative structure as some would have wished.

Other Issues

The 1973 legislation was vague on the question of when production *ob"edineniya* should be formed, stating merely that when ministries and the like are planning the creation of production associations, they should "foresee" the optimal level of specialization, cooperation, and so on. The 1974 legislation is equally nonspecific.[49]

The 1973 decree stipulated that the administration of the production *ob"edinenie* was simultaneously that of the head unit.[50] Thus there appeared to be a rejection of the concept of the *trest*, although the *ob"edinenie* would function rather like a trust in relation to autonomous enterprises. The decree did not stipulate that the administration of the head unit before and after the formation of the *ob"edinenie* would necessarily comprise the same personnel, and hence is open to interpretation. Moreover, the 1974 statute allowed for a separate (*spetsial'noe*) administration in exceptional cases; the *trest* was not necessarily to disappear after all.[51]

In none of the legislation is the problem of the choice of the head unit considered; hence there has been no authoritative ruling on this issue.

EAST GERMAN LEGISLATION

The Concept of the Association

In 1958, the meaning of the abbreviation "VVB" changed to symbolize both the greater level of integration between the VVB and its enterprises, and the more directive as opposed to purely administrative role of the VVB.[52]

By 1963, however, it was stated that the VVBs had, in fact, still been mainly concerned with administration rather than management since 1958.[53] It will be recalled from the last chapter that in order to symbolize their new role (e.g., the transfer to profit-and-loss accounting), they were now defined as "economic organs of management" (*oekonomische Fuehrungsorgane*). The definition of a VVB as an economic organ of management was retained in the 1967 draft decree on the VVBs.[54] However, in the first and only fully ratified decree on the VVBs, that of March 1973, these bodies are described as *wirtschaftsleitende Organe*, which translates unsatisfactorily as "organs for managing the economy";[55] the downgrading of the VVBs symbolized in their new definition is more obvious in the German than in the English.[56] This definition still applies, since the November 1979 legislation explicitly does not supersede the 1973 legislation vis-à-vis the VVBs.

The definition of the combine contained in the October 1963 legislation is not accessible; all we know, as pointed out earlier, is that a distinction was made between groupings of enterprises vertically (combines) and horizontally (amalgamated enterprises). The 1967 legislation on nationalized enterprises did not deal with the combines as sui generis, so that the first definition we have is that of October 1968. According to this, "The nationally owned combines have the legal position of nationally owned enterprises."[57] In other words, the combines were defined as a specific type of enterprise. Although there were marginal modifications in the status of the combines over the next few years, no new definition as such appeared until March 1973, when the combines were defined as "an economic unit in the field of material production, consisting of enterprises."[58] This was symbolic of the upgrading of the enterprises in combines that many legal specialists in particular had called for, and also meant that the earlier confusion in distinguishing between a combine and an enterprise had been overcome — in the legislation at least.

The legislation on the component parts of the combine reflects nicely the emerging awareness of illogicalities that were identified in Chapter 3. In other words, although the component unit might be called an enterprise at different times in the legislation, the similarities between the VEB and the enterprise in a combine have become greater over time, as legislators have appreciated the problem of using the same term both for bodies enjoying the status embodied in the February 1967 enterprise decree and for component units of a combine possibly enjoying very little autonomy. Thus, it is insufficient merely to point out that the component units were called enterprises; the actual extent of their rights also needs to be considered.

In the October 1968 legislation, the component units were called "enterprises" or "enterprise parts" (i.e., parts of the combine, itself seen as an enterprise).[59] There was little detail on the exact position of these bodies; in fact, it was up to the combine director to lay down the rights and duties of the enterprises in planning, R and D, the management of funds, commercial relations, concluding contracts, and relations with local state organs.[60] Moreover, it was stipulated that enterprises in a combine would have the rights of enterprises granted in the February 1967 decree and be legal persons only in exceptional cases; other enterprises in the combine were not to be legal persons.[61]

The May 1969 resolution attempted to give a more detailed, generally applicable picture of the relationship between the combine and its component parts. The component enterprises were now explicitly supposed to devise their own plans and their own means for obtaining funds for production, within the framework of the combine's general long-term plan. The new legislation also made the personal responsibility of the directors of combine enterprises for their unit's performance far more explicit than earlier decrees.[62] Finally, the legislation stipulated that, within limits, the combine enterprises could conduct commercial transactions on their own. This said, the autonomy of the component units was potentially severely limited by their dependency on the combine management's rulings on all important aspects of fund allocation.[63]

The December 1969 resolution was published with the express aim of plugging loopholes in earlier legislation.[64] This resolution also increased the rights of the component units. Thus, it was now stipulated that the enterprises of a combine could, within the framework of the plan and combine regulations, conclude contracts with third parties (i.e., outside the combine).[65] This was symptomatic of the more general point of the legislation, which was to reflect awareness of the fact that the legal position of the combine enterprises had not been seriously considered in earlier decrees, a situation which had led to problems.[66] For the first time in legislation, the notion that legal status was something a unit either possessed or did not possess (i.e., the idea that legal position was reflected in a unit either being a legal person or not) was abandoned. The more flexible concept of legal competence was now introduced, and it was made clear that the combine enterprise could enjoy a degree of legal competence without having as much as the combine.

According to the 1973 legislation on combines, the combine consists only of enterprises; although there was an escape clause stating that combines could consist exclusively of enterprise parts, the decree did not apply to them (they were to have individual regulations drawn up by their respective ministries, based on the decree).[67] Moreover, the decree stipulated that the legislation on nationalized enterprises applied to the enterprises in a combine to the extent that nothing to the contrary was included in the regulations on the combines.[68] Such a statement was no mere window dressing to ensure a modicum of enterprise autonomy, however. Further details on the position of the combine enterprises endorsed the general point. Thus, on the question of the right to conclude contracts, the combine director had to allow a certain amount of freedom to the component parts to conclude some contracts. Although the autonomy in this area was to be variable — the legislation envisaging more autonomy to larger units and/or units taking a key place in production and/or being located a long way from the head enterprise of the combine — there was a stipulation that only "certain" (but not all) economic contracts were to be concluded solely through the combine.[69] Clearly this was open to interpretation, but it did mean that the spirit of the legislation was to ensure some minimum level of autonomy for the parts of a combine.

As to the question of the names of units within combines, the legislation omitted reference to this for a long time, despite claims to the contrary by some East German writers.[70] The 1973 legislation did specify that the enterprise of a combine was to have its own name, although, "when necessary," this title could incorporate a reference to the fact that the enterprise was part of a combine.[71]

Legislation: The Micro Policy Formulation

All in all, the legislation revealed a gradual upgrading of the component parts of the combine from the late 1960s, although the 1973-1979 position was by no means devoid of ambiguities.

The general lack of concern about the number of tiers in East German industry has been reflected in the legislation in a total absence of references to this aspect of industrial administration. In this connection, it should be noted that whereas the 1973 Soviet legislation was intended to lead to major change in the running of Soviet industry — including a reduction of tiers in most branches — the simultaneous East German legislation was merely aimed at plugging certain loopholes in and coordinating the existing legislation.[72] Since previous legislation was essentially disjointed — in the sense that it did not constitute a fully interrelated set of regulations representing an overall strategy for the structure and development of industrial administration — the number of tiers was not dealt with there either.

Other Issues

We begin by considering legislation on the timing of the establishment of an association. Since VVBs have been responsible for whole subbranches of industry, their formation or disbandment has been in accordance with changes in the official structure of industry (in terms of the numbers and nomenclatures of branches or subbranches). The 1963 "guideline" was only concerned with the tasks of the VVB, not its formation — as were the 1967 draft decree on the VVBs and the 1973 decree.

In the case of the combines, the 1968 legislation stated that they were to be formed with the aim of improving the economic organization in comparison with the existing situation; the economic effect was to be projected before the establishment of a combine.[73] The May 1969 resolution stated that the creation of combines was to proceed from the basic principle that the functions of the combine consisted of effective concentration, centralization, cooperation, and combination of VEBs. The decision was to be based on scientific preparation, making full use of operations research and electronic data-processing.[74]

The tone of the March 1973 legislation was markedly more cautious on the question of when a combine should be established. Once again, the creation of combines was to be prepared "thoroughly and in a planned manner."[75] However, the legislation then stipulated that

> combines may only be formed if it has been established that, through the gradual deepening of the division of labor by means of concen-

tration, specialization, and cooperation or other measures, effective management of the unified production process is made possible, and a higher level of usefulness to the economy attained.[76]

This cautiousness reflects nicely the present East German leadership's initial lack of enthusiasm for the combines in comparison with Ulbricht's faith in them.

Since the main establishment period of the new VVBs (1958), nothing has been contained in the legislation regarding the formation of the staff in them.

In the October 1968 legislation on combines, no reference was made to the manner in which the combine administration was to be formed. In contrast, the May 1969 resolution stated clearly that the director of the combine was simultaneously the director of the main enterprise (*Stammbetrieb*) of the combine.[77] This represented a clear ruling on the question of whether or not a separate administration should be formed above all the component units of the combine.

In the March 1973 legislation on combines, however, the picture was less clear:

> The management of the combine is to be organized rationally and with low expenditure on administration. The director of the combine is *usually* at the same time director of the main enterprise. The same applies for the specialist directors, the chief accountant, and other leading functionaries [emphasis added].[78]

In other words, the possibility of an administration quite separate from all the production units is expressly allowed for in the 1973 legislation. While this was probably largely intended to cover the situation in which a VVB would be converted into a combine, it did reveal a certain lack of commitment to a very streamlined administrative hierarchy in East German industry. It is also unclear what the precise difference was to be between, on the one hand, a combine with an administration separate from all the production units and subordinate directly to a ministry and, on the other, a VVB. Seemingly, this distinction hinges largely on the level of autonomy of the subordinate units; but since this could now be high in combines, the difference in some cases must have been extremely marginal. In sum, there was more ambiguity in the 1973 than in earlier legislation.

Clearly, the question of choosing the head enterprise does not pertain to the VVBs. In the case of the combines, no guideline on the method of choosing the head enterprise of a proposed combine is contained in any of the legislation to which the Western researcher has access. This, it will be recalled, is probably linked to the fact that combines usually develop either from VVBs, in which case the combine can have a separate administration, or from product groups, in which case the head enterprise will already have emerged. However, it is not clear how an enterprise will be chosen for a combine replacing a VVB and not having a separate administration, or a combine not developing from a product group.

5.3. CONCLUSIONS

Despite the fact that when it did finally emerge, Soviet legislation on the associations was more detailed than the East German, it has also proved to be more open to interpretation on many issues — although we have also seen that the 1973 German legislation reopened some of the loopholes (especially concerning the combines) that had been closed at the end of the 1960s. It has also been shown that the 1974 Soviet legislation was more ambiguous than that issued in 1973. There are various ways of interpreting these findings, and we can make some introductory remarks on these at this point of the study.

First, the East Germans do appear simply to be more efficient than the Soviets at producing legislation. Certainly their legislative style is neater than the Soviets'. For instance, East German legislation on associations nearly always includes specific dates by which it becomes operative; Soviet legislation does so less often.[79] Any new East German legislation usually indicates which existing legislation is rendered inoperative; Soviet legislation rarely does, although the situation has improved in recent years. The level of integration of legislation on all the different tiers of East German industrial administration is much higher than in the USSR: Legislation on the Council of Ministers, the VVBs, the combines, the nationalized enterprises, and the local state organs all appeared within about ten months in the GDR, whereas the decrees and the like covering the structurally equivalent bodies in the USSR were issued over a period of nearly nine years. There has also been more and earlier interest in economic law in the GDR, manifested in the establishment of the relatively high number of bodies to deliberate on and integrate the large body of legislation on industrial administration; here too, though, the Soviets improved somewhat in the 1970s.[80]

Second, and closely related to all this, there does appear to be a difference in the process of legislating in the two states, although we still have insufficient evidence on the GDR to make definitive statements. Of particular importance is the role of leadership in the two states. In the GDR the legislative commissions appear frequently to have been headed by and composed of members of the Politburo and/or the Praesidium of the Council of Ministers. In contrast, the Soviet legislative process does not appear directly to involve members of the Politburo or other senior political actors. Hence, the distinction between stages 2 and 3 of our analytical framework has been less easy to sustain vis-à-vis the GDR than the USSR; the situation might have been changing in the smaller state during the 1970s, however. Although specialists[81] dominate the process in both countries — representatives not only from enterprises but even from branch ministries seem to have played a negligible role — we can say with certainty that the legislators in the USSR represented very differing views on many issues, whereas there appears to have been a more obvious division of labor between East German lawmakers, as inferred from an analysis of articles by identified members of the working parties. Moreover, the Soviet legislators seem to prefer (or to feel obliged) to reach mutually agreed, comprehensive legislation, even if this delays the process and leads to more ambivalent legislation. The East Germans, in contrast, have sometimes produced legislation quite rapidly, subsequently modifying it in response to problems arising in its implementation; this certainly pertains to the combine legislation of the 1960s.

We shall next consider in more detail how the policy outputs examined in this and the previous chapter have been put into practice.

NOTES

1. For details on the legislation, see Ch. 1, notes 3, 4, 7 and 34. The 1965 enterprise statute had been promised as early as the November 1962 plenum. See *Resheniya* . . . , Vol. 5, p. 248.

2. The November 1967 statute is not in *Resheniya* . . . , but is referred to in Taksir, *Upravlenie* . . . , p. 221. Not all legislation in the USSR is published; for a useful discussion of this and the reasons surrounding the decision to publish or not, see D. A. Loeber, "Legal Rules 'For Internal Consumption Only,' " *International and Comparative Law Quarterly*, No. 1, 1970, pp. 70-98, esp. 77-78. A Soviet decree promulgated on May 6 1980 seeks to make the publication of laws and resolutions more open, but it remains to be seen how practice will evolve. The *Minpribor* decree is entitled "Postanovlenie Soveta Ministrov SSSR 19 marta 1970 g. 'O dal'neishem sovershenstvovanii planirovaniya proizvodstvenno-khozyaistvennoi deyatel'nosti ministerstva priborostroeniya, sredstv avtomatizatsii i sistem upravleniya i povyshenii roli ekonomicheskikh metodov v ego rabote,' " and can be found in *Resheniya* . . . , Vol. 8, pp. 61-69. The decree on the chemical industry is entitled "Postanovlenie TsK KPSS i Soveta Ministrov SSSR 28 maya 1970 g. 'O sover-

shenstvovanii organizatsii upravleniya khimicheskoi promyshlennost'yu' "; see *ibid.*, pp. 126-130. The decree on the oil industry is entitled "Postanovlenie TsK KPSS i Soveta Ministrov SSSR 28 maya 1970 g. 'O sovershenstvovanii organizatsii upravleniya neftyanoi promyshlennost'yu,' " while that on the coal industry has exactly the same title except that the word *ugol'noi* replaces *neftyanoi*; for both decrees, see *ibid.*, pp. 130 and 130-131, respectively.

3. See "Richtlinie . . . ," pp. 1-47; "Richtlinie fuer die Bildung von Kombinaten und Vereinigten Betrieben in der volkseigenen Industrie im Bereich des Volkswirtschaftsrates," *Verfuegungen und Mitteilungen des Volkswirtschaftsrates der Deutschen Demokratischen Republik*, No. 12, 1963, p. 125ff.; "Verordnung ueber die Aufgaben, Rechte und Pflichten des volkseigenen Produktionsbetriebes," *GBl*, Pt. 2, No. 21, 1967, pp. 121-135; "Entwurf zur Verordnung ueber die Aufgaben, Rechte und Pflichten der Vereinigungen Volkseigener Betriebe," *Die Wirts.*, No. 13, (Beilage), 1967, pp. 1-8; "Verordnung ueber die Bildung und Rechtsstellung von volkseigenen Kombinaten," *GBl*, Pt. 2, No. 121, 1968, pp. 963-965; "Verordnung ueber das Verfahren der Gruendung und Zusammenlegung von volkseigenen Betrieben," *GBl.*, Pt. 2, No. 121, 1968, pp. 965-968; "Beschluss ueber die Verwirklichung des Oekonomischen Systems des Sozialismus bei der Bildung von volkseigenen Kombinaten in Industrie und Bauwesen und die Gestaltung der Beziehungen zwischen den volkseigenen Kombinaten und ihren Betrieben fuer 1969/70," *GBl.*, Pt. 2, No. 46, 1969, pp. 293-295; "Beschluss zur weiteren Gestaltung der Aufgaben, Rechte und Pflichten der volkseigenen Kombinate im Planjahr 1970," *GBl.*, Pt. 2, No. 5, 1970, pp. 19-24; Ch. 1, note 39. The guidelines are in fact what might be called quasi-legislation. For instance, in subsequent decrees and resolutions, they are not referred to as no longer valid, for the simple reason that they were never considered regular, normative pieces of legislation. The reason for their inclusion here was given in Ch. 4.

4. Referred to in "Richtlinie . . . ," p. 32, although we have been unable to obtain the actual resolution.

5. "Postanovlenie . . . 'O dal'neishem sovershenstvovanii planirovaniya . . . ,' " para. 1.

6. *Ibid.*, para. 21.

7. *Ibid.*, para. 22. The findings of the experiment in *Minpribor* were published in 1972; see "Otrasl' Na Khozraschete," *Ekon. Gaz.*, No. 22, 1972, p. 7. From this we learn that there had recently been a meeting of the *Gosplan* commission, at which it was decided that other ministries should transfer to the new management.

8. "Postanovlenie . . . O sovershenstvovanii . . . khimicheskoi promyshlennost'yu," para. 5.

9. *Ibid.*, para. 5.

10. Bachurin in Dumachev and Varsobin, *Opyt* . . . , pp. 79, 81-82.

11. Interview data; also, V. V. Laptev stated at the September 1971 East German gathering that work on a statute for the *ob"edineniya* was under way; see Kensy, "Wissenschaftliche Arbeitsberatung . . . ," p. 361.

12. Pevzner favored minimal integration of enterprises in associations; Panfilov favored maximal.

13. Dumachev has written at least three full-length studies of the *ob"edineniya* over the years, for instance. See his *Khozraschetnye Ob"edineniya . . . , Effektivnaya Sistema Organizatsii Proizvodstva i Upravleniya* (Moscow: Izd. Ekonomika, 1975); and *Partiinye Organizatsii i Proizvodstvennye Ob"edineniya* (Moscow: Politizdat, 1977).

14. We do not know if any one individual in the Ministry of Finance was particularly responsible for commenting on the draft legislation. If there was, it might, by analogy with the other three bodies, have been the Minister (V. Garbuzov) or the Deputy Minister (I. Guzhkov). The latter in particular has revealed himself to be less than enthusiastic about the *ob"edineniya* (see his paper in Bachurin, *Sovershenstvovanie* . . . , pp. 263-275, esp. p. 275).

15. "Postanovlenie . . . O nekotorykh meropriyatiyakh . . . ," para. 9.

16. It is noteworthy that three of the four original "ratifying bodies" were included in this list. The State Committee for Prices, however, was not. One possible explanation for this is that Sitnin had proved to be less prepared than Bachurin and Sukharevskii to reach a compromise with the Ministry of Finance. If this were the case, the fact that the latter was included on the newer list of bodies might indicate its greater influence in comparison with the State Committee for Prices. But this must remain speculation.

17. Vanneman shows that the decree (*postanovlenie*) often emanates from the Council of Ministers, while the statute (*polozhenie*) is not normally passed by any of the Supreme Soviet organs. Moreover, the Supreme Soviet commissions draft only laws (*zakony*), so that one would not expect there to have been such a body for the legislation being considered here. See Vanneman, *The Supreme Soviet*, passim, esp. pp. 52-59, 119-150.

18. On all this, see W. Berger and O. Reinhold, *Zu den Wissenschaftlichen Grundlagen des Neuen Oekonomischen Systems der Planung und Leitung* (Berlin: Dietz Verlag, 1966), esp. pp. 23-26; H. Beyer and H. Kanzig, "Die Genesis des neuen oekonomischen Systems in der Zeit vom VI. Parteitag der SED bis zur Wirtschaftskonferenz," *Wirts/wiss.*, No. 12, 1969, pp. 1761-1784; and Neugebauer, *Partei und* . . . , pp. 71-86.

19. Referred to in "Richtlinie . . . ," p. 32.

20. Beyer and Kanzig, "Die Genesis . . . ," p. 1769, and Neugebauer, *Partei und* . . . , pp. 73-74.

21. "Entwurf . . . ," p. 1.

22. Ulbricht, *Das Neue* . . . , p. 6, and Such, *VVB und* . . . , p. 9.

23. Neugebauer, *Partei und* . . . , p. 78.

24. "Entwurf . . . ," p. 1.

25. See (no title) *Die Wirts.*, No. 18, 1967, p. 12, and, for examples of articles still appearing, those by W. Horster and W. Beyer ("Gestoerte Kooperationsketten erfordern das Eingreifen der VVB"), K. Meissner ("Von objektiven Interessen der VVB ausgehen"), and H. Herold ("Die Aufgabenabgrenzung zwischen VVB and VEB gruendlich beraten"), *ibid.*, pp. 12-13.

26. Mittag, "Aus dem Bericht . . . an die 3. Tagung . . . ," p. 5.

27. W. Halbritter, "Hinweise und Empfehlungen zur Durchsetzung der Beschluesse zur Verwirklichung des oekonomischen Systems des Sozialismus in den volkseigenen Kombinaten 1969/70," *Die Wirts.*, No. 51/52, 1969, Beilage 2, pp. 1-12.

28. *Ibid.*, pp. 1-2.

29. *Ibid.*, p. 1.

30. See the "Auskuenfte" in *VS*, No. 10, 1967, p. 577, and an article by a member of the group at the beginning of 1968 (A. Richter, "Gestaltung der Erzeugnisgruppenarbeit mittels Wirtschaftsvertrag," *VS*, No. 1, 1968, pp. 5-11).

31. The interconnection of this legislation can be inferred from the fact that it was all published in one volume in 1974; see *Gesetz ueber den Ministerrat – Gesetz ueber die oertlichen Volksvertretungen und ihre Organe – Verordnung ueber die Aufgaben,*

Rechte und Pflichten der VEB, Kombinat und VVB (Berlin: Staatsverlag der Deutschen Demokratischen Republik, 1974). There are two reasons for inferring that this group was disbanded in mid-1972. First, it had jointly coedited the journal *Wirtschaftsrecht* since the latter's establishment in 1970, yet no reference to it was made in the editorial details from issue No. 4, 1972, on. Second, articles by erstwhile members of the group that were published in late 1972 and 1973 give details of the author's current post, and in no case refer to the working party (in contrast to the situation when the group existed). The disbandment, like that of Halbritter's group, was no doubt part of the new East German leadership's intention to end the Economic System of Socialism. Another symbol of this was Halbritter's removal from the Politburo in October 1973. It should, however, be pointed out that while some Western commentators interpreted Halbritter's fall in essentially the same way as we do here, others accepted his formal resignation at face value; compare K. Fricke, "DDR-Fuehrung neu formiert," *D.A.*, No. 10, 1973, p. 1010, and F. Oldenburg, "Ost-Berlin wieder auf haerteren Kurs. Zur 10. Tagung des ZK der SED." *D.A.*, No. 11, 1973, pp. 1121-1122.

32. See, for example, H. Boettcher, "Erfahrungen bei der Durchfuehrung von monatlichen Rechenschaftslegungen der Direktoren der volkseigenen Betriebe und Kombinate vor den Werktaetigen," *WR*, No. 3, 1971, pp. 134-139; the series of articles on different dimensions of the combines by K. Heuer, A. Panzer, M. Sauer, and B. Willma in *WR*, No. 4, 1970, pp. 206-221; and the series on economic law beginning with C. J. Kreutzer, "Zu einigen Fragen der Entwicklung des sozialistischen Wirtschaftsrechts," *Die Wirts.*, No. 13, 1969, pp. 16-17 (the series includes articles by K. Heuer in No. 14, p. 18, and S. Bergmann in No. 19, p. 14).

33. Supranowitz appears to have replaced Spitzner on the latter's death; see the references in *WR*, No. 1, 1970, p. 1, and No. 11, 1970, p. 661.

34. Details are in M. Wedler, "Bildung des Rates fuer wirtschaftsrechtswissenschaftliche Forschung der DDR," *VS*, No. 8, 1969, pp. 458-459.

35. See G. Klinger, "Zur Entwicklung des sozialistischen Rechts seit dem VIII. Parteitag der SED und Tendenzen der kuenftigen Rechtsentwicklung," *WR*, No. 3, 1974, p. 121, and U-J. Heuer, "Verfassung fuer den Sozialismus," *VS*, No. 6, 1968, p. 302.

36. (Unsigned), "Ministerrat beriet Verordnung ueber Aufgaben der Kombinate und Betriebe," *Die Wirts.*, No. 9, 1973, p. 10.

37. "Polozhenie o sotsialisticheskom . . . ," para. 10.

38. "Postanovlenie . . . 'O Nekotorykh . . . ," para. 4.

39. *Ibid.*, para. 4.

40. "Polozhenie o Proizvodstvennom . . . ," para. 6.

41. The term was used by S. N. Bratus'; see "Pravovoe polozhenie . . . ," p. 62.

42. "Postanovlenie . . . 'O Nekotorykh . . . ," para. 4, and "Polozhenie o Proizvodstvennom . . . ," para. 11.

43. "Postanovlenie . . . 'O Nekotorykh . . . ," para. 4.

44. "Polozhenie o Proizvodstvennom . . . ," para. 11.

45. *Ibid.*, paras. 124, 125.

46. *Ibid.*, para. 10, See too note 71 below.

47. "Postanovlenie . . . 'O Nekotorykh . . . ," paras. 2, 15.

48. *Ibid.*, para. 2.

49. "Postanovlenie . . . 'O Nekotorykh . . . ," para. 19; "Postanovlenie Soveta Ministrov SSSR 27 marta 1974 g. 'Ob Utverzhdenii Polozheniya o Proizvodstvennom Ob"edinenii (Kombinate),' " in *Resheniya . . .* , Vol. 10, pp. 136-138, para. 2; and "Polozhenie o Proizvodstvennom . . . ," para. 5.

50. "Postanovlenie . . . 'O Nekotorykh . . . ," para. 6; see too note 51 and accompanying text.
51. "Polozhenie o Proizvodstvennom . . . ," para. 17.
52. See Ch. 1, note 111.
53. See, for example, "Richtlinie . . . ," p. 36.
54. "Entwurf . . . ," para. 1.
55. "Verordnung ueber die VEB . . . ," para. 34.
56. On this see Lieser-Triebnigg, "Ein Neues Organisationsrecht . . . ," esp. p. 832.
57. "Verordnung ueber die Bildung . . . ," para. 7.
58. "Verordnung ueber die VEB . . . ," para. 24. In the November 1979 legislation, the combine is defined as "a basic economic unit of material production," so that there is once again more confusion between the combine and the enterprise. This is particularly obvious from the fact that the combine is defined as consisting of "combine enterprises or enterprise parts"; the combine enterprise is enigmatically defined as "an economically and legally autonomous unit within the framework of its position in the reproduction and management process of the combine." For details on all this, see "Verordnung ueber die volkseigenen Kombinate . . . ," paras. 1, 6. For a thorough Western analysis of the legislation and its background, see K. Erdmann and M. Melzer, "Die Neue Kombinatsverordnung in der DDR," Pt. 1, *D.A.*, No. 9, 1980, pp. 929-942, and Pt. 2, *ibid.*, No. 10, 1980, pp. 1046-1062.
59. "Verordnung ueber die Bildung . . . ," para. 7.
60. *Ibid.*, para. 14.
61. *Ibid.*, section 2 (esp. para. 10) and para. 14.
62. "Beschluss ueber die Verwirklichung . . . ," para. 3.
63. *Ibid.*, para. 3.
64. "Beschluss zur weiteren . . . ," and Heuer, "Die planmaessige . . . ," p. 207.
65. "Beschluss zur weiteren . . . ," para. 4.
66. Heuer, "Die planmaessige . . . ," pp. 207-210.
67. "Verordnung ueber die VEB . . . ," para. 24.
68. *Ibid.*, para. 25.
69. *Ibid.*, para. 30.
70. Schroeter, "Kombinate . . . ," p. 27.
71. "Verordnung ueber die VEB . . . ," para. 25.
72. Lieser-Triebnigg, "Ein neues Organisationsrecht . . . ," p. 825. Although on p. 826 Lieser-Triebnigg argues that the East Germans have an essentially three-tier system, this is based purely on inference and the study of practice.
73. "Verordnung ueber die Bildung . . . ," para. 1. The "Verordnung ueber das Verfahren . . . ," is concerned only with the legal mechanics of establishing combines, not the question of when one should be created.
74. "Beschluss ueber die Verwirklichung . . . ," para. 1.
75. "Verordnung ueber die VEB . . . ," para. 27.
76. *Ibid.*, para. 27.
77. "Beschluss ueber die Verwirklichung . . . ," para. 2.
78. "Verordnung ueber die VEB . . . ," para. 29.
79. This emerges from a comparison of the final parts of the various pieces of East German and Soviet legislation referred to in this study. It should be noted that Soviet practice has improved in this respect in recent years.
80. One early symbol of this was the issuance of the decree "Postanovlenie TsK KPSS i Soveta Ministrov SSSR 23 dekabrya 1970 g. 'Ob uluchshenii pravovoi

raboty v narodnom khozyaistve,' " to be found in *Resheniya* . . . , Vol. 8, pp. 277-281; especially important are paras. 7-10, in which there is a call for codification and better publicity of economic legislation over the coming years. Nevertheless, even after the issuance of all the legislation on the associations, there was still dissatisfaction among Soviet writers with the existing state of economic law; see V. Terebilov, "Ekonomika i Pravo," *Pravda*, 28 June 1974, p. 2, and V. V. Laptev, "Ekonomika i Pravo," *Sots. Ind.*, 9 October 1975, p. 2. Of course, the existence of a large number of bodies can be dysfunctional (because of confusion over responsibilities and so on), but this does not appear to have pertained to the East German case.

81. It should by now be clear that even some members of the senior party bodies in the GDR can be classified as "specialists."

Chapter 6

IMPLEMENTATION

The present chapter is relatively short, since some aspects of the development of associations were considered in Chapter 1. Nevertheless, if we examine the progress from a number of different angles, it emerges that implementation has been more problematic than mere numbers will reveal, especially in the USSR. These various approaches can be subsumed under two headings: the pace of development and the quality of development.

6.1. IMPLEMENTATION IN THE USSR

One way of considering how successful implementation has been is to examine the extent to which targets/deadlines have been met. Although most *general* policy statements on the Soviet associations have been vague in terms of target dates, this is not true of the 1973 decree. This contained several deadlines, many of which have been repeatedly extended in much the same way as they were following the announcement of the Economic Reform in 1965.

According to the decree, all branch ministries were to have introduced a predominantly two- or three-tier administrative structure between 1973 and 1975.[1] The first step of such a change was to have been the compilation by each ministry of a "general scheme of management," outlining the proposed arrangement. These schemes were to have been produced by early September 1973 and based on a guideline issued by *Gosplan* in April 1973.[2] Once produced, they were to have been considered by the Council of Ministers, following whose approval the schemes would be realized. In practice, only three of over thirty all-union and union-republic schemes had been approved by September 1974, a figure that had climbed to eight by May 1975.[3] By February 1976, all industrial ministries had submitted their schemes, and "the majority" had been confirmed.[4] But as late as the spring of 1977 the general schemes of some ministries were still being worked on, largely because the Council of Ministers had rejected the original proposals.[5] Seemingly, the process was not completed until 1979 — at least four years past the deadline.[6]

Some writers had by 1975 started referring to two separate processes in the restructuring of industry: the "general schemes" and, based on these, the "projects" for creating new associations.[7] This two-stage approach was not inherent in the original legislation, and can be seen to represent an attempt to make delays less obvious. Moreover, the fact that discussions of "good" approved schemes in the mid-1970s were usually of the arrangements in the coal and oil branches, is another manifestation of an attempt to cover up slow implementation.[8] The irony of citing these branches is that they had started transferring to something very akin to the new arrangement at the beginning of the 1970s (*before* the 1973 legislation).

Having said all this, an important point needs to be made. Although the implementation of the 1973 legislation has taken much longer than anticipated, the central authorities do now seem to be taking the question of industrial administration far more seriously and possibly more soberly than the imminent deadlines contained in the 1973 legislation might suggest. Thus, the tenth five-year plan (1976-1980) was the first to include a section specifically devoted to administrative changes that were to be introduced within the quinquennium.[9] Unfortunately, though, it still looks highly unlikely that the targets of completing the restructuring of industry by the end of 1980 and of having three-quarters of industrial production from a projected 5300 production *ob"edineniya* by that date will be met.[10] Although no figures on the *ob"edineniya* were given in the Prime Minister's report on the economy at the 26th Congress (February 1981) — itself an ominous sign — it was explicitly stated that the transfer to the two- and three-tier system of industrial administration was still being implemented (see N. A. Tikhonov's speech in *Pravda*, 28 February 1981, p. 4). It is interesting that speakers from whom one has come to expect positive comments on and advocacy of the *ob"edineniya*, such as Romanov, made no meaningful statements on them at the 26th Congress (see *Pravda*, 25 February 1981, p. 2, for Romanov's speech).

Another way we can see that the development of *ob"edineniya* progressed less rapidly and satisfactorily than many Soviets would have liked is in the presentation of figures on the growth of these bodies. It was shown in Chapter 1 that sources differ on the number of associations, the greatest discrepancy being between the figures of Gromov and Kamenetskii, on the one hand, and Kuznetsov and Tikhomirova, on the other, for the year 1966. Some of these differences are due simply to different classifications of associations (i.e., writers

Implementation

often disagreed on what should and should not be considered an association). Thise particularly pertains to the period before the 1973-1974 legislation. For instance, the inclusion by some writers of "amalgamated enterprises" under "*ob"edineniya*" was not acceptable to others, which clearly would lead to differing figures.[11] Others probably reflect the differences between the number of associations actually established at a given date and the number envisaged for that date. It is known, for example, that the all-union *sovnarkhoz* had anticipated a total of nearly 900 *firmy* by the end of 1964, whereas the number actually created by then was well below this figure.[12] It is not clear that there are "political" explanations for all the above cases, in the sense of writers consciously trying to exaggerate or play down the growth in numbers of associations in order to strengthen their argument. But there are instances where such motivations can scarcely be doubted, and we would argue that such overt attempts either to cover up difficulties or to make the growth in numbers look more impressive reflect, on one level, the awareness of some degree of failure. Perhaps the best example of the glossing over of development problems is the histogram that appeared in *Ekonomicheskaya Gazeta* in September 1972. This gave the impression that there had been constantly positive growth in the numbers of *ob"edineniya* since 1964, whereas many more associations were disbanded than created in the period 1965-1969 (i.e., there was negative growth).[13] Thus, according to data from the Central Statistical Office, 180 *ob"edineniya* were created and 270 disbanded in the period 1965-1969; of the latter, 240 disappeared between 1966 and 1969.[14] A further breakdown is not possible, although one source states that only 25 *ob"edineniya* were created in 1967 and only 29 in 1969.[15] Although the problem of differing definitions of the associations once again arises here, the *general* picture was summarized by one writer as follows:

> *Firmy* sprung up like mushrooms after the rain and, just like mushrooms, suddenly disappeared.[16]

Although there are numerous examples of distortion of the kind cited above, it should be pointed out that not all Soviet writers have been prepared to accept such misleading figures. In 1974, for instance, Markin criticized the fact that much of the economic literature on *ob"edineniya* either had not considered the reasons for the decline in numbers or had portrayed it incorrectly in order to imply that associations had developed better under the ministries than under the *sovnarkhozy*, which he disputed.[17]

In addition, the 1974 decree by which the 1974 statute was formally adopted stipulated that many large enterprises should be granted the rights of production associations. Presumably this meant they were also classified as the latter for statistical purposes.[18] Given this, and the fact that data on "production associations" since 1975 usually include the science-production associations, most if not all of the statistics available on sales, proportion of industrial output, and so forth since 1973, and even more so since 1975, are more impressive than they would be had only production associations proper been included.

The situation regarding numbers of industrial associations is also difficult to assess. There is always the problem of distinguishing industrial from production associations in the period before 1973. Since then, it is not clear how many industrial associations either the senior leadership or the advocates of a very streamlined industrial administration would like to see. All we can say is that if industrial associations are primarily considered as replacements for *glavki*, then we would expect the optimal number of the former to be considerably less than the latter. Certainly, advocates of the association policy have praised ministries that have drastically reduced their number of middle-link organizations; Drogichinskii did so in an important article published in 1975, for instance. According to this, the coal industry now had 7 as opposed to its former 56 middle-tier bodies, while the corresponding figures for the oil industry were 8 instead of 42, and for the gas industry 16 instead of 35.[19] However, these appear to have been the best ministries from this point of view. Thus, the Ministry of Tractor and Agricultural Machine Manufacture was criticized for retaining the same number of middle-tier bodies as before; and, according to Drogichinskii, even ministries adhering closely to the 1973 legislation in terms of the creation of primary-link production associations were trying to retain the same number of middle-tier bodies as before.[20] If we can thus assume that there should be considerably fewer industrial associations than there were *glavki*, a report on the structure of Soviet industry that appeared a few months before the 1973 decree is instructive. According to this report, there were over 280 *glavki* under the all-union ministries and *vedomstva* and approximately 400 *glavki* under the union-republic ministries of the union republics, while the republic ministries included "hundreds" of *glavki*.[21] From this we can only infer that there should be less than 280 industrial associations under central ministries, and so on. Since the "nearly five hundred" that existed in June 1977 included both all-union and republic, it seems that the numbers had become reasonably satisfactory in the two years since Drogichinskii wrote, a point borne out by a 1980 Soviet article.[22] But even if the figures are satisfactory, it should not be forgotten either that the original deadline for introducing new administrative arrangements was 1975, or that numbers in themselves by no means reveal all aspects of the success of implementation.

Let us return for the present to a consideration of the production associations, as far as possible. If it were the case that, while the growth rate in absolute numbers slowed down from 1965 at least until the early 1970s, the *average size* of such an association had increased considerably, then the total number could give a misleading impression. In fact, the average size of a production association in terms of numbers of component units *decreased* in the period 1964-1974. Thus, it was revealed at the 1975 conference that the average *ob"edinenie* comprised 4.6 component units on January 1, 1964, while the corresponding figure for July 1, 1974 was 3.9.[23] Margaret Miller has calculated that the average size in the middle of 1963 was 6 units, showing an even greater decline.[24] Furthermore, the average *ob"edinenie* in certain branches of industry in the mid-1970s (e.g., chemical engineering, tractor-building) consisted of only two factories.[25]

Yet this still does not tell us everything, since the average size of component units might have grown considerably over the period. It has not been possible to obtain a clear picture on this. However, as late as May 1974, over one-half of the 50,000 or so Soviet industrial enterprises were small, employing less than 200 people.[26] Given this statistic, the fact that at that time approximately 12 percent of factories were in production associations is not very impressive, even though this figure had risen from 5.5 percent in 1971;[27] that this percentage is very modest becomes more obvious when it is recalled that the majority of supporters of the associations consider them to be most beneficial when they link small and medium-sized units.

Thus, the growth of production *ob"edineniya* has been slow. The growth of industrial associations has also been slow if we consider that experimentation began in the mid-1960s, although it does look as if the situation regarding these less-integrated associations has improved markedly since 1973. Nevertheless, association policy has been implemented sufficiently slowly to prompt Brezhnev to express his dissatisfaction at the 25th Congress.[28]

Turning now from the pace to the quality of implementation, the picture becomes even less satisfactory. There is evidence, for instance, that some production *ob"edineniya* are so in name only. One example of this is the Belorussia Tractor Association. According to a report by the director of one of the component units of this association, there was at the time of writing no real difference in the relationship between the various factories in the *ob"edinenie* as compared with the situation before the *ob"edinenie* was formed.[29]

Another point is that some so-called associations are so small that one wonders how they could possibly be considered as qualitatively in the same class as giant organizations employing tens of thousands of people. Markin, for example, referred to seven *ob"edineniya* in Novosibirsk that employed between 40 and 63 people each,[30] and as late as 1975 almost 14 percent of *ob"edineniya* employed less than 500 workers.[31] On the other hand, despite the claims that large associations are very beneficial, some have experienced severe problems of coordination;[32] this is not surprising when it is borne in mind that some production *ob"edineniya* employ over 100,000 workers.[33]

Various more specific problems of implementation have also arisen within the production *ob"edineniya*. One example is that of the internal accounting systems. A late-1970s survey of 21 production associations and large enterprises in the automobile industry revealed that the indicators of the internal profit-and-loss system (the system operating between the component units) did not accord with the indicators of the basic *khozraschet* links in all but three of them.[34]

It is not only the production associations that have sometimes failed to match the claims made for them by their advocates; the industrial associations, too, have not always adhered to the spirit of the administrative reform. For instance, almost eight years after it had been transferred to the new economic methods, Sigma still had the same administrative structure as when it had been established.[35] Another aspect is that, although the 1973 legislation is quite clear that "nearer to production" means that the industrial associations should physically be located nearer to the enterprises they administer than the *glavki* had been, many industrial associations are in fact situated in the same location as their predecessors. The "new" industrial associations of the Ministry of Tractor and Agricultural Machine Manufacture, for instance, are located in the same offices in the ministry building in Moscow as the *glavki* they replaced — despite the fact that no tractors are produced in the capital — and are headed by the same people.[36]

While some industrial associations are criticized for being mirror images of the *glavki*, others are accused of actually having worsened the situation in industrial administration. Among the charges leveled against industrial associations in comparison with the *glavki* is that they have increased the size of their administrative apparatus and/or, contrary to stipulations in the 1973 legislation, have become even less involved in the technical development and administrative restructuring of their branches.[37]

There have also been criticisms of the practice of some industrial *ob"edineniya* of dealing directly with the component units of a production association, when they should be working only through the latter.[38]

Finally, there have been charges that particular industrial associations should never have been established in the first place, since production *ob"edineniya* would have been more appropriate.[39]

The problems of implementation have been most thoroughly investigated in the reports on association development commissioned by the State Committee for Science and Technology. In line with a requirement of the 1973 decree on administration, this State Committee established 17 study-groups in 1973.[40] These groups consisted of representatives from central *vedomstva* and ministries (including the Ministry of Finance and *Gosplan*), the USSR Academy of Sciences, *ob"edineniya* themselves, and so forth. They made a detailed study of 78 *ob"edineniya* (primarily production, but including some industrial) in late 1973 and early 1974. *Ob"edineniya* that were "typical" of various branches were selected for the investigation; in practice this meant that the study concentrated on both the biggest (these 78 accounted for over 15 percent of production sold by associations) and the best (well-established *ob"edineniya*, most of which had already been functioning for at least three years and which accounted for 44.6 percent of the profit from Soviet associations).[41] In choosing primarily the best associations, it is not surprising that many of the results of the study were impressive. In most of the associations, labor productivity and profitability were above the average for the branch, although in the timber- and wood-processing branch they were actually below.[42] The length of time needed for introducing the results of scientific research into production was in some cases reduced by one and one-half to two times, and the quality of production also improved.[43] Nevertheless, many disappointing results also emerged from the study. In 31 percent of the *ob"edineniya*, the proportion of specialized products had declined in comparison with the preassociation situation.[44] The number of auxiliary services was actually increasing in the majority of the associations. The anticipated improvement in administration — which appears to have been the major reason for the Central Committee's interest in the *ob"edineniya* at their December 1969 plenum — had not materialized. Thus, in 54 percent of the associations, the administrative structure remained essentially the same in comparison with the preassociation situation, while in 26 percent it became more complex. Although the number of administrative personnel did decline in a majority of associations, in no less than 43 percent the proportion of administrative staff to total work force increased.[45] Finally, the investigation revealed a high correlation between the territorial proximity of subordinate units to the head unit and legal/economic autonomy; the further a subordinate was from the center of the association, the more likely it was to enjoy a high level of independence.[46] It should be noted here parenthetically that practice since the investigation shows that the tendency to include autonomous enterprises in production associations probably increased in the mid-1970s. In 1974, 60 percent of the units in all production *ob"edineniya* retained their legal autonomy, a proportion that may have risen by 1977; even by 1980, 45 percent of enterprises in production *ob"edineniya* were still autonomous.[47] These figures — certainly those of the mid-1970s — probably compare quite unfavorably with the position in April 1964, when all of the enterprises/units in almost 60 percent of the *firmy* and some units in another 14 percent had forfeited their legal and considerable economic autonomy.[48] Unless the remaining 26+ percent were highly atypical, in the sense of incorporating a considerably higher mean average number of enterprises than the mean average in all *ob"edineniya*, it seems probable that the overall proportion of autonomous units in associations was lower in 1964 than in 1975.

In sum, the results of the official study of associations were far from satisfactory. When it is remembered that the study considered primarily the best associations, it may be inferred that the overall picture of association advantageousness is even less convincing. To some extent, this might be the result of "teething" problems (although the study itself concentrated on well-established associations), a function of branch differences (i.e., associations of differing types and scales being appropriate to different branches, and the optimality of such matching not yet being fully understood), and the result of poor preparatory work. Let us now briefly consider each of these in turn.

Regarding so-called teething problems, the fact that the associations (production at least) have been in existence since 1961, and that they have operated under the ministerial system since 1965, would suggest that problems still present are not merely the result of difficulties peculiar to the early stages of development. The decree and statute of 1973 and 1974, respectively, have theoretically ironed out some of these early problems (e.g., on the question of salaries; see Chapter 7), but there are still, as has been shown, sufficient loopholes for there to be difficulties in the associations for an indeterminate time to come. It is thus hardly surprising that there have been calls since 1973-1974 for modification of the legislation.[49]

On the question of branch differences, it was recognized almost from the beginning of the current generation of production associations that particular types were more appropriate to some branches than others;[50] indeed, it is precisely the acknowledgment of differences between branches that leads many Soviets to argue that a basically two-tier structure is appropriate for some ministries, while a three-tier arrangement is better for others. Nevertheless, it is evident from the study of different regions, towns, and the like that some form of amalgamation can be useful in virtually any branch if the officials forming it are sufficiently committed to the idea. Thus, areas such as the Ukraine and Leningrad have formed associations in most branches, whereas in an area of indifference or hostility (Uzbekistan on occasions in the laat fifteen or so years), the associations will not develop in many branches at all.[51]

Finally, there have been charges on various occasions since 1961 that the formation of particular *ob"edineniya* (primarily production) has not been preceded by sufficiently detailed preparation.[52] In fact, while a universally applicable answer to this charge is not available, we do know that two regions about which such criticisms were made (L'vov and Leningrad) did, in fact, produce highly detailed analyses of the criteria for creating associations.[53] It might be the case that such analyses did not, in the event, foresee every problem that might arise — indeed, it would be difficult to accept that this would be possible anyway[54] — but it is not true that the formation of associations in these regions was anywhere near as spontaneous and haphazard as some critics maintain.

In the case of the industrial *ob"edineniya* there was considerable, monitored experimentation prior to the 1973 legislation. The reader will recall that experiments in *Minpribor* had been suggested and implemented in the late 1960s; this was the first time since 1936 that the economic rights and responsibilities of the *glavki* had been revised, and the results were impressive.[55] The experiment reached a watershed in the early 1970s. In March 1970, the ministry itself transferred to profit-and-loss accounting, and one of its *glavki* became an all-union *ob"edinenie* (Soyuzchasprom). At the beginning of 1971, all of the ministry's *glavki* were transformed into "all-union state profit-and-loss industrial associations," and a three-tier structure (i.e., ministry-industrial *ob"edinenie*-enterprise) was implemented throughout the branch.[56]

Although *Minpribor* was the first ministry to experiment with all aspects of the post-1973 industrial administrative structure, it was not the only one to convert to the three-tier system or industrial associations. Thus, in line with the May 1970 decrees, the chemical, oil, and coal industries transferred to a three-link arrangement. In the case of the latter two branches, the middle tier was to be the production *ob"edinenie* or combine, and is therefore of marginal interest at this point.[57] The middle tier of the new all-union chemical branch, however, was not the production but the "all-union state industrial profit-and-loss *ob"edinenie*";[58] the Ukrainian Ministry of the Chemical Industry had abolished its *glavki* already in 1968, but for the next two years or so its middle tier was called the "production" rather than the "industrial" *ob"edinenie*.[59] Given the 1970 change of title and the fact that the legislation on the chemical industry appeared on the same day as that for the oil and coal industries, it is safe to assume that the legislators, at least, were by this time aware of the differences between what are now called the production *ob"edineniya* and the industrial *ob"edineniya*. This is further suggested by the fact that, although there is no detail whatever on either the production associations in the oil industry or the combines in the coal industry, there is considerable detail on the tasks of the new chemical industrial associations, again indicating the newness of these bodies.[60] Thus, at least two ministries had industrial associations in the sense of *glavk* replacements by 1973, when the general legislation for the whole of industry appeared, and others (including those for automobiles and timber) had experimented with a three-tier arrangement.[61] Moreover, most if not all of the experiments were closely monitored by an interdepartmental commission within *Gosplan*, which was established to evaluate experiments with both main types of *ob"edinenie*. In the case of the industrial associations, for example, this commission was charged with studying the experiment being conducted by *Minpribor*. The report on this was published in the middle of 1972, and was followed by many calls in the press for the transfer of more branches of industry to this arrangement.[62] There were also many reports on the innovations in the other branches mentioned, so that experiments were well publicized.[63]

In sum, the three reasons given above do not adequately explain the relatively poor implementation of Soviet association policy.

6.2. IMPLEMENTATION IN THE GDR

Once again, there is much less information on the GDR than on the USSR; if certain points made about Soviet implementation are not dealt with here, it is due to lack of data.

The East Germans appear to have been more successful than the Soviets in adhering to deadlines. For example, all VVBs transferred to some form of profit-and-loss accounting at the beginning of 1964, and many combines were set up quickly in the late 1960s.[64] This is not to say there have been no delays at all; for instance, the merging of the three VVBs of the lignite industry into one at the beginning of 1969 was several months behind schedule.[65] Moreover, within two years of the New Economic System's introduction, the original idea that "profit is the decisive criterion for judging the economic achievement of the VVB" had to be temporarily abandoned; several price reforms had not been completed, so that some VVBs, through no fault of their own, appeared to be functioning inefficiently, while others fared exceptionally well.[66] Therefore, until a price reform was completed in 1967 there were no profit-linked indicators for assessing the VVBs and their enterprises. But such delays have not been as long or as serious as comparable ones in the USSR, as far as we can tell. Having said this, an important point must be made. This is that the East Germans have not attempted such comprehensive, simultaneous change as the Soviets did in 1973. Although the East Germans have frequently included dates in legislation, these usually specify when a decree or like legislation becomes operative, which seems to be a less ambitious exercise than specifying a date by which organizations affected by legislation must themselves produce a relatively complex document such as a "general scheme of management."

In contrast to the situation in the USSR, there do not appear to have been differences in the GDR over the numbers of VVBs and combines. This is to some extent because East Germans do not seem to have had any basic disagreements on what either of these terms meant. However, it is also partially because the negative growth in numbers of production *ob"edineniya* in the latter half of the 1960s was not reflected in East German combine development, so that no attempt at presenting misleading information was considered necessary. Although there has been a decline in the number of VVBs since the late 1960s, this is in line with official policy (i.e., VVBs have usually been replaced by combines) — once again, no attempt to hide negative growth seemed appropriate.

As with Soviet statistics, the total number of VVBs and combines does not in itself reveal very much. Another quantitative way of examining their growing or declining significance is to consider their average size in terms of the number of subordinate units. In 1964 there were 80 industrial VVBs, with 1700 centrally administered enterprises directly subordinate to them; the mean size of a VVB was thus 21.25 units.[67] In 1966, 1576 centrally administered enterprises were under 82 VVBs, giving a mean average of 19.2 units.[68] Since we have been unable to distinguish between enterprises subordinate to combines with the status of a VVB and to actual VVBs since the end of the 1960s, no mean can be estimated for the period since then. Nor can we say how large the spread was about the computed mean in the mid-1960s. In other words, the data do not reveal very much. Moreover, data on the combines are even scarcer. We have discovered only two sources giving the average size of a combine: In 1976 the average combine (all types) had 7-10 enterprises and 25-30 nonautonomous subdivisions (*Betriebsteile*, or enterprise parts, and *Produktionsstaette*); in 1978 combines directly under ministries averaged just over 10 enterprises, whereas combines subordinate to VVBs had an average of almost 5 enterprises.[69] As in the USSR, some combines are relatively small in terms of the size of the work force. But although we know some combines are as small as 400 workers,[70] we have found no references to combines as small as the Novosibirsk ones mentioned earlier; the mean average number of workers in a combine directly subordinate to a ministry was over 2000 in 1974.[71] We have no details on changes in the average size of component units over time, although the East Germans — if not quite as often as the Soviets — are frequently critical of the fact that there are so many relatively small enterprises in their economy.[72]

In terms of the quality of implementation, the East Germans again appear to have experienced fewer difficulties. It was noted earlier that the VVBs really have been located "near to production," for instance. We have found no references to combines being so in name only, unlike some of the Soviet production associations, although at least one ministry seems to have considered planning by the combine to be of essentially the same nature as earlier planning by the VVB (that is, it could perceive no real difference between the two types of association on an important variable).[73] We have also discovered no detailed analysis of the East German associations revealing all the problems that the big Soviet study did. This might simply be because the East Germans are less willing than the Soviets publicly to discuss their difficulties. On the other hand, it should be noted that although the late 1960s were economically problematic for the GDR, the 1971-1975 plan period was the best ever. Thus, if research on the combines had not commenced by 1970-1971, the subsequent impressive economic performance — in addition to low leadership interest in these bodies — would hardly have prompted study of "problems" in the period considered here.

Implementation

The reader should not gain the impression that there have been no drawbacks in East German association development, however. The most obvious sign that there were indeed difficulties with the VVBs was Ulbricht's interest in the combines in 1967, as well as the development of the late 1970s. There have also been many criticisms of specific VVBs for underfulfilling their plans.[74] And although all the VVBs introduced some dimensions of profit-and-loss accounting in 1964, between one-fifth and one-quarter of them were still not operating satisfactorily on the new system by the end of 1965.[75]

Turning now to a consideration of the combines, we find complaints of bureaucratism in some of these bodies, a few of which have tried to increase rather than decrease the number of administrative tiers, for instance.[76] While some combines appear to have been very successful in becoming closely involved in the foreign sales of their products, others have been criticized for making insufficient use of their rights as commissioning agents of foreign-trade enterprises.[77] Not all combines have had a good record on plan fulfillment; indeed, one was criticized for treating models made for improving its work with contempt (seeing them as "platonic futuristic music") and, allegedly as a result, not fulfilling its plan.[78] Finally, Honecker did state at the 8th Congress in 1971 that there had been problems in establishing the combines, although the point was not made forcefully or at length;[79] nor have there been many important criticisms since then.

In sum, East German implementation has not been without problems, but these seem to have been less than those in the USSR. It could be objected that, since the East Germans modified laws so rapidly in the late 1960s, they clearly had many more problems in implementing association policy than are revealed in the available literature. This might be the case, but even if it were, the very fact that corrections were made so relatively rapidly suggests that the East Germans have coped better with difficulties.

But why have such problems as there have been arisen? It would be difficult to argue that the East Germans have approached association development in a disorganized way, which might have provided one explanation. Thus, before all the VVBs were transferred to the methods of the New Economic System, a well-publicized experiment had already been conducted in four VVBs (those for mining and conveying equipment; office equipment; foodstuffs, luxury items, and packing machines or *Nagema*; and woolen wear and hosiery).[80] This experiment started at the beginning of 1963 and did not proceed without problems. For example, the woolen wear and hosiery VVB experienced difficulties in taking over balancing functions from central organs, while the office equipment VVB encountered various problems in attempting to transfer to a new form of export contract.[81] But this is precisely what experimentation is intended to highlight, and the rapid evaluation of new methods and the broad publicity given to the findings meant that when the other VVBs were transferred to the new system at the beginning of 1964 they did already have a body of vicarious experience from which to draw. Similarly, a decision to extend the foreign-trade rights of the VVBs was preceded by a well-publicized experiment in the shipbuilding VVB.[82] Although this particular attempt greatly to increase the VVBs' responsibility does not appear to have progressed very far — itself a sign of problems — the groundwork had been laid and analysis made.[83]

The situation regarding experiments in the combines is somewhat different from that pertaining to the VVBs. Certainly there was experimentation with selected dimensions of combine work — notably in the field of foreign trade in the latter half of the 1960s.[84] Important, detailed theoretical contributions concerning these bodies were also published.[85] And it will be recalled that the East German leaders had by the late summer of 1967 established a working party to study, inter alia, the combines; reports of the work of this group were fairly regular until the early 1970s.[86] Thus, although the type of experimentation that preceded the transfer of the VVBs to the New Economic System in the early to mid-1960s was not conducted for the combines, much analysis of their work and some experimentation on selected dimensions of their operating methods was undertaken. It would seem, therefore, that problems encountered were to some extent teething ones, and would be expected in the experimental period — although there are also other reasons yet to be considered.

6.3. CONCLUSIONS

In brief, the East German implementation appears from many angles to have been more successful than the Soviet. It would be difficult to explain this solely in terms of the factors mentioned in this chapter. While the East Germans were certainly faster than the Soviets in evaluating experiments, several other variables need to be brought into the equation. Once again, the most appropriate place for assessing these is in the concluding chapter. But before this, we need to consider in depth one other factor that has contributed to the differing success rates of policy implementation in the two states: opposition to the associations.

NOTES

1. "Postanovlenie . . . O Nekotorykh Meropriyatiyakh . . . ," para. 2.
2. *Ibid.*, para. 3. The guideline was published in May 1973 (see "Ukazaniya o poryadke razrabotki general'nykh skhem upravleniya otraslyami promyshlennosti," *Ekon. Gaz.*, No. 19, 1973, p. 8), and is summarized and elaborated upon in D. A. Allakhverdyan and E. N. Slastenko, *Metodologicheskie Osnovy Formirovaniya Ob"edinenii v Promyshlennosti* (Moscow: Izd. Ekonomika, 1974), pp. 45-49.
3. G. A. Dzhavadov, "Potentsial Ob"edinenii," *Pravda*, 18 September 1974, p. 2, and V. Selyunin, "General'nye skhemy otraslei," *Sots. Ind.*, 28 May 1975, p. 2.
4. N. Drogichinskii, "Kak razvivat'sya ob"edineniyam," *Pravda*, 7 February 1976, p. 3.
5. Kashirina, "Srednee Zveno," p. 2, and "Po General'nym Skhemam," *Pravda*, 14 March 1977, p. 1.
6. Nagovitsin, "Effektivnost' Vsesoyuznykh . . . ," passim.
7. N. Drogichinskii, "Proekty General'nykh Skhem Upravleniya Otraslevymi Sistemami," *Plan. Khoz.*, No. 5, 1975, pp. 6-17.
8. For example, G. A. Dzhavadov, "Po General'nym Skhemam," *Pravda*, 26 December 1975, p. 3. See too note 57 below.
9. Kapustin and Subotskii, "Problemy Razvitiya Ob"edinenii," p. 7.
10. Figure from S. Khavina and V. Gerasimova, "Burzhuaznye Ekonomisty ob Ob"edineniyakh v Sotsialisticheskoi Promyshlennosti," *Vop. Ekon.*, No. 4, 1978, p. 77.
11. This hypothesis is borne out by Rakitskii, *Formy* . . . , p. 36.
12. Andreev and Margolis, *Leningradskie Firmy*, p. 118 and Table 1.
13. "Upravlenie Proizvodstvom," p. 1.
14. R. E. Leshchiner in Gvishiani and Kamenitser, *Vtoraya Vsesoyuznaya . . . Sbornik 3*, p. 118; Sazontov, *Sotsial'no-Ekonomicheskie Problemy* . . . , p. 209.
15. Lagutkin, *Proizvodstvennye Ob"edineniya* . . . , p. 45.
16. A. Sabov, "Otkazalis' Ot Podpisi . . . ," *Komsomol'skaya Pravda*, 14 July 1971, p. 2. It is interesting to note that the deputy editor of *Ekonomicheskaya Gazeta* stated in a 1970 East German article that production *ob"edineniya* first emerged in the USSR five years earlier. Apart from giving the impression that the development of these bodies was thus directly related to the present Soviet leadership and their Economic Reform of 1965, such a statement would also to some extent mask the "rise and fall" pattern of *ob"edinenie* development in the 1960s. See V. Polyakov, "Produktionsvereinigungen — Die Konzentration in der sowjetischen Industrie," *Die Wirts.*, No. 6, 1970, p. 20.
17. Markin, *Effektivnost'* . . . , p. 38.
18. "Postanovlenie . . . 'Ob Utverzhdenii . . . ," para. 7.
19. Drogichinskii, "Proekty . . . ," p. 8.
20. *Ibid.*, pp. 8-9.
21. Subotskii, "Ob Otraslevoi . . . ," p. 24.
22. Nagovitsin, "Effektivnost' Vsesoyuznykh . . . ," p. 87.
23. Subotskii in Yu. V. Subotskii, K. I. Taksir et al., *Problemy Razvitiya Ob"edinenii v Promyshlennosti – Kratkie Tezisy Dokladov* (Moscow: Institut Ekonomiki AN SSSR, 1975), p. 41. Even by 1977, according to the official statistical annuals, the average production *ob"edinenie* still comprised only 4.5 units.

24. M. Miller, *Rise of the Russian Consumer* (London: Institute of Economic Affairs, 1965), p. 159.
25. Kapustin and Subotskii, "Problemy Razvitiya Ob"edinenii," p. 7. Moreover, many of the associations formed in *other* branches as part of the post-1973 "general schemes" were very small (two or three factories).
26. N. Drogichinskii, "General'naya Skhema Otrasli," *Pravda*, 31 May 1974, p. 3. As of 1976, over 20 percent of Soviet enterprises employed less than 500 workers, according to C. Horváth, "A vállalati nagyságról," *Közgazdasági Szemle*, No. 4, 1979, pp. 428-443; translated as "On the Size of the Firm," *Eastern European Economics*, No. 3, 1980, p. 45. However, the latter figure is open to some doubt.
27. Taksir, *Upravlenie* . . . , p. 137, and Kapustin and Subotskii, "Problemy Razvitiya Ob"edinenii," p. 7.
28. Brezhnev in *XXV S'ezd* . . . , Vol. 1, pp. 62-63, 82-86.
29. M. Shimanskii, "Ministerstvo, Glavk. A Firma?" *Izvestiya*, 18 November 1972, p. 2.
30. Markin, *Effektivnost'* . . . , p. 58.
31. Drogichinskii, "Proekty . . . ," p. 12.
32. A. Lyakhov, "Za shchitom global'nykh idei," *Sots. Ind.*, 25 January 1976, p. 2.
33. G. Schroeder in U.S. Congress Joint Economic Committee (ed.), *The Soviet Economy in a Time of Change* (Washington, DC: U.S. Government Printing Office, 1980), p. 316.
34. P. Bunich, "Khozraschetnyi Mekhanizm vnutri Proizvodstvennykh Ob"edinenii," *Plan. Khoz.*, No. 5, 1978, p. 55.
35. V. I. Maksimenko and V. I. Kukin in *Vsesoyuznaya Nauchnaya Konferentsiya* . . . , Vol. 2, p. 135.
36. V. Parfenov, "Poisk vedet Ministerstvo," *Pravda*, 11 May 1978, p. 2.
37. "Po General'nym Skhemam," *Pravda*, 14 March 1977, p. 1, and V. Eliseev, "Novoe — Ne Po Nazvaniyu," *Sots. Ind.*, 13 April 1977, p. 2.
38. Kashirina "Srednee Zveno," p. 2.
39. *Ibid.*, p. 2.
40. "Postanovlenie . . . O Nekotorykh Meropriyatiyakh . . . ," para. 21. Details of this investigation are from Maksimenko and Kukin in *Vsesoyuznaya Nauchnaya Konferentsiya* . . . , Vol. 2, pp. 129-138, and V. I. Maksimenko, V. S. Sominskii, M. A. Gusakov, and V. I. Kukin, "Chto Pokazalo Obsledovanie?," *Ekonomika i Organizatsiya Promyshlennogo Proizvodstva (EKO)*, No. 2, 1977, pp. 61-70. The point about seventeen groups is from the former source, pp. 130-131.
41. *Ibid.*, p. 130 and "Chto pokazalo . . . ," p. 62. The 78 were responsible for almost 25 percent of all products made by Soviet *ob"edineniya* (former source, p. 133). It is perhaps reflective of growing pessimism about and/or criticism of the implementation of association policy that the earlier source called the *ob"edineniya* typical of their branches (p. 130), whereas the later one explicitly stated that the *better* associations of given branches were those selected for the research project, as well as those typical "of current tendencies of production" (p. 62).
42. Maksimenko and Kukin, *Vsesoyuznaya Nauchnaya Konferentsiya* . . . , pp. 133-134. For an example of an enterprise's performance (including productivity) worsening on becoming part of an *ob"edinenie*, see D. Morkhov, "Tolkach . . . v svoem ob"edinenii," *Sots. Ind.*, 9 May 1977, p. 2.
43. Maksimenko et al., "Chto Pokazalo . . . ," p. 68. New techniques normally take an average of 7-8 years to be introduced into the production of most branches of industry, according to Dumachev, *Khozraschetnye Ob"edineniya* . . . , p. 10.

44. Masimenko et al., "Chto Pokazalo . . . ," p. 69.
45. *Ibid.*, p. 67. It is possible that the *ob"edineniya* had replaced *glavki* as well as taken functions from the enterprises — in which case the figure would be less disappointing. But if this is so, neither of the reports on this research makes reference to this. It is noteworthy that some Soviets accept that the number of administrators will increase over the next ten to fifteen years, whatever happens. See, for example, F. A. Dronov in F. R. Borovik (ed.), *Problemy Intensifikatsii Promyshlennogo Proizvodstva* (Minsk: Izd. Nauka i Tekhnika, 1974), p. 209.
46. Maksimenko et al., "Chto Pokazalo . . . ," p. 66.
47. Drogichinskii, "General'naya Skhema Otrasli," p. 3; Laptev, "Mezhdu Tsekhom . . . ," p. 3; and Nagovitsin, "Effektivnost' Vsesoyuznykh . . . ," p. 88. According to the official TsSU statistics, however, the 1977 figure was 43 percent. The reason for this discrepancy is not entirely clear, although Laptev is known to favor more autonomy to enterprises in *ob"edineniya* and may therefore wish to give the impression that developments are in the direction he would prefer.
48. Figures are from Popov, *Sovershenstvovanie* . . . , p. 29.
49. See Ch. 1, note 13, and Ch. 3, note 125. For a similar complaint about the legislation on the science-production associations, see (lead article), "V edinom Komplekse," *Pravda*, 12 January 1978, p. 1.
50. For example, Drogichinskii, *Organizatsiya Upravleniya* . . . , p. 56.
51. By 1962, for instance, L'vov *sovnarkhoz* had plans to create *ob"edineniya* in all branches of industry (Meleshkin, *Pervye Sovetskie Firmy*, p. 4). In contrast, not a single *ob"edinenie* was created in any branch of industry in Uzbekistan from 1967-1970. See Sh. Yuldashev, "Firmy: Vygody i Perspektivy," *Pravda Vostoka*, 18 February 1971, p. 2.
52. For example, Radomysel'skii and Shifrin, *Firmy* . . . , p. 36.
53. On analyses in L'vov, see Alekseenko et al., "Proizvodstvennye kompleksy . . . ," p. 13 (where the authors do, however, admit that not all *ob"edineniya* throughout the USSR are sufficiently evaluated in advance), and the book of guidelines on the creation of *ob"edineniya* issued by the Project-Design Institute of L'vov *sovnarkhoz*: A. G. Alekseenko (ed.), *Skhemy Struktur Upravleniya Promyshlennost'yu L'vovskogo Ekonomicheskogo Raiona i Proizvodstvennykh Ob"edinenii v Period Ikh Organizatsii vo L'vovskom SNKh i v Drugikh Sovnarkhozakh Strany* (L'vov: Proektno-Konstruktorskii Institut L'vovskogo Sovnarkhoza, 1964). On Leningrad, see Andreev and Margolis, *Leningradskie Firmy*, pp. 43-45. On other preparatory work, see Taksir, *Upravlenie* . . . , p. 193.
54. This point is taken by Dumachev, for one; see his *Effektivnaya Sistema* . . . , pp. 113-114.
55. Taksir, *Upravlenie* . . . , p. 219, 221.
56. *Ibid.*, pp. 221-230.
57. On the oil and coal industries, see the paper by A. A. Zhdanov in *Vtoraya Vsesoyuznaya* . . . ," Vol. 4, Pt. 1, pp. 8-20, and Suprun and Bobrov, "Shakhterskaya Nov'," p. 2.
58. For details of the new structure in the chemical industry, see L. A. Konstandov, "Struktura Upravleniya i Effektivnost' Proizvodstva," *Ekon. Gaz.*, No. 32, 1970, pp. 3-4.
59. Yu. Gnedkov and V. Tsmel', "Problemy Upravleniya i Informatsiya," *Plan. Khoz.*, No. 9, 1968, pp. 93-94.
60. "Postanovlenie . . . "O sovershenstvovanii . . . khimicheskoi . . . ," passim, esp. paras. 2, 3.

61. "Kurs — Sozdanie Ob"edinenii," *Pravda*, 15 August 1973, p. 1, and "Trekhzvennaya Sistema," *Ekon. Gaz.*, No. 37, 1972, p. 8.
62. The report ("Otrasl' na Khozraschete") appeared in *Ekon. Gaz.*, No. 32, 1972, p. 7.
63. See notes 57 and 58 above; also B. F. Bratchenko, "Ot Uchastka do Ministerstva," *Ekon. Gaz.*, No. 37, 1972, p. 4.
64. For details on newly formed combines, see Gerstner, "Kombinat fuer Oberkleidung . . ."; "Kombinat im Spreewald," *B.Z.*, 7 January 1969; the announcement about three new combines in *N.D.*, 9 January 1969; and, of particular value, the "Sonderausgabe zur Leipziger Fruehjahrsmesse," of *Die Wirts.*, 1969 and 1970.
65. "Grosswerk Deuben-Profen soll 15 Mio Mark zusaetzlichen Gewinn bringen," *Die Wirts.*, No. 48, 1967, p. 4, and "Taeglich Kohle ueber dem Plan?" *Die Wirts.*, No. 5, 1969, p. 8.
66. Keren, "The New Economic System . . . ," pp. 565-566.
67. *Das Funktionelle Wirken* . . . , p. 14.
68. *Oekonomisches System und Interessenvertretung – Probleme der gewerkschaftlichen Fuehrungstaetigkeit bei der Verwirklichung des Oekonomischen Systems des Sozialismus*, Vol. 2 (Berlin: Verlag die Tribuene 1968), p. 511.
69. H. Trauer in R. Gerisch (ed.), *Leitungsorganisation in den Betrieben und Kombinaten* (Berlin: Dietz Verlag, 1976), p. 156; Melzer and Scherzinger, "Wirtschaftssystem der DDR . . . ," p. 381. On the *Betriebsteile* and *Produktionsstaette*, see Graichen and Rouscik, *Zur Sozialistischen* . . . , p. 77.
70. Gerisch, *Leitungsorganisation* . . . , p. 248.
71. See "25 Jahre DDR . . . ," p. 12.
72. See, for example, Graichen and Rouscik, *Zur Sozialistischen* . . . , pp. 159-166, and Gerisch, *Leitungsorganisation* . . . , pp. 123-125. In fact, the East Germans have the second highest proportion of small enterprises of all the East European CMEA states (Bulgaria has the most). In 1976, over 30 percent of East German enterprises employed up to 500 workers, and another 14.9 percent employed between 501 and 1000 workers; data are from Horváth, "On the Size of . . . ," p. 45.
73. Die Redaktion, "Nur ein modernes sozialistisches Planungssystem sichert Pionier- und Spitzenleistungen," *Die Wirts.*, No. 3, 1970, pp. 3-4, esp. p. 4.
74. For example, G. Mittag, "Aus dem Bericht . . . an die 3. Tagung . . . ," p. 4, and G. Mittag, *Erfahrungen bei der Durchfuehrung der Beschluesse des VIII. Parteitages zur Intensivierung der Producktion in Industrie und Bauwesen. Zu einigen Problemen der Leitungstaetigkeit* (Berlin: Dietz Verlag, 1975), p. 13.
75. Ulbricht, *Probleme* . . . , p. 389.
76. W. R., "Die Hauptsache ist die hoehere Effektivitaet," *N.D.*, 30 November 1970, p. 6.
77. A. Panzer, "Die Aufgaben, Rechte und Pflichten der Kombinate auf dem Gebiet der Aussenwirtschaft," *WR*, No. 4, 1970, p. 220.
78. G. Br., "Modelle nur platonisch?," *N.D.*, 21 January 1969, p. 2.
79. Honecker in *Protokoll der Verhandlungen des VIII Parteitages* . . . , Vol. 1, p. 92.
80. For details, see "Richtlinie . . . ," pp. 32-42 and mb, "Das Experiment," *Die Wirts.*, No. 9, 1963, pp. 18-19.
81. "Richtlinie . . . ," pp. 39, 41.
82. For example, Ziegenhals, "Erste Erfahrungen . . . ," p. 26, and A. Dudszus, "VVB Schiffbau experimentiert," Beilage to *Die Wirts.*, No. 49, 1967, p. 10.

83. In December 1970, a decree was passed which led to more centralized control of foreign trade; on this, see Leptin in Hoehmann, Kaser, and Thalheim, *The New Economic Systems* . . . , pp. 68-70.

84. Some of the most important experiments were those conducted by the VEB Carl Zeiss Jena, the VEB Uhrenkombinat Ruhla, and the VEB WMW-Kombinat "7 Oktober."

85. For example, Gerisch et al., "Organisatorische Probleme . . . ."

86. See Halbritter, "Hinweise und Empfehlungen . . . ," passim, and the reference in Graichen and Rouscik, *Zur Sozialistischen* . . . , p. 216.

Chapter 7

OPPOSITION TO THE ASSOCIATIONS

A major intention of this study is to show how interests can be of relevance in communist systems at least as much in policy implementation as in policy formulation. This aspect of the role of interests in communist systems has been rather neglected, despite the fact that it is in this area that we can obtain some of the most detailed and interesting data.

The approach adopted here is to categorize opposition to all types of association from different functional sources. This produces a clearer, less repetitive exposition than an attempt to show the hostility from all sources to one type of association, then to another, and so on. The final introductory point is that we include in this chapter details of *inferred* as well as overt opposition, since an understanding of the reasons for the differences in the success of association development in the USSR and GDR requires consideration of as many factors as possible.

7.1. OPPOSITION TO THE *OB″EDINENIYA* IN THE USSR

We have found no articles outrightly condemning the *concept* of the *ob″edinenie*, although references to individuals who are opposed to it have occasionally been made.[1] On the other hand, there is considerable evidence of some form of hostility to the associations — though less so since the 1973-1974 legislation than in the period preceding it.

OPPOSITION FROM HIGHER STATE ORGANS

Evidence of both lack of enthusiasm for and overt opposition to the *ob″edineniya* from higher state organs — ministries, *vedomstva*, *glavki*, and generally all bodies above the associations — is abundant; we consider all these bodies in one section since both Western and Soviet writers often treat them as a single entity.[2]

As early as 1959 it was argued that the branch administrations in the *sovnarkhozy* would eventually be made redundant as *firmy* developed.³ This point was made many times by senior *sovnarkhoz* officials and others during the next six years, so that it is hardly surprising that complaints appeared in the press about the negative attitude to be found among some branch administration officials toward the new *firmy*.⁴ The *firmy* were to be administered by the people who had previously worked in the component units, so that the administrators in the branch administrations would be without work — at least in their own field — as a result of the spread of *firmy*. This was openly admitted by some of the more honest advocates of the association.⁵

Since the ministries returned in 1965, there has been no shortage of evidence of opposition (both overt and inferred) from them to the *ob"edineniya*. As has so often been pointed out, however, Soviet officials and writers themselves were frequently seemingly unaware before 1973 of the essential distinction between what have come to be known as the industrial and production associations, so that it is not possible in other than a few cases to isolate the hostility to one rather than the other form of *ob"edinenie* in the prelegislation period.

A common criticism was that ministries were very slow in implementing proposals for the formation of *ob"edineniya* of various kinds. This slowness has often been interpreted as a form of opposition. Typical was the criticism by the head of the department of light and food industry for Cherkassk *obkom*, who complained of "incomprehensible passivity" on the part of many ministries and *vedomstva*, and a terrible slowness on their part to create new associations.⁶ One cause of this has been that the component parts of proposed *ob"edineniya* are subordinate to different ministries, in which case the ministries have often been loath to cooperate with each other.⁷ Another aspect of this slowness is that ministries and *glavki* can appear to be in favor of the formation of an *ob"edinenie* in theory, but do little actually to implement this (i.e., they do not work out practical plans for realizing the projected *ob"edinenie*).⁸ Indeed, as was shown in the last chapter, slowness in producing acceptable plans for the creation of associations has been one of the most criticized aspects of ministerial behavior since the 1973-1974 legislation.

In other cases, they have modified plans so extensively that many of the potential advantages of the *ob"edinenie* are effectively nullified. The Ryazan provincial party committee, for instance, suggested the creation of an *ob"edinenie* to the Ministry of Tractor and Agricultural Machine Manufacture, to which the latter appeared to react favorably. However, the ministry refused to allow a reduction in the administrative apparatus, thus effectively negating an important advantage of the *ob"edinenie*.[9] Another example is that of the Ministry of Engineering for the Light and Food Industry and Household Appliances when it agreed to establish the Soyuzsteklomash science-production association. In this case, the ministry created the *ob"edinenie* but permitted a ludicrous subordination arrangement:

> To cap it all, the *ob"edinenie* which has been created . . . is subordinate to Glavkhimlegmash, which has nothing to do with glass manufacturing. Soyuzsteklomash has merely been formally attached to a *glavk*. As a result, there is no help, and problems multiply.[10]

A complaint about this was made to the minister responsible, V. I. Doenin, who agreed that the *ob"edinenie* should be directly subordinate to the ministry. At the time of the writing of the article describing this case, however, nothing had in fact been done about the problem.[11]

In the cases so far cited, it is not possible to ascertain whether the action of the ministries was the result of incompetence, indecisiveness, or deliberate lack of cooperation. Simple inefficiency and/or difficulties in implementation that were not envisaged in the planning stage could account for some of these situations. But in other cases, party organs, factory management, economists, and others have made concrete suggestions for the creation of *ob"edineniya*, which the ministries refuse to acknowledge. Thus, a factory worker wrote to *Sotsialisticheskaya Industriya* in 1971 to complain that although managers and specialists had made concrete proposals for restructuring the administration of the textile industry along the lines of the *ob"edinenie*, the senior officials of the textile branch had made no comment on these proposals.[12] A similar criticism of the ministries for not helping in the creation of *ob"edineniya* was made by the First Secretary of Kalinin district party committee, E. Yudin. who wrote that

> amongst certain ministries, we have up to now found no support in so important a matter [i.e., the creation of *ob"edineniya* — LTH].[13]

The point here is that even if these ministries did experience difficulties in implementing suggestions, this does not excuse their refusal even to explain their position; bureaucratic delays are a partial but insufficient explanation of their behavior.

A different type of complaint is that ministries pursue development plans in their branch that run counter to the essence of the *ob"edinenie* policy. Once again, the Kalinin district party committee in Leningrad has been strongly critical of many ministries that, instead of reconstructing, reequipping, and developing existing production in line with the policy of specialization, concentration, and cooperation, actually built new workshops and enterprises.[14] And in Yaroslavl province, a party secretary criticized a ministry for siting two closely related electrical engineering factories next to each other without formally linking them in some way.[15]

A final point is that it appears that some heads of branch ministries and other *vedomstva* have not appreciated any real difference between the *glavki* and the industrial *ob"edineniya* — at least prior to the 1973 legislation.[16] Of those that did, some did not want to have their *glavki* transformed into associations. Typical was the head of the Ministry for the Electro-Technical Industry of the USSR, A. K. Antonov. In a paper he delivered at a conference in 1972, Antonov demonstrated clearly that he was not eager to disband his *glavki* and replace them with the newer bodies. He devoted much of his paper to an elaboration of the many ways in which the ministry and its *glavki* assisted the branch's enterprises, especially in the field of scientific-technical developments, and made no reference at all to the associations.[17] Even after the 1973 legislation, which meant that *ob"edineniya* could not be avoided, articles can be found in which *glavki* are directly or indirectly defended. Thus, the deputy head of a *glavk* reported in December 1973 on the very good work his office had done in creating *production* associations.[18] In other words, while he seemed loath to oppose *ob"edineniya* across the board, he could at least argue that his *glavk* was doing all that was expected of it in terms of creating associations; it will be recalled that an escape clause in the 1973 legislation allowed for the retention of *some glavki*, and it certainly looked as if this official was hoping to show that his own organization still had a raison d'être. It seems probable that such attitudes have been supported by some ministers, since, if the *glavki* were to be disbanded in the way recommended by most economists, then those ministers would no longer have such direct control over and contact with many of their best specialists. Such an interpretation is suggested by the following remarkably frank quotation from a republic minister in 1970:

> After all, we created *tresty* and administrations [it is clear from the context that the latter are ministerial subdivisions — LTH] in order not to lose the specialists who had worked in the *sovnarkhozy*.[19]

Hostility from ministries and other bodies above the associations has led some writers to argue in a similar vein to Markin, who maintains that because of wrong attitudes, departmental (*vedomstvennye*) difficulties, and even "direct resistance" to the *ob"edineniya* on the part of some ministries,

> the creation of each new *firma* is, as a rule, the result of the efforts of and a great deal of organizational work by district, town, provincial, and republic party organs.[20]

While it shall be shown that this is an idealized picture of at least *some* party organizations, it is still a damning criticism of the higher state organs and their role in the development of the associations.

Yet at times, in reading the criticisms of the ministries and central bodies, it looks like a case of "heads I win, tails you lose" on the part of the critics. When some ministries do create *ob"edineniya*, there are complaints that the latter are not sufficiently autonomous, that the measures have not gone far enough.[21] But other ministries can be accused of playing too small a role in the running of the associations. Thus a senior scientific worker at the Institute of Economics in the USSR Academy of Sciences argued that

> one must not imagine that with the creation of an *ob"edinenie* all that remains for a ministry to do is to "hand down" to it the plan and check on its implementation. On the contrary, with the appearance of large production-economic complexes, the role of ministries in the leadership (*rukovodstvo*) of industry increases significantly.[22]

On the basis of the evidence so far, can it be argued that the ministries and other central organs have been hostile to the *ob"edineniya*? The answer must be divided into four broad sections.

First, many of the articles in which ministries are criticized blame them for committing errors and lacking organizational ability. Thus, the fact that some *ob"edineniya* have been disbanded and others seem slow to materialize is in some cases due simply to poor conceptualization and difficulties optimalizing a structure.[23]

Second, some writers on the *ob"edineniya* see the main reason for the delays as being that people in ministries and elsewhere are used to the old ways — that they believe change must come slowly and only after there have been detailed orders and considerable paperwork. In other words, conservatism is linked with what can be called the "culture of bureaucratism" as much as with the defense of vested interests.[24]

Third, one must be wary of grouping all ministries and *vedomstva* together in a blanket fashion. Some ministries, such as the All-Union Ministry of the Electronics Industry and the all-union section of the

Union-Republic Ministry of Light Industry, have been praised for their innovatory measures, while many of the same names recur among those that are criticized (e.g., the All-Union Ministry of Tractor and Agricultural Machine Manufacture).[25] There does appear to have been some pattern here — namely, that in the case of union-republic ministries, the central body has tended to be more innovatory than its republic-level counterpart. The likely explanation for this is that the ministerial officials at republic level have been concerned that their link in the administrative hierarchy will eventually become redundant as a result of the spread of associations. It should be noted that such concern was not unjustified in the prelegislation period, as revealed in the following comment made at the beginning of 1973:

> At present there is a discussion on whether or not the union-republic ministry of the union republic should be included in these links of industrial administration.[26]

As we have seen, the legislation finally adopted did remove some of this fear, in that it specifically provided for, even if it did not encourage, the existence of such bodies.

Another aspect of this differentiation of ministries and central bodies is that there are some *nonbranch* ministries that have opposed the associations for rather different reasons from those of the branch ministries. By far the most frequently cited of these is the one whose position became clear at the legislation stage, the Ministry of Finance. A typical criticism was that made by D. A. Takoev at the May 1968 conference. Takoev (head of the Kuibysheft' oil *ob"edinenie*) suggested areas in which the ministry had in practice rights that he felt the association should have, such as determining the number of staff and the size of the wage fund. He accused the State Bank and even more so the Ministry of Finance of "hindering the broadening of the *ob"edinenie's* rights," relating this particularly to the question of the bonus fund and the production development fund.[27] The only speaker at the conference from the Ministry of Finance that we know of was the deputy minister, I. V. Guzhkov. He did not answer Takoev's charges, but some interesting points emerge from his paper which make it clear that many of these criticisms were well founded. For instance, although Guzhkov emphasized that enterprises should enjoy the full autonomy granted them under the 1965 reforms, he also frequently stressed that they did not always use their new rights properly. Consequently, he argued, the *central* organs (and particularly the Ministry of Finance!) should help and supervise the enterprises even more now than previously. Clearly this would impinge upon the autonomy of both the enterprises *and* the associations. Gushkov also referred specifically to some of the funds Takoev had mentioned, saying that enterprises and *ob"edineniya* did not always use them in the proper manner. In this context he cited a combine which had been using only 25 percent of its production-development fund for the purposes intended, thus implying that a body above the association was necessary for checking on the proper use of funds.[28] Hence, the Ministry of Finance has not been an advocate of the *ob"edineniya*, fearing that many of its rights vis-à-vis the individual production units might be lost to the new organizations.[29]

Finally, one must be careful to distinguish in some cases between ministries and their *glavki*. In 1969, for example, the Ukrainian Ministry of Light Industry suggested that the Zorya clothes *firma* be enlarged, and passed a resolution to this effect. However, the respective *glavki* of the ministry used various pretexts to evade both this and the suggestions of the L'vov province and town to create new *ob"edineniya*.[30] In another case, the Ministry of Machine-Tool Production ordered the creation of an *ob"edinenie* in Kharkov in April 1971. Despite this, the head of Glavosnastk (the *glavk* to which the *ob"edinenie* was subordinated) maintained that the association did not exist. In spite of official condemnations by the ministry, he obstructed the association management in various ways. As a newspaper correspondent wrote, the outcome of the situation was a cold war between the *glavk* and the *ob"edinenie*, contrary to the wishes of the ministry.[31] The reasons for this type of hostility are patently obvious to some Soviet writers. For instance, the indicators of *glavki* (and indeed some ministries) can be lowered by having to include scientific-technical organizations that before their inclusion in an *ob"edinenie* had been subordinate to another *glavk* or ministry.[32] Another factor is that *glavk* (as well as ministry) staffs have generally preferred to have many enterprises subordinate to them rather than a few *ob"edineniya*; this is because, under the system of "repeating accounts" (*povtornye schety*), output appears higher under the former arrangement.[33] It is largely due to this factor that so many enterprises in production *ob"edineniya* have been allowed to retain their autonomy.[34] Even more important, the creation of *ob"edineniya* can put the continued existence of *glavki* in question, and hence lead to fears of demotion among *glavk* workers. In this respect, the creation of industrial associations can be seen on one level as a means for assuaging opposition; as has been shown, many industrial associations are in practice little different from the *glavki* they are supposed to have replaced.

In sum, it is quite clear that some central bodies have been opposed to the associations, but also that one should be wary of excessive generalization.

OPPOSITION FROM MANAGEMENT IN "SECONDARY" ENTERPRISES

One source of opposition frequently cited is the management in what can be called "secondary" enterprises. These are enterprises that would become filials (i.e., lose most of their autonomy) if they were to be included in an *ob"edinenie*. Opposition from such managers is explained largely by the fact that they stand to lose much of their prestige and independence if subordinated to an *ob"edinenie*, and they seem to have been aware of this from the time of the earliest Soviet *firmy*.[35] Typical was the director of the Borisov agroengineering factory who feared

> being deprived of independence. Whatever the factory is like — all the same, it is one's own. And you are its director. A director, and not some head of a filial. There's a difference![36]

Typical criticism of such views is to be found in Dumachev's 1972 book, where the type of prestige and "perks" enjoyed by such directors is described in more detail than in most sources. Having complained that many management personnel and other white-collar workers claim to be generally in favor of the associations but in practice devise all sorts of reasons why their particular enterprise should not be included in one, Dumachev writes,

> From the mundane point of view, all this looks something like the following. There was an autonomous factory, the director of which was usually elected onto the local party and soviet organs, independently decided all questions concerning "his" enterprise ... made trips to the capital and sometimes even had the opportunity to call in on the minister personally with his rather trivial questions. After the creation of the association, the heads of enterprises lose a significant proportion of their autonomy, all questions are decided only through the management of the *ob"edinenie* or with its consent. In most cases, they are now no longer elected to local organs, do not sit on the presidia of district and town meetings, etc.[37]

In fact, however, practice has shown that these sorts of fears are not the only ones such managers can have — that it is not solely a matter of being a filial head as opposed to an enterprise director. Thus when Progress was established, it was said that component units (filials) would be directly subordinate to the director of the *firma*. In practice, however, they were managed by the Deputy Chief Engineer for Production, assisted by the Department of Production and Conjuncture.[38] It would not be surprising, therefore, if people who had been managers of an enterprise have resented taking orders from an engineer. Moreover, there is evidence that in some very centralized *ob"edineniya*, the consultative "council of directors" that is supposed to exist is not created.[39] The idea behind these councils is that managers from all component units in an association can meet regularly to discuss questions that affect the whole *ob"edinenie* or individual component parts of it. While they do not normally have a decision-making as opposed to an advisory role, such councils do at least give the former directors of autonomous enterprises a forum for discussing important matters and in which they can feel that they still have *some* role in major decision-making. When there is no such council, access to even this surrogate source of prestige is denied.[40]

Loss of prestige and power is not the only loss for many managers; salaries, too, have been affected. Because of an edict from the State Committee on Labor and Wages in the early 1960s, the salaries of leading personnel in filials of an *ob"edinenie* were in many cases reduced in order to help finance higher salaries for personnel in the head enterprise. The justification given for this by the State Committee was that the overall salary fund for leading personnel should not be increased, although the salaries of those people managing the *firma* as a whole should be greater than they had been when the same people were responsible only for the head enterprise.[41]

In the most extreme cases, former managers can lose not only prestige and earnings but their very jobs. Even in an association such as LOMO — often cited as a model to be emulated — there was such hostility to the formation of the association that many enterprise managers had to be transferred to "other" (unspecified) work altogether in order that the amalgamation could proceed.[42] And in some cases, the formation of an association has led to the closure of some units altogether.[43] In such cases, hostility from managers can be seen in terms of fear for their own jobs and for those of their workers as much as of personal prestige.

In all these cases hostility is aimed at the production associations; no evidence has been found of hostility from managers to the industrial associations. Since, as far as enterprises are concerned, there is little difference between a *glavk* and an industrial association (other than that the latter has to be more financially responsible for mistakes it makes that have a detrimental effect on its subordinate units), this is not surprising.

To some extent, some of the reasons for hostility to the associations were theoretically removed by the 1973 legislation. But these measures will be considered vis-à-vis all sources of opposition at the end of this section. For the present, it should be noted that opposition from enterprise management has been seen by Dumachev, for instance, as even *more* important to the slow development of associations than opposition from ministerial *glavki* and other central organs.[44] This sort of opposition constitutes a clear case of interest defense.

OPPOSITION FROM MANAGEMENT IN HEAD ENTERPRISES

While opposition from management in secondary enterprises would be expected, it is far less obvious that there would be opposition from the heads of large enterprises, who would become the head of a new *ob"edinenie*. In fact many such directors *do* welcome such a proposed "expansion."[45] But this is not always the case. When the director of what is now the head enterprise of the Frunze dairy combine (established in January 1968) first learned that an *ob"edinenie* was to be formed, he received the news "without particular enthusiasm." Such an attitude initially seems difficult to comprehend, since presumably his prestige would rise as head of an association. However, there was a sound reason for this director's lack of enthusiasm. He had headed his enterprise for twenty years, and it was very successful. The level of profitability was high, the equipment modern. In contrast, the other factories that were to be included in the *ob"edinenie* were small, poorly equipped, and their standards of hygiene "below criticism." Most important of all, few of them were profitable; those that were were only marginally so. The director of the head enterprise, S. D. Kuznetsov, knew that in the event of an association being formed the profits from his enterprise would be used to raise the level of the other enterprises. Following the formation of the *ob"edinenie*, this is precisely what happened. The journalist who reported this situation argued that the attitudes in the head enterprise were understandable in the circumstances, and it is noticeable that he did not say that these attitudes had changed since the formation of the association. While the reasons for such opposition are not elaborated in the article, it seems probable that since the head enterprise has had to help the other enterprises to develop by subsidizing them from its own funds, the bonus fund in the head enterprise would be less than it had been before the establishment of the association. Thus, economic factors appear to be the main explanation for opposition in this particular case.[46]

OPPOSITION FROM LOCAL STATE (SOVIET) ORGANS

From the start of the current phase of creating associations, some local soviet officials have opposed particular *ob"edineniya*. Some detailed explanations of why this should be so were given at the Leningrad seminar held in August 1970. Thus,

> Sometimes, individual local organs oppose the creation of *ob"edineniya* because in this case the district (or province) is deprived of deductions from profit into the budget.[47]

Since up to 15 percent of profit from local industry is directed to housing construction and welfare-amenity projects, and since money for this is to be at the disposal of the local soviet executive committee, it is understandable why, if an *ob"edinenie* is to be formed and subordinated to a province, the town and district soviets will suffer.[48] Likewise, some provinces are unwilling to create particular *ob"edineniya*, since they would suffer in doing so. This requires further explanation. If a factory is incorporated into a production association, the head enterprise of this often takes all of that factory's production. On the one hand, the province can suffer physical losses of production (and often a reduced range of products) to dispose of within its own boundaries when it allows a factory to be included in an *ob"edinenie*, the head enterprise of which is in another province. On the other hand, since the Central Statistical Office organs have often included the production of filials in the head enterprise's output, the production indices in that town or province in which the head enterprise is situated will rise, while in those that have only filials, there is a sudden drop.[49] While one might expect central organs to appreciate this, such assumptions cannot be taken for granted in a highly complex, large-scale economy such as the USSR's. Bearing in mind the fact that local soviet officials may thus be considered inefficient — with all that this might imply for them in terms of promotion and so on — a certain reticence is understandable. As one Soviet writer expressed it,

> As we see, even with a most critical attitude toward the position of the province organizations, it is impossible not to take their interests into consideration.[50]

A rather more specific criticism of the reluctance of local state (and party) officials relates to the establishment, by *ob"edineniya*, of new industrial plants in small towns and rural areas: It will be recalled from Chapter 3 that this has been cited by some as a major advantage of the associations. However, there have been reports in the Soviet press of hostility to this process, on the grounds that the establishment of such units can attract much-needed labor away from the fields, and also that new housing and other services necessitated by such developments are not properly provided by the *ob"edinenie*.[51] Such practices thus further help to explain opposition to the associations from some local soviet officials.

OPPOSITION FROM PARTY ORGANS

In an article published in 1972, the First Secretary of Leningrad *obkom*, G. Romanov, referred to the attitudes of certain officials of local party committees toward the associations. Such people

> often hold on to the independence of "their" enterprises, *perhaps even more strongly than do the ministries* [emphasis added].[52]

Although the reasons for such behavior are, unfortunately, not explained, such localism and possessiveness is clearly at odds with official party policy. Another Leningrad party official, A. Dumachev, made the same point as Romanov in a book published in 1972, and gave a concrete example of the effect of such attitudes. Evidently, local party officials from Pskov and Novgorod pressured various ministries, when the latter were reestablished, to remove many enterprises from Leningrad-based *ob"edineniya* and reestablish them as autonomous enterprises.[53] Thus, in this case, we see how particular party organs appealed to the ministries against the actions of other party organs. In some cases, party organs can actually oppose ministerial suggestions to create associations. This happened in Zakarpat'e, for example, where the provincial party committee objected to various ministerial proposals. Moreover, the *obkom* either raised no objections or else very weak ones when various existing associations were disbanded; one *Pravda* correspondent described this party committee's support for the associations as of a purely "Platonic" nature:

> In some cases, they [the provincial committee — LTH] did not protest against the disbanding of this or that *ob"edinenie*. In other cases they did protest — but insufficiently, not using all their authority and influence.[54]

In this particular case, such attitudes are explained as "the result of an insufficiently deep appreciation of all the progressiveness and significance of the new form of running industry."[55] Clearly, such attitudes do not become what is allegedly the "vanguard" element in Soviet society, and require further explanation. Once again, vested interests largely explain the phenomenon. While local party organs do not appear to be financed by local industry, there are two important reasons why local officials should be loath to lose "their" enterprises. To understand these reasons, we need first to explain the relationship of party bodies within *ob"edinenie* units to the local party organizations.

There is no unified pattern for restructuring the party organization following the creation of a production association; the situation described by Zdorov in 1970 still pertains:

> The structure of party organizations in associations may vary. It all depends on the concrete conditions and the specific type of production, the peculiarities of this or that actual *ob"edinenie*.[56]

Nevertheless, three basic patterns are discernible and have been officially sanctioned since 1976.[57] In the first, a new, unified primary party organization is created for the whole production association; at the beginning of 1977, 23 percent of these *ob"edineniya* had such an arrangement.[58] The new primary organizations are based on the head unit of the association.[59] Therefore, the party organs in those districts that contain only the filials of the *ob"edinenie* lose many of their functions to the local party organ responsible for the head unit. In the article by Romanov already cited, this point is made clearly when he says that all the communists in Leningrad enterprises that are now in associations have been transferred to the register (*uchet*) of the party committee responsible for the *ob"edinenie's* head unit.[60] Centralization in the second type is partial; only the primary party organizations of production units located in the same city or district as the head unit are merged, while the others retain their autonomous status and are subordinate to their local town or district party committee. In the third type, each production unit in the association retains its own primary party organization, and the subordination arrangement remains essentially unaltered.[61] Having made these points about territorial subordination, we can explain the reasons for hostility from some party organs.

In the case of type-one party structures, the loss of functions by some local officials is quite unambiguous. But some perception of a diminished role may arise among local *apparatchiki* even where associations have a type-two or type-three party structure. This is because many *ob"edineniya* — as of January 1977, some 20 percent of those with a type-two or type-three arrangement[62] — have established Councils of Party Committee Secretaries, which can impact upon local party committees. The idea behind these councils was to harmonize the work of separate party organizations within an association to the maximum extent possible. They consist of secretaries from all the primary party organizations in an *ob"edinenie*, and sometimes deputy secretaries and workshop secretaries too; they are usually convened four or five times per year.[63] The councils adopt recommendations, which are then supposed to be agreed upon with the relevant local party committees and confirmed by individual primary organization committees within the association. Although there is some disagreement as to whether or not such decisions become binding on all communists in the *ob"edinenie*,[64] the fact that some party secretaries have believed they do implies that local party officials may on occasion have felt that their role was being usurped by such councils. Thus, with all three types of party structure, local party officials can lose some of their former functions, a factor which could lead to fears of being considered superfluous by higher party organs — and hence to hostility. Since there is an official policy of reducing the numbers of party *apparatchiki*,[65] such fears are not without substance. To a limited extent, there is in practice a process of "swings and roundabouts" between different party bodies — "lose a few, gain a few"; but there is no inherent reason why the process of creating associations should ultimately lead to a redistribution of tasks between different party organizations in much the same proportions as the status quo ante.

Second, if it is the case that promotion within the CPSU apparatus is to some extent related to the economic success of one's particular territorial unit, then party officials will be loath to forfeit well-functioning enterprises to another party organ. Although this, too, can work in both directions (a party committee might also receive profitable and efficient enterprises from another and be able to dispose of less successful ones), there are undoubtedly cases where this factor explains hostility.

Thus, the attitudes of the party officials in Novgorod, Pskov, and elsewhere, referred to above, become more understandable if not necessarily justifiable.

What of party organs *within* the enterprises? We were not permitted to interview party officials in *ob"edineniya* and have no concrete evidence of opposition from this source. However, it is highly probable that some hostility to the associations has existed at this level, and certainly there are hints in Soviet writing of such attitudes.[66] What would lead to such views?

Above all, there is the point about structural reorganization already mentioned — for example, the creation of a *unified* primary party organization in a production association. Thus, it was decided to merge the primary party organizations of all the subdivisions of the Pozitron *ob"edinenie* in Leningrad into a single, unified organization. As the director of Pozitron made quite clear, "this means . . . that a decision taken by such a party organization will become obligatory for all communists."[67] Consequently, many communists will feel that they have less chance of participation in decision-making affecting their work place than before, unless they be included in the new, unified primary party organization. Even if they are on this body, it is likely that communists in "secondary" enterprises will be more aware than their comrades in the head enterprise of the drawbacks of being in the new organization. If party meetings are usually held in the head unit, it is obviously easier for the communists working there to attend than for those party members who have to travel from another factory; in territorially deconcentrated associations (which, at least until 1976, were able to create unified primary party organizations), this problem could well have been acute.

As we have seen, this problem has been partially dealt with in many associations by retaining "autonomous" party organizations in some units. However, such autonomy may in practice be severely circumscribed by the Councils of Party Committee Secretaries. Despite the necessity for confirmation of such councils' decisions by the committees of the individual party organizations, it is highly probable that, in practice, these councils of full-time, professional party functionaries frequently dominate decision-making, thus causing friction. Although many associations have created more workshop committees and party groups in order to increase opportunities for participation,[68] such measures can at best only partially overcome the feeling of alienation.

Finally, since the creation of production *ob"edineniya* sometimes leads to the closure of workshops and factories[69] — and hence to the disbandment of their party organizations — the points made earlier concerning cuts in the party apparatus and loss of prestige would apply; although some officials might be incorporated into bigger, more important party bodies, many would not.

It can therefore be seen that there are many reasons why particular party officials and ordinary party members will in some cases oppose the creation of associations.

SUGGESTED FURTHER SOURCES OF OPPOSITION

Not only managers but also many lower-ranking white-collar workers may well oppose the organizational changes involved when an association is established. The most important reason for this would be fear for one's position. One of the frequently cited "advantages" of the *ob"edinenie* is that in the process of centralization there is a reduction in the administrative apparatus and a consequent lowering of administrative costs. In the Plastpolimer association, for example, the number of departments was exactly halved from 52 to 26, and more than 200 technical and office workers were "released" from their posts.[70] Innumerable examples of similar reductions can be found in the Soviet press, and it is clear that white-collar workers must be aware that there is a real chance that their posts could be considered superfluous if their enterprise, R and D institute, and the like were to be incorporated into an *ob"edinenie*. Quite where all these "superfluous" people are transferred to is seldom explained. A report from Kirghizia did refer, however, to the transfer of hundreds of people from desk jobs to production work following the creation of an *ob"edinenie*.[71] The implications seem obvious. While some sociologists of the Soviet Union maintain that attitudes there are not the same as in Britain, for example — skilled blue-collar workers in the USSR enjoying greater social prestige than low-ranking white-collar workers[72] — it is unlikely that lower administrative personnel would suddenly be transferred to *skilled* production work, since much of the necessary expertise requires long training and experience. It is thus more probable that white-collar workers are transferred to unskilled or semiskilled production work, or else less prestigious white-collar posts. This would entail a loss not only of prestige, but probably of income too.

It is not only administrative reorganization that threatens white-collar workers when an *ob"edinenie* is formed. Even if they survive the initial centralization and rationalization process, the fact that automated administration systems (ASUP) are usually considered more beneficial and feasible in an *ob"edinenie* than in smaller enterprises could lead to fears of redundancy at a later date (if their work is mostly done by a machine) or of the necessity to learn a technical skill in later years (e.g. how to operate a computer).[73]

Focusing now on those personnel who do retain their posts, it is clear that the creation of an *ob"edinenie* can be financially disadvantageous to some of these people. As we saw earlier, unless there is a drastic "pruning" of the administration, a ruling by the State Committee on Labor and Wages that when a production association was formed, the administrative wage fund was not to become any larger than the sum of the wage funds of the component units, as these were prior to the formation of the association, has meant that some administrators have been worse off then they were when in single autonomous enterprises.⁷⁴ In other cases, managers, senior engineers, and administrative workers have received the same salary in the association as they did when they worked in autonomous enterprises, even though their workload and responsibility has increased.⁷⁵ In many science-production associations, the specialists and white-collar workers in the head unit (i.e., an R and D institute) have often received less than their functional equivalents in the "secondary" units, and less qualified specialists have received more than highly qualified ones.⁷⁶ Given the evidence we have on the reaction of other Soviet functionaries in similar situations, it can be inferred that if specialists and administrative workers believe they will have added responsibilities and an increased workload with the same or less income if they work for an association, at least some of them will oppose suggestions that their enterprise or institute be included in such an organization.

White-collar workers and specialists are not the only ones who may suffer when an *ob"edinenie* is formed. For example, when the repair services in the Soyuzkhimvolokno chemical-fibre association were centralized, nearly 5 percent of the repair workers lost their jobs, and in individual enterprises within the association this figure reached 15 percent.⁷⁷ Yet again, workers may fear redundancy as the association speeds up the automation of production.

Finally, it should be mentioned that trade union bodies as well as party bodies can be adversely affected through the formation of an *ob"edinenie*. In the Voskhod *firma*, for example, participation by the trade union in the overall running of the *firma* was weakened in comparison with its role in the individual enterprises prior to the formation of the association. This was because the local committees of filials were not directly subordinate to the local committee of the head unit, and contact between them was not systematized; consequently, the participation of filial trade union organizations in the association's decision-making process was very haphazard.⁷⁸

It is not only people whose position/function may be threatened by the formation of an association who oppose these bodies; many local trading organizations have also been hostile. There are two closely related reasons for this. The first is that they frequently prefer to obtain their goods directly from local enterprises, and this can be made more difficult if these are then incorporated into an association based on a head enterprise in another locality. Second, local enterprises can be encouraged to produce an even wider range of goods if they receive orders for them from local trading organizations. Such universalization of production usually has to cease and is replaced by specialization when an enterprise is incorporated into an association — which similarly leads to greater difficulties in obtaining some products.[79]

In our concluding chapter, the relevance of all these sources of opposition to the development of the *ob"edineniya* will be discussed. For the present, it is worth considering briefly the extent to which the reasons for opposition were removed, de jure at least, by the 1973 and 1974 legislation. Since financial interests have been so important as a source of hostility, what was done to overcome the problems that had arisen? The solutions adopted included the introduction of a requirement that the directors of production associations were to receive an increase of between 10 and 15 percent in their salaries, while the salaries and certain privileges of the senior administrative staff both in the head unit and in secondary units were not to be decreased as a result of the formation of an association; however, both of these "solutions" are subject to certain conditions.[80] Local state organs were to be compensated for any losses incurred as a result either of formerly autonomous enterprises and organizations being transformed into production units of a production association, or the transfer of enterprises and organizations from local subordination to all-union and republic industrial associations.[81] Despite these regulations, however, there is in addition to the ministerial resistance that still exists evidence of continued opposition to the *ob"edineniya* from both managers and local state and party bodies.[82] Apart from the fact that many staff may feel that they will lose financially despite the legislation (because it is ambiguously worded),[83] one reason that has been suggested for this continued hostility is that local cliques may fear the exposure of corrupt practices in all this change.[84] Finally, since the Soviet legislation envisaged as few enterprises as possible retaining autonomy in a production *ob"edinenie*, hostility engendered by the fear of losing prestige has not been satisfactorily dealt with (this explanation for the high number of autonomous enterprises is *in addition* to the point made earlier about the vested interests of the ministries).

Let us now compare all this with the situation in the GDR.

7.2. OPPOSITION TO THE VVBs AND COMBINES IN THE GDR

There is considerably less evidence of overt and enduring hostility to the associations in the GDR than in the USSR.[85] While this could simply reflect less open reporting in the smaller state, that the implementation has been more successful there implies that there has really been less opposition and/or that it has had less effect.

OPPOSITION FROM HIGHER STATE ORGANS

It seems probable that there was hostility toward the VVBs from some central state functionaries as early as 1958. The reason for such attitudes would be a familiar one — loss of prestige and/or earnings. An article in *Die Wirtschaft* in 1958 referred to the disbandment of a ministerial "chief administration" and its replacement by a VVB, under which the staff would drop from 120 to 85 employess.[86] The fact that the number of VVBs was greater than the number of chief administrations they replaced means that it is conceivable that the total number of VVB personnel would approximately equal the number of people working in the former chief administrations; however, the article explicitly stated that some of the people working in the administration would be transferred to *enterprises*.

Since that time we have found no evidence or even hints of opposition to either the VVBs or the combines on the part of the *branch* ministries after their reappearance at the end of 1965. The power of the ministries essentially remained static during the rest of the 1960s, and increased from about 1970 to 1979. Lack of opposition from this quarter is thus understandable. Moreover, much of the ministerial opposition in the Soviet Union had been from the republic branch ministries with only a few enterprises to manage; once again, there are no functional equivalents of these in the much smaller GDR.

However, there have been criticisms of the nonbranch ministries and other central organs. The Ministry of Finance and the Ministry of Foreign Trade in particular have been attacked for their actions and attitudes toward the associations. Since it was these bodies that had most to lose when the VVBs and later the combines were to be granted more rights in pricing and foreign trade, and because of being on profit-and-loss accounting, this opposition emerges clearly as an example of interest defense. Thus the Minister of Finance himself, Boehm, admitted at a conference in 1967 that many of the people working in the finance organs were not succeeding in reorienting their attitudes (*Umdenkungsprozess*) as they should do under the Economic System of Socialism (ESS).[87] While the minister did not relate this specifically to the VVBs, the head of the Central Committee's Department for Problems of State and Law (also a member of the State Council), Klaus Sorgenicht, was at the same conference highly critical of the attitudes of several named central bodies for their lack of interest in granting the VVBs more autonomy. He spent some time elaborating this by reference to the VVB Shipbuilding. This was the first VVB to be transferred onto the full application of ESS, one of the main aspects of which was that it had new rights in the field of foreign trade. The Minister for Heavy Industry and Equipment Installation, Zimmermann, was responsible for all the coordinatory work involved in implementing this decision. However, when he convened a meeting of the various bodies that were to have been involved in this change (including the Ministry of Foreign Trade, the Ministry of Finance, and the State Planning Commission), they either sent along relatively low-ranking officials or no representative at all. Unfortunately, Sorgenicht did not name the bodies that fall into the latter category. He did, however, emphasize that this was no isolated case.[88] Clearly, then, several central organs were decidedly lacking in their enthusiasm for raising further the status of the VVBs.

This hostility to the new methods and roles inherent in the New Economic System/Economic System of Socialism had been foreseen right at the beginning of the change. At the June 1963 conference, for instance, Erich Apel had warned that the danger in NES lay not in the granting of too high a level of autonomy to the VVBs, but in that the central state organs might be unable to fit in with the intentions and spirit of the reform. In this context Apel was particularly critical of the National Economic Council and the Ministry of Finance.[89] At the same conference, a VVB deputy general director, Fritz Teuscher, elaborated on the problems his VVB had experienced (it was one of the four in which experiments were being conducted in 1963) from these and other central organs. His main complaint was of the excessive number of directives and regulations coming from above, especially concerning investment. He singled out four bodies that had been particularly guilty in this connection: the National Economic Council, the Ministry of Finance, the Ministry for Construction, and the Central Office for Statistics. Teuscher argued that one of the problems was that the industrial (i.e., specialized branch) departments of the National Economic Council were to have a new, more general coordinatory and long-term role under NES, which the people working in these bodies did not always appear to have grasped.[90] Apel agreed with Teuscher's analysis of the problem, while Ulbricht went considerably further at this conference in his criticism of the National Economic Council's attitude toward the new role of the VVBs, making it quite clear that there had been opposition from this body to the concept of greater autonomy for the VVBs. Thus, against the spirit of NES, the Council and other central bodies had continued to send vast numbers of detailed instructions to the VVBs instead of performing their intended role of coordination and supervision. The reason soon becomes obvious: Ulbricht argued that as the role of the VVBs became more significant, so the apparatus of the Council could be reduced. The best of the functionaries were to go from the general departments (*Querschnittabteilungen*) either to the Council's industrial departments or to the VVBs themselves, so that gradually most of the general departments would disappear. If this were to be the fate of the best of these people, the question arose of the future of their less able colleagues. Ulbricht did not answer this question directly, but did give a hint on their fate. Many would be retrained and given jobs commensurate with their new skills. If this meant demotion, so be it; the First Secretary was quite explicit that development, even in a socialist society, could not always proceed without conflict.[91]

It is instructive to compare the sort of criticisms made by leading politicians and others of the central state organs at this crucial meeting on NES with the speeches by representatives of the organs under attack. Thus, Alfred Neumann, Politburo member and Chairman of the National Economic Council, paid lip service to the general line of increasing the rights and responsibilities of the VVBs, also saying that the industrial departments of the Council would have to change their workstyle. Rather than agree with the suggestion that the general departments be disbanded, however, Neumann argued merely that their activity would have to be better coordinated with the production principle. He also counterattacked the VVBs themselves, saying that there were VVB directors with a very limited knowledge of profit-and-loss accounting, the new methods of balancing and sales.[92] Although this did not represent an explicit rejection of Ulbricht's criticisms, the nature of Neumann's language and the emphasis strongly suggest that the Chairman of the National Economic Council was piqued at this criticism of his own staff. In similar Aesopian language, the then Minister of Finance, Willy Rumpf, supported the general policy of devolving decision-making within the industrial administrative hierarchy while at the same time arguing that local finance organs (i.e., directly under his ministry) could assume many of the functions that the central finance organs had formerly discharged. In other words, while talking of decentralization, he ensured that this was in such a way that the lower levels would still be very much under the direct supervision of his ministry. He was thus the only speaker at the conference who argued that financial questions formerly decided by central organs would now be resolved *either* by the VVBs or by the local finance organs.[93] This evoked a response from Apel, who in his concluding remarks at the conference stated that it was far from clear to him from the Minister of Finance's speech exactly what concrete changes the minister envisaged in the work of the finance organs, thus implying that there appeared to be none.[94]

Criticisms of the central organs' attitudes and actions continued for some time. For instance, Ulbricht attacked the industrial departments of the National Economic Council "and other organs" in

February 1964 for continuing to take decisions for which the VVBs should be responsible.[95] However, the attacks became weaker, so that by the time of the speech evaluating the success of the first stage of the implementation of the New Economic System (December 1965), Ulbricht did not make any specific criticisms of the central organs' activities vis-à-vis the VVBs. Indeed, he argued that with the clearer delineation of rights between the (new) ministries, VVBs etc., the autonomy and initiative of both the general-directors of the VVBs and the managers of the nationalised enterprises had made good progress.[96] This said, it could be argued that the excuse Ulbricht gave at this session for replacing the industrial sections of the National Economic Council with eight ministries (namely, that very often decisions were taken further up the industrial hierarchy than they ought to have been) should be accepted at face value. However, three factors militate against such acceptance. First, the number of complaints had declined previous to this speech. Second, it seems very clear from its timing that the East German introduction of ministries was, superficially at least, mere emulation of the Soviet changes. Third, if there really was concern that too many decisions were being taken by the Council's departments, why were they transformed into ministries rather than being abolished completely (i.e., instead of being replaced by functional equivalents)?[97]

Later criticisms of the poor functioning of NES/ESS focused mainly on the VVBs themselves rather than the bodies above them, so that it does look as if the branch ministries were not being excessively difficult with the VVBs.[98] As we have also seen, the same cannot be said of, in particular, the Ministry of Finance and Ministry of Foreign Trade in relation to both the combines and the VVBs.[99] In the 1970s, however, the fact that both investments and foreign trade have largely been recentralized suggests that our inability to find criticisms of these bodies' attitudes toward either type of association reflects the actual situation. One question that arises at this point is whether the very fact of recentralization itself was a reflection of pressure from the central organs, or at least of a perception by the leadership that it could not ultimately force these bodies to implement its wishes. This is, of course, a possibility; but since, as we saw in Chapter 4, there were senior leaders (including Honecker) who had their misgivings about the combines and who were more interested in the enterprises and the ministries, this suggestion is not convincing.

OPPOSITION FROM THE VVB MANAGEMENT

It may appear incongruous to write of VVB opposition to associations; it must therefore be clarified that in this section we are looking at opposition from VVB directors to the new role expected of them under NES as well as to the combines.

While there is scant evidence of unwillingness of VVB directors to accept the new responsibilities accorded them by NES, Mittag was not the only one to point to such lack of enthusiasm in the early days.[100] For instance, Ulbricht himself referred in 1963 to an unwillingness on the part of some VVBs to accept greater responsibility for scientific-technical progress in their branches.[101] After that, there is little evidence. The fact that at least sixteen VVBs had new directors in the period 1963-1965 could suggest grave dissatisfaction with the directors that were replaced, but the incomplete data we have on the movement of such people show that in many cases the reverse was true; i.e., the VVB directors were promoted, presumably as a reward for good performance.[102] Thus this does not appear to have been a major source of opposition to association policy.

There is rather more evidence of and reason to infer opposition of VVB management to the combines. At the 1967 seminar, for instance, Ulbricht stated that the Ruhla combine had had changes made in its structure against the wishes of the appropriate VVB.[103] The director of this combine, Wedler, himself indirectly explained why the VVB should be hostile. He made the point that by eliminating the VVB in the administration of his part of industry, not one but three links were removed:

> Under the old management structure, a decision concerned with research and technology, for instance, had to go from the enterprise to the product group management, from the product group to the specialist section of the VVB, from the specialist section to the management section (*Direktionsbereich*) of the VVB; there, the appropriate institutes and establishments were consulted, then the decision went to the general director of the VVB and then it went the second round.
>
> The present management structure saves weeks and months of "decision time."[104]

Wedler did not actually suggest that the VVBs were superfluous, but he did say that there could be improvements in their operating methods (e.g., similar shortened decision-making paths). He further argued that his combine performed the tasks of a VVB without any addition to the administrative work force; VVBs with a volume of production similar to Ruhla's at that time employed between 50 and 250 workers.[105] The implication was that the VVBs were overstaffed and/or superfluous, which almost certainly would have led to feelings of hostility among at least some VVB personnel. Since, as we have seen, some VVBs were indeed replaced by combines, such hostility based on fear for one's position was sometimes well founded.

At the same time (1967), Ulbricht was explaining that VVBs were to implement the Economic System of Socialism more fully, one aspect of which was that they were to create more combines and product groups.[106] This meant that the VVBs themselves would no longer be the direct superiors of as many enterprises. Thus, the VVBs were threatened in two ways at this time by the combines: They might be replaced by them, or else they might have to transfer some of their work to them. Since Ulbricht explicitly stated that VVB personnel rendered superfluous by such changes would be sent to combines or enterprises, it again becomes clear why opposition to the combines might arise.

At the end of 1969, legislation appeared that transferred additional tasks to the combines from the VVBs. The Council of Ministers' resolution set out in detail how combines directly subordinate to a ministry would have *most* of the rights of a VVB. These included patenting rights and the right to supervise product groups. Of course, since these rights applied to the combines already directly subordinate to ministries, they were possibly not perceived as a major new threat to the VVBs. Of greater significance, therefore, was the stipulation in the resolution that some combines subordinate to a VVB could, by prior agreement with the minister (*not* the VVB), also be granted these rights if this was considered to be in the interests of greater efficiency.[107] This would clearly have constituted a threat to the VVBs, and in fact was to some extent illogical. Since most of these rights were ones that the VVBs themselves had enjoyed, a transfer of them to the combines obviously put the whole raison d'être of the VVBs in question, leaving them directly in charge only of the smaller, less important enterprises not yet in a combine. The same resolution also allowed for the possibility of both kinds of combine (those directly under a ministry and those under a VVB) having the full rights of a VVB in foreign trade and pricing; and it stipulated that seminationalized enterprises hitherto supervised by a VVB (i.e., through being in product groups) could henceforth be subordinate to a combine if the product group supervision were to be transferred to the combine, and subject to the agreement of the enterprise manager and the relevant ministry(-ies).[108] Clearly, the threat of the combines to the VVBs was growing, and it seems likely that this would have led to much opposition to the newer type of association from within the VVBs. As we have seen, however, both types of association were very soon to start losing power to the ministries, so that the position did not last very long.

OPPOSITION FROM MANAGEMENT IN SECONDARY ENTERPRISES

We have found no evidence of opposition from enterprise managers to the expanded role of the VVBs as such; in that the VVBs were to take powers from the central organs rather than from the enterprises, this is what would be expected.

However, there is evidence of hostility or at least a lack of enthusiasm for both the product groups (the combine predecessors) and the combines. Thus, at the 1963 conference there was a complaint about the reluctance of some personnel from locally administered enterprises to have their factories included in a product group; apparently, they feared losing much of their autonomy or else "had other ideas."[109] The meaning of the latter phrase was not explained, but it is possible that it referred to the tendency, mentioned by Scheler in 1967, for the management of some nationalized enterprises to attempt to expand their own units rather than join with other units to form a combine or product group. In fact, Scheler said that the *majority* of enterprises were still attempting to develop extensively, when labor shortages and party policy called for intensive development.[110] It is probable that experience of similar attitudes lay behind Thieme's call in 1970 for more positive attitudes toward the combine in many component units of such associations.[111]

It was not only managers in nationalized enterprises who lacked the desired enthusiasm for being included in product groups. Apparently, directors of private enterprises were often either skeptical about having their unit included in such an arrangement or else accepted it, expecting it to be only a temporary measure.[112] If this was the attitude toward product groups, there was probably even less enthusiasm for combines.

Having said all this, there is evidence that the interests of individual units going into combines were not always observed in the manner the legislators intended. Thus, in blatant contradiction of the regulations on this, some combines changed the names of component units from their former enterprise names; given the East German interest in this aspect of combine development, such actions must have led to hostility and fear among enterprise directors whose factories were not yet included in a combine.[113] In addition, it is clear that some combines have deprived component units of rights that senior party officials felt these enterprises should have retained,[114] which has undoubtedly also led to friction.

OPPOSITION FROM MANAGEMENT IN THE HEAD ENTERPRISES OF COMBINES

Although we have no hard evidence of opposition to their new role from the management of head enterprises, it seems likely that the sort of situation described in the Soviet Union has also arisen in the GDR. In the NARVA combine, for instance, the backward enterprises were developed at the expense of the more advanced ones, particularly the head enterprise. The directors of the combine also had more work than they had had previously.[115] Moreover, Walter Halbritter argued in 1970 that many combine directors needed to change their attitudes and accept that they were responsible for the whole combine, not merely its head enterprise.[116] Such managerial attitudes can hardly have been conducive to good relations within the combines, and reflect the reluctance of some directors to accept their new, expanded role.

OPPOSITION FROM LOCAL STATE ORGANS

There is some evidence that Regional Economic Councils have not always been cooperative with the VVBs in terms of encouraging the inclusion of locally administered enterprises in product groups — in all probability for the same reasons that local state organs in the Soviet Union were loath to lose "their" enterprises. In 1963, for example, Teuscher praised one council for its cooperativeness in this matter (Karl-Marx-Stadt), while Leipzig Council was strongly criticized for its refusal to work with the VVB Woolen Wear and Hosiery.[117]

There is also evidence of opposition on the part of local state functionaries toward the combines. Thus a deputy chairman of the State Planning Commission complained in 1969 that some combines (and enterprises) were paying insufficient attention to local conditions, and were attempting to give local state bodies the passive role of "suppliers of the proper production conditions." Quite what is meant by this term is not explained, but the implication is clear that some combines have tried to downgrade the role of the local state organs in industrial administration.[118] In a 1972 article, moreover, the director of social affairs of a combine enterprise admitted that his enterprise and the combine as a whole had in the past often paid far too little attention to the representatives of the local state organs when the latter had approached the combine on issues such as housing for the combine's work force.[119] Finally, it seems probably that the local state organs were not entirely satisfied with the 1973 legislation on the combines: The original March legislation was modified in August so as to limit still further the role of the local state bodies in the administration of the combines, reducing their rights to be involved in matters concerning the welfare of the combines' work forces.[120]

OPPOSITION FROM PARTY ORGANS

Regretfully, inference must again dominate hard evidence in this section.

One possible source of friction within the party concerns the VVBs' increased role under the New Economic System. In order to ensure that the party organizations within the VVBs fully understood their new role and saw to the implementation of NES from 1963 on, the Central Committee Secretariat sent party organisers from the central party headquarters to some of the key VVBs.[121] It is possible that this interference from above, resulting from the upgraded role of the VVBs, led to resentment among some party officials. This pattern could well have been reflected down the administrative hierarchy. Thus the VVB party secretaries were instructed to involve themselves considerably more in the work of the enterprises below them, which could have irritated enterprise party secretaries.[122] However, it should also be pointed out that there is another side to this development. One enterprise party secretary, for instance, was critical of the fact that under the new arrangement, enterprise secretaries had to attend too many meetings, commissions, and so on outside the production unit.[123] In other words, the greater involvement and responsibility expected of enterprise party secretaries also led to some resentment among them.[124]

Moreover, not all *local* party organs have always been cooperative with the VVBs. Mittag referred at the 1963 conference to a VVB that had wanted to rationalize its branch, a process that involved converting a particular enterprise to more specialized production. But the VVB was hindered in this by the first secretary of a district party organization, since the conversion would have involved problems for the enterprise in the transitional period. Mittag further criticized those party functionaries who avoided change to avoid conflict, such as those who shied away from rationalization measures when these involved a reduction in the number of administrative personnel.[125] While this would not have applied to combines to any meaningful extent in 1963, it can be inferred that such resistance also occurred with the development of these bodies later in the decade.

Finally, since the East Germans too have had Councils of Party Secretaries since 1973,[126] the suggestions concerning these in the Soviet Union would presumably also apply to the GDR. However, a more fundamental restructuring of the SED's "base organizations" along the lines of the changes introduced in the Soviet functional equivalents (the primary party organizations) does not appear to have been made, so that less hostility would be expected.

SUGGESTED FURTHER SOURCES OF OPPOSITION

As in the USSR, so in the GDR the fact that industrial concentration and centralization can lead to even less participation of workers (both blue-collar and white-collar) in decision-making may well lead to feelings of hostility toward the associations. The VVBs had advisory bodies called Technical-Economic Councils until 1963, which were then disbanded; these bodies seem to have been ineffective.[127] In December 1965, senior politicians appeared to acknowledge that the running of the VVBs could and should become more democratic, when it was announced at the 11th plenum of the Central Committee that "social councils" were to be established in all VVBs. These councils were to have wider powers than their predecessors, in that they were not only to advise the general directors on social as well as technical matters, but also to check that management responded to their recommendations.[128] However, these bodies too were eventually dissolved in 1973, partially because it was felt that there was excessive duplication of bodies for realizing socialist democracy and, in particular, to strengthen the role of the trade unions.[129] There had certainly been complaints from trade unionists that the trade union committee in some VVBs had not been heeded by management,[130] but this also pertained to the social councils. Apparently,

> these councils were clearly not sufficiently successful in the practice of management precisely because the collective deliberation of the managers (*Leiter*) and the involvement of the workers, engineers, etc. in management were more or less formally, institutionally bound up with each other. It seems better to give the manager the possibility of linking these two aims with optimal effect in this or that way according to the content of the task.[131]

If the arrangement was not working well before the 1973 legislation, it would certainly seem that workers and lower management have had even fewer opportunities for involvement in decision-making in the VVB since then, as there is now not even a minimum formal requirement that they be consulted. These changes in the VVBs in recent years cannot have been well received by all employees.

In the combines, there were until 1973 several organizations for representing and, more important, involving the workers; these included the production committees, the scientific-economic councils, and the "permanent production consultative bodies."[132] Despite all these organs, there had been problems in involving employees in the running of the combines, a fact the senior leadership acknowledged at the 13th plenum of the Central Committee in 1970.[133] A a result of this and of other meetings at which the problem of raising "combine consciousness" was discussed, the Council of Ministers decreed in September 1970 that the directors of combines and combine enterprises (as well as ordinary enterprises) should give monthly reports to their workers;[134] hitherto, directors had normally delivered their reports on the general progress and future development of the combine only to the (senior) functionaries, not the workers.[135] However, it would appear that concern about a lack of socialist democracy was only one, and not necessarily the major, reason for the passing of the decree. Several speakers had complained at the July 1970 meeting on combines of a lack of enthusiasm for the new associations — particularly among blue-collar workers — and of the effect this was having on the *efficiency* of these bodies.[136] This interest in economic performance probably contributed as much to the 1970 decree as the concern about democracy. Similarly, the abolition of several of the representative bodies in 1973 — simultaneous with such developments in the VVBs[137] — can be seen at least as much in terms of a desire for greater efficiency as for more involvement of the work force in decision-making. The 1973 changes left only the trade union organizations to represent the interests of the workers.[138] Although Zimmermann's research into the East German trade unions suggests that their role has increased somewhat in the 1970s (seen, for instance, in the new Code of Labor Law, which became operative at the beginning of 1978), it is in practice largely their responsibilities which have increased rather than their rights and influence in decision-making. Zimmermann himself acknowledges that the role of the trade unions in combines and enterprises can only be understood in the context of one-person management, democratic centralism, and the political primacy of the SED.[139]

Moreover, the trade unions have generally supported rationalization measures involving, inter alia, the creation of combines and the abolition of VVBs (as part of the reorganization of the branch structure).[140] Given the poor combine consciousness referred to above, it can be assumed that various rationalization measures, particularly connected with combines, have been received with hostility in some quarters, and that trade union support for such measures has led to frustration and alienation among workers. Let us consider two well-known examples; both concern the often acute labor shortages in the GDR and the measures taken to reduce the size of work forces (while maintaining or improving output and quality) and/or to redistribute workers. Such measures are usually seen as most appropriate in large units — combines and amalgamated enterprises — where production lines and various forms of automated administrative systems can be installed, and which would be impracticable in small enterprises.[141] The first example is from the Leuna chemical combine. By 1973, the combine employed in excess of 30,000 people, and this number was not to rise before 1980 at the earliest. On the other hand, considerable expansion of production was envisaged. As a consequence, two new production units were under construction within the combine, and these would lead to the creation of 467 new jobs. This apparent dilemma was to be solved by rationalizing the administration within the combine and transferring former white-collar workers to production work. The number of administrative posts was thus to decline by 11 percent, primarily by increasing the load and the responsibility of the administrators remaining. In 1972, 206 administrative posts were abolished. In addition, 329 so-called black office-workers (*schwarze Angestellte*) — former production workers who had been transferred to desk jobs — were returned to production. It is unlikely that everyone affected by this development accepted it gracefully! Moreover, the number of cadres with a completed higher education going into production work rather than administration had been rising steadily within the combine, from 130 in 1970 to 300 in 1973. The majority of these people were young and had a degree in engineering. It is highly probable that some of these, too, resented the situation in the combine, in which upward mobility channels were becoming increasingly narrow.[142]

The second example is the Schwedt petrochemical combine, which in recent years has pursued a well-publicized policy of "fewer produce more." As a result, 1443 workers throughout the combine were to have been "released" for "new, interesting tasks in other production areas" in 1980 alone, a development fully supported by the chairman of the combine's trade union committee, Max Tschirner.[143] It is far from clear that such trade union attitudes would help to raise enthusiasm for combines — i.e., improve combine consciousness — among many workers.

East German legislators have dealt with the problem of salaries in associations more rapidly and probably more efficiently than their Soviet counterparts, and have thereby lessened conflict. Basically, the East German approach has been to leave most of the decisions on this to be settled by the individual combine, and in the 1968 legislation it was overtly stipulated that all questions relating to salaries and wages were to be agreed upon with the trade unions *before* the establishment of a combine.[144] There is certainly evidence of dissatisfaction with incomes in the GDR,[145] but we have been unable to relate this specifically to the associations. Moreover, since the East Germans have produced so much legislation — which is frequently intended specifically to overcome problems arising from the implementation of earlier decrees and the like — the fact that none of this has related directly to incomes suggests that this was not perceived as a significant problem.

Moreover, since the enterprises in an East German combine seem to have enjoyed more autonomy than the component units of a production *ob"edinenie*, it is unlikely that the Germans have faced the same problems over management prestige as the Soviets. Linked to this is the fact that the East Germans have not raised expectations of greater enterprise autonomy to the extent that the Russians did in 1965; consequently, there are unlikely to have been the same feelings of bitterness in the GDR as in the USSR when associations have taken rights from individual enterprises. This said, the rationalization measures that usually accompany the formation of a combine/ production *ob"edinenie* have led to identical problems and some hostility in both states.

Local party and state functionaries have sometimes been opposed to associations in the USSR, seemingly less so in the GDR. One noticeable difference between the two states, however, has been the role of the branch ministries and their subdivisions in defending their interests against the associations, and it is likely that this source of opposition has been a major contributory factor to the differing rates of association development in the USSR and the GDR. On the other hand, certain nonbranch ministries have played virtually identical roles in both countries; the conservative nature of the Ministries of Finance is particularly obvious. In sum, vested interests have led to hostility to the associations, which in turn has had a definite effect on their progress. Let us now pull all these, and other, strands of the policy process together.

NOTES

1. Bobrov, "Sovetskaya Firma," p. 2; A. Golenishev, "Partkom i Ob"edinenie," *Pravda*, 30 August 1973, p. 2; and Pevzner, *Khozraschet v* . . . , p. 22.
2. K. Ryavec in Skilling and Griffiths, *Interest Groups* . . . , passim; Schroeder, "Soviet Economic Reform . . . ," passim; and Pospelova, "Khozraschetnye Ob"edineniya . . . ," p. 132.
3. Bobrov, "Sovetskaya Firma," p. 2.
4. For example, Grushetskii, "Sovetskie Firmy . . . ," p. 3.
5. Ivonin, "Vygoda Dokazana," p. 3. In some cases, specialists from branch administrations were to be transferred to the enterprises of *firmy*; see Slusarenko and Krupenchik in Meleshkin, *Pervye Sovetskie Firmy*, p. 14.
6. V. Shkvorets, "Kak rasti ob"edineniyu," *Pravda*, 11 August 1972, p. 2.
7. B. Shchegolev, "Shtab Tekhnicheskogo Progressa," *Sots. Ind.*, 21 February 1971, p. 2.
8. V. Burtsev, "Molchanie — Ne Luchshii Otvet," *Sots. Ind.*, 14 March 1971, p. 2.
9. I. Divnogortsev, "Za Svoim Zaborom," *Sots. Ind.*, 3 January 1971, p. 2.
10. Kovalenko, "Shagi Ob"edineniya," p. 2.
11. *Ibid.*, p. 2.
12. Burtsev, "Molchanie . . . ," p. 2.
13. E. Yudin, "Kompleksnyi Podkhod, Vsestoronnyi Analiz," *Pravda*, 30 May 1972, p. 3.
14. "Kompleksno, S Perspektivoi," p. 18.
15. N. Morozov, "Na Puti K Ob"edineniyam," *Pravda*, 27 March 1972, p. 2.
16. Baibakov, "Zadachy Sovershenstvovaniya . . . ," esp. pp. 5, 7. According to Dzhavadov and Dunaev (*Proizvodstvennye Ob"edineniya* . . . , pp. 47-48), some such heads also did not notice the difference between *glavki* and production *ob"edineniya*.
17. Antonov in Gvishiani and Kamenitser, *Problemy* . . . , 1974, pp. 161-169.
18. V. Pivovarov, "Lider potoka — Kombinat," *Pravda*, 2 December 1973, p. 2.
19. L. Ryzhenko, cited in Nevelyuk, "Firmy . . . ," p. 2.
20. Markin, *Effektivnost'* . . . , p. 41.
21. Shchegolev, "Shtab . . . ," p. 2.
22. E. Pospelova, "Uspekh ne prikhodit Samotekom," *Sots. Ind.*, 13 October 1972, p. 2.
23. Shchegolev, "Shtab . . . ," p. 2, and Bakalo, "Nerealizovannye Vygody," p. 2.
24. Dumachev, *Khozraschetnye Ob"edineniya* . . . , p. 101.
25. Other "good" ministries include the All-Union section of the Union-Republic Ministry of the Meat and Dairy Industry and of the Union-Republic Ministry of the Timber and Woodworking Industry. Other "bad" ones include the All-Union Ministry of Machine-Tool and Instrument-Making, the All-Union Ministry for the Light and Food Industries and Household Appliances, and the Ministry of Heavy, Transport and Energy Engineering. See Smirnov, "Slovo — za Ministerstvami," p. 7; "Kurs — Sozdanie Ob"edinenii," p. 2; V. Andreev, "Otkhody Lesa

— Tsennoe Syr'e," *Sots. Ind.*, 11 March 1971, p. 2; criticisms by Ryabov, Akulintsev, and Smirnov at the 1970 seminar in Dumachev and Varsobin, *Opyt Organizatsii* . . . , pp. 160, 184, 190-191; and V. Gusev and A. Khachaturyan, "Upravlenie v Podotrasli," *Sots. Ind.*, 3 November 1976, p. 2.
    26. V. G. Vishnyakov, "Problemy Sovershenstvovaniya Upravleniya Promyshlennost'yu," *Pravovedenie*, No. 1, 1973, p. 26.
    27. Takoev in Bachurin, *Sovershenstvovanie Planirovaniya* . . . , pp. 73-74.
    28. Guzhkov, *ibid.*, pp. 263-275.
    29. This hypothesis seems to be supported by a reference in Dumachev, *Effektivnaya Sistema* . . . , p. 104.
    30. Nevelyuk, "Firmy . . . ," p. 2.
    31. Selyunin, "Logika . . . ," p. 2.
    32. Dumachev, *Khozraschetnye Ob"edineniya* . . . , p. 101.
    33. For an explanation of this anomaly, see Popov and Petrov, "Na Putyakh k Ob"edineniyam," p. 2.
    34. Dumachev, *Partiinye Organizatsiya* . . . , p. 104.
    35. N. Volokh in Meleshkin, *Pervye Sovetskie Firmy*, p. 65.
    36. Shimanskii, "Ministerstvo . . . ," p. 2. See too Lenev and Apse, "Ob"edinenie v Puti," p. 2, and Morozov, "Na Puti . . . ," p. 2.
    37. Dumachev, *Khozraschetnye Ob"edineniya* . . . , pp. 102-103; evidently the picture still pertained into the late 1970s; see an almost identical quotation in Dumachev, *Partiinye Organizatsii* . . . , p. 17.
    38. "Sovetskie Firmy," p. 13.
    39. Dzhavadov and Dunaev, *Proizvodstvennye Ob"edineniya* . . . , pp. 78-79. According to the authors, a Council of Directors is not feasible in all *ob"edineniya*, but their explanation of why this should be is shallow. (Their basic argument is that there is little need for one in very centralized *ob"edineniya*!)
    40. On the Councils of Directors, see Savitskaya in Meleshkin, *Pervye Sovetskie Firmy*, p. 102; Radomysel'skii and Shifrin, *Firmy* . . . , pp. 122-123; Chuplinskas and Baranauskas, *Tak Rabotaet* . . . , pp. 17-19, 28-31, 55; Pevzner, *Khozraschet v* . . . , pp. 50-52; Dunaev, *Ob"edineniya Predpriyatii* . . . , p. 19; and the papers in *Vsesoyuznaya Nauchnaya* . . . , Vol. 4.
    41. Radomysel'skii and Shifrin, *Firmy* . . . , pp. 43-46.
    42. Markin, *Effektivnost'* . . . , p. 42.
    43. Pospelova, "Khozraschetnye Ob"edineniya . . . ," p. 133. See, too, note 69.
    44. Dumachev, *Effektivnaya Sistema* . . . , p. 120.
    45. See A. Lyakhov, "Zavod i NII," *Sots. Ind.*, 16 February 1971, p. 2.
    46. Malevanyi, "Effekt Obshchikh Usilii," p. 3.
    47. D. A., "Proizvodstvennye Ob"edineniya . . . ," p. 154. For an early example of such hostility, see Ivonin, "Vygoda Dokazana," p. 3.
    48. Yu. Kuznetsov, "Firmy Mestnoi Promyshlennosti," *Izvestiya*, 21 May 1972, p. 3.
    49. A. Baranov, "Vmesto Trestov — Ob"edineniya," *Ekon. Gaz.*, No. 8, 1970, p. 10.
    50. *Ibid.*, p. 10
    51. V. Glukharev, "Golovnoe Predpriyatie i Filial," *Sots. Ind.*, 11 February 1977, p. 2, and B. Khorev, "Bol'shaya Stroika v malom Gorode," *Pravda*, 16 April 1978, p. 2.
    52. Romanov, "Novye Usloviya . . . ," p. 51. Romanov has been on the Politburo since April 1973, and a full member since March 1976. While ambiguous attitudes among party leaders toward the *ob"edineniya* could be used to "excuse"

opposition to these bodies from lower party officials, this would not pertain after the December 1969 plenum or, at the very latest, the 24th Congress (Spring 1971).
53. Dumachev, *Khozraschetnye Ob"edineniya* . . . , p. 102.
54. Nevelyuk, "Firmy . . . ," p. 2.
55. *Ibid.,* p. 2.
56. Zdorov, "Proizvodstvennye Ob"edineniya . . . ," p. 4. On party finances see L. Schapiro, *The Communist Party of the Soviet Union* (London: Methuen, 1970), p. 587.
57. For details, see T. Dunmore, "Local Party Organs in Industrial Administration: The Case of the Ob"edinenie Reform," *Soviet Studies*, No. 2, 1980, pp. 200-210; Yu. Khristoradnov, "V Usloviyakh Proizvodstvennogo Ob"edineniya," *Kommunist*, No. 14, 1978, pp. 105-115; (Unsigned). "Konsul'tatsiya — Sovet Sekretarei Partorganizatsii Proizvodstvennogo Ob"edineniya," *Part. Zh.*, No. 18, 1978, pp. 45-50. This change in the party statutes followed two party directives of 1976 (the Central Committee's decree of 16 August, "O rabote partiinykh organizatsii Gor'kovskogo avtomobil'nogo zavoda v usloviyakh proizvodstvennogo ob"edineniya," and the notes of various central committee departments, "O nekotorykh voprosakh organizatsionnogo postroeniya i formakh raboty partiinykh organizatsii v usloviyakh proizvodstvennykh ob"edinenii v promyshlennosti"). Such practice was already operative in the Leningrad *ob"edineniya* by the mid-1970s. See Dumachev, *Effektivnaya Sistema* . . . , p. 124.
58. Dunmore, "Local Party Organs . . . ," p. 202.
59. For example, Smirnov, "Slovo . . . ," p. 7, and "Konsul'tatsiya — Sovet Sekretarei . . . ," passim.
60. Romanov, "Novye Usloviya . . . ," p. 58.
61. Dunmore, "Local Party Organs . . . ," pp. 200-210.
62. Based on figures in Dunmore, *ibid.*, p. 202.
63. *Ibid.*, p. 206, and "Konsul'tatsiya — Sovet Sekretarei . . . ," p. 46.
64. Cf. Dumachev, *Effektivnaya Sistema* . . . , p. 139, and *Partiinye Organizatsii* . . . , p. 97; Khristoradnov, "V Usloviyakh . . . ," p. 113; and A. Novikov, "Partorganizatsiya v Usloviyakh Proizvodstvennogo Ob"edineniya," *Part. Zh.*, No. 12, 1978, p. 41.
65. See the program of the CPSU in *Pravda*, 2 November 1961, p. 9. See also Brezhnev in *XXIV S'ezd* . . . , Vol. 1, p. 123, where he refers to a reduction of more than 20 percent in the professional party apparatus during the preceding fourteen years.
66. See, for example, Dumachev, *Effektivnaya Sistema* . . . , p. 140. Lack of evidence seems strange, given the information we have on hostility from other quarters. It is possible, although unlikely, that this means there is no opposition. A more convincing explanation is that Soviet writers concentrate on what they perceive to be significant opposition (that which is hindering the development of the associations). This in itself would be important in assessing the political significance of the lowest levels of the party.
67. Golenishev, "Partkom i Ob"edinenie," p. 2.
68. However, see Dunmore, "Local Party Organs . . . ," pp. 207-209. He suggests that many "new" bodies are, in fact, merely renamed and gutted PPOs.
69. Romanov, "Novye Usloviya . . . ," p. 58.
70. Taksir, "Nauchno-Proizvodstvennye Ob"edineniya," p. 46.
71. A. Vasil'ev, "Izlishestvu Shtatov — Zaslon," *Sov. Kirg.*, 9 September 1970, p. 2. For an up-to-date analysis of how to deal with the problem within one

ob"edinenie, see B. I. Maksimov, *Kak Upravlyat' Peremeshcheniem Kadrov v Ob"edinenii* (Leningrad: Lenizdat, 1979).

72. F. Parkin, *Class Inequality and Political Order* (London: Paladin, 1972), pp. 147-149. Not all would agree with this analysis, it should be noted; see D. Lane, *The End of Inequality?* (Harmondsworth: Penguin, 1971), passim, esp. pp. 78-79.

73. On ASUP generally, see "ASU — Na Sluzhbu Pyatiletke," *Ekon. Gaz.*, No. 28, 1973. pp. 7-8.

74. On this, see Radomysel'skii and Shifrin, *Firmy . . .* , pp. 43-44, and Markin, *Effektivnost' . . .* , pp. 42-44. See too note 80, below.

75. Pospelova, "Khozraschetnye Ob"edineniya," p. 133.

76. Taksir, "Nauchno-Proizvodstvennye Ob"edineniya," p. 49. The reason for this is not fully explained by Taksir, but seems to be because the engineers and the like in the factories (i.e., producing units) receive more bonus than those in "mere" research institutes. See too Komlev, *Promyshlennye Ob"edineniya . . .* , p. 21.

77. F. Markov, "Bez Dvoevlastiya na Remonte," *Sots. Ind*, 21 September 1972, p. 2.

78. Popov, *Sovershenstvovanie System . . .* , pp. 206-207. Into the mid-1970s there were complaints that no new model structure for the "permanent production conferences" (one form of worker participation) or for the trade union committees in production *ob"edineniya* had been approved, which meant that many such bodies functioned poorly or not at all when an association was formed. Although this problem was partially dealt with by the issuance of a decree on the trade union committees late in 1976, problems have persisted. See Yu. Baranov, "Avtoritet PDPS Ob"edineniya," *Ekon. Gaz.*, No. 41, 1975, p. 14; V. N. Polivanov, "Profkom Ob"edineniya," *Trud*, 11 November 1976, p. 2; and (unsigned) "Profkom Ob"edineniya," *Trud*, 3 August 1977, p. 1.

79. See, for example, E. Pospelova "Idet Eksperiment," *Sots. Ind.*, 9 May 1978, p. 2.

80. See "Postanovlenie . . . Ob Utverzhdenii . . . ," paras. 3, 4, esp. the final sentence of para. 4. See too the conditions stipulated in "Polozhenie o Proizvodstvennom . . . ," paras. 115, 116.

81. "Postanovlenie . . . O Nekotorykh . . . ," para. 8. However, details of the compensation arrangements are not given; these were to be the responsibility of *Gosplan* and the Ministry of Finance. We have been unable to trace any such document.

82. Sh. Khodzhaev, "Pochemu medlenno sozdayutsya ob"edineniya," *Pravda*, 14 January 1974; Dumachev, *Effektivnaya Sistema . . .* , pp. 118-120, and Glukharev, "Golovnoe Predpriyatie . . . ," p. 2.

83. The problem also applies to industrial *ob"edineniya*; on all this see G. San'kov, "Stimulirovanie v Podotrasli," *Sots. Ind.*, 12 October 1976, p. 2, and E. Polisyuk, "Real'nost' Prav," *Sots. Ind.*, 13 May 1977, p. 2.

84. S. Pomorski, "The Soviet Economic Associations: Some Problems of Legal Status and Organisation after the 1973 Reform," *Review of Socialist Law*, No. 3, 1976, p. 114. Unfortunately, Pomorski does not produce any evidence to endorse his hypothesis.

85. Zimmermann, "Wandel von Industrieverwaltungen . . . ," pp. 136-137, also failed to find evidence of conflicts in the VVB organizations: "It emerged that only very little — and no concrete information — on latent and manifest conflicts in the VVB organizations finds its way into publications, so that nothing can be said about the informal processes."

86. H., "Vor Gruendung . . . ," p. 3.
87. S. Boehm in *Der Weg zur Durchfuehrung* . . . , pp. 46-47.
88. K. Sorgenicht, *ibid.*, pp. 27-30, esp. p. 28.
89. E. Apel in *Das Neue Oekonomische System* . . . , pp. 278-280, 284.
90. F. Teuscher, *ibid.*, pp. 154-155.
91. W. Ulbricht, *ibid.*, pp. 20-21, 82-89, 115.
92. A. Neumann, *ibid.*, pp. 174-181.
93. W. Rumpf, *ibid.*, pp. 254-260.
94. E. Apel, *ibid.*, p. 284.
95. W. Ulbricht at the 5th plenum of the Central Committee, in *Zum Neuen Oekonomischen System* . . . , p. 412.
96. *Ibid.*, pp. 671-674, esp. p. 673. The only, marginal criticism is to be found on pp. 669-670.
97. On the establishment of the ministries and the reasons for this given by Ulbricht, see *ibid.*, pp. 663-751, esp. pp. 704-711.
98. However, see G. Leptin in Hoehmann, Kaser, and Thalheim, *The New Economic Systems* . . . , p. 51; unfortunately, it is unclear whether Leptin is referring at this point to the general ministries or the industrial branch ministries. Even if it is the latter, see the point in text accompanying note 116 to Ch. 1.
99. See, for example, H. Wedler, in *Der Weg zur Durchfuehrung* . . . , p. 44.
100. G. Mittag in *Das Neue Oekonomische System* . . . , p. 163.
101. Ulbricht, *ibid.*, p. 100.
102. This information is from our own collection of data on the VVBs and their directors.
103. Ulbricht, "Der Weg zur Durchfuehrung . . . ," p. 4.
104. Wedler, *Der Weg zur Durchfuehrung* . . . , p. 43.
105. *Ibid.*, p. 44.
106. Ulbricht, "Der Weg zur Durchfuehrung . . . ," p. 6; he referred in this context to the progressive role being played by the VVB EBM and the VVB Electrical Appliances.
107. "Beschluss zur weiteren . . . ," para. 1.
108. *Ibid.*, paras. 1, 3.
109. F. Teuscher in *Das Neue Oekonomische System* . . . , p. 151.
110. M. Scheler in *Der Weg zur Durchfuehrung* . . . , p. 33.
111. See Ladwig and Kiermeyer, "Das Niveau . . . ," p. 5. Criticism of the essentially insular and "antisocial" attitudes of enterprises, as well as of the tendency in some to inflate their administrative staffs, has not been uncommon in the GDR; see, for example, Kroemke and Rouscik, *Konzentration* . . . , p. 104, and S. Boehm in *Der Weg zur Durchfuehrung* . . . , pp. 47-48.
112. "mge," "Mit Skepsis empfangen — aber Vorteile ueberzeugten," and H. Misselwitz, "Zur Einbeziehung halbstaatlicher Betriebe," both in *Die Wirts.*, No. 3, 1964, pp. 16-17.
113. W. R., "Die Hauptsache . . . ," p. 6. This source also describes how a combine virtually liquidated an enterprise, against official policy.
114. U. L., "Volkseigene Kombinate," p. 11.
115. H. Riess and Dr. Lehmann, "Mehr Licht: Effektiver durch Konzentration," *Die Wirts.*, No. 50, 1973, pp. 4-5.
116. Halbritter, "Leistungsstarke Kombinate . . . ," p. 5.
117. F. Teuscher in *Das Neue Oekonomische System* . . . , p. 152.
118. Mueller, "Betriebe . . . ," p. 25.
119. U. Harnapp, "Was gehen das Werk die Wohnungen an?" *N.D.*, 24 January 1972, p. 3.

120. Compare para. 10, section 4 of the March version of "Verordnung ueber die VEB . . ." with the August modification (details on the location of this legislation are in note 39 to Ch. 1).

121. W. Ulbricht in *Das Neue Oekonomische System* . . . , pp. 93-94.

122. *Ibid.*, p. 94. At the same conference, one such organizer describes his work; see the paper by R. Ramolla, *ibid.*, pp. 232-235. One other paper of particular interest on this point is that by Mittag on pp. 160-170, *ibid*.

123. P. Liehmann, *ibid.*, p. 199.

124. A further possible source of irritation to party members was Mittag's statement in 1963 that party cells should hold their meetings outside of working hours under the New Economic System; this was to be for all levels of industry, however, and was not peculiar to VVBs and combines. See. G. Mittag, *ibid.*, pp. 166-167.

125. *Ibid.*, pp. 163-164, 168.

126. Rossmann, *Geschichte der SED*, p. 607. A general directive on these was passed by the Central Committee Secretariat in June 1975 (i.e., *before* the comparable Soviet directive).

127. Zimmermann, "Wandel von Industrieverwaltungen . . . ," p. 139.

128. A useful, brief description of these social councils can be found in Bundesministerium, *A bis Z . . . 1969*, p. 244.

129. Heuer and Klinger, "Einige Fragen . . . ," pp. 1073-1074.

130. See Heinrich, "Konsequenzen einer harten Kritik," *Die Wirts.*, No. 21, 1967, p. 3.

131. Heuer and Klinger, "Einige Fragen . . . ," p. 1074.

132. *Ibid.*, pp. 1073-1074.

133. Several of the papers from this plenum were published in *N.D.*, 11, 12, and 13 June 1970.

134. "Beschluss ueber die Durchfuehrung von monatlichen Rechenschaftslegungen der Direktoren der volkseigenen Betriebe, Kombinate und der Betriebe der Kombinate vor den Werktaetigen ihres Verantwortungsbereiches vom 17. September 1970," *GBl.*, Pt. 2, No. 78, 1970, pp. 547-549. It should be noted that para. 2 allowed for the possibility of such reports being given only to *representatives* of the workers; but it is also clear that these are not to be middle managers.

135. Ladwig and Kiermeyer, "Das Niveau der Leitung . . . ," p. 6.

136. See *ibid.*, pp. 4 and 6, and Halbritter, "Leistungsstarke Kombinate . . . ," p. 6. On the importance of management discussing the formation of a combine in advance with the workers to be affected, see U. L., "Mit Elan die neuen Aufgaben loesen," *Die Wirts.*, No. 23, 1969, p. 13; and on the formal rights of the workers in connection with such proposals, see K. Woche, "Zum Fuehrungsprozess bei der Bildung von Kombinaten," *WR*, No. 2, 1971, p. 102 (it is unclear whether such rights have often been exercised).

137. Heuer and Klinger, "Einige Fragen . . . ," pp. 1073-1074.

138. On all this, see H. Zimmermann in Ludz, *DDR Handbuch*, pp. 351-362.

139. *Ibid.*, p. 358.

140. *Ibid.*, p. 359.

141. On automated management systems and jobs lost ("several tens of thousands since the 8th Congress"), see Gerisch, *Leitungsorganisation* . . . , p. 216. One method used by the East Germans to overcome the human problem of rationalization is to give workers a training in a second skill, so that they have something to offer if their original skills are no longer required. See H. Naumann and M. John, "Eine grosse Zeit fuer Rationalisatoren," *N.D.*, 28 September 1972, p. 3.

142. E. Slangen and E. Mueller, "Wo Leuna Arbeitskraefte fuer zwei neue Betriebsteile findet," *N.D.*, 28 March 1973, p. 3.

143. (Unsigned), "Gewerkschaftliche Vertrauensleute beschlossen anspruchsvolle Ziele," *N.D.*, 3 January 1980, p. 3.

144. The relevant legislation is to be found in "Verordnung ueber die Bildung . . . ," para. 4, pt. 2; "Verordnung ueber das Verfahren . . . ," para. 7; "Beschluss ueber die Verwirklichung . . . ," para. 3, pt. 4; "Beschluss zur weiteren . . . ," para. 5; "Verordnung ueber die Aufgaben . . . ," para. 19, pt. 3, para. 25, pt. 2, para. 31 and para. 32 (where, in pt. 3, there is the only example we have discovered of potentially antagonistic legislation on income).

145. See, for example, Mitzscherling, *DDR-Wirtschaft* . . . , p. 238.

Chapter 8

CONCLUSIONS

We have now considered many of the similarities and differences between the development of the associations in the USSR and the GDR. Before attempting to draw an overall picture of the political process and these bodies, we need now to examine factors, other than internal "demands," leadership politics, and interest defense, that have contributed to the different developments in the two states.

INDUSTRIAL STRUCTURES AND PROBLEMS

In the light of the foregoing analysis, it does appear that one of the reasons the political process is often more problematic in the USSR relates to the federal structure of the larger state. Reflecting the attempt to grant the republics some real decision-making powers in industry, there is in the Soviet Union a very complicated ministerial system — which has undoubtedly been one of the main causes of problems in the implementation of association policy. Certainly the relationship between center and periphery in the GDR is not always clear or trouble-free, but there do appear to be fewer problems of optimalization than in the USSR.

Related to this is the fact that the sheer scale of the Soviet economy necessitates more subdivisions than the East German. Thus, the types of production that can be administered by one industrial ministry in the GDR might require five or six more specialized industrial ministries in the USSR. While it would be ingenuous to infer some neat exponential progression of complexity in this, it is nevertheless clear that the *potential* for conflicting interests increases the more organizations are involved in any process.

A third difference between the USSR and the GDR is that the latter state has faced even more acute problems of labor shortages in industry than the former; the East Germans now have their Polish *Gastarbeiter* just as the West Germans have their Turks, Yugoslavs, and so on.[1] Ceteris paribus, this would suggest that the East Germans

TABLE 6   Annual Increase in Gross Industrial Production in the GDR (percentages)

Year	
1956 1957 1958 1959 1960	Av. 9.1
1961	6.2
1962	6.1
1963	4.3
1964	6.8
1965	5.5
1966	6.8
1967	6.3
1968	6.0
1969	6.9
1970	7.0
1971	5.5
1972	6.2
1973	6.8

SOURCES: See Ch. 8, note 2.

have even less room for mistakes, fewer possibilities for "muddling through" in industrial administration than the Soviets.

Fourth, we must now consider in more detail the impact of declining growth rates as a factor in the development of the associations. Since we are concerned with industry rather than the economy generally, the most useful data to consider are those on the annual percentage increase in gross industrial production. For the GDR, official statistics give the picture in Table 6.[2] From the table it is clear that there were problems in the early 1960s that would have encouraged the leadership to look for ways to improve the running of the economy.[3] Thereafter, the worst years were 1965 and 1971, which *might* be correlated with the 1967 and 1973 developments, but which do not obviously do so. Let us now compare this with the Soviet picture (see Table 7).[4]

As in the GDR, the early 1960s showed a definite slowdown in growth in comparison with the 1950s; after that, there was a noticeable decline following the boom year of 1967 (bottoming in 1969), a reversal of the decline in 1970, followed by a steady decline. Thus, the concern shown at the December 1969 plenum would correlate well with such developments, while there must have been real concern by 1973. In sum, with the notable exception of the early 1960s, the impact of industrial growth figures on leadership interest in the associations would seem to have been greater in the USSR than in the GDR.

TABLE 7   Annual Increase in Gross Industrial Production in the USSR (percentages)

1956	10.6
1957	10.2
1958	10.3
1959	11.4
1960	9.4
1961	9.2
1962	9.6
1963	8.1
1964	7.4
1965	8.7
1966	8.7
1967	10.0
1968	8.2
1969	7.1
1970	8.5
1971	7.8
1972	6.5
1973	6.1

SOURCES: See Ch. 8, note 4.

Nevertheless, growth rate figures are also very important in the smaller state. Although the comparisons with Western states have not recently been made nearly so often in the GDR (or the USSR) as they were in the 1950s, the East German leaders must be sensitive to growth figures at least as much as their Soviet counterparts; whereas the Soviet population has no foreign state against which to make direct comparisons of Soviet performance, the East German populace — whether fairly or otherwise — often compare their state's performance with West German.[5] This factor (leadership perception of popular assessments of the economy) could also help to explain the differing nature of the development of associations in the two states — and, perhaps, the less open reporting of problems in the East German press.

Closely linked to the question of growth is that of foreign trade, to which we now turn.

FOREIGN TRADE STRUCTURE AND PROBLEMS

One of the reasons why the development of associations in the GDR has been less erratic than in the USSR might be that foreign trade is by many criteria much more important there than in the larger state, so that changes have to be more carefully made and supervised.[6] In many ways, foreign trade constitutes a crucial test of the economic system of a country if this trade is of major importance. This would imply a greater emphasis on efficiency in the more trade-oriented economy and possibly more "piecemeal" changes with careful experimentation before such changes were made. It is also significant that there has been far more experimentation with and discussion of the role of the associations in foreign trade in the GDR, symptomatic of the importance of this sector to the East German economy.

Moreover, it is instructive to note that during the period 1960-1974, the GDR had a favorable trade balance in all years except 1962, 1966, 1970, 1973, and 1974. Recalling that the New Economic System was announced in 1963, that its name was changed and Ulbricht's interest in the combines became obvious in 1967, and that most Western observers argue that 1970-1971 marked the beginning of the recentralization of East German industrial administration, an interesting pattern emerges. Major changes have occurred very soon after the emergence of foreign trade deficits, so that it is quite feasible that the latter was one of the factors leading to the former.[7]

EXTERNAL INFLUENCES ON POLICY

Ultimately, the question of who influenced whom cannot be fully satisfactorily answered, since much of the required information (e.g., on meetings between East German and Soviet legislators and/or leaders concerned with the question of industrial administration) is not available. However, the following observations can be made.

First, the *senior leadership's* enthusiasm for both types of association developed first in the GDR. Certainly Ulbricht was aware of Soviet experience when he praised the idea of the combine for local industry and construction in the early 1960s, shortly after Khrushchev had done so. However, when Ulbricht became significantly interested in the combines for centrally administered industry (in 1967), there was no reference to Soviet experience; indeed, the Soviet leadership was not particularly interested in the associations at that time. Moreover, Ulbricht himself wrote an article for *Pravda*, published in January 1964, in which he described for Soviet readers the New Economic System and the role of the VVBs in this. Although he referred in that article to the influence of Lenin and the CPSU's 22nd Congress, these are only brief, insignificant references and nothing is related specifically to East German policy.[8] And, of course, one could interpret the article as an attempt to influence the Soviets — which is hardly compatible with the the notion of the latter imposing policies on the East Germans. The East German leadership since 1971 has unquestionably been more sycophantic toward the Soviets than Ulbricht was in his later years. In addition, the appearance of the legislation on the associations in the GDR just a few days after similar legislation appeared in the Soviet Union must surely have been synchronized, and East German legislators in the 1970s seem to have had more contact with their Soviet counterparts than they did in the 1960s.[9] Having said this, we have also seen that the Soviet and East German legislation differs in several important ways and that work had started on the East German legislation in the late 1960s; although it may well have been changed during the Honecker period, it would be wrong to assume that the East Germans produced legislation solely because the Soviets had done so. Finally, it should not be forgotten that the East German legislation on the combine *preceded* the full legislation on the production *ob"edinenie*, nor that legislation on both types of association appeared as part of a comprehensive package on industrial administration that first began to appear in October 1972 — i.e., before the new round of Soviet legislation on administration.

East German influence on the Soviet leadership was probably marginal at most. The 1965 Soviet Economic Reform did not look particularly similar to the East German New Economic System — certainly with regard to industrial administration — and Soviet leaders have not referred to East German experience. We know that the East German leaders were definitely aware of Soviet association development, but cannot say with certainty that most of the Soviet leaders knew of the *details* of what was happening in the GDR. However, it is likely that Kosygin, at least, did know of such details. His son-in-law, D. M. Gvishiani, has given papers on management to the East German CISEM (Central Institute of Socialist Economic Management); he has organized two of the most important conferences on industrial administration that have taken place in the USSR, at both of which East German experience was considered; and he was the chief editor of a two-volume work on the associations in the Comecon countries, which was compiled in 1973.[10] Gvishiani is one of the leading management specialists in the USSR, and, although his own writings reveal him to be more interested in theories of management than in the associations as such, it seems highly probable that East German experience has been mentioned in conversations he would have had on administration and management with his father-in-law.

If leadership influence on either side does not appear to have been very important other than in rather superficial ways (i.e., timing of legislation as opposed to content of legislation),[11] does it look as if the people involved in the subleadership debates have influenced each other and hence perhaps their respective leaderships? Once again, we must restrict ourselves to intelligent inference based on the information available.

Without any doubt, East German specialists in law and economics have been very aware of administrative developments in the USSR, and Soviet specialists also often refer to East German experience.[12] Moreover, as with the East German leadership, so East German specialists have become far more sycophantic toward the USSR since about 1971. Nevertheless, three points need to be made. First, the question of words and actions again arises; even in the writings of those German specialists who praise Soviet developments, actual proposals for change do not often appear to emulate such developments. Second, some East German specialists have stated explicitly, both in the 1960s and in the 1970s (though less so in the later period), that what is suitable for the Soviets is not necessarily appropriate for the East German economy, and that one should not wait for guidance from Moscow. For example, in a 1962 discussion in *Die Wirtschaft* of the views of the Soviet economist Liberman, Dr. K-H. Jonuscheit of the German Academy of Sciences argued,

> Unfortunately, this discussion in our country has not gone far enough. Many economists evidently want to wait to see which way the wind blows in the Soviet Union. But we will not progress with such attitudes.[13]

Later on in the same article, having again emphasized that there needed to be a real discussion in the GDR, he argued,

> But we must start this, and not wait for the Soviet comrades to solve the problem for us.[14]

On the Soviet side, while some writers argue that the USSR could learn much from the GDR, others feel that East German experience is essentially irrelevant to Soviet requirements.[15] Third, both East German and Soviet specialists also look elsewhere for inspiration when attempting to make suggestions for improving industrial administration. Such alternative sources include the works of Marx, Engels, and Lenin; past experience in one's own country; the advanced capitalist states; and other communist states — although it is perhaps reflective of the GDR's pioneering role in association development that specialists there have much less frequently referred to influences from abroad or the past than their Soviet peers, the most commonly cited sources of inspiration being Central Committee plena! All these sources help to influence views, and there is no satisfactory quantitative method for measuring such influence. In sum, it is far from clear that the leaderships and/or the specialists in either country have been heavily influenced by their peers in the other state.

Apart from mutual influence, however, we need also to consider the role of the Council for Mutual Economic Assistance on policies, since both the USSR and the GDR are members of this organization.

During our interviews in the Soviet Union, we asked whether there had been any CMEA directives on associations. All the interviewees, including the three who had been members of the commission that produced the 1973-1974 legislation on the *ob"edineniya*, stated categorically that there had been no such directives. Obviously, it was not possible to obtain such a statement in the GDR because of the lack of interviews, although there is no inherent reasons to suppose that if the Soviet legislators did not receive directives from the CMEA the East Germans did; this inference is further borne out in the very differences between the East German and the Soviet legislation.[16] Nevertheless, it seems unlikely that either state would have adopted policies at great variance with policies in other member states of Comecon, since both — especially the GDR — have been among the strongest advocates of increased integration within and an expanded role for the organization. Certainly, writers from both states have called for a more standardized industrial management structure within the CMEA member states.[17] Moreover, it seems certain that at least some of the legislators were aware of the statements on management structures in the all-important Complex Programme of 1971. According to that document, member states of the CMEA were to pursue policies of concentration, specialization, and centralization from enterprise level, and to exchange experiences and views in this field.[18] Such a statement is very general, however.

THE CULTURAL FACTOR

Many writers on the policy process in communist states — including Archie Brown, Henry Morton, and Andrzej Korbonski — have pointed to the necessity to include in any analysis the climate of political attitudes in which the process is conducted.[19] We would certainly agree with the argument that a consideration of the role of political culture (attitudes toward authority, efficiency, order, and so on) should be included in any attempt at a comprehensive explanation of differences between the policy process in the two states. Both the Germans and the Russians are often argued to be more respectful of authority and social hierarchy than, for instance, the British or the Americans, while the Germans are said to be more efficiency-oriented than the Russians and more disposed to formal codification of the norms of social behavior.[20] While there may well be some truth in such views, they are difficult to prove empirically, particularly given the very real problems of conducting opinion surveys in the USSR and the GDR. Furthermore, it would be difficult to assess the relative importance of such attitudes in the political process. Consequently, given that we have so many other factors that seem to explain developments in the two states, the possibility of the cultural factor playing a role is allowed for here, without any attempt to suggest how much significance should be attached to it.

THE IDEOLOGICAL FACTOR

Another factor in the policy process, often referred to by commentators, is the role of ideology. There is some truth in Joravsky's contention that, partially as a function of the closed nature of politics in the USSR (and, to a large extent, in other communist states), we can only make very general inferences about the role this factor plays.[21] However, a few points can be made.

As Meyer has pointed out, students of communist politics differ in their views as to whether ideology plays primarily an initiating/guiding role (inspiring action and policies) or an ex post facto justificatory role — though a third group of writers maintains that it can and does perform both functions, and that the primacy of one or the other varies according to the time, place, and policy area.[22] Part of this disagreement can be explained in terms of different interpretations of the concept of communist ideology. What might be called the narrow approach limits the consideration of the term to the ideas and methods of Marx, Engels, and Lenin. A broader definition, and the one preferred here, includes not only the ideas of the "classic" theoreticians, but also Marxist-Leninist jargon, the "scientific" approach more generally understood,[23] and what can be referred to as the normative propagation of leadership policies (i.e., details of policies are widely disseminated not merely for informational purposes but also in order to justify policies as being "good for society").

Applying first the narrow conception to our policy area, we can repeat the point made earlier, that there have been references to the views of Marx, Engels, and particularly Lenin[24] on industrial administration in the debates and leadership statements. It is possible to construe these as examples of the use of classic communist theories as a guide to action (i.e., ideology as initiator). However, we would argue that, even employing the narrow definition, the use of the ideology here is primarily for justification — that is, the references to Lenin and so on are made to lend support and legitimacy to a current leadership's and/or specialists' proposals for change. The broader conception by definition places considerable emphasis on the justificatory role of the ideology. Hence, in the present study, the limited evidence available suggests that ideology — whether narrowly or broadly understood — has played more of a justificatory than a motivatory role.[25]

But this does not render the ideological factor irrelevant or only marginally significant. The effectiveness of the ideology in legitimizing a policy can be of considerable consequence to the success of its implementation. In this connection, it is worth noting the more prolific, prolonged, and unambiguous leadership campaign in favor of associations in the GDR in comparison with the Soviet Union,[26] which could well constitute part of the explanation for the greater success of the policy in the smaller state. Although it is not possible to determine whether the East German people accepted the proposals for changes in industrial administration more willingly than the Soviet, the very nature and scale of the East German campaign made it more difficult for people involved in the policy implementation to impede the development of these organizations. Therefore, while we would agree with writers like Smith that moves toward incrementalist policy-making (see below) in a communist state are incompatible with the ideological approach to policy *making*,[27] it must be made quite clear that evidence of such moves does not necessarily render the ideological factor irrelevant to the policy process as a whole.

A final point is that, in view of the fundamental similarity of industrial structures and policies in the two states (and elsewhere in Eastern Europe, with the partial exception of Yugoslavia),[28] we would tend to agree with writers like Brown[29] and Dawisha[30] that the ideology does perform a limiting function — that it sets parameters that are not to be transgressed. In the case of this particular policy, for instance, it is highly improbable that the Soviets or East Germans would attempt to solve problems of industrial administration by abandoning the planned and nationalized economy in favor of selling factories and associations to foreign, private entrepreneurs, even if there were a persuasive argument that this would increase productivity and so on. This said, it must also be emphasized that the parameters are very broad, and that the ideology is, clearly, sufficiently malleable in communist states to permit quite radical policy shifts; this has emerged from the present analysis as well as from many other studies.[31]

THE INDUSTRIAL ADMINISTRATION POLICY PROCESS: A SUMMARY

In the light of all the foregoing, let us now briefly examine association policy in the two states again, using our systems approach, in order finally to assess the significance of demands, interest groups, interests, and so forth. Considering first the GDR, we see that in the early 1960s declining growth rates and then foreign-trade deficits made the leadership look for ways to improve the economy. Before then, specialists making suggestions for ways to improve industry that were unacceptable to the leaders were discouraged to the extent of losing their posts. But in the two or three years preceding the announcement of the New Economic System, the leadership itself established work groups and convened conferences to examine alternatives and produce recommendations. It also promoted leading economists to high party positions, thus ensuring excellent access to the senior politicians.[32] Thus, stage one ("demand" input) was activated by stage two (leadership calls), while an external influence (Liberman's proposals and the Soviet reactions to these) *may* have encouraged the leadership to convert ideas into concrete policies. When the New Economic System was introduced, the First Secretary strongly advocated a greatly enhanced role for the VVBs. While formal legislation on these bodies — in the form of a decree or resolution — did not appear at this time, not only the "guideline" but also the leader's statements on them were highly detailed and presented as if they had full legislative authority (i.e., stages two and three are blurred). Implementation of the new policy on VVBs (stage four) was comparatively rapid and trouble-free. Nevertheless, by 1967 at the latest, the leadership felt that not all VVBs were operating as well as had originally been hoped — while 1966 had also witnessed a foreign-trade deficit. In this situation, a draft decree on the VVBs that the leadership had called for was rejected by Ulbricht; here legislation (stage three) was clearly dependent on leadership statements (stage two). Simultaneously, Ulbricht became seriously interested in the combines. He had shown mild interest in these in the early 1960s, and specifically stated that he was aware of the suggestions from the

Conclusions

Hettstedt combine, which, he said, had been made on evaluation of Soviet experiences.[33] However, the leader said little else at that time; a form of legislation was issued later that year (1963), but does not appear to have been normative in the particular sense of being a statement of intent to create more combines. There was, moreover, no criticism from the leadership of poor development of the combines. Generally, the question of combines was of marginal significance to both leadership and, judging from the lack of discussion, subleadership levels in the mid-1960s. But with Ulbricht's new interest in these bodies, there was discussion of them both at party meetings and at conferences called by central party and state organs — at which senior leaders were present. Papers on them were given at such gatherings; but these were probably encouraged by Ulbricht himself rather than being self-motivated calls from management to the leadership. As in the pre-1963 period, working parties were also established by the leadership to consider aspects of the combines. Legislation on these bodies (stage three) appeared rapidly — apparently without public discussion — and implementation, in the sense of creating many new combines, seems to have proceeded rapidly and relatively smoothly. By this time, subleadership debates on the VVBs had virtually ceased and been replaced by debates on the combines.

The change of leader in the GDR was accompanied by a decline of interest at all levels in both types of association. But the new leadership was not anxious openly to renounce too much of Ulbricht's economic policy. This fact, plus, perhaps, awareness of the Soviet leadership's new enthusiasm for associations and a feeling that the associations had *some* role to play, meant that the VVBs and the combines continued to exist. However, the new East German leadership had shown itself already in the Ulbricht period to be more interested in the ministries and, to some extent, the enterprises, and this orientation was revealed in the sometimes ambiguous legislation of 1972-1973. This legislation did not usher in any new policy on the associations, and indeed one did not emerge until about 1977.

There are several points to be borne in mind in considering the role in the policy examined of demands, interest groups, and interests in the GDR. The first concerns the timing of subleadership debates. Of all the units analyzed in the chapter on debates, *very* few appeared *before* the senior leadership (usually Ulbricht) had called for suggestions and given some indication of the lines along which such proposals were to be made. Indeed, one East German source states that even members of the various working parties *instructed* to produce ideas for the New Economic System approached their work "very timorously" until they had been given the full go-ahead for a radical solution by representatives of the Central Committee.[34] This leads us to the point that the debates have nearly always been conducted within the parameters laid down by the leaders. When very differing views did appear at the end of the 1960s, this reflected differences among members of the senior leadership. Third, the majority of participants in such debates are either members of working parties established by the leadership to consider aspects of the associations, or professional commentators on economic policy (e.g., journalists working for *Die Wirtschaft*), or they are people who may well have been prompted to speak on the associations by the leaders (e.g., combine directors at economic conferences or a party Congress). Fourth, strong calls for the associations from people who can be seen to have a clear, vested interest in the development of such bodies are very rare; those examples we have found, as has already been pointed out, seem to be from directors and the like, who are giving empirical evidence of the benefits of their combine or upgraded VVB, in order to strengthen a leadership call for such bodies. Such directors may well criticize central state organs above them, but this too will be in line with what the head of the party wants. There is *some* evidence of interest defense at the debate stage, however, mainly from central state bodies (notably the Ministry of Finance). Calls for legislation have been made by people who could be seen to have vested interests in making such calls, but the significance of these in terms of being able to secure such legislation is unclear. Either the legislation has not appeared, or else it has been produced but reflects leadership calls or the views of specialists called upon by the leaders to produce legislative proposals at least as much as requests from subleadership interested parties. If we take the Oxford dictionary definition of a demand as "a request made as of right or peremptorily," then we have found requests, suggestions — but not demands. And, of course, such requests and suggestions are not in practice strengthened by sanction powers (e.g., withdrawal of labor), as they often are in liberal democracies. At the legislative stage, we have relatively little to go on. We can say that the compilation of the 1963 guideline involved subleadership levels — under the control of the leadership — but did not reveal serious conflicts of interests. Moreover, the nonratification of the draft statute on the VVBs in 1967 was a reflection of differences within the leadership (notably between Ulbricht and Stoph) at least as much as the result of any differences between the leadership and the subleadership levels. Another point about the legislation is that it has often, possibly usually, been supervised by a senior political actor

Conclusions

(Stoph, and probably Halbritter); this may have changed after 1971, but we have no evidence on this. Finally, invitations to comment on legislative proposals were either very limited in scope — both temporally and in terms of who was to be involved in such discussions — or were nonexistent. At the implementation stage, there is hard evidence of some form of hostility to the party leader's views on the associations, primarily from senior state bodies of ministerial level or above. Such hostility has been identified by members of the Politburo, and can reasonably be construed as exemplifying interest defense. Yet this activity can be seen as interest-group activity only in a very narrow sense. It is not able to promote change, but can only attempt to prevent it; even the success at blocking development was very limited. Finally, such groups are very much "within-system" even by communist standards; in fact, they are often part of the central governmental machine. Hence, the "bureaucratic" model of politics would be a more appropriate term to describe this stage of the process than the "interest-group" approach.

In the USSR, there is no doubt that the first important calls for the *ob"edineniya* were made at the *sovnarkhoz* level. A major impetus for these was dissatisfaction with the senior leadership's policy on industrial administration, a point inherent in the following quotation from Gromov and Kamenetskii:

> Essentially the organization of production *ob"edineniya* was to a certain extent an attempt to establish the leadership of branches, destroyed in the conditions of the *sovnarkhozy*.[35]

The local level not only advocated the creation of associations, but was also able to implement its wishes while the leadership remained vague about such bodies and there was no legislation on them. Hence, stages one and four were under way while stages two and three were unclear or nonexistent. Soon after the local levels had become interested in the *ob"edineniya*, however, central state bodies became involved in their further development, and the Central Committee gave approval to them. Thus, developments occurred despite the absence of strong leadership support — although not, of course, actually against leadership wishes. At this stage, moreover, the views of specialists, managers, *sovnarkhoz* officials, and others were articulated and aggregated at the Central Committee level and possibly higher still by party secretaries from these areas.

Following the ouster of Khrushchev, the innovatory role of local officials declined. There were two main reasons for this. First, the leadership abolished the *sovnarkhozy*, thus removing the main institutional base of these people. The other reason was that the senior leadership now produced a major new industrial policy. The later Khrushchev period was characterized by an increasingly confused policy, with centralization of the *sovnarkhoz* structure occurring at the same time Liberman's proposals were being made and empirically evaluated. Now, however, the leadership seemed to have a clearer idea of what it wanted. In some ways the *ob"edinenie* concept clashed with the ideas behind the 1965 Economic Reform. Yet the fact that there was a brief reference to them both in the announcement of the Reform and in the 1965 legislation on the enterprises was sufficient for the advocates of such bodies to justify keeping the debate on them alive in the late 1960s. At this stage, however — and in contrast to the situation of the early 1960s — the debate was largely theoretical, with little opportunity for implementing ideas; the earlier congruence of advocates and implementers no longer pertained. On the one hand, the people who might have aggregated and articulated these views for the legal and economic specialists, managers, and the like, did not do so at, for instance, the 1966 Congress. On the other, the ministries were often loath to establish the associations. Here, then, interest defense on the part of central state bodies became a major obstacle to the development of the *ob"edineniya* in the absence of clear and/or detailed policy statements and/or legislation to check them.

In 1968, a major economic conference was held, at which several members of the Politburo were present. There was some advocacy of the associations, but no obvious leadership response to such calls. Yet by the end of 1969, it was clear that the Economic Reform was less successful than had been anticipated — industrial growth was again decelerating. At this point, the Leningrad party boss in particular appears once again to have argued the case for the associations to a senior leadership searching for solutions to a problem. The Central Committee Secretariat agreed to convene a meeting of senior government officials and others, to be held in Leningrad. The seminar was apparently important in convincing many senior state and party officials of the advantageousness of the *ob"edineniya*, and in a real sense represented a case of stage two encouragement of stage one. This was followed by more significant and public policy statements (stage two) than had been made in December 1969. Following the statements of the party head and the premier at the 1971 Congress, legislation eventually appeared. This legislation, in contrast to that in the GDR, not only described the position of the associations but also

Conclusions

specifically called for more associations; stage three was thus more normative than it has ever been in the smaller state. Furthermore, since the Soviet leadership had never gone into detail on the associations in the same way that Ulbricht had done, there was room for differing views — some based on vested interests, some on seemingly purely academic grounds — to be reflected in highly ambiguous legislation. Such legislation could be used to hinder rapid and efficient implementation of the policy. But although vested, identifiable interests could obstruct the policy to some extent, the fact that the senior leadership was now clearly committed to the associations and a simplified administrative structure meant that their role was less significant than it had been in the second half of the 1960s. Although the implementation of association policy was far from satisfactory in many ways, nevertheless the numbers of these bodies increased noticeably; leadership and some of the vested interests were in conflict, but leadership wishes were proving to be the stronger force.

What general points concerning demands, interest groups, and interests emerge from this Soviet picture? First, new developments in the USSR are *not* invariably the result of leadership calls. The associations were promoted by groups — more territorially than functionally based[36] — and created by local organs. These organs and groups did have certain vested interests in the associations, and from this point of view can be seen as promotional interest groups. However, there is an important point to be made about the use of this term to describe the Soviet activities in the early 1960s. This is that they were not achieving their end in clear opposition to official policy/leadership views. Thus, although we do have evidence here of a form of promotional interest-group activity in the USSR, this is not of the same nature or range as interest-group activity in the liberal democracies. Nor is there any evidence that there have been real demands (as defined above) for the associations under the present leadership. Rather, when the leadership wanted suggestions, arguments in favor of the *ob"edineniya* were soon forthcoming. However, there is an important distinction to be made between this process and the East German one. Although we cannot know for certain that the idea of associations was not debated and discussed among East German specialists *in private* before leadership calls were made, our evidence shows that public debates and advocacy almost invariably appeared in the GDR after leadership encouragement of new ideas. The Soviet specialists, on the other hand, were discussing the associations before leadership became seriously interested in them. From this point of view, they were still more autonomous than their East German counterparts, even if they were less able to implement their ideas than they had been under Khrushchev.[37]

Second, we can consider the role of defensive interests at the implementation stage. It is clear that in the late 1960s, the vested interests of ministerial-level bodies were able seriously to impede the development of *ob"edineniya* in the absence of an official, firm policy to create them. Even if it were the case that the economic and legal specialists who were calling for the associations in the latter half of the 1960s were in some cases actually articulating and aggregating the vested interests of, for instance, ambitious enterprise managers or local party officials, the impact of such calls was negligible in the face of widespread (though not universal) ministerial opposition. In the 1970s, interest defense on the part of central state bodies not only affected the development of associations at stage four (implementation), but also at stage three (legislation). Here, the branch ministries were less able to defend their interests than some of the nonbranch ministries — notably the Ministry of Finance. Even in the case of the latter body, however, we would argue that it would not have had the success it did in delaying legislation and ensuring that its own interests were partially reflected in the statute that finally emerged, had the Politburo been firmer and clearer in its views on the associations.

Another point about interest defense is that expectations concerning enterprise autonomy were raised in the USSR by the Economic Reform and subsequently dashed. One effect of this was that it led in some cases to hostility to the *ob"edineniya* from enterprise management, although it was not *only* the managers who reacted in this way. Thus, we would argue that many of the debates between Soviet legal and economic specialists can be explained in terms of differing views on how to achieve a common end. It is clear that in some cases, proponents of the less integrated *ob"edinenie* have been so largely because they have wanted to maximize the level of enterprise autonomy promised in the 1965 Reform. Conversely, many supporters of the more integrated forms of *ob"edinenie* have also wanted to ensure the producing unit more autonomy vis-à-vis the central organs, but have felt that the best way to ensure this was to strengthen and enlarge the enterprise.[38] The irony is that these very differences between the specialists could be exploited by the central organs, the powers of which *both* "schools" were anxious to limit. It is for this reason that we cannot call specialists such as Pevzner "conservative," since they were so only in a very particular sense. All this is, of course, in marked contrast to the East German picture. There, the reforms of the 1960s never placed as much emphasis on the individual enterprise as the Soviet reform did, so that neither managers nor specialists could feel as cheated as they did in the USSR. This undoubtedly constitutes a major reason for the different success rates in the two states.

Finally, we have discovered something about the process by which suggestions can reach the senior leadership in the USSR; unlike the East German situation under Ulbricht, specialists were not so obviously promoted to leading party and state organs, so that we have to look for alternative channels. Sometimes, senior leaders acknowledge suggestions made from the local level, although we can only speculate that these are made to leaders on visits to enterprises and the like, or through letters, or through the Secretariat informing the leadership. Sometimes suggestions are made directly, at conferences, although this is rare, and we have found no conferences at which Khrushchev or Brezhnev or Kosygin was present. Sometimes, conferences are attended by leading personnel from the Central Committee staff and/or ministers, who probably convey the suggestions made at such gatherings to the Politburo and/or the Council of Ministers' Praesidium. Yet another path is via senior party officials articulating views on behalf of people from their province at Central Committee plena. There is a problem here of distinguishing a call to the leadership and a policy statement from the leadership; Podgorny's comments at the November 1962 plenum represent a good example of this. However, particularly when such views are at odds with those of the First/General Secretary, we would argue that they are an input at least as much as an output — although clearly no definitive answer to this problem can be given, and we can see here yet another example of overlap between our stages (here, between stages one and two). A final channel of access is the informal one, about which we can again only speculate. In the policy area studied here, for instance, it seems highly probable that Gvishiani discussed ideas on the *ob"edineniya* with his father-in-law and possibly other members of the Politburo.

SOME GENERAL OBSERVATIONS ON THE
COMMUNIST POLICY PROCESS

We begin this section by reminding the reader that we are concerned with the domestic policy process in a noncrisis situation in the older, industrially developed communist states, the implication being that this could well be the general pattern which will eventually emerge in the newer and/or less industrially developed communist states. It was also pointed out very early in the study that we have deliberately chosen a policy that is of major importance to the leadership (i.e., one over which they will want and need to keep a high level of control), while at least one of these states (the GDR) is often considered to be one of the most authoritarian of the communist states. In doing this, we would argue that the limited and specific form of pluralism we have discovered is likely to represent the *minimum* level of this kind of political activity in such systems. We would, however, endorse the arguments of Brown, Hough, and others, that it is most important to recognize that there are very differing degrees and types of pluralism,[39] and that the discovery of evidence to show that, for instance, interests can and do play an important part in such states in no way implies that they either have or are moving toward political systems that are basically similar to those of the so-called first world states. Their political systems are sui generis, neither totalitarian nor pluralist, as this term is used of Western states.

It is not the intention to present here a detailed overview of the many and varied hypotheses on and analyses of the policy process in mature communist states; this would not only be a major task, but would almost inevitably lead to tautology, in that many writers have made basically similar points. Instead, we will consider what seem to be some of the most important and/or contentious hypotheses, and compare these with the findings of the present study.

First, we would agree that political culture probably plays some role in the communist policy process and that it might help to explain the differences between states. But we would also maintain that notwithstanding the bold and interesting attempts that have been made to do so[40] there is still a wide range of problems to be overcome in trying to discover whether a dominant political culture really exists, what its salient features are, and, most difficult of all, what impact it has on the policy process in communist states. For the time being, the variable must be used sparingly and cautiously.

Second, we would argue on the basis of our findings that there is little evidence to suggest that specific policies in the Soviet-oriented communist states are essentially dictated by Moscow.[41] The reader will recall that one of the reasons for choosing the GDR for this study was precisely that it, along with Bulgaria, is usually considered to be the most loyal and emulative of the Soviet-oriented states. In fact, such emulation as exists is generally superficial and/or in the interests of the smaller state as perceived by its leadership. We would therefore maintain that the domestic policy process in other communist states would be at least as autonomous. It would, of course, be ingenuous to imply that the USSR plays no role whatsoever in the internal politics of many communist states; it is necessary only to consider the events in Hungary in 1956, Czechoslovakia in 1968, possibly Afghanistan in 1979, and conceivably Poland in late 1980 or 1981 to realize that a generalized framework for the political system *is* determined by the Kremlin, and in this we would agree with Fejtö.[42] But it must also be emphasized that to accept this is quite different from accepting that domestic policies adopted in smaller communist states are in some sense based on a Moscow blueprint. The leaderships in most communist states have a fundamentally similar ideological perspective, and this fact can explain similarities in structures at least as well as any notion of imposed policies. Moreover, we have seen that the relationship could well be two-way on occasions; i.e., the USSR almost undoubtedly takes heed of experiments and policies in other communist states, as well as vice versa.[43] Bearing this in mind, let us consider the internal political process. We begin by considering the two most commonly accepted ideal types of the policy process.

At one end of the spectrum is what has variously been described as the "synoptic," the "rational comprehensive," or the "teleological" ideal type.[44] According to this, policy makers gather at the center as much data as possible on any given problem or for a particular development; carefully consider the measurable (and, to the extent possible, nonmeasurable) costs and benefits of alternative policy choices relative to the desired end; relate these to other policies and to a distant, general goal (e.g., "communism"); make their policy; and ensure that it is properly implemented. The approach is thus based on careful and comprehensive evaluation rather than being a spontaneous response to urgent problems and/or interest groups. At the opposite end of the spectrum there is what is usually known as the "incrementalist" or "muddling through" ideal type.[45] In this case, policy makers are faced with the need to reach a decision because of a problem that has arisen and/or the need to deal with one or several interest groups. Their deliberations are not to any meaningful extent related to a long-term, general goal. The decision adopted for solving the problem only marginally, or incrementally, changes existing policies, and its possible ramifications are not thoroughly analyzed. If the new policy fails to solve the problem or is only partially successful in doing so, then another incremental decision can be made. Such a process will probably also be disjointed in two ways. First, decision-making can take place in several locations (i.e., it is not highly centralized). Second, attempts to relate one area of policy to another are minimal. With these ideal types in mind, we can consider the communist policy process.

According to one of the very few attempts at a genuinely comparative analysis of the policy process in communist states, Gary Bertsch argues that,

> Relative to the First and Third World states, the Communist-run states of the Second World are best equipped to make policy according to the synoptic mode. Centralised political leadership within an authoritarian system of government facilitates long-term planning, coordinated decision-making, and effective implementation and execution. A small group of decision-makers are relatively free to weigh competing goals, study alternative actions to attain them, and decide on those that appear to be in the collective interest.[46]

Certainly, the emphasis in recent years in so many of the mature communist states on cybernetics and the scientific-technical revolution would lend weight to this image of a high potential for rational comprehensive policy-making.[47] However, despite this potential, Bertsch also concludes that

> the more developed states of eastern Europe display the blend of rational comprehensive decision-making and muddling through characteristic of the Soviet Union.[48]

Clearly, then, Bertsch is arguing that the policy process in the maturer communist states contains elements of both types, a hypothesis the present study would support. For instance, administrative change has now been incorporated into the Soviet five-year plans (symptomatic of the synoptic approach), whereas legislation on the East German combines was produced and changed remarkably rapidly in the late 1960s (suggestive of the incrementalist approach). Numerous other examples could be cited, but the general point has been made.

Having decided this, the next questions to be answered are why such a blend exists, and what factors lead the process nearer to the incrementalist or the synoptic mode. Given that an authoritarian policy process in a technologically advanced society is argued to have the greatest potential for the synoptic mode, and that the pluralist approach will necessarily tend toward incrementalism, a related but different question can be put: What factors lead to more or less participation of subleadership levels in the policy process?

Without any doubt, the single most important factor in both of these is the role of leadership; it is a highly complex variable. We would tend to agree with Henry Morton that the USSR — and, it can be inferred, other communist regimes — will at any given point in time possess one of three possible leadership configurations, each of which can affect the policy process.[49] In the first, there is one supreme leader, who can terrorize his peers and who certainly dominates the policy process to a very high degree. This kind of situation — to the extent that it has existed, anyway[50] — is of marginal relevance here, since none of the leadership arrangements in the mature communist states can be so described.[51] The second type is where there is a "first among equals"; this is typified by both the Khrushchev and the Ulbricht periods. The third is one of collective leadership — which is, more or less, what the Soviets have had since 1964 and the East Germans since 1971. This does not preclude the possibility of one leader being above the others for symbolic purposes, but there is far less dominance of the policy process by one man than in the first two types.

Considering type two first, we would argue that the *style* of the leader will have an important impact on the kind of political process. For instance, the level of arbitrariness of a first among equals, plus the level of his interest in a given policy area, will affect the extent to which subleadership levels will be able to play a role in that area. Looking at this from another angle, it should by now be quite clear that the mere existence of a relatively strong leader does *not* in itself ensure a synoptic mode, nor does it necessarily minimize the possibilities for subleadership interests to play a role in the policy process. Conversely, moves toward incrementalism in this type of leadership arrangement do not necessarily lead to greater pluralism. The comparison of the policy process under Khrushchev and Ulbricht has shown clearly the big differences that can exist.

Turning now to a consideration of type three, we would agree with Morton when he rejects Lowenthal's argument that collective leadership necessarily produces less clear-cut policies than one-person leadership;[52] in fact, there can be ambiguous and unambiguous policies under one-person leadership in just the same way as there can be under collective leadership.[53] Part of the reason for this is that there are at least three different kinds of collective leadership. The first is "total" collectivity, in which all members of a group of leaders will consider all major questions as equals; this form of collectivity undoubtedly contains the greatest potential both for delays in reaching decisions and for ambiguous policies (because of the need for compromise). In the second type, what might be called "selective" collectivity, there is a division of labor between leaders. The third type consists of a blend of types one and two. Other things being equal, collective leadership of the second type should be able to produce at least as clear-cut and efficient policy-making as the single leader. Indeed, since there is a division of labor, and thus a distribution of policy areas, there would appear to be *greater* potential for efficient policy-making across a range of policies than where one person tries to cope with a wide range of policy areas. Bearing this in mind, type-three collective leadership — which is typical of most of the mature communist states — could well produce as rapid and unambiguous policy-making as one-person leadership.

One of the principal reasons we are interested in the factors leading to ambiguous policies is that the greater the ambiguity, the greater the potential for subleadership levels to impact upon the success of these policies — i.e., the greater chance for a higher degree of pluralism. The type of leadership, the style of leadership, and the level of leadership interest — all these factors help to explain ambiguity. But there is one other important variable to be added to this list; this can be called the "practical range of options." It would seem feasible that the leaderships of the mature communist states feel increasingly over time that their scope for maneuver in any given policy area is lessening. For example, taking the policy area analyzed in this study, the East European leaderships have now tried so many variations along the centralization-decentralization and territorial-branch axes that the possibilities for real novelty must by now appear extremely limited; there *are* still radical alternatives (e.g., anarcho-syndicalism), but these are such anathema to the ideology of the planned economy and a party state run along the lines of democratic centralism that they would require revolutionary change — a consideration of the possibility and results of which is beyond the scope of this study. Hence it is quite conceivable that this awareness of limitations in the number of possibilities for change within the existing parameters constitutes part of the explanation for incrementalism, delays, ambiguity, and hence the possibility for subleadership interest-defensive activity to lead to the relative failure of policies. In addition, the increasing complexity of communist societies (e.g., the ever-growing division of labor and increasingly sophisticated expectations among the population) suggests that, even allowing for improvements in the technology of planning, the problem of overload will affect communist leaderships in a fashion similar to the way it is often argued to be affecting leaderships in the liberal democracies.[54] This, in turn, leads to the point that the larger (in terms of population, diversity of the economy, and so on) communist states will, ceteris paribus, experience greater problems of coordination than smaller ones. We would thus argue that synopticism in a mature communist state becomes increasingly difficult the larger that state is.

It is in the context of all these factors that, irrespective of ideological views on pluralism and interest groups, subleadership interests can and do play a very important role in the policy process. Moreover, these interests can play a role *whether or not* they are articulated and/or aggregated (i.e., whether or not there are self-conscious interest groups). It would also appear to be the case that if interest groups are not perceptible, then the most important role of interests is at the policy implementation stage. Once it is recognized that specific interests can play a role in the policy process, it must be acknowledged that this will affect the capacity of a leadership to adhere to the synoptic mode; moves toward incrementalism are a necessary outcome of conflicting interests playing a role in the policy process. Moreover, it would be advisable for communist leaderships to recognize this fact. If they contemplate relatively far-reaching policy changes, they must include in their calculations the likely reaction of interested parties. If such reactions are likely to be strongly negative, then the policy makers either are going to have to decide upon a more incremental change, or are going to have to purge various functional groups to a sufficient extent to prevent members of these groups from blocking a policy. For various reasons, the latter path seems to have become ever less attractive to the leaders of the maturer communist states in recent years.

One other point — made in parentheses — about interests and interest groups is that it is clear that there are often important differences of interest between members of any particular functional group, whether they be ministers, managers, economists, party officials, or whatever. Hence, the policy process approach may well produce a picture of less homogeneity in functional or social groups than the social background approach to such groups.

Moves toward incrementalism are not per se undesirable. It could certainly be argued, for instance, that this represents a more humane form of socialism than the rational, "scientific" approach to policy-making and implementation. Indeed, in taking heed of interests (which is not to be equated with weak submission to the selfish interests of powerful groups) policies could be more successfully implemented. This, in turn, can help to legitimize a leadership. This must surely be more desirable than producing radical policies that alienate important interests, are therefore in all probability poorly implemented, and which therefore undermine the legitimacy of the policy makers.

Summarizing this section on the role of leadership, it should by now be clear that to argue that this role is all-important is not to imply that leadership either does or can dominate all stages of the policy process. Rather, it is to suggest simply that the leadership is involved in most important developments in society, and that it has a better chance than any other group of being able to introduce change into that society.

The policy process in the mature communist states is a complex amalgam of political culture, ideology, problem-responsiveness, leadership politics, bureaucratic politics, subleadership interests, foreign influence, and perhaps even Tolstoy's unknown X factor — so that we would reject *all* essentially monocausal models, ideal types and approaches, and agree with A. H. Brown that the most useful approach to the study of communist politics is the eclectic one.[55] This may be the least tangible and systematized approach, but it is also the most honest and the only genuinely comparative one. If it is not precise enough for some readers, then they have failed to recognize that the process varies from time to time, country to country, policy area to policy area. Some generalizations can be — and have been — made here; no others seemed to us to be justifiable.

NOTES

1. On the problems of East German labor shortages in the 1960s see N. N. Popov, *Po Puti Sovershenstvovaniya* . . . , pp. 16-17. The situation has improved since the late 1960s, largely through the increase in the number of females employed (see Mitzscherling, *DDR – Wirtschaft* . . . , pp. 36-37) and in numbers of foreign workers (see Ludz, *DDR Handbuch* . . . , pp. 55-56), but there are still some difficulties.

2. The 1956-1960 average is from N. N. Popov, *Po Puti Sovershenstvovaniya* . . . , p. 15; the rest have been calculated by the author on the basis of data in the *Statistical Pocket Book* . . . *1975*, p. 35. There is a slight discrepancy between the latter and the figures from 1961-1963 given by Popov, but the differences are marginal.

3. Ulbricht himself acknowledged that there were problems with the development of the economy in an interview he gave to *N.D.*, 1 January 1962; the plan for 1961 was not fulfilled, even though the original plan targets had been substantially lowered. On all this see Jaenicke, *Der Dritte Weg*, p. 175.

Conclusions 281

4. Figures through 1971 are from R. A. Clarke, *Soviet Economic Facts 1917-70* (London and Basingstoke: Macmillan, 1972), p. 9. Data for 1972 are from *Pravda*, 30 January 1973, and for 1973 from *Pravda*, 28 January 1974.

5. This statement is based primarily on the author's own experiences in East Berlin. Although many Western observers, with the notable exception of Ludz, have argued that the East Germans identified and compared themselves with the West Germans ever less after 1961 (the "Year of the Wall"), there are signs that this was changing in the 1970s, largely because of closer contact between the GDR and the FRG. Such contact can hardly be seen to have been seriously dysfunctional to the East German leadership in the early 1970s, when the economy was booming and the GDR finally secured full international recognition. But with the economic problems of the GDR in the latter part of the 1970s, such contact and comparisons became an increasing embarrassment to the East German regime. See H. Zimmermann, "The GDR in the 1970s," *P of C*, No. 2, 1978, esp. pp. 22-25, 35-39.

6. There is no universally accepted method of measuring the importance of trade. One sometimes taken is the export quotient (exports relative to national income); the GDR's export quotient for 1974 was 22.6 percent, while that for the USSR was 10.2 percent, possibly suggesting the greater importance to the smaller state of exporting. However, a full analysis would also have to consider the *nature* of imports and exports (e.g., how dependent a particular country was on the products it imported) and is beyond the scope of this study. Still, in addition to the points made about trade in the text, it should also be borne in mind that the USSR, with its massive supplies of natural resources, should be ever less threatened by international trady cycles and possible boycotts than the resource-deficient GDR.

7. There were again trade deficits in the GDR in 1975 and 1976; unfortunately, in recent years the East Germans have usually given only the overall trade turnover figures rather than separate figures on imports and exports.

8. W. Ulbricht, "Primenenie Leninskikh Printsipov Sotsialisticheskogo Upravleniya v GDR," *Pravda*, 9 January 1964, pp. 3-4.

9. This inference is based on discussions the author has had with Western specialists on the GDR in West Berlin, and on the reference by I. Dudinskii to a deliberative body, composed of representatives of the CMEA-states, which has been set up since 1971 to consider legal questions relating to economic cooperation. See Dudinskii's *Das Komplexprogramm als strategischer Plan fuer die sozialistische Integration* (Moscow: APN, 1973), p. 131.

10. See "Wissen fuer die Zukunft," *effekt*, No. 3, 1969, p. 37; the details on the 1966 and 1972 conferences in note 18 to Ch. 2; and Gvishiani, Irasek and Kamenitser, *Upravlenie Sotsialisticheskimi* . . . .

11. As we have seen, in other areas of industrial administration there appears to have been a higher level of emulation. It would be ingenuous to argue that the abolition of the ministries in 1958 and their reintroduction in 1965 were not primarily inspired by similar developments in the USSR. But it appears to us that the East Germans have copied only aspects of Soviet changes that they felt were appropriate to their conditions and/or were "low-cost" (the term "cost" being broadly understood). We have found no examples of "high-cost" gestures of loyalty by the East Germans in the policy area studied, while we would argue that even the "low-cost" gestures can ultimately be explained in terms of self-interest.

12. Apart from the fact that there are specialist journals in the GDR consisting solely of translations of Soviet articles, there are plenty of articles in the more readily

available press about Soviet associations. See, for example, "Sowjetische Firmen," *Die Wirts.*, No. 15, 1963, p. 30; details on the experiment in *Minpribor* in *Die Wirts.*, No. 10, 1969, p. 22; and the references to Soviet experience at the September 1971 conference. For examples of Soviet references, see Nagovitsin, "Promyshlennye Ob″edineniya . . . ," passim; Gromov and Kamenetskii, *Proizvodstvennye Ob″edineniya* . . . , passim; and Aleksandrov at the 1968 conference in Bachurin, *Sovershenstvovanie Planirovaniya* . . . , p. 88.

13. See K-H. Jonuscheit under "In Vorbereitung des VI. Parteitages," *Die Wirts.*, No. 51/52, 1962, p. 7.

14. *Ibid.*, p. 7. For a warning in the post-Ulbricht period not to follow Soviet ideas (on the relationship between local state organs and combines) too closely, see K. Schubert, "Zur Rechtsgestaltung der Beziehungen zwischen oertlichen Staatsorganen und Kombinaten, Betrieben und wirtschaftsleitenden Organen," *WR*, No. 2, 1972, p. 91.

15. The latter point is hinted at in Dzhavadov and Dunaev, *Proizvodstvennye Ob″edineniya* . . . , p. 57, and was made explicitly to us in an interview.

16. Our interview data are endorsed by the comments in M. Senin's *Socialist Integration* (Moscow: Progress, 1973), passim, esp. pp. 218-226.

17. This is usually related to the argument that international planning will then become easier. See, for example, G. Schuerer, *Die Aufgaben bei der Verwirklichung der sozialistischen oekonomischen Integration* (Berlin: Dietz Verlag, 1975), esp. pp. 20-31, and M. N. Os′mova, *Sotsialisticheskaya Ekonomicheskaya Integratsiya i Effektivnost′ Proizvodstva* (Moscow: Politizdat, 1975), esp. pp. 17-47. See too Gvishiani, Irasek, and Kamenitser, *Upravlenie Sotsialisticheskimi* . . . , Vol. 1, pp. 6-7. One concrete manifestation of the policy further to integrate planning was the creation in 1971 of the Committee of the CMEA for Cooperation in the Field of Planning, while joint Soviet-East German planning for selected areas of industry began in 1973 (note in *Die Wirts.*, No. 6, 1973, p. 24).

18. See "Komplexprogramm fuer die weitere Vertiefung und Vervollkommnung der Zusammenarbeit und Entwicklung der sozialistischen oekonomischen Integration der Mitgliedlaender des RGW" in *Sozialistische Aussenwirtschaft*, No. 9, 1971, pp. 2-39 (esp. Ch. 2, sections 3 and 4, pp. 6-7 and 10-11; Ch. 2, section 8, pp. 21-22; Ch. 3, section 10, p. 23; Ch. 4, sections 15 and 16, pp. 37-38). For details on the Complex Program — its genesis, content, and the first stages of its implementation — see Dudinskii, *Das Komplexprogramm* . . . , passim. For a detailed, up-to-date analysis of the CMEA, see van Brabant, *Socialist Economic Integration*, passim.

19. Brown and Gray, *Political Culture* . . . , passim; H. W. Morton in Juviler and Morton, *Soviet Policy-Making*, pp. 6 and 14-19; A. Korbonski, "Leadership Succession and Political Change in Eastern Europe," *Studies in Comparative Communism*, Nos. 1 and 2, 1976, esp. pp. 6-7, 12-14.

20. For two studies of Soviet political culture by the same person but with some important methodological differences, see S. White in Brown and Gray, *Political Culture* . . . , pp. 25-65, and White's book, *Political Culture and Soviet Politics* (London: Macmillan, 1979). Probably the most useful — and certainly the most cautious — analysis of political culture in the GDR is G. Schweigler's *National Consciousness in Divided Germany* (London: Sage, 1975), esp. pp. 89-140; although Schweigler is primarily concerned with a dimension of East German culture of marginal relevance to us at this point, he does cite three authors (J. Smith, A. Kohlschuetter, and E. Richert) who have noted the presence of most of these "traditional German" attitudes in the GDR (see pp. 108, 110, and 125). Traditional

Conclusions

Russian scorn for the alleged cold efficiency of the Germans comes out nicely in Pushkin's treatment of "Herman the German" in *The Queen of Spades*.

21. D. Joravsky, "Soviet Ideology," *Soviet Studies*, No. 1, 1966, pp. 12-13.

22. A. G. Meyer, "The Functions of Ideology in the Soviet Political System," *Soviet Studies*, No. 3, 1966, p. 275.

23. By this we mean that there should be inclusion of the emphasis of many communist leaders on cybernetics and the scientific-technical revolution. For further details, see note 47, below.

24. This finding is in line with J. Armstrong's argument in his *Ideology, Politics and Government in the Soviet Union* (London: Nelson, 1973), passim, esp. p. 28.

25. For one of the most refined analyses of the different functions played by ideology in the policy process, see K. H. Dawisha, "The Roles of Ideology in the Decision-Making of the Soviet Union," *International Relations*, No. 2, 1972, pp. 156-175.

26. On the GDR campaign as part of the more general campaign to legitimize the New Economic System, see Baylis, "Economic Reform as Ideology . . . ," pp. 211-229.

27. G. B. Smith in Smith, *Public Policy* . . . , p. 11.

28. Yugoslavia has a form of planned economy, and social rather than private ownership of production, and in this sense her industry is similar to that in other East European communist states. However, decision-making is generally far less centralized in Yugoslavia than elsewhere. For instance, whereas the other East European states were tending to concentrate and centralize industrial production and administration in the 1970s — via the creation of associations — Yugoslavia adopted a policy in 1971 of breaking down large production units into smaller ones. In recent years an increasing number of articles have appeared in the Soviet Union and Eastern Europe in which it is argued that there is a useful place in any national economy for small enterprises as well as the larger associations. See Yu. Subotskii, "Maloe Predpriyatie," *Pravda*, 20 July 1978, p. 2, and Horváth, "On the Size of the Firm," pp. 34-62.

29. A. H. Brown, "Policy-Making in the Soviet Union," *Soviet Studies*, No. 1, 1971, passim, esp. p. 129.

30. Dawisha, "The Roles of Ideology . . . ," esp. pp. 169, 172.

31. To take but two of many examples from other communist states, there is the decollectivization of agriculture in Poland after the 1956 troubles and the present Chinese leadership's rejection of so many of Mao's policies.

32. On "cooptation" policy, see P. C. Ludz, *The Changing Party Elite in East Germany* (Cambridge, MA: MIT Press, 1972), passim, and esp. pp. 276-286. Ludz also very soon noted the early moves away from such a policy under the present East German leadership; see his "Continuity and Change . . . ," esp. p. 65.

33. Ulbricht in *Protokoll der Verhandlungen des VI Parteitages* . . . , Vol. 1, p. 114.

34. Berger and Reinhold, *Zu den Wissenschaftlichen* . . . , pp. 25-27, quoted in Baylis, *The Technical Intelligentsia* . . . , p. 237. There are some remarkable similarities between the East German process and that vis-à-vis economic reform in Czechoslovakia in the mid-1960s; see A. Korbonski in L. J. Cohen and J. P. Shapiro (eds.), *Communist Systems in Comparative Perspective* (New York: Anchor, 1974), pp. 358-378, esp. 370-371. A full-length study of the development of the Polish associations has recently been completed, so that it will soon be possible to compare the details of the Polish process with the Soviet, East German, and Czechoslovak;

see J. Woodall, *The Policy of Industrial Concentration and Amalgamation in Poland since 1958* (Cambridge, England: Cambridge U.P., forthcoming).

35. Gromov and Kamenetskii, *Proizvodstvennye Ob"edineniya* . . . , p. 10.

36. That is, a few individuals in each territorial unit dominated the calls for the associations, but these advocates did not represent any particular functional group, nor do they appear to have attempted to link up in any significant way with functional peers in other areas.

37. As was mentioned earlier, there is some evidence that the East German specialists have started to become a little more autonomous in recent years, but the question needs considerably more research before a reasonably satisfactory and convincing answer can be produced.

38. This point is made explicitly in Popov, *Sovershenstvovanie* . . . , p. 9, and is implied in Omarov, "XXIV S'ezd KPSS . . . ," p. 102.

39. Brown, "Policy-Making in the Soviet Union," p. 121; J. F. Hough, "The Soviet System: Petrification or Pluralism?" *P of C*, No. 2, 1972, esp. pp. 27-29. David Lane is another writer who maintains that there is a difference between pluralism in communist states (though he prefers to call these countries "state socialist") and the liberal democracies; see his *The Socialist Industrial State*, p. 69.

40. See Brown and Gray, *Political Culture* . . . , passim.

41. A similar kind of relationship to that which exists between the USSR and several communist states might now be developing elsewhere in the communist world, e.g., between Vietnam and Kampuchea.

42. See note 8 to the Introduction.

43. It would not be surprising if the developments in East German industry in the late 1970s were to be mirrored in the USSR in the 1980s; this would involve the abolition of the Soviet industrial associations and the further development of the production associations. The main alternative is a return to something like the *sovnarkhoz* arrangement, which would no doubt also negatively affect the industrial associations.

44. See note 44 to the Introduction and G. K. Bertsch, *Power and Policy* . . . , pp. 133-145.

45. *Ibid.*, pp. 133-145.

46. *Ibid.*, p. 144.

47. It should, however, be pointed out that some of the East European states — including Czechoslovakia and the GDR — modified their attitudes toward the scientific-technical revolution (STR) in the 1970s, as part of a program to reassert the supremacy of the party and its Marxist-Leninist ideology; but we would interpret these developments as representing a desire for more political control of the STR, *not* its rejection. On the STR in the GDR, see Ludz, *The Changing Party Elite* . . . , pp. 367-407, and H. Zimmermann, "Politische Aspekte in der Herausbildung, dem Wandel und der Verwendung des Konzepts 'Wissenschaftlich-technische Revolution' in der DDR," *D.A.* (Sonderheft), 1976, pp. 17-51.

48. Bertsch, *Power and Policy* . . . , p. 144. Bertsch further argues that the Indochinese communist states, while more authoritarian than the East European ones, do not make policy in a rational comprehensive way either.

49. Morton, in Juviler and Morton, *Soviet Policy-Making*, pp. 7-14, 19-25.

50. By this we mean that there is increasing evidence to show that Stalin had less real power than was once widely believed; see, for example, T. Dunmore, *The Stalinist Command Economy* (London: Macmillan, forthcoming).

51. For analyses of communist leaderships (including leadership configurations, not all of which are essentially the same as that given here), see R. Barry Farrell (ed.),

Conclusions

Political Leadership in Eastern Europe and the Soviet Union (Chicago: AVC, 1970); Carl Beck et al., *Comparative Communist Political Leadership* (New York: McKay, 1973); and Korbonski, "Leadership Succession . . . ," passim.

52. Morton, in Juviler and Morton, *Soviet Policy-Making*, p. 23. For Lowenthal's argument, see "Replies," *P of C*, No. 4, 1965, p. 76. T. H. Rigby appears to adopt a position similar to Lowenthal's in "The Soviet Leadership: Towards a Self-Stabilizing Oligarchy," *Soviet Studies*, No. 2, 1970, pp. 190-191.

53. For instance, we would argue that literary policy — what can and cannot be published — has been less volatile and from the individual writer's point of view less ambiguous under the present Soviet leadership than it was under Khrushchev.

54. See, for example, A. King in A. King (ed.), *Why is Britain Becoming Harder to Govern?* (London: British Broadcasting Corporation, 1976), pp. 8-30.

55. Brown, *Soviet Politics and Political Science*, passim, esp. p. 104. Although Brown is here referring exclusively to Soviet politics, a similar view on politics in the communist world generally can be inferred from his review article, "Policymaking in Communist States," passim.

GLOSSARY AND LIST OF ABBREVIATIONS

The following is a list of the foreign terms and the abbreviations used more than once in this book and/or those the reader wishing to follow up references is likely to encounter; more detailed analyses of most of the concepts are to be found in the main text. Where appropriate, the plural form is given in parentheses, in the format adopted in most dictionaries. An "R" in brackets after a term signifies that it is Russian, a "G" that it is German.

Agrarno-promyshlenn|-oe (-ye) ob"edineni|-e (-ya) [R]	Agroindustrial association
APO [R]	See Agrarno-promyshlennoe ob"edinenie
Apparatchik (-i) [R]	Professional, full-time functionary in the party or state apparatus
ASUP [R]	Automated systems for the administration of production
Betrieb (-e) mit staatlicher Beteiligung [G]	Seminationalized enterprise
Betriebsteil (-e) [G]	Nonautonomous component part of combine or enterprise
Bezirk (-e) [G]	Region
Bezirkswirtschaftsrat (-̈e) [G]	Regional Economic Council
BWR [G]	See Bezirkswirtschaftsrat
CMEA	Council for Mutual Economic Assistance
CPSU	Communist Party of the Soviet Union
Edinonachalie [R]	One-person management
EDV [G]	Electronic data-processing
Einzelleitung [G]	One-person management
Erzeugnisgruppe (-n) [G]	Product group
ESS	Economic System of Socialism

Fabrik|-a (-i) [R]	Factory
Filial (-y) [R]	Filial (one type of component unit of a production association)
Firm|-a (-y) [R]	Firm (a type of production association)
Glavk (-i) [R]	Chief administration (subdivision of a ministry)
Gorkom (-y) [R]	CPSU committee at town level
Gosbank [R]	State Bank
Gosplan [R]	State Planning Committee
Gossnab [R]	State Committee for Material Technical Supplies
Gostsen [R]	State Committee for Prices
Hauptverwaltung (-en) [G]	Chief administration (subdivision of a ministry)
Khozraschet [R]	Profit-and-loss accounting
Kolkhoz (-y) [R]	Collective farm
Kombinat (-e) [G]	Combine (approximate equivalent of Russian proizvodstvennoe ob"edinenie)
Kombinat (-y) [R]	Combine (a type of production association)
Kooperationsgemeinschaft (-en) [G]	Cooperation collective
Kooperationskette (-n) [G]	Cooperation chain
Kooperationsverband (-̈e) [G]	Cooperation group
Kra|-i (-ya) [R]	Province
Kraikom (-y) [R]	CPSU committee at provincial level
Kreis (-e) [G]	District
KWO [G]	Kabelwerk Oberspree (a particular combine)
Leitbetrieb (-e) [G]	Head enterprise of a product group
Minpribor [R]	Ministry of Instrument Manufacture, Means of Automation and Administrative Systems
Nauchno-proizvodstvenn|-oe (-ye) ob"edineni|-e (-ya) [R]	Science-production association
NES	New Economic System
NPO [R]	See Nauchno-proizvodstvennoe ob"edinenie
Ob"edineni|-e (-ya) [R]	Association
Ob"edinenn|-oe (-ye) predpriyati|-e (-ya) [R]	Amalgamated enterprise
Oblast|-' (-i) [R]	Province
Obkom (-y) [R]	CPSU committee at provincial level
Orgkomitet (-y) [R]	Organizing Committee (e.g., of a conference)

Glossary/Abbreviations

PO [R]   See Proizvodstvennoe ob"edinenie
Produktionsstaette (-n) [G]   Nonautonomous component part of combine or enterprise
Proizvodstvenn|-oe (-ye) ob"edineni|-e (-ya) [R]   Production association
Proizvodstv|-o (-a) [R]   Production (one type of component unit of a production association)
Promyshlenn|-oe (-ye) ob"edineni|-e (-ya) [R]   Industrial association
Promyshlenno-torgov|-oe (-ye) ob"edineni|-e (-ya) [R]   Industrial-trade association
Raikom (-y) [R]   CPSU committee at district level
Raion (-y) [R]   District
R and D   Research and development
Rechtsfaehigkeit [G]   Legal competence
RGW [G]   Council for Mutual Economic Assistance
RPO [R]   Republic promyshlennoe ob"edinenie
SED [G]   Socialist Unity Party
SEV [R]   Council for Mutual Economic Assistance
Sovkhoz (-y) [R]   State Farm
Sovnarkhoz (-y) [R]   Economic Council
Stammbetrieb (-e) [G]   Main enterprise of a combine
Stroibank [R]   Construction bank
Trest (-y) [R]   Trust
Vedomstv|-o (-a) [R]   Central organ (literally, department)
VEB [G]   See Volkseigener Betrieb
VEK [G]   See Volkseigenes Kombinat
Volkseigen|-er (-e) Betrieb (-e) [G]   Nationally owned (state) enterprise
Volkseigen|-es (-e) Kombinat (-e) [G]   Nationally owned (state) combine
Volkswirtschaftsrat [G]   National Economic Council (*or* Council of National Economy)
VPO [R]   All-union promyshlennoe ob"edinenie
VVB [G]   Association or Union (between 1952-1958, Administration) of nationally owned enterprises
VWR [G]   See Volkswirtschaftsrat
Werk (-e) [G]   Works (i.e., factory)
Wirtschaftliche Rechnungsfuehrung [G]   Profit-and-loss accounting
Zavod (-y) [R]   Works (i.e., factory)

BIBLIOGRAPHY

Alekseenko, A., Patrotskii, T., and Kamenetskii, V., " Proizvodstvennye kompleksy deistvuyut," *Ekon. Gaz.,* No. 46, 1962.
Alekseenko, A. G. (ed.), *Skhemy Struktur Upravleniya Promyshlennost'yu L'vovskogo Ekonomicheskogo Raiona i Proizvodstvennykh Ob"edinenii v Period Ikh Organizatsii vo L'vovskom SNKh i v Drugikh Sovnarkhozakh Strany* (L'vov: Proektno-Konstruktorskii Institut L'vovskogo Sovnarkhoza, 1964).
Allakhverdyan, D. A. and Slastenko, E. N., *Metodologicheski Osnovy Formirovaniya Ob"edinenii v Promyshlennosti* (Moscow: Izd. Ekonomika, 1974).
Andreev, B. S. and Margolis, D. A., *Leningradskie Firmy* (Leningrad: Lenizdat, 1965).
Andreev, V., "Otkhody Lesa — Tsennoe Syr'e," *Sots. Ind.,* 11 March 1971.
Armstrong, J., *Ideology, Politics and Government in the Soviet Union* (London: Nelson, 1973).
"ASU — Na Sluzhbu Pyatiletke," *Ekon. Gaz.,* No. 28, 1973.
Aus den Diskussionsreden auf der 9. Tagung des ZK der SED (Berlin: Dietz Verlag, 1973).
Avtorkhanov, A., *The Communist Party Apparatus* (Chicago: Henry Regnery Co., 1966).
Avtorkhanov, A., "The New Phase of Soviet Expansionist Policy," *Bulletin of the Institute for the Study of the USSR,* No. 12, 1971.
Azrael, J., *Managerial Power and Soviet Politics* (Cambridge, MA: Harvard U.P., 1966).
Bachurin, A., " Nauchno-Proizvodstvennoe Ob"edinenie," *Ekon. Gaz.,* No. 9, 1976.
Bachurin, A. V. et. al. (eds.), *Sovershenstvovanie Planirovaniya i Uluchshenie Ekonomicheskoi Raboty v Narodnom Khozyaistve* (Moscow: Izd. Ekonomika, 1969).
Baibakov, N. K., "Po Voskhodyashchei Linii," *Pravda,* 1 August 1972.
Baibakov, N. K., "Zadachi Sovershenstvovaniya Planirovaniya i Uluchsheniya Ekonomicheskoi Raboty y Narodnom Khozyaistve," *Ekon. Gaz.,* No. 21, 1968.
Baikov, N. D. et. al., *Otraslevye Proizvodstvennye Ob"edineniya v Promyshlennosti* (Moscow: Izd. Ekonomika, 1966).
Bakalo, R., "Nerealizovannye Vygody," *Sots. Ind.,* 11 July 1972.
Baltrusch, E., " Dispute in Rahnsdorf," *effekt,* No. 2, 1968.
Baranov, A., "Vmesto Trestov — Ob"edineniya," *Ekon. Gaz.,* No. 8, 1970.
Baranov, M., "Problemy Formirovaniya i Razvitiya Agrarno-Promyshlennykh Ob"edinenii," *Vop. Ekon.,* No. 9, 1972.

Baranov, Yu., "Avtoritet PDPS Ob"edineniya," *Ekon. Gaz.*, No. 41, 1975.
Baylis, T. A., "Economic Reform as Ideology: East Germany's New Economic System," *Comparative Politics*, No. 3, 1971.
Baylis, T. A., *The Technical Intelligentsia and the East German Elite* (Berkeley: University of California Press, 1974).
Beck, C. et al., *Comparative Communist Political Leadership* (New York: McKay, 1973).
Benjamin, M., Moebis, H., and Penig, L., *Funktion, Aufgaben und Arbeitsweise der Ministerien* (Berlin: Staatsverlag der Deutschen Demokratischen Republik, 1973).
Berger, W. and Reinhold, O., *Zu den Wissenschaftlichen Grundlagen des Neuen Oekonomischen Systems der Planung und Leitung* (Berlin: Dietz Verlag, 1966).
Berri, L. Ya., *Spetsializatsiya i Kooperirovanie v Promyshlennosti SSSR* (Moscow: Gosudarstvennoe Izd. Politicheskoi Literatury, 1954).
Berri, L., *Spezialisierung und Kooperation in der Industrie der UdSSR* (Berlin: Verlag Die Wirtschaft, 1955).
Bertsch, G. K., *Power and Policy in Communist Systems* (New York: John Wiley, 1978).
"Beschluss ueber die Durchfuehrung von monatlichen Rechenschaftslegungen der Direktoren der volkseigenen Betriebe, Kombinate und der Betriebe der Kombinate vor den Werktaetigen ihres Verantwortungsbereiches vom 17. September 1970," *GBl.*, Pt. 2, No. 78, 1970.
"Beschluss ueber die Verwirklichung des Oekonomischen Systems des Sozialismus bei der Bildung von volkseigenen Kombinaten in Industrie und Bauwesen und die Gestaltung der Beziehungen zwischen den volkseigenen Kombinaten und ihren Betrieben fuer 1969/70," *GBl.*, Pt. 2, No. 46, 1969.
"Beschluss zur weiteren Gestaltung der Aufgaben, Rechte und Pflichten der volkseigenen Kombinate im Planjahr 1970," *GBl.*, Pt. 2, No. 5, 1970.
Bethkenhagen, J. and Machowski, H., *Integration im Rat fuer gegenseitige Wirtschaftshilfe* (Berlin: Berlin Verlag, 1976).
Beyer, H. and Kanzig, H., "Die Genesis des neuen oekonomischen Systems in der Zeit vom VI. Parteitag der SED bis zur Wirtschaftskonferenz," *Wirts/wiss.*, No. 12, 1969.
Beyme, K. von, "A Comparative View of Democratic Centralism," *Government and Opposition*, No. 3, 1975.
Biermann, W., "Ein Kombinat ist mehr als die Summe seiner Betriebe," *N.D.*, 24 July 1972.
Blyakhman, L., "Ob"edineniya: Opyt i Perspektivy," *Pravda*, 1 January 1971.
Bobrov, A., "Sovetskaya Firma," *Isvestiya*, 21 October 1959.
Boettcher, H., "Erfahrungen bei der Durchfuehrung von monatlichen Rechenschaftslegungen der Direktoren der volkseigenen Betriebe und Kombinate vor den Werktaetigen," *WR*, No. 3, 1971.
Boldin, V., "Vazhnoe Zveno," *Pravda*, 15 March 1972.
Borodin, P., "Gigant i Ego Sputniki," *Sots. Ind.*, 24 February 1971.
Borovik, F. R. (ed.), *Problemy Intensifikatsii Promyshlennogo Proizvodstva* (Minsk: Izd. Nauka i Tekhnika, 1974).
Brabant, J. W. van, *Socialist Economic Integration* (Cambridge, England: Cambridge U. P., 1980).
Bratchenko, B. F., "Ot Uchastka do Ministerstva," *Ekon. Gaz.*, No. 37, 1972.
Bratus', S. N., "Reforma i Pravo," *Ekon. Gaz.*, No. 4, 1967.

Braybrooke, D. and Lindblom, C. E., *A Strategy for Decision* (New York: Free Press, 1970).
Brezhnev, L. I., *Ob Osnovnykh Voprosakh Ekonomicheskoi Politiki KPSS Na Sovremennom Etape: Rechi i Doklady*, 2 vols. (Moscow: Politizdat, 1975).
Brezhnev, L. I., "Rech' Pervogo Sekretarya TsK KPSS Tovarishcha L. I. Brezhneva," *Ekon. Gaz.*, No. 40, 1965.
Bromke, A. and Rakowska-Harmstone, T. (eds.), *The Communist States in Disarray 1965-1971* (Minneapolis: University of Minnesota Press, 1972).
Brown, A. H., "Policymaking in Communist States," *Studies in Comparative Communism*, No. 4, 1978.
Brown, A. H., "Policy-Making in the Soviet Union," *Soviet Studies*, No. 1, 1971.
Brown, A. H., *Soviet Politics and Political Science* (London: Macmillan, 1974).
Brown, A. and Gray, J. (eds.), *Political Culture and Political Change in Communist States* (London and Basingstoke: Macmillan, 1977).
Bruce, J. B., *The Politics of Soviet Policy Formation* (Denver: University of Denver Graduate School of International Studies, 1976).
Brzezinski, Z. and Huntington, S. P., *Political Power – USA:USSR* (New York: Viking Compass, 1965).
Brzezinski, Z. K., *The Soviet Bloc: Unity and Conflict* (Cambridge, MA: Harvard U. P., 1967).
Brzezinski, Z., "The Soviet Past and Future," *Encounter*, No. 3, 1970.
Bundesministerium fuer gesamtdeutsche Fragen (eds.), *A bis Z – Ein Taschen- und Nachschlagebuch ueber den anderen Teil Deutschlands* (Bonn: Deutscher Bundes-Verlag, 1969).
Bundesministerium fuer gesamtdeutsche Fragen (eds.), *SBZ von A bis Z* (Bonn: Deutscher Bundes-Verlag, 1960).
Bunich, P., "Khozraschetnyi Mekhanizm vnutri Proizvodstvennykh Ob″edinenii," *Plan. Khoz.*, No. 5, 1978.
Burghardt, K. H., Pobuda, C., and Weber, K., *Organisation von Konferenzen und Beratungen* (Berlin: Verlag Die Wirtschaft, 1973).
Burtsev, V., "Molchanie — Ne Luchshii Otvet," *Sots. Ind.*, 14 March 1971.
Cherkovets, V., "Predpriyatie v Sisteme Sotsialisticheskogo Obshchestvennogo Proizvodstva," *Plan. Khoz.*, No. 5, 1979.
Chuplinskas, A. B. and Baranauskas, V. A., *Tak Rabotaet Ob″edinenie "Sigma"* (Moscow: Izd. Ekonomika, 1967).
Clarke, R. A., *Soviet Economic Facts 1917-1970* (London and Basingstoke: Macmillan, 1972).
Cohen, L. J. and Shapiro, J. (eds.), *Communist Systems in Comparative Perspective* (New York: Anchor, 1974).
D. A., "Proizvodstvennye Ob″edineniya: Opyt i Perspektivy," *Vop. Ekon.*, No. 11, 1970.
Dallin, A. and Breslauer, G. W., *Political Terror in Communist Systems* (Stanford: Stanford U. P., 1970).
Das funktionelle Wirken der Bestandteile des neuen oekonomischen Systems der Planung und Leitung der Volkswirtschaft (Berlin: Dietz Verlag, 1964).
Das Neue Oekonomische System der Planung und Leitung der Volkswirtschaft in der Praxis (Verlin: Dietz Verlag, 1963).
Dawisha, K., "The Roles of Ideology in the Decision-Making of the Soviet Union," *International Relations*, No. 2, 1972.
Dellin, L. A. D. and Gross, H. (eds.), *Reforms in the Soviet and East European Economies* (Lexington, MA: D. C. Heath, 1972).

Der Weg zur Durchfuehrung der Beschluesse des VII. Parteitages der SED auf dem Gebiet der Wirtschaft, Wissenschaft und Technik (Berlin: Dietz Verlag, 1967).

"Diabolical Social-Imperialist Face of the Soviet Revisionist Renegade Clique," *Peking Review*, No. 43, 1968.

Die Redaktion, "Nur ein modernes sozialistisches Planungssystem sichert Pionier- und Spitzenleistungen," *Die Wirts.*, No. 3, 1970.

Die Redaktion, "Kombinatsleitung kein Dachorgan," *VS*, No. 8, 1969.

Divnogortsev, I., "Za Svoim Zaborom," *Sots. Inds.*, 3 January 1971.

Doernberg, S., *Kurze Geschichte der DDR* (Berlin: Dietz Verlag, 1965).

"Dokumentation — Das 7. Plenum des ZK der SED (24. und 25. November 1977), 'Aus dem Bericht des Politbueros,'" *D.A.*, No. 1, 1978.

Domdey, S. and Albrecht, D., "Mit dem neuen Instrumentarium lassen sich wichtige aussenwirtschaftliche Probleme loesen," *Die Wirts.*, No. 15, 1967.

Domdey, S. and Hohl, S., "Ein Experiment im Dienste hoeherer Effektivitaet," *Die Wirts.*, No. 4, 1967.

Drogichinskii, N. E., "General'naya Skhema Otrasli," *Pravda*, 31 May 1974.

Drogichinskii, N., "Kak razvivat'sya ob"edineniyam," *Pravda*, 7 February 1976.

Drogichinskii, N., "Nazrevshie Voprosy Sovershenstvovaniya Upravleniya Promyshlennost'yu," *Plan. Khoz.*, No. 5, 1962.

Drogichinskii, N. E., *Organizatsiya Upravleniya Promyshlennost'yu i Planirovaniya na Sovremennom Etape* (Moscow: Izd. Ekonomika, 1965).

Drogichinskii, N., "Proekty General'nykh Skhem Upravleniya Otraslevymi Sistemami," *Plan. Khoz.*, No. 5, 1975.

Dudinskii, I., *Das Komplexprogramm als strategischer Plan fuer die sozialistische Integration* (Moscow: APN, 1973).

Dudszus, A., "VVB Schiffbau experimentiert," *Die Wirts.*, No. 49 (Beilage), 1967.

Duesterwald, M., "Genauere Leistungsrechnung der Kombinate," *Die Wirts.*, No. 1, 1980.

Dumachev, A. P., *Effektivnaya Sistema Organizatsii Proizvodstva i Upravleniya* (Moscow: Izd. Ekonomika, 1975).

Dumachev, A. P., *Khozraschetnye Ob"edineniya v Promyshlennosti* (Leningrad: Lenizdat, 1972).

Dumachev, A. P., (ed.), *Leningradskie Khozraschetnye Ob"edineniya* (Leningrad: Lenizdat, 1975).

Dumachev, A. P., *Partiinye Organizatsii i Proizvodstvennye Ob"edineniya* (Moscow: Politizdat, 1977).

Dumachev, A. P. and Varsobin, A. K. (compilers), *Opyt Organizatsii i Raboty Khozraschetnykh Ob"edinenii v Promyshlennosti* (Leningrad: Lenizdat, 1970).

Dunaev, E. P., *Ob"edineniya Predpriyatii Kak Forma Obobshchestvleniya Proizvodstva* (Moscow: Izd. Moskovskogo Universiteta, 1974).

Dunmore, T., "Local Party Organs in Industrial Administration: The Case of the Ob"edinenie Reform," *Soviet Studies*, No. 2, 1980.

Dunmore, T., *The Stalinist Command Economy* (London: Macmillan, 1980).

Dzhavadov, G. A., "Po General'nym Skhemam," *Pravda*, 26 December 1975.

Dzhavadov, G. A., "Potentsial Ob"edinenii," *Pravda*, 18 September 1974.

Dzhavadov, G. and Dunaev, E., *Proizvodstvennye Ob"edineniya i Khozraschet* (Moscow: Moskovskii Rabochii, 1971).

Easton, D., *A Systems Analysis of Political Life* (New York: John Wiley, 1965).

Ebbecke, H-D. and Niebelschuetz, J., "Nochmals zur Rechtsstellung der Kombinate und der Kombinatsbetriebe," *WR*, No. 11, 1970.

"Effektivnost' Nauchnykh Soveshchanii," *Pravda*, 15 May 1975.

"Ekonomicheskii Eksperiment Podtverzhdaet: Firmy — Eto Khorosho," *Ekon. Gaz.*, No. 27, 1963.
Ekonomicheskii Ezhegodnik (Moscow: various years).
Eliseev, V., "Novoe — Ne Po Nazvaniyu," *Sots. Ind.*, 13 April 1977.
Ellman, M., *Economic Reform in the Soviet Union* (London: P.E.P., 1969).
Engibaryan, G., "Luchi 'Armelektrosveta,' " *Sots. Ind.*, 11 March 1971.
"Entwurf zur Verordnung ueber die Aufgaben, Rechte und Pflichten der Vereinigungen Volkseigener Betriebe," *Die Wirts.*, No. 13 (Beilage), 1967.
Erbe, G. et. al., *Politik, Wirtschaft und Gesellschaft in der DDR* (Opladen: Westdeutscher Verlag, 1980).
Erdmann, K., " Das Ende des Neuen Oekonomischen Systems," *D.A.*, No. 9, 1968.
Erdmann, K. and Melzer, M., " Die neue Kombinatsverordnung in der DDR," Pts. 1 and 2, *D.A.*, Nos. 9 and 10, 1980.
"Erfahrungen aus Kombinate," *Die Wirts.*, No. 12, 1979.
Evans, A. B., " Developed Socialism in Soviet Ideology," *Soviet Studies*, No. 3, 1977.
F. K., " Das Kombinat," *N.D.*, 10 January 1968.
Farrell, R. B. (ed.), *Political Leadership in Eastern Europe and the Soviet Union* (Chicago: AVC, 1970).
Faude, E., "Zur Rolle der Kombinate in der Aussenwirtschaft," *Sozialistische Aussenwirtschaft*, No. 6, 1968.
Faude, E. and Heinze, M., "Internationale oekonomische Organisationen sozialistischer Laender," *Einheit*, No. 6, 1975.
Fejtö, F., *A History of the People's Democracies* (Harmondsworth: Penguin, 1974).
Fricke, K., " DDR-Fuehrung neu formiert," *D.A.*, No. 10, 1973.
Friedrich, G., *Aufgaben und Arbeitsweise der VVB* (Berlin: Verlag Die Wirtschaft, 1959).
"25 Jahre DDR — ein Vierteljahrhundert Kampf fuer Frieden, Demokratie und Sozialismus," *Die Wirts.*, No. 15, 1974.
G. Br., "Modelle nur platonisch?" *N.D.*, 21 January 1969.
Gerisch, R. (ed.), *Leitungsorganisation in den Betrieben und Kombinaten* (Berlin: Dietz Verlag, 1976).
Gerisch, R. and Hofmann, W., "Aufgaben und Probleme der Entwicklung in den Kombinaten zur Erhoehung der volkswirtschaftlichen Effektivitaet," *Wirts/wiss.*, No. 2, 1979.
Gerisch, R., Hofmann, W., Krieg, J., and Mueller, E., "Organisatorische Probleme der Kombinatsbildung," *Die Wirts.*, No. 15 (Beilage), 1968.
Gerstner, K-H., "Kombinat fuer Oberkleidung wird gebildet," *B.Z.*, 17 July 1968.
" Gesetz ueber den Ministerrat der Deutschen Demokratischen Republik," *GBl.*, Pt. 1, No. 16, 1972.
Gesetz ueber den Ministerrat – Gesetz ueber die oertlichen Volksvertretungen und ihre Organe – Verordnung ueber die Aufgaben, Rechte und Pflichten der VEB, Kombinate und VVB (Berlin: Staatsverlag der Deutschen Demokratischen Republik, 1974).
" Gesetz ueber die oertlichen Volksvertretungen und ihre Organe in der Deutschen Demokratischen Republik," *GBl.*, Pt. 1, No. 32, 1973.
"Gewerkschaftliche Vertrauensleute beschlossen anspruchsvolle Ziele," *N.D.*, 3 January 1980.
Glaess, K., Goerner, G., and Tauscher, H., *Lehr- und Studienmaterial zum Wirtschaftsrecht*, Vol. 6 (Berlin: Staatsverlag der Deutschen Demokratischen Republik, 1974).
Glukharev, V., " Golovnoe Predpriyatie i Filial," *Sots. Ind.*, 11 February 1977.

Gnedkov, Yu. and Tsmel', V., "Problemy Upravleniya i Informatsiya," *Plan. Khoz.*, No. 9, 1968.
Golenishev, A., "Partkom i Ob"edinenie," *Pravda*, 30 August 1973.
Gorlin, A. C., "The Soviet Economic Associations," *Soviet Studies*, No. 1, 1974.
Graichen, D. and Rouscik, L., *Zur Sozialistischen Wirtschaftsorganisation* (Berlin: Verlag Die Wirtschaft, 1971).
Granick, D., *Enterprise Guidance in Eastern Europe* (Princeton: Princeton U.P., 1975).
Grant, W. P., "Insider and Outsider Groups " (presented at ECPR workshop on Interest Groups, Berlin, March 1977).
Graupner, K-H. and Krzyzanowski, W., "14. Tagung des Wissenschaftlichen Rates fuer die wirtschaftwissenschaftliche Forschung," *Wirts/wiss.*, No. 9, 1975.
Gripp, R. C., *The Political System of Communism* (London: Nelson, 1973).
Gromov, V. I. and Kamenetskii, V. Ya., *Proizvodstvennye Ob"edineniya V SSSR* (Moscow: Izd. Ekonomika, 1967).
Grossmann, R., "Unser Experiment orientiert Aussenhandelsunternehmen und VVB auf ein gemeinsames Ziel," *Die Wirts.*, No. 8, 1967.
" Grosswerk Deuben-Profen soll 15 Mio Mark zusaetzlichen Gewinn bringen," *Die Wirts.*, No. 48, 1967.
Grote, G., "Zur Verwirklichung der Mitverantwortung von VVB und VEB fuer den Export," *Die Wirts.*, No. 1, 1964.
Grushetskii, I., "Sovetskie Firmy — Ikh Nastoyashchee i Budushchee," *Izvestiya*, 18 February 1962.
Gusev, V. and Khachaturyan, A., "Upravlenie v Podotrasli," *Sots. Ind.*, 3 November 1976.
Gvishiani, D. M. et. al. (eds.), *Materialy K Vsesoyuznoi Nauchno-Teknicheskoi Konferentsii "Problemy Nauchnoi Organizatsii Upravleniya Sotsialisticheskoi Promyshlennost'yu,"* 7 vols. (Moscow: 1966).
Gvishiani, D., Irasak, Ya., and Kamenitser, S. (eds.), *Upravlenie Sotsialisticheskimi Promyshlennymi Ob"edineniyami i Predpriyatiyami*, 2 vols. (Moscow: Izd. Progress, 1974).
Gvishiani, D. M. and Kamenitser, S. E. (eds.), *Problemy Nauchnoi Organizatsii Upravleniya Sotsialisticheskoi Promyshlennost'yu* (Moscow: Izd. Ekonomika, 1968).
Gvishiani, D. M. and Kamenitser, S. E. (eds.), *Problemy Nauchnoi Organizatsii Upravleniya Sotsialisticheskoi Promyshlennost'yu* (Moscow: Izd. Ekonomika, 1974).
H., "Echte Partner der zentralen Planung und Fuehrung," *N.D.*, 25 January 1969.
H., "Vor Gruendung der VVB Baumwolle," *Die Wirts.*, No. 13, 1958.
Halbritter, W., "Hinweise und Empfehlungen zur Durchsetzung des Beschluesse zur Verwirklichung des oekonomischen Systems des Sozialismus in den volkseigenen Kombinaten 1969/70," *Die Wirts.*, No. 51/52, 1969, Beilage 2.
Halbritter, W., "Leistungsstarke Kombinate — bedeutsamer Faktor bei der Erhoehung der Effektivitaet unserer Volkswirtschaft," *Die Wirts.*, No. 31, 1970.
Hammond, T. T. (ed.), *The Anatomy of Communist Takeovers* (New Haven: Yale U.P., 1975).
Hanhardt, A. M., *The German Democratic Republic* (Baltimore: Johns Hopkins Press, 1968).
Hanson, P., "Economic Development in the Soviet Union in 1972 " (presented at NASEES Conference, Cambridge, Spring, 1973).

Harasymiw, B., "Nomenklatura: The Soviet Communist Party's Leadership Recruitment System," *Canadian Journal of Political Science*, No. 3, 1969.
Harnapp, U., "Was gehen das Werk die Wohnungen an?" *N.D.*, 24 January 1972.
Haupt, A., "Probleme der oertlich geleiteten Industrie Leipzigs," *Die Wirts.*, No. 43, 1962.
Heilbroner, R. L., "The multinational corporations and the nation-state," *New York Review of Books*, No. 2, 1971.
Heinrich, "Konsequenzen einer harten Kritik," *Die Wirts.*, No. 21, 1967.
Herold, H., "Die Aufgabenabgrenzung zwischen VVB und VEB gruendlich beraten," *Die Wirts.*, No. 18, 1967.
Hesse, K., Mueller, K., and Richter, H., *Lehr- und Studienmaterial zum Wirtschaftsrecht*, Vol. 5 (Berlin: Staatsverlag der Deutschen Demokratischen Republik, 1974).
Heuer, K., "Die planmaessige Weiterentwicklung der Rechtsstellung der volkseigenen Kombinate," *WR*, No. 4, 1970.
Heuer, K. and Klinger, G., "Einige Fragen der Verordnung ueber die Aufgaben, Rechte und Pflichten der volkseigenen Betriebe, Kombinate und VVB," *S und R*, No. 7, 1973.
Heuer, U-J., "Rechtsfragen der Leitung," *Wirts/wiss.*, No. 6, 1966.
Heuer, U-J., "Verfassung fuer den Sozialismus," *VS*, No. 6, 1968.
Heuer, U-J., "Zur weiteren Entwicklung der Wirtschaftsrecht in der DDR," *N.D.*, 9 February 1968.
Hilbert, K., "Firmennamen und Warenzeichen — Symbole fuer Wertarbeit und Weltmarktfaehigkeit der Erzeugnisse," *Die Wirts.*, No. 36, 1969.
Hilbert, K., "Kombinatsbildung und Effektivitaet," *Die Wirts.*, No. 24, 1969.
Hill, R. J., *Soviet Politics, Political Science and Reform* (Oxford: Martin Robertson, 1980).
Hodnett, G., "Succession Contingencies in the Soviet Union," *P of C*, No. 2, 1975.
Hoehmann, H. H., Kaser, M., and Thalheim, K. C. (eds.), *The New Economic Systems of Eastern Europe* (London: C. Hurst and Co., 1975).
Holmes, L. T., "Democratic Centralism in the GDR," ECPR Conference Paper, April 1975.
Holmes, L. T. (ed.), *The Withering Away of the State?* (London and Beverly Hills: Sage, 1981).
Honecker, E., "Aus dem Bericht des Politbueros an die 8. Tagung des ZK der SED," *N.D.*, 25 May 1978.
Honecker, E., *Aus dem Bericht des Politbueros an die 9. Tagung des ZK der SED* (Berlin: Dietz Verlag, 1973).
Honecker, E., "Aus dem Bericht des Politbueros an die 10. Tagung des ZK der SED," *N.D.*, 29 April 1969.
Hopkins, M. W., *Mass Media in the Soviet Union* (New York: Pegasus, 1970).
Horster, W. and Beyer, W., "Gestoerte Kooperationsketten erfordern das Eingreifen der VVB," *Die Wirts.*, No. 18, 1967.
Horváth, C., "On the Size of the Firm," *Eastern European Economics*, No. 3, 1980.
Hough, J., *The Soviet Prefects* (Cambridge, MA: Harvard U.P., 1969).
Hough, J. F., "The Soviet System: Petrification or Pluralism?" *P of C*, No. 2, 1972.
Hough, J. and Fainsod, M., *How the Soviet Union is Governed* (Cambridge, MA: Harvard U.P., 1979).
Huntington, S. P., "Transnational Organisations in World Politics," *World Politics*, No. 3, 1973.

Il'in, I. K., "Promyshlennye ob"edineniya i sovershenstvovanie upravleniya proizvodstvom," *SGiP*, No. 11, 1973.
Il'inskii, I. P. et. al., *GDR – Osnovy Gosudarstvennogo Stroya* (Moscow: Yuridicheskaya Literatura, 1971).
Institute of World Economy of the Chinese Academy of Social Science, "Soviet Social Imperialism — Most Dangerous Source of World War," *Peking Review*, No. 29, 1977.
"Intensivierung der Sozialistischen Reproduktion — Teil 2 — Diskussion," *Sitzungsberichte der Akademie der Wissenschaften der DDR*, No. 12/2, 1973. (Berlin: Akademie-Verlag, 1974).
Ionescu, G., *Comparative Communist Politics* (London: Macmillan, 1972).
Ionescu, C., *The Break-Up of the Soviet Empire in Eastern Europe* (Harmondsworth: Penguin, 1965).
Ivonin, I. P., "Vygoda Dokazana," *Izvestiya*, 11 May 1962.
Jaenicke, M., *Der Dritte Weg* (Cologne: Neuer Deutscher Verlag, 1964).
Jarowinsky, W., *Aus dem Bericht des Politbueros an die 6. Tagung des ZK der SED* (Berlin: Dietz Verlag, 1972).
Johnson, C. (ed.), *Change in Communist Systems* (Stanford: Stanford U.P., 1970).
Jonuscheit, K-H., "In Vorbereitung des VI. Parteitages," *Die Wirts.*, No. 51/2, 1962.
Joravsky, D., "Soviet Ideology," *Soviet Studies*, No. 1, 1966.
Juviler, P. H. and Morton, H. W. (eds.), *Soviet Policy-Making* (London: Pall Mall, 1967).
K. S., "Eine Million Bauarbeiter ohne Beschaeftigung," *Die Wirts.*, No. 14, 1962.
Kalweit, W. and Reinhold, P., "Zum Erscheinen des Buches 'Politische Oekonomie des Sozialismus und ihre Anwendung in der DDR,'" *Wirts/wiss.*, No. 10, 1969.
Kapustin, E. and Subotskii, Yu., "Problemy Razvitiya Ob"edinenii," *Ekon. Gaz.*, No. 17, 1975.
Kardelj, E., *Democracy and Socialism* (London: Summerfield Press, 1978).
Kashirina, M., "Srednee Zveno," *Pravda*, 11 June 1977.
Kashmanov, A., "Kontsentratsiya Podskazyvaet," *Sots. Ind.*, 9 April 1972.
Kensy, U., "Wissenschaftliche Arbeitsberatung zu Rechtsfragen der Kombinate bei der Durchfuehrung der Beschluesse des VIII Parteitages der SED," *WR*, No. 6, 1971.
Keren, M., "The New Economic System in the GDR: An Obituary," *Soviet Studies*, No. 4, 1973.
Khavina, S. and Gerasimova, V., "Burzhuaznye Ekonomisty ob Ob"edineniyakh v Sotsialisticheskoi Promyshlennosti," *Vop. Ekon.*, No. 4, 1978.
Khodzhaev, Sh., "Pochemu medlenno sozdayutsya ob"edineniya," *Pravda*, 14 January 1974.
Khorev, B., "Bol'shaya Stroika v malom Gorode," *Pravda*, 16 April 1978.
Khristoradnov, Yu., "V Usloviyakh Proizvodstvennogo Ob"edineniya," *Kommunist*, No. 14, 1978.
King, A. (ed.), *Why Is Britain Becoming Harder to Govern?* (London: British Broadcasting Corporation, 1976).
Kiperman, G. Ya., *Tsentralizm i Samostoyatel'nost' Predpriyatii* (Moscow: Izd. Politicheskoi Literatury, 1969).
Klampfl, W. and Lehmann, H., "Rationalisierung der Leitungsprozesse verlangt wissenschaftlich begruendete Organisationsarbeit," *Die Wirts.*, No. 46, 1962.
Klinger, G., "Die neue Kombinatsverordnung — ein wichtiges Instrument zur weiteren Vervollkommung der Leitung und Planung," *S und R*, No. 3, 1980.

Klinger, G., "Zur Entwicklung des sozialistischen Rechts seit dem VIII. Parteitag der SED und Tendenzen der kuenftigen Rechtsentwicklung," *WR*, No. 3, 1974.
Klinger, G. and Panzer, W., "Sozialistisches Wirtschaftsrecht und Organisationsstruktur der Volkswirtschaft," *VS*, No. 2, 1969.
Knirsch, P., "Stand und Entwicklungstendenzen der Sowjetwirtschaft," *Osteuropa*, Nos. 8-9, 1971.
"Kombinat der Kabelwerke," *Die Wirts.*, No. 5, 1967.
"Kombinat im Spreewald," *B.Z.*, 7 January 1969.
Komlev, A. I. et. al., *Promyshlennye ob"edineniya i Firmy Odesshchiny* (Odessa: Izd. Mayak, 1973).
"Kompleksno, s Perspektivoi," *Part. Zh.*, No. 10, 1972.
"Komplexprogramm fuer die weitere Vertiefung und Vervollkommnung der Zusammenarbeit und Entwicklung der sozialistischen oekonomischen Integration der Mitgliedlaender des RGW," *Sozialistische Aussenwirtschaft*, No. 9, 1971.
Konin, N. M., "Sovershenstvovanie Pravovogo Regulirovaniya Organizatsii i Deyatel'nosti Khozyaistvennykh Ob"edinenii," *SGiP*, No. 2, 1969.
Konstandov, L. A., "Struktura Upravleniya i Effektivnost' Proizvodstva," *Ekon. Gaz.*, No. 32, 1970.
"Konsul'tatsiya — Sovet Sekretarei Partorganizatsii Proizvodstvennogo Ob"edineniya," *Part. Zh.*, No. 18, 1978.
Korbonski, A., "Leadership Succession and Political Change in Eastern Europe," *Studies in Comparative Communism*, Nos. 1 and 2, 1976.
Kosar', A., "Ot Zamysla do Vnedreniya," *Sots. Ind.*, 29 January 1971.
Kormnov, Yu. F. and Evstigneev, R. N. (eds.), *Struktura Upravleniya Promyshlennost'yu v Stranakh SEV* (Moscow: Izd. Mysl', 1973).
Kosygin, A. N., "Ob Uluchshenii Upravleniya Promyshlennost'yu, Sovershenstvovanii Planirovaniya i Usilenii Ekonomicheskogo Stimulirovaniya Promyshlennogo Proizvodstva," *Pravda*, 28 September 1965.
Kosygin, A. N., "Povyshenie Nauchnoi Obosnovannosti Planov — Vazhneishaya Zadacha Planovikh Organov," *Ekon. Gaz.*, No. 16, 1965.
Kovalenko, V., "Shagi Ob"edineniya," *Sots. Ind.*, 14 May 1972.
Koziolek, H., "Oekonomisches System und sozialistische Wirtschaftsfuehrung," *effekt*, No. 3, 1968.
Kozlov, N., "Fond Razvitiya," *Sots. Ind.*, 28 April 1972.
Kreutzer, C. J., "Zu einigen Fragen der Entwicklung des sozialistischen Wirtschaftsrechts," *Die Wirts.*, No. 13, 1969.
Kroemke, C. and Rouscik, L., *Konzentration, Spezialisierung, Kooperation und Kombination in der Industrie der DDR* (Berlin: Verlag Die Wirtschaft, 1959 and 1961).
Krylova, V., *Osobennosti Analiza Khozyaistvennoi Deyatel'nosti Promyshlennykh Ob"edinenii* (Moscow: Ekonomika, 1971).
"Kurs — Sozdanie Ob"edinenii," *Pravda*, 15 August 1973.
Kuznetsov, I. and Tikhomirova, A., "Voprosy Effektivnosti Organizatsii Upravleniya Otrasl'yu Promyshlennosti," *Vop. Ekon.*, No. 11, 1970.
Kuznetsov, Yu., "Firmy Mestnoi Promyshlennosti," *Izvestiya*, 21 May 1972.
Ladwig, E. and Kiermeyer, D., "Das Niveau der Leitung und Wirtschaftsfuehrung bestimmt massgeblich den Konzentrationseffekt," *Die Wirts.*, No. 31, 1970.
Lagutkin, V. M. (ed.), *Proizvodstvennye Ob"edineniya: Problemy i Perspektivy* (Moscow: Izd. Mysl', 1971).

Lane, D., *Politics and Society in the USSR* (London: Martin Robertson, 1978).
Lane, D., *The End of Inequality?* (Harmondsworth: Penguin, 1971).
Lane, D., *The Socialist Industrial State* (London: Allen & Unwin, 1976).
Lane, D. and Kolankiewicz, G. (eds.), *Social Groups in Polish Society* (London: Macmillan, 1973).
Langer, H., Pflicke, G., and Streich, R., "Theoretische Aspekte der gesetzlichen Regelung der Rechtsstellung der volkseigenen Betriebe," *S und R*, No. 2, 1967.
Lapp, P. J., *Der Staatsrat im politischen System der DDR 1960-1971* (Opladen: Westdeutscher Verlag, 1972).
Lapp, P. J., *Die Volkskammer der DDR* (Opladen: Westdeutscher Verlag, 1975).
Laptev, V. V., "Ekonomika i Pravo," *Sots. Ind.*, 9 October 1975.
Laptev, V. V., "Khozyaistvovanie i Khozyaistvennoe Pravo," *Kommunist*, No. 1, 1975.
Laptev, V. V., "Mezhdu Tsekhom i Zavodom," *Sots. Ind.*, 5 January 1977.
Laptev, V. V., "Pravovoe polozhenie ob"edinenii v promyshlennosti," *S GiP*, No. 8, 1973.
Lazutkin, A., "Rukovoditeli Vystupaet Pered Rabochimi," *Part. Zh.*, No. 11, 1972.
Legters, L. H. (ed.), *The German Democratic Republic – A Developed Socialist Society* (Boulder, CO: Westview Press, 1978).
Lektsii po Partiinomu Stroitel'stvu – Vypusk 1 (Moscow: Izd. Mysl', 1971).
Lenev, O. and Apse, T., "Ob"edinenie v Puti," *Pravda*, 24 January 1972.
Levinson, C., *Vodka Cola* (Horsham: C. Levinson, 1980).
Lieser-Triebnigg, E., "Ein neues Organisationsrecht fuer die Wirtschaft in der DDR," *D.A.*, No. 8, 1973.
Lodge, M. C., *Soviet Elite Attitudes Since Stalin* (Columbus, OH: Merrill, 1969).
Loeber, D. A., "Legal Rules 'For Internal Consumption Only,'" *The International and Comparative Law Quarterly*, No. 1, 1970.
Loos, R. E., "Die VVB muss fuer die weitgehende Uebereinstimmung zwischen Zweig, Betrieb und Volkswirtschaft sorgen," *Die Wirts.*, No. 14, 1967.
Lowenthal, R. (under "Replies"), *P of C*, No. 4, 1965.
Ludz, P. C., "Continuity and Change since Ulbricht," *P of C*, No. 2, 1972.
Ludz, P. C. (ed.), *DDR Handbuch* (Cologne: Verlag Wissenschaft und Politik, 1979).
Ludz, P. C., *The Changing Party Elite in East Germany* (Cambridge, MA: MIT Press, 1972).
Ludz, P. C., "Widersprueche im Neuen Oekonomischen System: Organisatorische Probleme der Erzeugnisgruppen," *SBZ-Archiv*, No. 7, 1964.
Ludz, P. C. and Croan, M., "Meinungen zum Fuehrungswechsel in der SED," *D.A.*, No. 6, 1971.
Lyakhov, A., "Za shchitom global'nykh idei," *Sots. Ind.*, 25 January 1976.
Lyakhov, A., "Zavod i NII," *Sots. Ind.*, 16 February 1971.
mb, "Das Experiment," *Die Wirts.*, No. 9, 1963.
mge, "Mit Skepsis empfangen — aber Vorteile ueberzeugten," *Die Wirts.*, No. 3, 1964.
Maksimenko, V. I., Sominskii, V. S., Gusakov, M. A., and Kukin, V. I., "Chto Pokazalo Obsledovanie?" *Ekonomika i Organizatsiya Promyshlennogo Proizvodstva (EKO)*, No. 2, 1977.
Maksimov, B. I., *Kak Upravlyat' Peremeshcheniem Kadrov v Ob"edinenii* (Leningrad: Lenizdat, 1979).

Bibliography

Malevanyi, A., "Effekt Obshchikh Usilii," *Sov. Kirg.*, 15 December 1970.
Manaev, V., "Ob"edinenie i Otrasl'," *Pravda*, 17 November 1973.
Markin, A. A. (ed.), *Effektivnost' Khozyaistvennykh Ob"edinenii* (Leningrad: Izd. Leningradskogo Universiteta, 1974).
Markov, F., "Bez Dvoevlastiya na Remonte," *Sots. Ind.*, 21 September 1972.
Marr, H., "Detailfragen eigenverantwortlich loesen," *Die Wirts.*, No. 14, 1967.
McCauley, M., *Marxism-Leninism in the German Democratic Republic* (London: Macmillan, 1979).
Meissner, B., "Die Sowjetunion auf dem Wege zum XXIV. Parteitag (I)," *Osteuropa*, No. 6, 1971.
Meissner, K., "Von objektiven Interessen der VVB ausgehen," *Die Wirts.*, No. 18, 1967.
Meleshkin, M. T. (ed.), *Pervye Sovetskie Firmy* (L'vov: Knizhkovo-Zhurnal'ne Vidavnitstvo, 1962).
Melzer, M. and Scherzinger, A., "Wirtschaftssystem der DDR im Umbau?," *Vierteljahrsheft zur Wirtschaftsforschung*, No. 4, 1978.
Meyer, A. G., "The Functions of Ideology in the Soviet Political System," *Soviet Studies*, No. 3, 1966.
Miller, D. and Trend, H. G., "Economic Reforms in East Germany," *P of C*, No. 2, 1966.
Miller, M., *Rise of the Russian Consumer* (London: Institute of Economic Affairs, 1965).
Minagawa, S., "The Functions of the Supreme Soviet Organs, and Problems of Their Institutional Development," *Soviet Studies*, No. 1, 1975.
"Ministerrat beriet Verordnung ueber Aufgaben der Kombinate und Betriebe," *Die Wirts.*, No. 9, 1973.
Misselwitz, H., "Zur Einbeziehung halbstaatlicher Betriebe," *Die Wirts.*, No. 3, 1964.
Mittag, G. "Aus dem Bericht des Politbueros an die 3. Tagung des ZK der SED," *N.D.*, 24 November 1967.
Mittag, G., "Die Durchfuehrung des Volkswirtschaftsplanes im Jahre 1970," *N.D.*, 11 and 12 June 1970.
Mittag, G., *Erfahrungen bei der Durchfuehrung der Beschluesse des VIII. Parteitages zur Intensivierung der Produktion in Industrie und Bauwesen. Zu einigen Problemen der Leitungstaetigkeit* (Berlin: Dietz Verlag, 1975).
Mittag, G., "Vorzuege des Sozialismus fuer hoehere Effektivitaet nutzen," *N.D.*, 26/27 August 1978.
Mittag, G., "Zielstrebige Verwirklichung der Hauptaufgabe," *Einheit*, No. 10, 1978.
Mitzscherling, P. et. al., *DDR-Wirtschaft – eine Bestandsaufnahme* (Frankfurt am Main: Fischer Verlag, 1974).
Moran, T. H., "Multinational Corporations and Dependency: A Dialogue for Dependentistas and Non-Dependentistas," *International Organisation*, Winter 1978.
Morkhov, D., "Tolkach . . . v svoem ob"edinenii," *Sots. Ind.*, 9 May 1977.
Morozov, M., "Na Puti K Ob"edineniyam," *Pravda*, 27 March 1972.
Mothes, W. (under "Leserwort"), *VS*, No. 3, 1968.
Mueller, K. and Such, H., "Zur Rechtsstellung des Kombinats und der Kombinatsbetriebe," *WR*, No. 6, 1970.

Mueller, R., "Betriebe, Kombinate und Bezirke," *effekt*, No. 4, 1969.
Nagovitsin, A., "Effektivnost' Vsesoyuznykh Promyshlennykh Ob"edinenii," *Vop. Ekon.*, No. 4, 1980.
Nagovitsin, A., "Promyshlennye Ob"edineniya v GDR," *Plan. Khoz.*, No. 2, 1974.
Naumann, H. and John, M., "Eine grosse Zeit fuer Rationalisatoren," *N.D.*, 28 September 1972.
9. Tagung des Zentralkomitees der Sozialistischen Einheitspartei Deutschlands (Berlin: Dietz Verlag, 1961).
Neugebauer, G., *Partei und Staatsapparat in der DDR* (Opladen: Westdeutscher Verlag, 1978).
Nevelyuk, V., "Firmy: Ekonomika, Organizatsiya," *Pravda*, 19 May 1970.
Nikishova, V., "Ob"edinenie — Osnovnoe Zveno Otrasli," *Vop. Ekon.*, No. 12, 1972.
Nove, A., *The Soviet Economic System* (London: Allen & Unwin, 1977).
Nove, A., "The Soviet Industrial Reorganisation," *P of C*, No. 6, 1957.
Novikov, A., "Partorganizatsiya v Usloviyakh Proizvodstvennogo Ob"edineniya," *Part. Zh.*, No. 12, 1978.
"Ob"edineniya: Ikh Raznovidnosti, Obshchee i Spetsificheskoe v Ikh Deyatel'nosti," *Sots. Trud*, No. 10, 1972.
"Obshchee polozhenie o mezhkhozyaistvennom predpriyatii (organizatsii) v sel'skom khozyaistve," *Resheniya . . .* , Vol. 11.
"Obshchee polozhenie o ministerstvakh SSSR," *Resheniya . . .* , Vol. 6.
"Obshchee polozhenie o vsesoyuznom i respublikanskom promyshlennykh ob"edineniyakh," *Resheniya . . .* , Vol. 9.
"Oekonomisches System in den Kombinaten," *N.D.*, 18 July 1970.
Oekonomisches System und Interessenvertretung – Probleme der gewerkschaftlichen Fuehrungstaetigkeit bei der Verwirklichung des Oekonomischen Systems des Sozialismus, 2 vols. (Berlin: Verlag Die Tribuene, 1968).
Oksenberg, M. C., "Policy Making under Mao Tse-tung, 1949-1968," *Comparative Politics*, No. 3, 1971.
Oldenburg, F., "Ost-Berlin wieder auf haerteren Kurs. Zur 10. Tagung des ZK der SED," *D.A.*, No. 11, 1973.
Omarov, A., "XXIV S'ezd KPSS ob Ekonomicheskoi Politike Partii na Sovremennom Etape," *Plan. Khoz.*, No. 9, 1972.
Os'mova, M. N., *Sotsialisticheskaya Ekonomicheskaya Integratsiya i Effektivnost' Proizvodstva* (Moscow: Politizdat, 1975).
"Otrasl' Na Khozraschete," *Ekon. Gaz.*, No. 32, 1972.
Panfilov, M., *Sovetskaya Firma Deistvuet* (Leningrad: Lenizdat, 1964).
Panzer, A., "Die Aufgaben, Rechte und Pflichten der Kombinate auf dem Gebiet der Aussenwirtschaft," *WR*, No. 4, 1970.
Parfenov, V., "Poisk vedet Ministerstvo," *Pravda*, 11 May 1978.
Parkin, F., *Class Inequality and Political Order* (London: Paladin, 1972).
Penig, L., "Entwicklungstendenzen in der Wirtschaftsfuehrung," *VS*, No. 1, 1969.
Penig, L., "Rechtsbeziehungen der Planung und Leitung volkseigener Industriekombinate," *VS*, No. 11, 1967.
Pevzner, A. G., *Khozraschet v Proizvodstvennykh Ob"edineniyakh* (Moscow: Izd. Ekonomika, 1968).
Pevzner, A. G. and Subotskii, Yu. V., *Pravovye Osnovy Upravleniya Promyshlennost'yu* (Moscow: Izd. Ekonomika, 1966).
Pivovarov, V., "Lider Potoka — Kombinat," *Pravda*, 2 December 1973.
Plenum Tsentral'nogo Komiteta Kommunisticheskoi Partii Sovetskogo Soyuza 19-23 Noyabrya 1962 g. - Stenograficheskii Otchet (Moscow: Gosudarstvennoe Izd. Politicheskoi Literatury, 1963).

Pleyer, K., "Die rechtliche Stellung der VVB in Neuen Oekonomischen System," *D.A.*, No. 2, 1968.
Ploss, S., *Conflict and Decision-Making in Soviet Russia* (Princeton: Princeton U.P., 1965).
"Po General'nym Skhemam," *Pravda*, 14 March 1977.
Pohlan, G., "Warenzeichen und firmenrechtliche Probleme bei der Kombinatsbildung beachten," *Die Wirts.*, No. 22, 1969.
Pohlan, G. and Schmiechen, "Zur Rechtsstellung der Teilsysteme eines sozialistischen Industriekombinates und zur kombinatsinternen Kooperation," *WR*, No. 7, 1970.
Pokrovskii, V., "Rabochaya Baza Nauki," *Sots. Ind.*, 16 April 1976.
Polisyuk, E., "Real'nost' Prav," *Sots. Ind.*, 13 May 1977.
Politische Oekonomie des Sozialismus und ihre Anwendung in der DDR (Berlin: Dietz Verlag, 1969).
Polivanov, V. N., "Profkom Ob"edineniya," *Trud.*, 11 November 1976.
"Polozhenie o Nauchno-Proizvodstvennom Ob"edinenii," *Resheniya* . . . , Vol. 11.
"Polozhenie o postoyanno deistvuyushchem proizvodstvennom soveshchanii," *Resheniya* . . . , Vol. 9.
"Polozhenie o proizvodstvennom ob"edinenii (Kombinate)," *Resheniya* . . . , Vol. 10.
"Polozhenie o sotsialisticheskom gosudarstvennom proizvodstvennom predpriyatii," *Resheniya* . . . , Vol. 5.
Polyakov, D., "Ne Tol'ko Posrednik," *Sots. Ind.*, 7 January 1971.
Polyakov, V., "Produktionsvereinigungen — Die Konzentration in der sowjetischen Industrie," *Die Wirts.*, No. 6, 1970.
Pomorski, S., "The Soviet Economic Associations: Some Problems of Legal Status and Organisation After the 1973 Reform," *Review of Socialist Law*, No. 3, 1976.
Popov, G. Kh. (ed.), *Sovershenstvovanie Sistemy Vnutrifirmennogo Upravleniya* (Moscow: Izd. Moskovskogo Universiteta, 1972).
Popov, G. and Petrov, N., "Na putyakh k ob"edineniyam," *Pravda*, 12 September 1973.
Popov, N. N., *Po Puti Sovershenstvovaniya – Primenenie Novoi Sistemy Planirovaniya i Rukovodstva vo Vneshnei Torgovle i v Promyshlennosti GDR* (Moscow: Izd. Mezhdunarodnya Otnosheniya, 1967).
Pospelova, E., "Khozraschetnye Ob"edineniya po Proizvodstvu Prodovol'stviya v Strane," *Vop. Ekon.*, No. 9, 1972.
Pospelova, E., "Idet Eksperiment," *Sots. Ind.*, 9 May 1978.
Pospelova, E., "Uspekh ne prikhodit Samotekom," *Sots. Ind.*, 13 October 1972.
"Postanovlenie Plenuma TsK KPSS, 29 sentyabrya 1965 g. 'Ob uluchshenii upravleniya promyshlennost'yu, sovershenstvovanii planirovaniya i usilenii ekonomicheskogo stimulirovaniya promyshlennogo proizvodstva,'" *Resheniya* . . . , Vol. 5.
"Postanovlenie Soveta Ministrov SSSR 19 marta 1970 g. 'O dal'neishem sovershenstvovanii planirovaniya proizvodstvenno-khozyaistvennoi deyatel'nosti ministerstva priborostroeniya, sredstv avtomatizatsii i sistem upravleniya i povyshenii roli ekonomicheskikh metodov v ego rabote,'" *Resheniya* . . . , Vol. 8.
"Postanovlenie Soveta Ministrov SSSR, 14 aprelya 1977 g. 'Ob utverzhdenii obshchego polozheniya o mezhkhozyaistvennom predpriyatii (organizatsii) v sel'skom khozyaistve,'" *Resheniya* . . . , Vol. 11.
"Postanovlenie Soveta Ministrov SSSR, 2 marta 1973 g. 'Ob utverzhdenii obshchego polozheniya o vsesoyuznom i respublikanskom promyshlennykh ob"edineniyakh,'" *Resheniya* . . . , Vol. 9.

"Postanovlenie Soveta Ministrov SSSR, 30 dekabrya 1975 g. 'Ob utverzhdenii polozheniya o nauchno-proizvodstvennom ob"edinenii,' " *Resheniya* . . . , Vol. 11.
"Postanovlenie Soveta Ministrov SSSR, 27 marta 1974 g. 'Ob utverzhdenii polozheniya o proizvodstvennom ob"edinenii (kombinate),' " *Resheniya* . . . , Vol. 10.
"Postanovlenie Tsentral'nogo Komiteta KPSS i Soveta Ministrov SSSR, "Ob uluchshenii planirovaniya i usilenii vozdeistviya khozyaistvennogo mekhanizma na povyshenie effektivnosti proizvodstva i kachestva raboty," *Sobranie Postanovlenii Pravitel'stva Soyuza Sovetskikh Sotsialisticheskikh Respublik*, No. 18, 1979.
"Postanovlenie TsK KPSS, 28 Maya 1976 g. 'O dal'neishem razvitii spetsializatsii i kontsentratsii sel'skokhozyaistvennogo proizvodstva na baze mezhkhozyaistvennoi kooperatsii i agropromyshlennoi integratsii,' " *Resheniya* . . . , Vol. 11.
"Postanovlenie TsK KPSS i Soveta Ministrov SSSR, 2 marta 1973 g. 'O nekotorykh meropriyatiyakh po dal'neishemu sovershenstvovaniyu upravleniya promyshlennost'yu' " *Resheniya* . . . , Vol. 9.
"Postanovlenie TsK KPSS i Soveta Ministrov SSSR 28 maya 1970 g. 'O sovershenstvovanii organizatsii upravleniya khimicheskoi promyshlennost'yu' " *Resheniya* . . . , Vol. 8.
"Postanovlanie TsK KPSS i Soveta Ministrov SSSR 28 Maya 1970 g. 'O sovershenstvovanii organizatsii upravleniya neftyanoi promyshlennost'yu,' " *Resheniya* . . . , Vol. 8.
"Postanovlenie TsK KPSS i Soveta Ministrov SSSR 28 maya 1970 g. 'O sovershenstvovanii organizatsii upravleniya ugol'noi promyshlennost'yu,' " *Resheniya* . . . , Vol. 8.
"Postanovlenie TsK KPSS i Soveta Ministrov SSSR, 4 oktyabrya 1965 g. 'O sovershenstvovanii planirovaniya i usilenii ekonomicheskogo stimulirovaniya promyshlennogo proizvodstva,' " *Resheniya* . . . , Vol. 5.
"Postanovlenie TsK KPSS i Soveta Ministrov SSSR 23 dekabrya 1970 g. 'Ob uluchshenii pravovoi raboty v narodnom khozyaistve,' " *Resheniya* . . . , Vol. 8.
"Postanovlenie TsK KPSS i Soveta Ministrov SSSR, 30 sentyabrya 1965 g. 'Ob uluchshenii upravleniya promyshlennost'yu,' " *Resheniya* . . . , Vol. 5.
"Pravovoe polozhenie proizvodstvennogo ob"edineniya (kombinata) i proizvodstvennogo edinets," *SGiP*, No. 9, 1974.
"Profkom Ob"edineniya," *Trud.*, 3 August 1977.
Programm der Sozialistischen Einheitspartei Deutschlands (Berlin: Dietz Verlag, 1963).
Programme of the Communist Party of the Soviet Union (Moscow: Foreign Languages Publishing House, 1961).
Pronina, V. S., *Tsentral'nye Organy Upravleniya Narodnym Khozyaistvom* (Moscow: Yuridicheskaya Literatura, 1971).
Protokoll der Verhandlungen des VI. Parteitages der Sozialistischen Einheitspartei Deutschlands, 4 vols. (Berlin: Dietz Verlag, 1963).
Protokoll der Verhandlungen des VII. Parteitages der Sozialistischen Einheitspartei Deutschlands, 4 vols. (Berlin: Dietz Verlag, 1967).
Protokoll der Verhandlungen des VIII. Parteitages der Sozialistischen Einheitspartei Deutschlands, 2 vols. (Berlin: Dietz Verlag, 1971).
Protokoll der Verhandlungen des IX. Parteitages der SED, 2 vols. (Berlin: Dietz Verlag, 1976).

Pyper, T. R., "The Central Committee Apparatus of the Soviet Communist Party," unpublished M. A. Dissertation, University of Essex, December 1973.
Radomysel'skii, M. I. and Shifrin, I. A., *Firmy – Novaya Forma Upravleniya Proizvodstvom* (Moscow: Ekonomizdat, 1963).
Rakhmilovich, V. A., "Khozraschet v promyshlennykh ob"edineniyakh," *SGiP*, No. 8, 1973.
Rakitskii, B. V., *Formy Khozyaistvennogo Rukovodstva Predpriyatiyami* (Moscow: Izd. Nauka, 1968).
Remnek, R. B. (ed.), *Social Scientists and Policy Making in the USSR* (New York: Praeger, 1977).
Resheniya Partii i Pravitel'stva po Khozyaistvennym Voprosam, 11 vols. (Moscow: Izd. Politicheskoi Literatury, 1968-1978).
Richert, E., *Die DDR – Elite oder Unsere Partner von Morgen?* (Reinbek bei Hamburg; Rowohlt, 1968).
Richert, E., *Macht ohne Mandat* (Cologne and Opladen: Westdeutscher Verlag, 1963).
Richter, A., "Gestaltung der Erzeugnisgruppenarbeit mittels Wirtschaftsvertrag," *VS*, No. 1, 1968.
"Richtlinie fuer das neue oekonomische System der Planung und Leitung der Volkswirtschaft," *N.D.* (Sonderbeilage), 16 July 1963.
"Richtlinie fuer die Bildung von Kombinaten und Vereinigten Betrieben in der volkseigenen Industrie im Bereich des Volkswirtschaftsrates," *Verfuegungen und Mitteilungen des Volkswirtschaftsrates der Deutschen Demokratischen Republik*, No. 12, 1963.
Riess, H. and Lehmann, "Mehr Licht: Effektiver durch Konzentration," *Die Wirts.*, No. 50, 1973.
Rigby, T. H., "The Soviet Leadership: Towards a Self-Stabilizing Oligarchy," *Soviet Studies*, No. 2, 1970.
Romanov, G., "Novye Usloviya — Novye Trebovaniya k Kadram," *Kommunist*, No. 5, 1972.
Rosovsky, H. (ed.), *Industrialisation in Two Systems* (New York: John Wiley, 1966).
Rossmann, G. et al., *Geschichte der SED – Abriss* (Berlin: Dietz Verlag, 1978).
Sabov, A., "Otkazalis' Ot Podpisi . . . ,' " *Komsomol'skaya Pravda*, 14 July 1971.
Sandford, J., *The Mass Media of the German-Speaking Countries* (London: Oswald Wolff, 1976).
San'kov, G., "Stimulirovanie v Podotrasli," *Sots. Ind.*, 12 October 1976.
Sazontov, G., *Sotsial'no-ekonomicheskie Problemy Kontsentratsii i Razmeshcheniya Promyshlennogo Proizvodstva* (Moscow: Izd. Ekonomika, 1971).
Schapiro, L., *The Communist Party of the Soviet Union* (London: Methuen, 1970).
Schnitzer, M., *East and West Germany: A Comparative Economic Analysis* (New York: Praeger, 1972).
Schoenermark, J., "Konzentrierter Einsatz des Forschungspotentials durch Integration," *Die Wirts.*, No. 10, 1975.
Schoth, O., "Kombinate — Zentren der Leistungskraft unserer Gesellschaft," *N.D.*, 19 July 1970.
Schramm, L., "Rechtsfragen der Leitung," *VS*, No. 3, 1965.
Schroeder, G., "Soviet Economic Reform at an Impasse," *P of C*, No. 4, 1971.
Schroeter, S., "Kombinate, Warenzeichen und Namen," *effekt*, No. 3, 1970.
Schubert, K., "Zur Rechtsgestaltung der Beziehungen zwischen oertlichen Staatsorganen und Kombinaten, Betrieben und wirtschaftsleitenden Organen," *WR*, No. 2, 1972.

Schuerer, G., *Die Aufgaben bei der Verwirklichung der sozialistischen oekonomischen Integration* (Berlin: Dietz Verlag, 1975).
Schulz, H-D., "Fortsetzung des NOeSPL in Sicht?" *D.A.*, No. 2, 1978.
Schweigler, G., *National Consciousness in Divided Germany* (London: Sage, 1975).
Seickert, H., "Die Wissenschaft als Faktor oekonomischen Wachstums," *Wirts/wiss.*, No. 3, 1969.
Seleznev, A., "Khozyaistvennyi Raschet i Deyatel'nost' Organov Upravleniya Promyshlennykh Ob"edinenii," *Ekonomicheskie Nauki*, No. 10, 1974.
Selyunin, V., "General'nye skhemy otraslei," *Sots. Ind.*, 28 May 1975.
Selyunin, V., "Logika Nelogichnikh Reshenii," *Sots. Ind.*, 17 October 1972.
Senin, M., *Socialist Integration* (Moscow: Progress, 1973).
Shakhbazyan, R., "Ot Prostogo k Slozhnomu," *Sots. Ind.*, 16 September 1972.
Shchegolev, B., "Shtab Tekhnicheskogo Progressa," *Sots. Ind.*, 21 February 1971.
Shimanskii, M., "Ministerstvo, Glavk. A Firma?" *Izvestiya*, 18 November 1972.
Shkvorets, V., "Kak rasti ob"edineniyu," *Pravda*, 11 August 1972.
Shtundyuk, V. D., *Khozraschetnye Proizvodstvennye Ob"edineniya* (Moscow: Moskovskii Rabochii, 1973).
Shtundyuk, V., "Vygody Ochevidny," *Sots. Ind.*, 10 March 1971.
Skilling, H. G., "Interest Groups and Communist Politics," *World Politics*, No. 3, 1966.
Skilling, H. G., *The Governments of Communist East Europe* (New York: Crowell, 1966).
Skilling, H. G. and Griffiths, F. (eds.), *Interest Groups in Soviet Politics* (Princeton: Princeton U.P., 1971).
Slangen, E. and Mueller, E., "Wo Leuna Arbeitskraefte fuer zwei neue Betriebsteile findet," *N.D.*, 28 March 1973.
Slastenko, E. and Guseva, N., "Magistral'nyi Put," *Sots. Ind.*, 19 February 1971.
Smirnov, A., "Slovo — za Ministerstvami," *Ekon. Gaz.*, No. 37, 1970.
Smith, G. B. (ed.), *Public Policy and Administration in the Soviet Union* (New York: Praeger, 1980).
Smolinskii, L., "Towards a Socialist Corporation: Soviet Industrial Reorganisation of 1973," *Survey*, No. 1, 1974.
Soelle, H., "Neue Schritte auf dem Wege zu wachsender aussenwirtschaftlicher Effektivitaet," *Die Wirts.*, No. 8, 1967.
Solomon, P. H., *Soviet Criminologists and Criminal Policy* (New York: Columbia U.P., 1978).
"Sovershenstvovat' Upravlenie Proizvodstvom," *Pravda*, 4 April 1973.
"Sovetskie Firmy," *Ekon. Gaz.*, No. 6, 1963.
"Soviet Social Imperialism in 1974: More Exposure of its True Colours," *Peking Review*, No. 5, 1975.
Sovnarkhoz i Zhizn' (Kharkov: Knizhnoe Izd., 1959).
"Sowjetische Firmen," *Die Wirts.*, No. 15, 1963.
Starrels, J. M. and Mallinckrodt, A. M., *Politics in the German Democratic Republic* (New York: Praeger, 1975).
Statistical Pocketbook of the German Democratic Republic (Berlin: Staatsverlag der Deutschen Demokratischen Republik, annual).
Statistisches Jahrbuch der Deutschen Demokratischen Republik (Berlin: Staatsverlag der Deutschen Demokratischen Republik, annual).
Statistisches Taschenbuch der Deutschen Demokratischen Republik (Berlin: Staatsverlag der Deutschen Demokratischen Republik, annual).
Statut der Sozialistischen Einheitspartei (Berlin: Dietz Verlag, 1977).

Bibliography

Streich, R., "Sozialistische Wirtschaftsfuehrung und Recht," *Wirts/wiss.*, No. 1, 1968.
Streich, R., "Zur Rechtsstellung der VVB in der zweiten Etappe des neuen oekonomischen Systems," *S und R*, No. 2, 1967.
Studieneinfuehrung fuer die Seminare zum Studium der politischen Oekonomie des Sozialismus und der Wirtschaftspolitik der SED – 2. Studienjahr (Berlin: Dietz Verlag, 1972).
Subotskii, Yu., "Ob Otraslevoi Tsentralizatsii i Spetsializatsii v Promyshlennosti," *Vop. Ekon.*, No. 7, 1972.
Subotskii, Yu., "Ob"edineniya v Sisteme Ekonomiki Razvitogo Sotsializma," *Kommunist*, No. 13, 1973.
Subotskii, Yu., "Maloe Predpriyatie," *Pravda*, 20 July 1978.
Subotskii, Yu. V., Taksir, K. I. et al., *Problemy Razvitiya Ob"edinenii v Promyshlennosti – Kratkie Tezisy Dokladov* (Moscow: Institut Ekonomiki AN SSSR, 1975).
Such, H., *VVB und Wissenschaftlich-Technischer Fortschritt* (Berlin: Staatsverlag der Deutschen Demokratischen Republik, 1964).
Suprun, P. and Bobrov, V., "Shakhterskaya Nov'," *Sots. Ind.*, 25 February 1971.
"Taeglich Kohle ueber dem Plan?" *Die Wirts.*, No. 5, 1969.
Taksir, K. I., "Nauchno-Proizvodstvennye Ob"edineniya," *Vop. Ekon.*, No. 11, 1972.
Taksir, K. I., *Upravlenie Promyshlennost'yu SSSR v Sovremennykh Usloviyakh* (Moscow: Izd. Vysshaya Shkola, 1972).
Terebilov, V., "Ekonomika i Pravo," *Pravda*, 28 June 1974.
Thalheim, K. C. and Hoehmann, H-H. (eds.), *Wirtschaftsreformen in Osteuropa* (Cologne: Verlag Wissenschaft und Politik, 1968).
Tikhomirov, A. and Novikov, V., "Effektivnost' Upravleniya Cherez Proizvodstvennoe Ob"edinenie," *Plan. Khoz.*, No. 8, 1972.
Tikhomirov, S., "Ot Idei do Voploshcheniya," *Sots. Ind.*, 16 January 1971.
Toma, P. A. and Volgyes, I., *Politics in Hungary* (San Francisco: Freeman, 1977).
"Trekhzvennaya Sistema," *Ekon. Gaz.*, No. 37, 1972.
Tryakin, A., "Ukreplenie Gosudarstvennoi Planovoi Distsipliny vo vsekh Zvenyakh Khozyaistva," *Plan. Khoz.*, No. 3, 1978.
TsSUSSSR, *Narodnoe Khozyaistvo SSSR v 1979 g.* (Moscow: Statistika, 1980).
Tuldashev, Sh., "Firmy: Vygody i Perspektivy," *Pravda Vostoka*, 18 February 1971.
U. L., "Mit Elan die neuen Aufgaben loesen," *Die Wirts.*, No. 23, 1969.
U. L., "Volkseigene Kombinate," *Die Wirts.*, No. 22, 1969.
U.S. Congress Joint Economic Committee (ed.), *The Soviet Economy in a Time of Change* (Washington, DC: U.S. Government Printing Office, 1980).
"Ukazaniya o poryadke razrabotki general'nykh skhem upravleniya otraslyami promyshlennosti," *Ekon. Gaz.*, No. 19, 1973.
Ulbricht, W., "Der Weg zur Durchfuehrung der Beschluesse des VII. Parteitages der SED auf dem Gebiet der Wirtschaft, Wissenschaft und Technik — Schlusswort," *Die Wirts.*, No. 41, 1967.
Ulbricht, W., "Primenenie Leninskikh Printsipov Sotsialisticheskogo Upravleniya v GDR," *Pravda*, 9 January 1964.
Ulbricht, W., *Probleme der Sozialistischen Leitungstaetigkeit* (Berlin: Dietz Verlag, 1968).
Ulbricht, W., *Zum Neuen Oekonomischen System der Planung und Leitung* (Berlin: Dietz Verlag, 1967).
Ulč, O., *Politics in Czechoslovakia* (San Francisco: Freeman, 1974).
"Upravlenie Proizvodstvom," *Ekon. Gaz.*, No. 37, 1972.

Ustav Kommunisticheskoi Partii Sovetskogo Soyuza (Moscow: Izd. Politicheskoi Literatury, 1971).
Utkin, E., "K Voprosu o Firmakh," *Vop. Ekon.*, No. 10, 1963.
"V edinom Komplekse," *Pravda*, 12 January 1978.
"V Tsentral'nom Komitete KPSS i Sovete Ministrov SSSR," *Pravda*, 3 April 1973.
Vanneman, P., *The Supreme Soviet: Politics and the Legislative Process in the Soviet Political System* (Durham, NC: Duke U.P., 1977).
Vasil'ev, A., "Izlishestvu Shtatov — Zaslon," *Sov. Kirg.*, 9 September 1970.
Vasin, M. and Zakharov, Yu., "Kto Upravlyaet Firmoi?" *Pravda*, 13 June 1972.
Velichko, P. and Shevyakov, F., "Razvitie Proizvodstvennykh Ob"edinenii v Promyshlennosti GDR," *Vop. Ekon.*, No. 7, 1972.
"Verordnung ueber das Verfahren der Gruendung und Zusammenlegung von Volkseigenen Betrieben," *GBl.*, Pt. 2, No. 121, 1968.
"Verordnung ueber die Aufgaben, Rechte und Pflichten des volkseigenen Produktionsbetriebes," *GBl.*, Pt. 2, No. 21, 1967.
"Verordnung ueber die Bildung und Rechtsstellung von volkseigenen Kombinaten," *GBl.*, Pt. 2, No. 121, 1968.
"Verordnung ueber die VEB, Kombinate, VVB," *GBl.*, Pt. 1, No. 15, 1973, and *GBl.*, Pt. 1, No. 39, 1973.
"Verordnung ueber die volkseigenen Kombinate, Kombinatsbetriebe und Volkseigenen Betriebe vom 8. November 1979," *GBl.*, Pt. 1, No. 38, 1979.
Vishnyakov, V. G., "Problemy Sovershenstvovaniya Upravleniya Promyshlennost'yu," *Pravovedenie*, No. 1, 1973.
Volgyes, I. (ed.), *Political Socialization in Eastern Europe* (New York: Praeger, 1975).
Vorotnikov, V., (Report), *Plan. Khoz.*, No. 9, 1970.
Vtoraya Vsesoyuznaya Nauchno-Tekhnicheskaya Konferentsiya "Problemy Nauchnoi Organizatsii Upravleniya Sotsialisticheskoi Promyshlennost'yu," 11 vols. (Moscow: 1972).
Vsesoyuznaya Nauchnaya Konferentsiya "Problemy Razvitiya Ob"edinenii v Sisteme Otraslevogo Upravleniya" – Tezisy Dokladov, 5 vols. (Moscow: Institut Ekonomiki AN SSSR, 1975).
W. H., "Erfahrungen aus dem vergangenen Jahr," *Die Wirts.*, No. 1, 1964.
W. R., "Die Hauptsache ist die hoehere Effektivitaet," *N.D.*, 30 November 1970.
Wedler, M., "Bildung des Rates fuer wirtschaftsrechtswissenschaftliche Forschung der DDR," *VS*, No. 8, 1969.
Welsh, W. A., "The Usefulness of Social Stratification, Input-Output, and Issue-Processing Models in the Study of Communist Systems in Eastern Europe," presented to the 66th APSA Conference, Los Angeles, September 1970.
White, S., *Political Culture and Soviet Politics* (London: Macmillan, 1979).
"Wirtschaftskonferenz," *N.D.*, 7 and 8 December 1962.
"Wissen fuer die Zukunft," *effekt*, No. 3, 1969.
"Wissenschaftliche Arbeitsberatung zu Rechtsfragen der Kombinate bei der Durchfuehrung der Beschluesse des VIII. Parteitages der SED," *WR*, No. 6, 1971.
Woche, K., "Zum Fuehrungsprozess bei der Bildung von Kombinaten," *WR*, No. 2, 1971.
Woerterbuch der Oekonomie Sozialismus (Berlin: Dietz Verlag, 1973).
Wolf, H., "Die Rolle der Eigenverantwortung im Oekonomischen System," *effekt*, No. 2, 1969.
World Communism 1967-1969: Soviet Efforts to Re-establish Control (Washington, DC: U.S. Government Printing Office, 1970).

XXII S'ezd Kommunisticheskoi Partii Sovetskogo Soyuza – Stenograficheskii Otchet, 3 vols. (Moscow: Gosudarstvennoe Izd. Politicheskoi Literatury, 1962).
XXIII S'ezd Kommunisticheskoi Partii Sovetskogo Soyuza – Stenograficheskii Otchet, 2 vols. (Moscow: Politizdat, 1966).
XXIV S'ezd Kommunisticheskoi Partii Sovetskogo Soyuza – Stenograficheskii Otchet, 2 vols. (Moscow: Izd. Politicheskoi Literatury, 1971).
XXV S'ezd Kommunisticheskoi Partii Sovetskogo Soyuza – Stenograficheskii Otchet, 3 vols. (Moscow: Izd. Politicheskoi Literatury, 1976).
Yudin, E., "Kompleksnyi Podkhod, Vsestoronnyi Analiz," *Pravda,* 30 May 1972.
Yuldashev, Sh., "Firmy: Vygody i Perspektivy," *Pravda Vostoka,* 18 February 1971.
"Zakon ob izmenenii sistemy organov upravleniya promyshlennost'yu i preobrazovanii nekotorykh drugikh organov gosudarstvennogo upravleniya," *Resheniya . . . ,* Vol. 5.
"Zakon Soyuza Sovetskikh Sotsialisticheskikh Respublik. O Sovete Ministrov SSSR," *Pravda,* 6 July 1978.
Zdorov, P. A., "Proizvodstvennye Ob"edineniya i Effektivnost' Proizvodstva," *Ekon. Gaz.,* No. 33, 1970.
Zimmermann, H., "The GDR in the 1970s," *P of C,* No. 2, 1978.
Zimmermann, H., "Politische Aspekte in der Herausbildung, dem Wandel und der Verwendung des Konzepts 'Wissenschaftlich-technische Revolution' in der DDR," *D.A.* (Sonderheft), 1976.
Zimmermann, H. B., "Wandel von Industrieverwaltungen in Sozialistischen Laendern Dargestellt am Beispiel der Vereinigungen Volkseigener Betriebe der DDR," unpublished thesis for degree of Diplomsoziologe; presented to the Free University of Berlin, February 1970.
Zschunke, H., "Erste Erfahrungen in Leipzig mit der zweigmaessigen Leitung der oertlichen Industrie," *Die Wirts.,* No. 48, 1962.

INDEX

Academy of Sciences, GDR 113, 262; USSR 88, 128, 147, 175-176, 178, 204, 223
Access, channels of, 81, 95, 273
Accounting, 24, 28, 36, 38, 40, 41, 45, 46, 49, 52, 59, 60, 96, 107-108, 121, 124, 127, 129, 152-154, 164, 185, 204, 209, 211, 225, 237, 239
"Administrations," 44, 222
Afghanistan, 275
Agrarno-promyshlennoe ob"edinenie. See *Ob"edinenie* (Agroindustrial)
Agroindustrial association. See *Ob"edinenie*
Albania, 16
Aleksandrov, A., 84, 111, 127, 177
Alekseevskii, E., 149
Aliev, G., 148
All-Union Council of the National Economy. See *Sovnarkhoz*
Amalgamated enterprise, GDR, 61, 113, 173, 186, 248; USSR, 38, 201
Amalgamated industrial undertakings, 165
Anarchosyndicalism, 278
Antonov, A., 222
Apel, E., 152-153, 179, 238, 239
Apparatchiki, 25, 231-232, 252
Archangel, 38
Ashimov, B., 149
Association, general, 11, 12, 19, 20, 23-24, 266-273. See also Amalgamated enterprises; Combine; Firm; *Ob"edinenie;* Trust; *Vereinigung*

Association of Nationalized Enterprises. See *Vereinigung volkseigener Betriebe*
ASUP. See Automated systems for the administration of production
Automated systems for the administration of production, 121, 146, 234
Avtorkhanov, A., 45
Azerbaidzhan, 148

Bachurin, A., 177
Badestein, H., 182
Bagehot, W., 22
Baibakov, N., 84, 128-129, 132
Banks, GDR, 54; USSR, 45, 108, 175, 178, 224
Behavioralism, 21
Behrens, F., 113
Belorussia, 147, 203
Benary, A., 113
Bentham, J., 22
Bergmann, S., 182
Berlin, East, 51, 59, 60, 112, 182
Berri, L., 125
Bertsch, G., 276
Betriebsteil, definition of, 210
Bezirkswirtschaftsrat. See Regional Economic Council (GDR)
Bifurcation. See Communist Party of the Soviet Union
"Black office workers," 248
Bobrov, A., 106
Bodyul, I., 168
Boehm, S., 179, 237

310

Index

Boettcher, H., 182
"Borisov," 226
Borna, 60
Branch administrations, 56-57, 220
Brandt, W., 24
Braybrooke, D., 26
Brezhnev Doctrine, 16
Brezhnev, L., 15, 21, 23, 97, 141, 142-150, 164, 165, 203, 273
Brown, A., 15, 263, 265, 274, 280
Brzezinski, Z., 21-22
Budinskii, A., 176
Bulgaria, 216, 274
"Bureaucratic" model, 269, 280
BWR. See Regional Economic Council (GDR)

Cadres, 52, 118-119
Campbell, R., 19
Capitalist states, 18, 262. See also Liberal democracies; First World
"Carl Zeiss," 48, 217
Censorship, 83-85
Central Committee. See Communist Party of the Soviet Union; Socialist Unity Party
Central Institute of Socialist Economic Management, 102, 119, 183, 261
Centralization, 20, 40, 49, 50, 107-108, 116, 117, 120-121, 124-125, 153, 189, 234, 263
Central Statistical Office, GDR, 113, 238; USSR, 175, 178, 201, 229
Chemnitz, 60
Cherkassk, 220
Chief administrations, GDR, 13, 53, 58-59, 116, 126-127, 237; USSR, see Glavk
China, People's Republic of, 16, 283
Chuplinskas, A., 176
CISEM. See Central Institute of Socialist Economic Management
CMEA. See Council for Mutual Economic Assistance
Code of Labor Law (GDR), 247
Cold War, 21
Collegiality, 40-41
Combine, GDR: average size of, 210; claimed advantages of 124-127, 155-162; debates on, 112-119; definition of, 12, 20, 48, 110, 113-6, 186-191, 196; development of, 28, 46, 60-64, 209-212, 266-269; directorate, 159; enterprises, position of component, 113-116, 187-190, 196; leadership views on, 23, 155-162, 260-261; legislation on 46, 129-130, 173-174, 186-191, 261; opposition to, 236-250 (passim); policy, official, 164-166; status of, 40, 48-51, 53, 186-191. See also Ob"edinenie, production
Combine, USSR: claimed advantages of, 122, 125; definition of, 38; development of, 55; enterprises, position of component, 38, 183-184; leadership views on, 141-142, 148; legislation on, 183-184; policy, official, 163. See also Ob"edinenie, production
Combine-enterprise. See Combine, enterprises, position of
Comecon. See Council for Mutual Economic Assistance
Commissariats (USSR), 55
Committee of People's Control, 175
Communist Party of the Soviet Union, bifurcation, 141; Central Committee (General), 24, 25, 139-150 (passim), 269, 273; Central Committee (Plena), 141-149, 163, 166, 168-169, 205, 252, 258, 270, 273; Congress (General), 25, 28, 36, 64, 97, 139-140, 143-147, 149-150, 161, 163-164, 166, 200, 203, 252, 260, 270; councils of Party committee secretaries, 232-233; local organs, 221, 223, 230-233, 236, 249, 272; Politburo, 25, 45, 82, 90, 139-150 (passim), 192, 270, 272, 273; primary Party organizations, 231-233; program, 163; Secretariat (of Central Committee), 45, 90, 176, 270, 273
Communist states, 11, 15, 16, 18-24, 45, 81, 84, 174, 262, 264, 266, 274-280. See also Second World
Complex program, 19, 263
Computers, 121, 147, 234
Concentration, 20, 24, 50, 110, 117, 120-121, 124-125, 141, 143, 153, 156, 159, 165, 189, 222, 263
Conferences, general and comparative, 82-95 (passim), 97-99, 129-137 (passim); GDR, 91-94, 112-119

(passim), 124-127, 129, 152-162
(passim), 179-180, 237-238, 241, 243,
245, 247, 266-267, 268; USSR, 87-90,
106-112 (passim), 119-124 (passim),
127-129, 224, 229, 261, 270
Congresses. See Communist Party of
the Soviet Union; Socialist Unity
Party
"Conservatives," 117, 134, 272
Content analysis, 94-99, 105
Contracts, 53, 59, 107, 125, 126, 156, 184,
187-188, 212
Convergence theory, 21
Cooperation, 41, 50, 117, 120-121,
124-125, 143, 153, 156, 158-159, 163,
185, 189, 222
Cooperation chains, 50, 156
Cooperation collectives, 50-51
Cooperation groups, 50-51, 119, 158
Corporation, 12, 19
Corruption, 236
"Costs," 281
Cottbus, 60
Council for Mutual Economic
Assistance, 19, 42, 52-53, 126, 261,
263
Council of Directors, 227
Council of Ministers (GDR), 54, 91, 118,
139, 151, 157, 164, 179-180, 182-183,
191, 192, 247
Council of Ministers (USSR), 24, 36,
43-45, 57, 139, 142, 163, 175, 178, 199,
273
Council of National Economy (GDR).
See National Economic Council
Council of National Economy (USSR).
See *Sovnarkhoz*
Councils of Party Committee
Secretaries. See Communist Party of
the Soviet Union
Councils of Party Secretaries. See
Socialist Unity Party
Council of Research into Economic
Law, 182
CPSU. See Communist Party of the
Soviet Union
"Culture of bureaucratism," 223
Cybernetics, 276
Czechoslovakia, 16, 159-160, 275,
283-284

Dawisha, K., 265
Deineko, O., 176
"Demands," 25-27, 29, 81-137 (passim),
266-273 (passim); definition of, 268
Democratic centralism, 16, 84, 247, 278
Détente, 19
Developed socialism, 30
Directors. See Managers
Doenin, V., 221
Don (River), 38
Dresden, 60
Drogichinskii, N., 109, 175-176, 202
Dumachev, A., 177, 226, 228, 230
Dunaev, E., 176
Dzhavadov, G., 110, 176

Easton, D., 25-26
Ebbecke, H., 114-115
"Eclectic" approach, 280
Economic Council, 151-152
Economic groups, 133
Economic Law Group, 183
Economic Reform (USSR), 19, 36-37,
55, 57, 120, 134, 142, 144-145, 147, 165,
199, 213, 261, 270, 272
Economic System of Socialism, 155, 158,
161, 181, 237-240, 242
Economists, Comparative, 137;
(definition), 279; GDR, 61, 113, 116,
130, 180, 262, 266; USSR, 22, 97, 107,
110, 130, 137, 144, 175, 222, 262, 270,
272
Edinonachalie. See Management,
USSR
Einzelleitung. See Management, GDR
Eisleben, 60
Ellman, M., 19
Engels, F., 19, 262, 264-265
Enterprise, general, 21
Enterprise, GDR, general, 20, 58-64
(passim), 112-119 (passim), 153-162
(passim), 186-191, 196, 216, 243-244,
249; "secondary," 243-244;
nationally owned (VEB), 46-47,
49-51, 53, 113, 125, 134, 173, 174. See
also Enterprise, general
Enterprise, USSR, general, 20, 36-37,
47, 106-112 (passim), 127-128, 141-150
(passim), 175-176, 183-186, 203, 206,
214, 226-228; "secondary," 226-228,

Index

235. See also Amalgamated enterprise; *Betriebsteil;* Factory, Filials
"Enterprise part." See *Betriebsteil*
Erfurt, 48, 60
Erzeugnisgruppe. See Product-group
ESS. See Economic System of Socialism
Europe, Eastern, 16-24, 83, 216, 265, 276, 278, 284; Western, 21
Experimentation, GDR, 164-165, 179, 211-212, 260; USSR, 174-175, 207-208
Export quotient, 281

Fabrika. See Factory
Factory (USSR), 68, 106, 184
Farms, Soviet: state, 40; collective, 41, 123
Federalism, 18, 257
Federal Republic of Germany. See Germany, Federal Republic of
Feedback loop, 26
Fejtö, F., 17, 275
Filials, 37, 108, 125, 226-227, 229, 231, 235
Firm (Soviet), 12, 38, 55, 98, 108, 111, 127, 131-132, 141-142, 165, 183-184, 201, 206, 220, 223, 226, 227, 235. See also *Ob"edinenie,* production
Firma, see Firm (Soviet)
First Secretary, CPSU: See Brezhnev, L.; Khrushchev, N. SED: See Honecker, E.; Ulbricht, W.
First World, 274, 276. See also Capitalist states; Liberal democracies
Five-year plan, GDR, 210; USSR, 142, 163, 164, 200, 276
Foreign influence, 260-263, 267, 280
Foreign workers, 257
France, 17
Frankel, T., 22
FRG. See Germany, Federal Republic of
Frohn, W., 171
Frunze, 120, 228

Gallerach, E., 156, 158
Garbuzov, V., 194
Gastarbeiter. See Foreign workers
General scheme of management, 199-200, 209
General Secretary, CPSU: See Brezhnev, L.; Khrushchev, N. SED: See Honecker, E.; Ulbricht, W.
German Central Administrations, 58
German Economic Commission, 58
Germany, Federal Republic of, 17, 18, 259
Gerstner, K-H., 125
Glavk, 13, 28, 41, 44, 53, 56-57, 64, 84, 96-97, 106, 108-110, 116, 124, 128, 143, 146, 163, 173, 184-185, 202, 204, 207, 219-226 (passim)
"Glavkhimlegmash," 221
"Glavosnastk," 225
Gor'kii, 148
Gosplan. See State Planning Committee
Grass, K., 182
Great Britain, 22, 81, 83, 234, 264
Griffiths, F., 23
Gromov, V., 176, 200, 269
Groups, functional, 21-23, 27, 130, 271, 279; insider, 25; institutionalized, 25; interest, 21-23, 25-27, 29, 81, 130, 266-273 (passim), 275-280 (passim); opinion, 94-96, 109, 130; pressure, 27; social, 279. See also Economic Groups; Economic Law Group)
Growth rates, 18-19, 258-259, 266, 270
Guideline (on the New Economic System), 153, 164-165, 173, 179-180, 189, 266, 268
Guzhkov, I., 194, 224-225
Gvishiani, D., 101, 261, 273

Hager, K., 162
Halbritter, W., 63, 179-181, 195, 244, 269
"Haldex," 19
Halle, 60
Hardt, J., 22
Hauptverwaltungen. See Chief administrations (GDR)
Hettstedt, 267
Heuer, K., 182
Heuer, U-J., 183
Hoffmann, B., 182
Honecker, E., 24, 63, 158, 160-162, 166-167, 211, 240, 261
Horizontal linkage, 37-38, 39, 50, 113, 157, 186
Hough, J., 274
Hungary, 18, 275

Huntington, S., 21-22

Ideology, 16, 21-22, 83-84, 264-266, 275, 278, 280, 284
Ilmenau, 60
Imperialism (Soviet), 16-17
Incrementalism, 26, 258, 265, 275-280
Indochina, 284
Industrial association. See *Ob"edinenie*
Industrial structure, 35-79, 257-259
Industrial trade association. See *Ob"edinenie*
Institute of Economic Sciences, 113
Institute of Economics, 108, 223
Institute of State and Law, 128
Interests, 18, 22-27, 81, 108, 130, 219, 223, 228, 230, 237, 243, 249, 257, 266-273 (passim), 274-280 (passim)
International Economic Organizations, 19
"Involved-person perception," 94-95

Japan, 19
Jena, 48, 217
Jonuscheit, K-H., 262
Joravsky, D., 264
June 1953 Uprising, 150

"Kabelwerk Oberspree," 61, 118, 157, 159
Kalinin, 221-222
Kamenetskii, V., 200, 269
Kamenitser, S., 109, 132, 176
Kampuchea, 284
Kapustin, Ye., 108
Karl-Marx-Stadt, 60, 244
Kassof, A., 21
Kazakhstan, 148-149
Kazanets, I., 149
Keldysh, M., 147
Kharkov, 225
Khozraschet. See Accounting
Khrushchev, N., 18, 55, 141-142, 143, 165, 260, 269-270, 272, 273, 277, 285
Khudaiberdyev, N., 148
Kirghizia, 234
Kiselev, I., 148-149
Klinger, G., 115, 183
Knupfer, W., 182
Kombinat. See Combine
Konotop, V., 147

Kontrol', 44
Kooperationsgemeinschaften. See Cooperation collectives
Kooperationsketten. See Cooperation chains
Kooperationsverbaende. See Cooperation groups
Korbonski, A., 263
Kosygin, A., 101, 142-150, 154, 161, 166, 172, 261, 273
Kozlova, O., 176
Krasnodar, 149
Kreutzer, C., 182
Kruk, D., 176
Krupenchik, B., 111
Kuibysheft', 224
Kunaev, D., 148-149
Kuznetsov, I., 200
Kuznetsov, S., 228
KWO. See "Kabelwerk Oberspree"

Labor shortages, 248, 257-258
Lagutkin, V., 176
Lane, D., 23
Laptev, V., 95, 109, 115, 116, 176
Lassak, S., 182
Leadership, concept, 139-140; general role in communist states, 277-280
Legal Commission, GDR, 180; USSR, 175
Legal person, concept of, 107, 115-116, 188
Legal specialists, definition of, 137; GDR, 113-116, 129, 130, 180, 262; USSR, 107, 130, 137, 144, 175, 262, 270, 272
Legislative commission (Soviet), 94-95, 128, 175-178
Legitimacy, 18-19, 26, 280
Leipzig, 60, 156, 244
Lenin, V., 136, 260, 262, 264-265
Leningrad, 55-56, 87, 106, 110, 141-142, 144, 146, 148-150, 165, 176, 207, 222, 229, 230, 231, 233, 252, 270
Leuna, 48, 248
Leuschner, B., 151-152
Liberal democracies, 21, 25, 83, 268, 271, 279. See also Capitalist states; First World
Liberman, E., 262, 266, 270
Lindblom, C., 26

Index

Lisitsyn, V., 176
Literary policy, 23, 285
Lithuania, 57, 147
"L′nopravlenie," 55
Local councils, GDR, 47, 244-245, 249, see also Regional Council; USSR, 229-230, 236, 249
"LOMO," 38, 227
Lowenthal, R., 277
Luebeck-Oberfrohna, 60
L′vov, 55-56, 87, 108, 123, 142, 207, 225

Magdeburg, 60
Management, GDR, 46, 48-53 (passim), 118, 159, 190, 240-244, 246, 247, 267; USSR, 36-37, 40, 41-42, 90, 163, 226-228, 261
"Managerialism," 151-152
Managers, general, 279; GDR, 23, 25, 27, 46-53 (passim), 82, 118, 129, 130, 154, 160, 179-180, 187, 190, 239-244, 246, 268, 273; USSR, 22-23, 25, 27, 36-37, 40, 121, 130, 142, 175, 221, 226-228, 236, 269-270, 272
Mansfeld, 48
Mao Zedong, 283
Markin, A., 84, 109, 110-111, 112, 201, 204, 222-223
Markowitsch, E., 179
Marks and Spencer, 19
Marx, K., 19, 262, 264-265
Marxism-Leninism, 52, 83-84, 264, 284
Masherov, P., 147
Mature socialism. See Developed Socialism
Meerane, 60
Meissen, 60
Meissner, B., 145
"Melodiya," 57, 103
Meyer, A., 11, 21, 264
"Mikroelektronik," 48
Military (Soviet), 22
Miller, M., 203
Ministers, general, 279; GDR, 130, 140, 180, 237-240; USSR, 84, 90, 95, 130, 140, 148-149, 164, 219-226 (passim)
Ministries, GDR: general, 21, 23, 53, 59-60, 154-162 (passim), 181, 192, 210, 237-240, 249, 257, 281; finance, 54, 92, 237-240, 249, 268; foreign trade, 54, 92, 127, 237-240, 267; interior, 93; justice, 182.

Ministries, USSR: general, 12, 21, 23, 42-44, 45, 53, 55, 60, 85, 88, 97, 109, 128-129, 147, 164, 175, 177, 188, 201, 202, 205, 207-208, 219-226, 230, 257, 270, 272, 281; all-union, 42-43, 202; branch, 142-144, 192, 199, 249, 272; finance, 44, 89, 128, 174-175, 177-178, 205, 224-225, 249, 272; justice, 178; *Minpribor*, 13, 57, 84, 147, 173-175, 207-208; republic, 42-43, 202; union-republic, 42-43, 143, 202, 224
Minpribor. See Ministries, USSR
Mittag, G., 152-153, 159, 161-162, 179, 181, 241, 245
Morton, H., 263, 277
Moscow, 55, 110, 124, 146-148 (passim), 176
Mothes, W., 118
"Muddling through." See Incrementalism
Mueller, K., 114-115
Multinationals, 19-20
Mytishchin, 38

"Nagema," 211
"NARVA," 244
National Economic Council (GDR), 24, 60, 61, 153-156, 179, 238-240
National socialism, 58
Nationalization, 35, 45-47, 64, 125, 155
NES. See New Economic System
Neumann, A., 153-154, 166, 169, 239
New Economic System, 19, 23, 28, 60, 113, 127, 153-155, 157, 161-162, 164, 170, 173, 179-180, 209, 211-212, 238-241, 245, 260-261, 266, 267
Niebelscheutz, J., 114-115
Nomenclature system, 37
"Nonreference," 96-98
Novgorod, 230, 232
Novosibirsk, 204, 210
NPO. See *Ob″edinenie*, science-production

Ob″edinenie, general: analysis of, 205-206; average size of, 203; claimed advantages of, 119-124, 129-130; debates on, 84, 89, 97-98, 106-112, 129-130; definition of, 12, 106-110, 183; development of, 28, 54-58, 199-208, 269-271; enterprises, position of component, 37-40, 106-112 (passim), 184-185; leadership views on, 97, 141-150, 165-166; legislation on, 127-130, 173, 183-186; opposition to, 84, 219-236; policy, official, 163-164, 166-167; status of, 37-42, 183-186. See also Amalgamated enterprises; Combine; Firm; Trust

Ob"edinenie, types of: agroindustrial, 40, 122-123; industrial, 20, 23, 24, 28, 39, 41-42, 43, 56-57, 64, 96-98, 107-112 (passim), 119, 123-124, 145-146, 150, 163, 184, 202, 203, 204, 205, 207, 284; industrial trade, 40, 122; production, 20, 23, 36, 37-40, 50-51, 54-55, 57-58, 64, 96, 97, 106-112 (passim), 119-124, 128, 145, 150, 163, 184, 202, 203, 204, 205, 206, 249, 269, 284; science-production, 39-40, 112, 122, 123, 126, 128, 144, 146-147, 150, 163, 164, 202, 221, 235. See also Amalgamated enterprise; Combine; Firm; Trust

Ob"edinennoe predpriyatie. See Amalgamated enterprise, USSR
Oelssner, F., 151-152
Office for Prices, 53
Oligin-Nesterov, V., 176
Omarov, A., 176
"Options, Practical Range of," 277
Organisationsbuero, See Organizing committee, GDR
Organizing committee, GDR, 92; USSR, 89-90
Orgkomitet. See Organizing committee, USSR
Overload, 278-279
Oznobin, N., 176

Panfilov, M., 111, 176-177
Panzer, A., 182
Panzer, W., 115
Penig, L., 115, 118
People's Chamber, 54
Permanent production conferences, 253
Permanent production consultative bodies, 247
Petrov, A., 176
Pevzner, A., 95, 107, 109, 110, 176-177, 272
PGH. See Trade-production cooperative

Planning, general, 278, 282; GDR, 46-47, 49-50, 52, 60, 154-156; USSR, 36, 41, 44
"Plastpolimer," 234
Plato, 18
Plauen, 60
Plena. See Communist Party of the Soviet Union; Socialist Unity Party
Pluralism, 21-23, 26, 274-280 (passim)
Podgorny, N., 141-142, 144, 146, 149, 163, 273
Poland, 275, 283, 284
Police, GDR, 93; USSR, 22
Policy leverage, 17
Policy process, ideal types defined, 275; East German summarized, 266-269, 272-273; Soviet summarized, 269-273
Politburo. See Communist Party of the Soviet Union; Socialist Unity Party
Political culture, 16, 263-264, 274, 280
Popov, G., 110-111, 120, 176
Population, GDR, 18; USSR, 18
"Pozitron," 233
Press, The, 19, 82-85, 95, 99, 112, 113
Pricing, GDR, 46, 53, 60, 117, 209, 237, 242; USSR, 36
Primary party organization. See Communist Party of the Soviet Union
Product groups, 48, 50-51, 52, 63, 117, 119, 125, 156, 158-162 (passim), 165, 166, 191, 241, 242-244
Production association. See *Ob"edinenie*
Production committees, 247
Productions, 37
Produktionsstaette, 210
"Progress," 55, 226-227
Proizvodstva. See Productions
Proizvodstvennoe ob"edinenie. See *Ob"edinenie*, Production
Promyshlennoe ob"edinenie. See *Ob"edinenie*, industrial
Promyshlenno-torgovoe ob"edinenie. See *Ob"edinenie*, Industrial-trade
Promyslov, V., 148
Pronina, V., 44
Pskov, 230, 232
Pyper, T., 45

Quedlinburg, 60

Index 317

R and D. See Research and Development
Radeburg, 60
Radio, 82
Radomysel'skii, M., 106
Rakitskii, B., 132, 176
Ramminger, B., 182
"Rassvet," 55
Rasylov, D., 149
"Rational comprehensive" approach. See Synoptic approach
Regional council (GDR) 51, 180
Regional Economic Council, GDR, 51, 156, 180, 244; USSR, see *Sovnarkhoz*
Research and Development, 20, 39, 41, 49, 55, 118, 121, 123, 124, 126, 127, 136, 154, 155, 157, 160, 187, 234-235
Research Council, 152, 180
Richert, E., 151, 153
Richter, A., 182
Romania, 16, 126
Romanov, G., 146-147, 149-150, 200, 230, 231, 251
Rudnev, K., 84, 142, 147, 174
"Ruhla," 157, 217, 241
Rumpf, W., 239
Ryazan, 220

Salaries, GDR 249; USSR 123, 227, 234-235, 236
Sauer, M., 182
Savitskaya, A., 127
Sazontov, G., 110-111
Scheler, M., 243
Scholl, Dr., 181
Schramm, L., 182
Schuerer, G., 179
Schwedt, 248
Science-production association. See *Ob"edinenie*
Science-production complex, 69
Scientific Council for Economic Research, 91
Scientific-economic councils, 247
Scientific-Technical Centers, 136, 157
Scientific-Technical Revolution, 156, 276, 283, 284
Second World, 12, 276. See Communist states
Secretariat (of Central Committee). See Communist Party of the Soviet Union; Socialist Unity Party
SED. See Socialist Unity Party
Selbmann, F., 151-152, 153
Self-administration, 160
Serpukhov, 38
Shakhirov, M., 168
Shashin, V., 148-149
Shcherbitskii, V., 147-149
Shelest', P., 144, 146
Shifrin, I., 106
Shubnikov, A., 176
"Sigma," 57, 103, 204
Sindermann, H., 162
Sino-Soviet relations, 16, 83
Sitnin, V., 177
Slezinger, G., 176
Slyusarenko, V., 111
Smith, G., 265
Smolinskii, L., 23
Snechkus, A., 147
Social councils, 246
Social organizations, 36
Socialist Unity Party, general, 247; base organizations, 245-246; Central Committee, general, 54, 82, 91, 139-141, 151, 152, 179, 180, 263, 268; plena, 47, 59, 151-162, 169, 170, 246, 247; Congress, general, 25, 139-140, 268; 5th (1958), 152; 6th (1963), 153, 155, 164-165, 267; 7th (1967), 154, 156, 157, 158, 165, 182; 8th (1971), 63, 161, 162, 165, 211; 9th (1976), 28, 64, 140, 162, 165; 10th (1981), 33; councils of party secretaries, 246; local organs, 245, 249; Politburo, 25, 54, 81, 91, 93, 139-140, 151-162, 179-180, 182, 192, 269; program, 164, 165; Secretariat (of Central Committee), 54, 159, 162, 245, 255
Solov'ev, V., 131
Sorgenicht, K., 237-238
Soviet Military Administration for Germany, 58
Soviets. See Local councils, USSR; Supreme Soviet
Sovnarkhoz, 55-56, 60, 85, 108, 127, 142, 151, 201, 220, 222, 269-270, 284
"Soyuzchasprom," 207
"Soyuzkhimvolokno," 235
"Soyuzmargarinprom," 57
"Soyuzparfumerprom," 57

"Soyuzsteklomash," 221
Specialization, 20, 41, 50, 53, 110, 117, 119-121, 124-125, 141-150 (passim), 153, 163, 185, 222, 236, 263
Spitzner, O., 182
Stalinism, 17, 21
State Arbitration Board, 128
State committees (USSR), general, 44; for Labor and Social Questions, 45; for Labor and Wages, 45, 128, 174-175, 177-178, 227, 234; for Light Industry, 128; for Material-Technical Supplies, 44, 128, 175, 176, 178; for Prices, 44, 174, 177, 194; for Science and Technology, 44, 88-89, 174, 178, 205
State Council, 54, 180
State Planning Commission (GDR), 49, 52, 53, 60, 92, 125, 151-152, 157, 158, 238, 244
State Planning Committee (USSR), 44, 84, 87, 94, 97, 128-129, 131, 132, 142, 145, 174-178, 199, 205, 208
State Secretariat for Labor and Wages (GDR), 53
Stoph, W., 156, 158-159, 161-162, 166, 179-180, 268-269
STR. See Scientific-Technical Revolution
Structural policy, 61, 126, 130
Structure-determining tasks, 77, 158
Subotskii, Yu., 108, 131, 176
Such, H., 114-115
Suhl, 159
Sukharevskii, B., 177
Supranowitz, S., 182
Supreme Soviet, general, 43, 45, 54, 144, 178; commissions, 45, 194
"Svetlana," 75
"Synoptic" approach, 26, 275-280
Systems approach, 25-29, 266-273 (passim)

Tadzhikistan, 149
Takoev, D., 224
Tatevosyan, M., 176
Technical-Economic Council, 246
Technological determinism, 21
"Teleological" approach. See "Synoptic" approach
Television, 82

Teuscher, F., 238, 244
Thieme, B., 243
Third World, 276
Tiers in industrial administration, number of, GDR, 116, 161, 189; USSR, 109-110, 161, 164, 185, 189, 199-200, 207-208
Tikhomirov, S., 142
Tikhomirova, A., 200
Tikhonov, N., 172, 200
Tolerances, 52
Tolstikov, V., 141-142, 144-146, 148, 149, 163
Tolstoy, L., 280
Trade, foreign, 17, 60, 84, 92, 117, 126-127, 130, 155-162 (passim), 164, 177, 210, 212, 237, 240, 242, 259-260, 266
Trade-production cooperative, 47-48
Trade Unions, GDR, 54, 180, 246-249; USSR, 45, 123, 174, 175, 177-178, 235, 253
Transnationals, 12, 19
Trest. See Trust
Trust, 38-39, 54-55, 183-184, 185-186, 222
Tschirner, M., 248
Tsekh (autonomous), 68
Tsentrmebel', 38
TsSU. See Central Statistical Office, USSR

Ukraine, 55, 111, 141-142, 144, 146, 147-150, 165, 207, 208, 225
"Ukrlakokraska," 112
Ulbricht, W., 18, 23, 61, 93, 113, 129, 142, 151-161, 164-166, 179, 190, 211, 238-242, 260-261, 266-267, 268, 271, 273, 277
United States of America, 18, 21, 81, 264
Upravleniya. See Administrations
Uzbekistan, 123, 148, 207

Vanneman, P., 178
VEB. See Enterprise, GDR
Vedomstva, 44, 88, 128, 164, 175, 202, 205, 219-226 (passim)
VEK. See Combine, GDR
Vereinigung Volkseigener Betriebe, average size of, 209-210; claimed advantages of, 125-127; debate on, 82, 112-118; definition of, 12, 20, 110,

Index

186; development of, 23, 24, 28, 58-64, 209-212, 266-269; leadership views on, 23, 150-162, 166, 268; legislation on, 24, 46, 129-130, 173-174, 186, 189-191; location of, 59-60; opposition (from and to), 237-249 (passim); policy, official, 164-166; status of, 20, 24, 42, 50, 51-53
Vertical linkage, 37-38, 50, 113, 118, 157-158, 186
Verwaltung Volkseigener Betriebe. see *Vereinigung Volkseigener Betriebe*
Vietnam, 284
Vladivostok, 94
Volkskammer. See People's Chamber
Volkswirtschaftsrat. See National Economic Council
Vologodsk, 38
'Voskhod', 235
VVB. See *Vereinigung Volkseigener Betriebe*
VWR. See National Economic Council

Wages. See Salaries
"Walter Ulbricht," 48
Warnemuende, 60
Wedler, H., 116, 117, 118, 156, 158, 241
Wedler, M., 182
Welsh, W., 25
Werk, See Works, GDR

Western states. See Liberal democracies
"Wilhelm Pieck," 48
Willma, B., 182
Wirtschaftsverbaende. See Economic groups
Withinputs, 33
Wittik, H., 179
Worker participation, GDR, 127, 246-249; USSR, 123, 233, 253
Workgroup on the Formation of the Economic System of Socialism, 102, 181, 195
Working Party on Constitutional and Economic Law, 181-182
Works, GDR, 115; USSR, 68, 106, 184
WTZ. See Scientific-Technical Centers

Yaroslavl, 222
Yudin, E., 221
Yugoslavia, 16, 265

Zakarpat'e, 230
Zavod. See Works, USSR
Zdorov, P., 176, 231
Ziller, G., 151
Zimmermann, G., 238
Zimmermann, Hartmut, 247
Zimmermann, H. B., 112
Zolotukhin, G., 149
"Zorya," 225
Zorza, V., 166

LIBRARY OF DAVIDSON COLLEGE

Books on regular loan may be checked out for **two weeks**. Books must be presented at the Circulation Desk in order to be renewed.

A fine is charged after date due.

Special books are subject to special regulations at the discretion of the library staff.